Rewi

Rewi

Āta haere, kia tere

Jeremy Hansen
and Jade Kake

Contents

| 6 | He mihi |
| 11 | Introduction |

Homes
Ngā whare tūhāhā
28	Thompson House
49	Wishart House
66	West Coast Studio

Multi-unit housing
Ngā kāinga nohoanga
92	Laurelia Place state houses
109	Ngāti Whātua housing
118	Everyday Homes

Interviews — practice
Ngā uiuinga — mahi ngaio
132	Kevin O'Brien
136	Pip Cheshire
139	Patrick Clifford, Malcolm Bowes and Michael Thomson
142	Nicholas Dalton

Civic and public realms
Whaitua tūmatanui
146	Canopy, altar and Papal throne
152	Ōtara Town Centre canopies
167	Capital Discovery Place Te Aho a Māui
174	City to Sea Bridge
187	Museum of New Zealand Te Papa Tongarewa competition entry

Health and corrections
Ngā whare whakaora
204	Tiaho Mai Acute Mental Health Facility, Middlemore Hospital
209	Mason Clinic
223	Kaitāia Hospital redevelopment
228	Northland Region Corrections Facility

Education
Ngā whare wānanga
| 245 | Puukenga, Unitec Institute of Technology |
| 258 | Waikato-Tainui College for Research and Development |

Interviews — pedagogy
Ngā uiuinga — mahi ako
268	Deidre Brown
271	Karamia Müller
275	Lama Tone
279	Amber Ruckes
283	Mike Austin

Exhibitions
Ngā whakaaturanga
| 288 | Triennale di Milano |
| 296 | *Future Islands*, Venice Architecture Biennale |

Speculative and unbuilt
Ngā kaupapa kore hanga
308	Ngāti Pōneke Marae/Hometown Museum
312	Cape Rēinga redevelopment
316	FirstCorp Tower
318	Horouta ki Pōneke Marae Society
320	Rotorua Cultural Centre
324	Pacific Island Business and Cultural Centre
328	Coastal Lodge
332	Te Wero Bridge
335	Campbell House

KOHA — creative responses
Ngā whakahoki auaha ā-tuhi
353	essa may ranapiri
354	Samuel Te Kani
358	Gina Cole

Design philosophy
Tautake hoahoa
364	Architecture and translation
370	Māori architecture — a myth
372	New Zealand in America

Creative process
Te hātepe auaha
| 377 | |

446	About the authors
447	Acknowledgements
448	Index

He mihi

We battle, strive and live to tame
this great fish that Māui caught.
Our youthfulness allows us to
be playful, energetic, lively,
enthusiastic, experimental,
and not overburdened by the
weight of our past.

Our architecture is about the
land, the sea and the sky . . .
sometimes submerged,
grounded, suspended,
but always in a continuous
process of negotiation,
experimentation, enthusiasm . . .

Kei roto i te āhuatanga o te ao
Mai i te mana me te tū rangatira
Mai i te aroha me te māhaki

Tēnā koutou, tēnā koutou,
tēnā koutou katoa.

From within our place/world
With dignity and respect
With love and humility

Rewi Thompson (Ngāti Porou, Ngāti Raukawa)
Fragment of a mihimihi for *Future Islands*, the New Zealand
exhibition at the 15th Venice Architecture Biennale, 2016

Rewi Thompson, photographed
in 2016. *Jane Ussher*

Ko ttitanga fe amang
Ko Waia k. aue
Ko Te Ai kanga a Ita
Ko Te Bo a whaou

Introduction

Kōrero tīmatanga

He ika kai ake i raro, he rapake ake i raro
As a fish nibbles from below, so the ascent
of a hill begins from below

A book of conversations: Jeremy Hansen

I first met Rewi Thompson in the mid-2000s, early in my 11-year stint editing *HOME* magazine. I sought him out because I wanted to publish his house, which had been chosen as one of New Zealand's 50 best by Douglas Lloyd Jenkins and Bill McKay in a previous issue of the magazine. The article was illustrated with a single photograph of Rewi's house, a building so mysteriously aloof that I wanted to try to understand what was going on inside it, as well as in the mind of its architect. So I called Rewi and asked if I could come over.

Rewi demurred on the opportunity of a visit to his place and of publishing it in full, saying it still needed a bit of work. Instead, he suggested I publish a house he'd designed for a friend on a slender site in Newmarket. I happily agreed: while Rewi's own home is a bold and intriguing piece of sculpture, the Newmarket house is a quiet presence in its street, with a similarly gentle, ethereal interior (the original owners still live there and are giving the house a freshening up, so we couldn't photograph it for this book).

When I visited the Newmarket house with Rewi, he told me how he'd paid careful attention to the way it might nurture family dynamics — a void in the centre allowed easy communication between upstairs and downstairs, for example, and spaces were unconventionally flexible instead of rigidly programmed, allowing the patterns of life within to evolve organically over time. This was architecture as a nurturing, adaptive presence, refusing to impose a specific style of living on its occupants. Yet the building also possessed a quiet strength, conscious of its role in offering privacy and protection to the family. Like all of Rewi's work, it was simple but complex, layered but straightforward. It also appeared to confidently embrace these contradictions.

I was an architectural novice (I trained as a journalist, not an architect); Rewi was kind and interesting and never seemed inclined to draw attention to my naivety. I enjoyed talking to him, partly because conversations with him were often intriguingly oblique and gossamer-like, their meaning sometimes seeming to hover tantalisingly out of reach. At the time we first met he was working with Ngāti Whātua Ōrākei on its housing strategy. I was interested in the vision of medium-density living he suggested for the papakāinga and his confidence that it would help build a solid future on land the hapū had fought so hard to retain.

We met occasionally over the next few years, once at the Wishart House on the Hokianga Harbour — a home that features in this book and of which he was rightfully proud — and other times at various architectural gatherings. I last spoke to him in 2016 about his Everyday Homes project, a group of over 50 state-owned houses he'd designed for the Tāmaki Makaurau Auckland suburb of Northcote in his then-new job at Isthmus Group. He seemed energised and optimistic, and I was glad to see that, after years of working solo, he'd found a firm that understood his talents and had the scale and resources to support them. I was excited about the projects he and the Isthmus team might tackle next, and he seemed to feel this way, too. Sadly, he died suddenly just a few months later.

—

The Sumich House in Newmarket, Tāmaki Makaurau Auckland, photographed by James Stokes and featured in the October/November 2006 issue of *NZ Home & Entertaining* (later *HOME*) magazine. Rewi also designed the home's dining table.

Leona, Rewi and Lucy Thompson at the Thompson House, Tāmaki Makaurau Auckland, around 1989–90.
Lucy Thompson collection

Architectural careers are usually measured by the volume and quality of built work. Rewi's completed buildings were never sufficient in number to make him a figure of popular acclaim like his friends and contemporaries Ian Athfield and Roger Walker. Yet he created some remarkable, nationally important structures, including Te Whanganui-a-Tara Wellington's City to Sea Bridge, the striking canopies at the Ōtara Town Centre, and Puukenga, the School of Māori Studies at Auckland's Unitec Institute of Technology Te Whare Wānanga o Wairaka. His work in designing rehabilitative buildings for the incarcerated or the mentally unwell was radical and humane and is still shaping the way these facilities are created today.

Introduction

His designs broke the binary that associates Māori with the natural world and Pākehā with the urban, showing that Māori narratives were just as relevant and potent in creating urban forms. While working as an adjunct professor at the School of Architecture at the University of Auckland, he was at the vanguard of a cultural shift, his studio classes giving a generation of Māori, Pasifika, Pākehā and Tauiwi students the confidence to engage with Māori design principles in their work. Now some of his former students are sharing his approach with subsequent generations as teachers, and most large architecture and landscape design firms have Māori design units within them. Not all of this is due to Rewi, but his contributions to this transformation cannot be underestimated.

Rewi was beloved in the architecture profession and revered by many of his students. But whenever I showed my non-architect friends images of the exterior of Rewi's home they expressed amazement that they had never heard of him. When I told them about some of the speculative drawings in his archives — prismatic buildings on water with a *Tyrannosaurus rex* inside, for example, or the Te Papa proposal Rewi created with Ian Athfield and the Canadian-American architect Frank Gehry — they were fascinated and wanted to know more.

In late 2019, my friend Jade Kake and I spoke of our shared admiration for Rewi and the way his buildings and his teaching had advanced the possibilities of what architecture in Aotearoa New Zealand could be. A prevailing modesty in this country's architectural climate has meant its buildings are often grounded in the pragmatics of form and function. In stark and ambitious contrast, many of Rewi's designs are fearlessly conceptual. His references to Māori narratives are not decorative but deeply embedded; there is also an inherent generosity in his work that means it feels like an exploration of the possibilities of a positive post-colonial future. Rewi's approach to architecture, wrote University of Auckland professor Deidre Brown in an obituary for her friend and colleague, was 'fundamentally concerned with land and people, and conviction that architecture could return identity and well-being to people suffering from cultural estrangement'.

Jade and I discussed how a book about Rewi might further this conversation by introducing his work to a wider audience. We also hoped it might ensure that his contributions as a teacher, designer and collaborator were better remembered. We began by asking Rewi's daughter, Lucy, if she was comfortable with the idea of us making this book about her father and his work; she was supportive and has worked with us throughout.

Neither Jade nor I was interested in the idea of a so-called definitive biography, mostly because the idea of defining Rewi seemed antithetical to his multi-faceted and slightly dreamy way of being. Instead, we thought it would be more interesting and accessible to create a book full of conversations with Rewi's friends, collaborators and students, all of whom knew him better than we did. We also spent many hours in Rewi's archives at the University of Auckland, leafing through designs from straightforward villa renovations to fantastical schemes such as those towards the end of this book.

Our method of putting together this book was organic rather than comprehensive, the result of following our instincts and interests in attempting to gather a group of people and projects that showcase the breadth of Rewi's gifts and achievements. We selected drawings from the archives that caught our eyes, that revealed some of the evolution of his completed and unbuilt designs or that were just straight-out beautiful. We hoped that by combining this archival material with photographs of some of Rewi's completed projects we could create a book that offers multiple perspectives on a fascinating architect and the scope of his imagination.

—

Rewi was as passionate about rugby as he was about architecture. His long association with Wellington's Oriental-Rongotai club included a stint as team vice-captain in 1972.
Lucy Thompson collection

Rewi was born in 1954. He was of Ngāti Raukawa and Ngāti Porou descent and was raised in Wellington, where his father worked as a bus driver. 'My parents were poor and we lived a sheltered life,' Rewi wrote in a 1987 essay for *NZ Architect* magazine, 'but we knew the fundamental qualities of integrity, and I'm proud of that.' He first trained as a civil and structural engineer at Wellington Polytechnic, then worked as a structural draughtsperson at Structon Group in Wellington. He gravitated towards the architecture team, some of whom encouraged him to go to architecture school. He graduated with honours from the School of Architecture at the University of Auckland in 1980, becoming one of just a handful of Māori architects in the country's history at the time.

His architectural verve was evident early in his time at the school. Former students told us stories of rushing down to Brick Studio to check out his drawings as word spread of their bravery and originality. Around the time he graduated, he won the AAA/Monier Design Award for Ngāti Pōneke Marae, a breathtaking, dream-like conceptual structure with a lean linear form that emerges from Wellington Harbour to rest on the side of Tangi-te-keo Mount Victoria. The project fused Māori design principles with a bold futurism akin to the superstructures being dreamed up by the Japanese Metabolist movement around that time. It gained Rewi national media attention and signalled the arrival of a significant new talent.

Introduction

From left: Rewi in a kapa haka group in Wellington when he was a child; his wedding day with Leona in 1981; in his Auckland studio in the 1980s. *Lucy Thompson collection*

Rewi's career got off to a roaring start: as well as the projects listed above, he designed homes and home alterations; rugby clubrooms for Oriental Rongotai, his old Wellington club (rugby was a passion as enduring as architecture); marae complexes in Matauri Bay, Ōtara and Glen Innes; 20 state houses at Wiri; temporary canopies in the Auckland Domain for Pope John Paul's 1986 visit; offices and a warehouse for a pharmaceutical company in Manukau City; the Capital Discovery Place Te Aho a Māui children's museum in Wellington; and proposals for a new visitor centre at Te Rerenga Wairua Cape Rēinga, a cultural centre in Rotorua, and much more.

In the late 1980s this momentum stalled. When we began this book, I often thought about the buildings Rewi might have made had his career continued on its early trajectory. How would the country be different, for example, had the scheme Rewi developed for Te Papa with Athfield and Gehry been realised? Could the experimental state houses he designed in Wiri have been used as a model for higher-density housing elsewhere? How different might our built environment look and feel if people had listened more closely to his advocacy for a strong response to landscape, and taken courage from the bravura way he seized opportunities and crafted unique responses to them?

We asked many people why Rewi's prolific output hadn't continued at the pace of his early career. The variety of answers suggests a confluence of circumstances. The 1987 stock market crash froze the construction industry, putting many architects out of work. Later, Rewi's wife Leona, whom he had met in Wellington in 1973 and who worked as a teacher, was ill with cancer for long periods before she died. Rewi moved his office home so he could care for her; for a long time after she died, a number of people we spoke to noted how he seemed, quite understandably, lost in a fog of grief.

The economy improved a few years later, but Rewi seemed unable to regain the momentum he'd established. He didn't have the financial means to rebuild a team of a size that would allow him to confidently take on larger commissions, and his work shifted from schemes he was leading to projects led by other firms on which he provided advice, often as a cultural consultant. He was also diabetic and had challenges managing his health.

He didn't fit the visible stereotype of an architect; he had a casual demeanour and speaking declaratively wasn't his style. We heard one excruciating anecdote in which a public servant mistook him for a state housing tenant instead of an architect who was there to discuss the new state homes he was designing. Some people we spoke to — both Māori and Pākehā — acknowledged racism as a career-limiting possibility but did not believe it played a decisive influence in Rewi's case, pointing to the number of significant projects he won early in his career as evidence of a culture that was ready and able to welcome his point of view.

—

Now I look back on all the questions I asked about what might have been had Rewi's career not stalled in this manner and realise I was missing quite a lot of the point. It's true that, had things been different, he might have designed some tremendous buildings. But his diminished built output doesn't mean his influence waned. The opportunity to teach at the University of Auckland as an adjunct professor in 2002 undoubtedly came at the right time for Rewi — some people we spoke to said it was a lifeline for him, financially and emotionally — but it is also the area where his impact has arguably been the greatest.

His teaching empowered a generation of students to feel comfortable grappling with Māori design concepts, looking to the land and its history as the foundations of their architectural narratives. Students like Karamia Müller, now a lecturer at the University of Auckland's School of Architecture herself, attest not just to the sense of possibility opened up by a brown face in a senior position at the university, but also to the confidence Rewi's teaching could bring to the act of creating architecture in this colonised land. This, perhaps, is Rewi's most profound contribution, echoing and multiplying through generations and helping architects strive to make places that feel as if they belong here.

Rewi's notion of belonging, of course, was different to many of his contemporaries. There is a strand of architectural thinking in this country that prides itself on blending in, of receding into the bush, buildings that, to borrow the words of influential Australian architect Glenn Murcutt, 'touch the earth lightly'. This is entirely valid as an approach, possessing a kind of deference that appears to acknowledge the primacy of landscape — so much so that these attempts at camouflage can feel like apologies for occupying the land at all.

Rewi's buildings never tried to hide: he often advocated for an architectural response as strong as the landscape around it. One of the last buildings he designed was a studio for artist Katharina Grosse on a beautiful coastal site prone to dramatic storms. In our interview, Katharina mentioned that many buildings in the area seemed determined to disappear into the landscape as much as possible, but that Rewi was not interested in this approach. 'He thought you can be very powerful here,' she said. At the same time, he didn't aspire to permanence. Instead, he was comfortable with the idea of buildings assuming new lives or, more radically, eventually crumbling to dust.

Since the Architectural Group issued its 1946 manifesto espousing the creation of a uniquely New Zealand style of architecture, people have wrestled with the question of what, if anything, makes architecture from this country distinctive. (In The Group's case, this meant lightweight timber structures that rejected uptight English-style blueprints and relaxed into Auckland's balmy climate.) These attempts at cultural simplification — they happen in literature and other creative fields, too — and their whiff of insecure parochialism can get dull and reductive. But they also explore issues of what it means to live here and how architecture might ask questions that lead to a better understanding of ourselves and this place.

There's a clear line between the gentle approach advocated by The Group and the recessive structures many New Zealand architects design today, a line Rewi's bold buildings appear happy to cross. Rewi's buildings are different, too, from the neo-Colonial approaches for which Athfield and Walker became famous in the 1970s, in which they rejected sleek modernist style and playfully sampled the country's vernacular heritage. It's true that Rewi's buildings were partly grounded in the post-modern context in which he was educated, defined by its rejection of modernism's rectilinear orthodoxy, but many buildings from the post-modern era now read as empty provocations. Rewi's designs may possess a similar enthusiasm for the spectacular, but they also feel as though they have a deeper reason for being.

Rewi didn't write frequently — his preferred mode of thinking seemed to be endless doodling in his notebooks — but he left behind some intriguing articles that reveal something of the development of his unique architectural approach. His designs possessed a deep sense of confidence from the start, but friends such as Mike Barns — who is also Māori and who became friends with Rewi in Wellington, starting architecture school shortly before him — say Rewi's work was an ongoing exploration of his identity, an identity in which he was less secure than his confident designs might have suggested. 'I think he felt like taura here [a domestic migrant] in the city: I'm in the city, but I don't really understand my roots,' Mike told us.

—

Rewi 'was always drawing', his daughter Lucy says, and rarely went anywhere without a notebook. They are an insight into Rewi's creative process and Lucy has kept many of them. *Samuel Hartnett*

Rewi's rapid rise to prominence as one of the few Māori architects in the country meant he was often asked (by Pākehā architects and journalists, for the most part) to define not only his own architectural approach but also Māori architecture as a whole, something he understandably bridled against. In 'Māori Architecture — A Myth', an article published in *NZ Architect* magazine in 1987, his frustration bubbled over into italics. 'As individuals we have the freedom to choose our own approach to our work,' he wrote. 'For instance, because I'm Maori, that doesn't necessarily mean that my work is Maori architecture. Sure, there are times when Maori influence is appropriate, *but not all the bloody time mate*.'

It was something he had to reconcile at his own pace. By 1988, an article Rewi wrote in *The Landscape*, the magazine of the New Zealand Institute of Landscape Architects Tuia Pito Ora, seems to display a greater level of comfort with referencing Māori influences in his work:

> It is no secret that ties to our ancestral land are very important and significant. The acknowledgment of this can be expressed in my parents' return to their Marae, and reinforced in our tribal legends, beliefs and cultural heritage. For these reasons, the means of land or environment has a more human and spiritual significance; a source of life and development of one's own wairua (spirit) and peace of mind. It is this spiritual connection with our land that is often the inspiration for design.

Rewi expanded on this line of thought in the academic journal *Transition* in 1995:

> From a Maori perspective there is a different value system. That is, for Maoris the affiliation with the land is spiritual as opposed to an understanding that is commercial which pervades a western viewpoint. This leads to a different interpretation of architecture relative to the site. Here we take the site as being New Zealand, not only as a place but as a culture . . . In this sense the site or context of the work is the land but also the culture because the land is cultural. The land or the site can be seen to be an emblem of these divergent expectations. The works we do are not posed as solutions or as a resolution to this, but are part of an ongoing process and therefore are unfinished.

Rewi's work asks questions for all of us about what it means to occupy this land, questions many would prefer to ignore or to have him do the work of explaining. In this context, the blank face of his house becomes a refreshing act of refusal, in which a man sometimes defined by his agreeability refuses to play games of glib explanation and suburban gentility, and decides to issue a challenge instead.

Rewi's home is a place that refuses to privilege this country's scenic beauty as a triumphal force, instead delving into darker histories of volcanic eruptions and territorial battles. 'Auckland is a violent place, that is not only in geological terms of the volcanic cores, or even the Maori myths of the volcanos, or historically where it has been the site of wars — Maori vs Maori and later Maori vs the colonials,' Rewi told the architecture lecturer Ross Jenner for a story in the academic journal *Lotus International* in 2000. 'But now it is violent, where people fight over land, they fight a war for a view of the water . . . The house or the project . . . is the object of negotiation. The object is a part of this reconciliation that is central to the process of culture: they have to get used to it or burn it down.'

Even now, after spending hours in his archives and talking to his friends and colleagues, Rewi's house remains a mystery to me, which may be part of the point: Jenner described Rewi's buildings as 'a call to attend to the limits of one's thinking. And to the encounter with what lies outside one's own thinking.' They are a challenge for all of us to think about our places here: how we fit and how, with a clear-eyed view of history and a bold look to the possibilities of the future, we might get better at doing so.

Jenner also wrote: 'Thompson's practice is devoted to exploring what bi-culturalism might mean architecturally. He recognises that, in such a context architecture must be the site of complex cultural negotiation, a daring act of becoming.'

The words 'a daring act of becoming' rang in my ears as I first read them because they explain something of what makes Rewi such a compelling figure. His designs are not feel-good narratives, but rather deeply personal buildings that make us contemplate the complex nature of living here. Their bravery and their imperfections — the way they thumb their nose at the commonly held architectural goal of resolving every aspect of a building so it leaves no questions open for debate — embrace of the inherent messiness of the act of becoming. They also acknowledge that, whether you're an individual or a multicultural nation, the act of becoming will be challenging, frustrating, at times uplifting — and eternally incomplete.

Always the architect: Jade Kake

When Jeremy and I first discussed the idea of writing a book on Rewi Thompson, my first thought (as it often is) was, 'Am I the right person to be doing this?' I had met Rewi only a handful of times. The first was in 2013 in Carin Wilson's office (I was working with Carin on a project for the Independent Māori Statutory Board, which would later lead to Te Aranga principles and design methodology being integrated into Auckland Council policy and processes); Rewi and Carin were finishing a meeting. The last time was at a Ngā Aho wānanga at Waipapa Marae at the University of Auckland, when we were working together towards what would become Te Kawenata o Rata, the covenant between Ngā Aho and Te Kāhui Whaihanga New Zealand Institute of Architects. There may have been other encounters in between, but those were the first and last, and the ones that left an impact on me.

Although the question lingered in my mind, the response to my pātai was 'Mēnā kāhore au e mahi pērā, mā wai atu?' 'If not me, then who?' In some ways, I felt that being someone who was not close to Rewi, but who was undoubtedly a beneficiary of the work he and others such as Mike Barns, Tere Insley, and later Rau Hoskins and Derek Kawiti, had laid down in the generations before, was an advantage. I was familiar with his work, and as a student and graduate I was fast becoming embedded in the kind of work that Rewi had been among the first to do. It was not lost on me that the young Māori architects and designers of my generation (and those who follow) are able to stand as Māori and have the kind of Māori-centric careers we have because of the foundational work of Rewi and others.

Something I discovered is that Rewi did not always have an easy relationship with his own ahurea Māori, particularly in how this related to architecture. I was interested to understand Rewi in his context, as someone who started working in architecture at the beginning of the Māori renaissance and whose career matured in the decades that followed. Although my grandfather was not an architect, I was often reminded of my koro as I listened to people describe Rewi: a gentle man, a humble man, softly spoken but commanding respect. They both loved rugby, and loved their families. My koro, too, was close to his daughter(s) and heartbroken when his wife passed. But the other thing they had in common was that they were both navigating an overwhelmingly Pākehā world as men who were visibly Māori.

—

In this context, it's easier to understand Rewi's reluctance to be labelled as a 'Māori architect' when to be labelled Māori may have meant to be considered less than, or else tokenised within a majority Pākehā environment. This isn't to minimise the many genuine and close relationships Rewi had with his Pākehā friends and colleagues. Particularly in the early stages of his architectural career, Rewi wanted to be taken seriously as an architect, not as a Māori

This photograph of a model of Ngāti Pōneke Marae, the award-winning conceptual design by Rewi, was published in a 1988 edition of *The Landscape*, the magazine of the New Zealand Institute of Landscape Architects.

"... tired and hungry, we hauled our canoe onto the beach, it had carried our people, and contained within its hull, our culture. We had arrived home ..."

architect, which was fraught and carried all of these connotations at a time when Māori architecture was not considered architecture and instead confined to the realms of anthropology.

At that time, Professor Mike Austin was one of those lone voices advocating for the legitimacy of Māori and Pacific architecture. Mike was also one of Rewi's lecturers at the School of Architecture and Planning in the 1970s. As Mike recalls: 'I was with Rewi one night, and I said, "Rewi, you need to start taking this Māori architecture seriously." And he said, "No, I don't want to do that." I think I said, "Why don't you involve yourself in this?" He said very clearly to me, "I don't want to be a Māori architect, Mike. I want to be an architect."'

Rewi entered the architecture school at the University of Auckland in 1977. The school admitted around 90 students each year and at the time he enrolled Rewi, with Mike Barns (Tūwharetoa ki Kawerau) and Tere Insley (Ngāti Porou, Te Whānau-ā-Apanui), was one of three openly Māori students. He may have been only the fourth or fifth ever to have enrolled at that time. We don't know whether Rewi had any direct involvement, but the burgeoning Māori political awareness had reached the university by then. In 1979 the Māori students group He Taua (including Hilda Halkyard, Hone Harawira and Ben Dalton) challenged the engineering students' racist mock haka.

In 1980, as a student, Rewi also created the Ngāti Pōneke Marae scheme as a competition entry (there is more about this later in the book). The scheme won the AAA Monier Tile Award and according to Mike Barns (a judge for the competition alongside Kerry Morrow and John Scott), it was a critical point in Rewi's understanding and strengthening of his own Māori identity: 'I think it confirmed his validity as a Māori commentator, and probably gave him a lot more confidence in those early days around his architectural capability.'

Rewi rarely wrote about his own work (he preferred drawing, and allowing the work to speak for itself), but some of his writing from the late 1980s explicitly addresses his relationship with this nebulous idea of 'Māori architecture': 'the notion of developing a Pākehā or Māori Architecture sounds absurd . . . For instance, because I'm Māori, that doesn't necessarily mean that my work is Māori Architecture.'

Rewi and his friends at social gatherings and working together on DIY projects. These images are from an album of photographs from the 1970s compiled by Rewi's friend Allan Stevenson for Lucy, Rewi's daughter, after Rewi's death in 2016.
Lucy Thompson collection

If Rewi and Mike were among a very small number of Māori architecture students, then upon graduation they faced becoming the only Māori within their professional architectural firms. Rewi was the only Māori at Structon Group, the architecture and engineering firm, when he worked there as a graduate from 1978 to 1982.

When Rewi launched his own practice in 1983, he was beginning to establish himself as an architect, but also growing to understand his own Māori identity in relation to his work. It would be too simplistic to characterise Rewi's work during this period as a rejection of his Māoritanga. It would be more accurate to describe his developing attitudes and experiences as a journey. As the society around him changed, Rewi became more anchored in his Māoritanga, and the opportunities to openly practise as a Māori architect — without fear of dismissal — began to emerge. As Mike Barns notes, 'He was finding his Māoriness through his architecture but he never claimed to be an expert in tikanga or Māori architecture. He expressed what he knew and it was unfolding as he grew in life. His architecture was his own personal journey and his Māoriness was becoming more and more evident.'

Through the late 1980s and into early 1990s, he began to produce explicitly cultural work, mostly through large-scale civic work, such as the Ōtara Town Centre Canopy and a series of significant civic works in Te Whanganui-a-Tara. This would mark the beginning of a consultant model or collaborative approach to architecture, whereby Māori perspectives and skills were incorporated as part of the wider project team.

By the mid-1990s, he was collaborating with health planners and specialist health architects to inject the cultural dimension. This was the beginning of Rewi's work bringing a Māori perspective to larger, complex institutional projects.

Rewi may not have been involved in more direct political activism, but he was political in and through his work. His involvement in the design of Northland Region Corrections Facility at Ngāwhā (1999–2005), in collaboration with Mike Barns, Stephenson & Turner and Cox Group, was another critical point in both Rewi's career and his emerging sense of himself as an architect who was Māori. The project was contentious, and not supported by mana whenua hapū Ngāti Rangi in the beginning. Rewi and Mike, in particular, were motivated by a belief that Māori needed to be doing this work for Māori. At its core, the project was about restorative justice and healing for incarcerated people, the overwhelming majority of whom were (and are) Māori.

Rewi was also involved in several education projects that considered kaupapa Māori approaches to education and alternative visions for sharing and co-creating knowledge. In these projects, Rewi worked alongside highly

Introduction

regarded kāumatua, such as Haare Williams and Hare Paniora, and tribal leaders such as Sir Robert Mahuta. In relation to the Waikato-Tainui college project, Rewi's whakapapa to Ngāti Raukawa and the connections to the Kīngitanga were seen as particularly important in terms of his ability to understand and interpret Sir Robert Mahuta's expansive vision for the project as well as the cultural themes and motifs of significance to Waikato-Tainui.

—

Although his built projects have been significant, Rewi's influence extends far beyond the physical realm. Arguably, his most important contributions have been as a thinker and an educator. His philosophical contributions to architecture included an intentionally slow, careful process whereby you listened to the land, to what the whenua was trying to tell you. Many of the people we interviewed spoke of Rewi's quiet, gentle nature, but also of his commanding presence. When he spoke, people listened. Colleagues and students who knew Rewi during his time as an educator at the university considered him to be a brilliant conceptual thinker, and a great architect. They also directly acknowledged Rewi's cultural expertise and grounding in this space, for which he had become widely known and respected by this time.

Rewi's relationship to his Māori identity was not always straightforward, and at times complex. I get the sense from our interviews and Rewi's own writings that he arrived at this identity through his work, and in his own time. Rewi's reluctance to be labelled as a Māori architect came at least partially from his desire to be taken seriously as an architect, and at least partially from his humility. As an urban Māori raised away from the hau kāinga, he perhaps felt a degree of insecurity in his identity, as well as a desire to 'get things right', because of his reverence and respect for his culture.

Where he gained his grounding, his place to stand, was in his profession as an architect. Through his architectural training and skillset, he was able to express himself spatially, and give spatial expression to, at times, radical ideas. He didn't necessarily want to be considered the expert in this space, and would much rather that the ideas, the architecture, speak for themselves.

Rewi was a product of his time, and of a society that was moving through a period of rapid change, but he was also an active agent in shaping and changing our society: through his architecture, and through his engagement with mātauranga Māori and his own Māori culture.

In April 2023, shortly before this book went to print, I had the privilege of visiting Ūawa Tolaga Bay for the first time. On this brief trip, I visited Te Rāwheoro Marae (which belongs to Ngāti Patuwhare of Te Aitanga-a-Hauiti) and the adjacent urupā, where Rewi is at rest with his wife, Leona, and his parents, Bobby and Mei Thompson. There's a lane close by, opposite the marae, where the Thompson whānau ūkaipō, or ancestral lands, are located and where many of the Thompson whānau still live. On this visit, I learned of Te Rāwheoro as a whare wānanga. Established in the fifteenth century by Hīngāngāroa, the father of Hauiti, the wānanga specialised in visual arts, alongside karakia and whakapapa. Whakairo, i te ao kikokiko, ā-wairua hoki — both physical and spiritual — was a particularly significant kaupapa of this whare wānanga. I felt this additional context was the missing piece for me in understanding Rewi and his legacy. In retrospect, it seems an obvious and natural extension of this whakapapa that Rewi should have pursued architecture in the ways that he did.

On the notion of legacy, Mike Austin sums it up simply: 'That's his legacy and everybody who came in touch with him felt this. He lifted architecture in people's minds. He was always the architect. He was never anything else.'

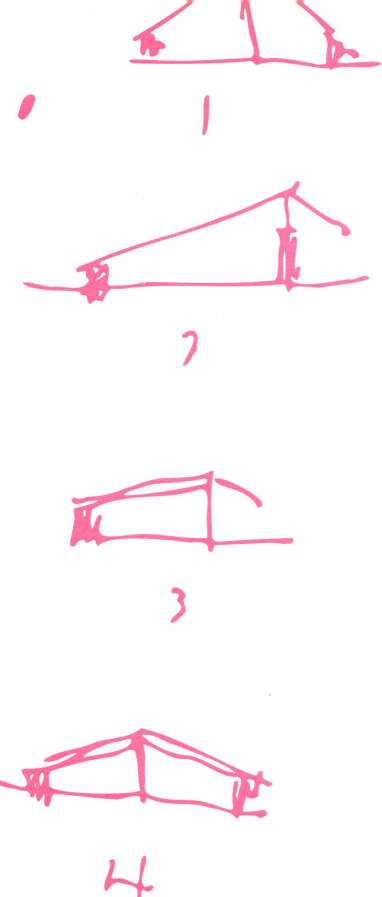

Homes

Ngā whare tūhāhā

Ka hanga whare te tangata, ka hanga tangata te whare
Those who build the house are also built by the house

Thompson House

Kohimarama
Tāmaki Makaurau
Auckland

1986

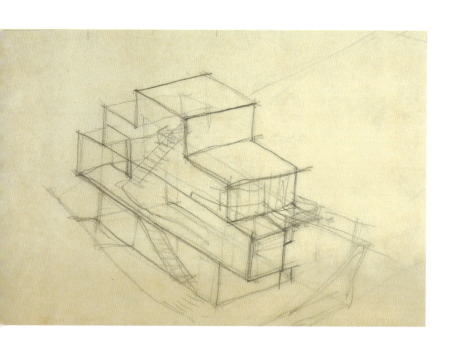

Left: A sketch of the Thompson House from Rewi's archives. *Architecture Archive, University of Auckland*

Opposite: The Thompson House, photographed after Rewi's death in 2016. *David Straight*

Left: The Thompson House turns an impassive face to its suburban surrounds. *David Straight*

Below: A sketch from Rewi's archives showing the planned planting scheme of a row of nīkau or cabbage trees in front of the house. *Architecture Archive, University of Auckland*

Homes

Rewi Thompson's best-known work is the home he designed for himself, his wife, Leona, and their daughter Lucy in the Auckland suburb of Kohimarama. The home faces the street with an impassive façade of plywood panels and a ziggurat form that Professor Deidre Brown likens to the poutama (stairway to heaven) tukutuku pattern. The rear of the house has windows facing the hill and bush behind it. It is a home that is both impassive and poetic, inviting and intimidating. Rewi lived there until he passed away in 2016.

Rewi lived in the house but never fully completed it, which meant its interior was never formally photographed and it was in poor repair at the time of his death. After Rewi died, Lucy sold the house, which is now being renovated by new owners.

In the archives, there is a document written by Rewi offering architectural services to Te Kura Kaupapa Māori o Te Rawhiti Roa in Te Tai Tokerau in 1999. In listing some of his notable projects, he describes the house and some of the responses to it, positioning the building as a statement contrary to the prevailing search for an Auckland vernacular. We haven't edited the text, so the spelling, punctuation and line breaks are all preserved from the original document. It serves as a useful introduction to his feelings about the house.

```
34 Southern Cross Road.

Essentially, the underlining theme refers to family (whanau),
but engages this idea with the context of site and community.

Picking a place or site for ones family to live is crucial
to their well being and development.

As discussed, the house metaphorically, stands as a face
(elevation), that expresses the feels about the well being
ones family. Space is extracted from the elevation.

While the 'eyes' are seemly closed, the skin (surface) and
elevation (form), bare scars of indifference, and marks of
identity.

Beneath the skin lies irritations and blood.

It has never been our intension for our neighbours to
understand the messages expressed in the thinking behind
the house.

I never ask anyone what they think of my work, or my house.
My work is not about being accepted. I do what I have to do.
Architecture can be a lonely business.
```

I know people hate my house. I guess it's too different from people's idea of a house in Kohimarama, or too defensive or challenging or pure cultural shock!

However, it does engage with the community and broader site, whether directly or indirectly, as compared to other houses in the street that hide their faces behind foliage.

Site and Auckland vernacular

I've never seen the house as violent or aggressive, but it does refer to Auckland as a place of violence Inwardly, the house is peaceful, as it reflects the whanau (family), aroha (affection), awhi (embrace) concepts. Is this reflected externally? Do the crinkles in the skin reflect this?

Traditionally, Auckland has, and still is a desirable place to live. The Maori name Tamaki Makaurau is interpreted as Tamaki of a hundred lovers or desirable by many. Many wars fought and blood spelt for the occupation of Tamaki Makaurau. Wars are still being fought.

The harbours provided an abundance of food, the harbours provided a means of voyaging, the climate was warm, and the nature of the terrain provided fortification against enemy.

Auckland has a violent past both geologically and culturally.

The interior when finally completed will reflect this.

The landscaping refers to Kohimarama beach.

My view of the sky tower, is that it has identifies the inner city as a landmark, as, a entity.

However, Rangitoto will always stand as the identity and landmark of Auckland.

Identifying and understanding the Auckland vernacular has always been unclear to me. This relates particularly to new work.

Vernacular is a language.

To develop a vernacular, one has to develop a language, that relates back to the language of our cultural roots. From this position, a vernacular can grow.

Consequently, we see our house as a integral part of a language, that discusses ourselves, place, expectations, possibilities, dreams, visions etc. — rather like a punctuation 'mark'.

Cities by their very nature are public. They are to do with community and engagement. From this point of view, our house adds to the formal language of the city, albeit in a more 'cultured' way.

A drawing of the Thompson House from Rewi's archives.
Architecture Archive, University of Auckland

Windowless (walls), buildings are a part of the urban language. As our cities become more dense, privacy becomes an issue. We start to build walls and look to the heavens for space and release. There are signs of this happening.

This raises further questions about ourselves. We need to listen more to our needs, and feel the irritations that are under our skin. Until we become truthful, then Auckland will always be soulless, or gutless, or both.

Lucy Thompson is Rewi and Leona's daughter. She moved into the house with her parents when she was three or four years old. Here, she recounts her memories of the house, her parents and drawing with her dad.

Jeremy Hansen
Lucy, a good place to start might be to ask you about the house you grew up in, which Rewi designed. What are your memories of it?

Lucy Thompson
It was probably an idea in his head for goodness knows how long before I was around. But I know that we moved in when I was three or four, I'm pretty sure. He and Mum would've probably bought the land in Kohimarama not long before that, when I was a toddler. It was still being built when we moved in.

It was always a work in progress. I remember when the permanent stairs were put in — the new stairs, not the temporary plywood stairs — and one of the things that was great until it got painted was that I was allowed to draw on the walls, which is very lucky as an architect's daughter who thought she was quite creative. I had free rein in my room, which was wonderful, but eventually it all got painted over, so if anyone was to peel back the paint in some parts of the house they'd probably see some of my masterpieces from that time. I've got really fond memories of growing up in the house.

Jeremy
Did you consciously compare it to your friends' places?

Lucy
I guess I just thought, that's your house, that's my house. It wasn't until I was about seven or eight and friends would come and have a sleepover, and they would be like, 'Whoa, your house is so different. You don't have walls in your house.' And there were massive drop-aways, which I'd grown up with, drops down to nothing with no barrier. Mum and Dad had just said, 'Never go one metre past there, you can't go back.' It was very nice being in the bush as well. I spent a lot of time out the back climbing trees. It was a nice experience.

Jade Kake
This isn't about my childhood, but it sounds very much like my childhood. Because my dad wasn't an architect, but he did build the house that I grew up in. And so I had that same thing where I'd lived in this house in the bush that my dad built and then people would come over and say, 'Oh, your house is really different.' I really related to a lot of what you were saying, and the random quirks where the house isn't legal or safe, exactly, but it works. Our house was always a work in progress as well.

Lucy
Well, that's what they say: architects rarely live in a finished house, or they finish it and then they move on to the next one.

Jeremy
Neither of us got to meet your mum, but I've noticed how people talk a lot about 'Rewi and Leona' in our interviews, which suggests they were a pretty tight unit. Can you tell us a little bit about your mum, and what you know about how they met and got together? And what do you remember them being like together?

Lucy
Mum was introduced to Dad by a friend, Anne Harris, in Wellington in 1973. They first met at the Ories Club [the Oriental Rongotai Rugby Club], when Anne took Mum along one night. From what I know they were a team from the start. I have a photo up in my room from this era — Mum, youthful and bright-eyed, and Dad rocking a floral shirt/plaid jacket/ massive tie combo with a generous head of hair and moustache. They look happy and in love, and it always brings a smile to my face. Another one of Dad's close friends from Wellington, Allan Stevenson, has printed me out an album of photos from 'the glory days' and they are great! Special memories to have.

My personal memories of my parents' relationship are warm, happy and filled with love. They were

Left: Rewi and Leona at a party in Wellington in 1975.
Lucy Thompson collection

Below: The Thompson House under construction in the mid-1980s. 'It was always a work in progress,' Lucy Thompson says.
Lucy Thompson collection

'I was quite involved in him being an architect,' says Lucy Thompson, who used to join her father in his working area at home after school and write in his notebooks.
Lucy Thompson collection

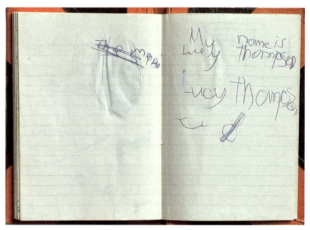

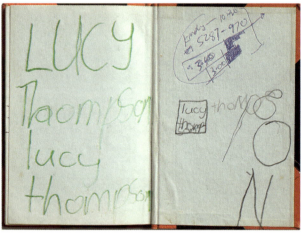

soulmates. They used to call each other 'Fred' or 'Freddie', and I never found out the origin of where that came from. When Mum became unwell in later years, Dad would go and visit her every day after work, cook her dinners, pick up her books from the library: he doted on her. When she passed away, sadly, he was never the same again. To help channel his grief, he poured his energy into his work, and I think it really helped with his healing. But he always missed her. Now they are together, which is a comforting thought for me, even though I miss them both every day, too. I will always cherish all the happy times we had as a family — summers spent with whānau and friends in Tolaga Bay, holidays overseas to Disneyland and Rarotonga, and our time living at Southern Cross Road.

Jeremy
What was your mum's input into the design of the house? Do you have a sense of their interactions when they were discussing it?

Lucy
No, unfortunately not, I was too young. But from what I could tell, and what I do know, it was only 100 per cent support. They were a team. Because Mum was living in a not-completed house for a number of years, as well. It wasn't just me and Dad.

Jeremy
I like hearing you being so matter-of-fact about a house other people are reverential about.

Lucy
I just didn't think it was any different. Growing up, it even took me a while to get my head around it. People would be like, 'Oh, you live in that house?' I'd be like, 'Yeah, I guess it is quite unusual.'

Jade
I think it's interesting because I've heard people describe the house you grew up in as our Villa Savoye.[1] I'm not saying that's wrong, but I've always been so much more interested in architectural

---

1   Villa Savoye is a modernist villa in Poissy, France, designed by Swiss architects Le Corbusier and Pierre Jeanneret, and is widely regarded as one of the most significant contributions to modernist architecture.

Homes

The house in Southern Cross Road under construction. *Lucy Thompson collection*

Homes

The Thompson House presented a windowless face to the street, concentrating its gaze on the tree-lined bank behind it, as seen in this drawing from Rewi's archives.
Architecture Archive, University of Auckland

spaces that people actually live in and occupy, rather than them being a symbol. And so I think the story of how you lived in the house and what it was like for you is more interesting than what it means for it to be Architecture with a capital A.

Lucy

One of the things I've said to a number of people is that it might be this famous architectural icon, one of the most poignant pieces of Dad's work, but ultimately at the end of the day, it was just a home, and it was a happy home. And now it's finished its first stage of its journey, and it's gone on to have its second journey, which is really cool. Dad always used to say, 'Structures are never meant to be permanent forever and ever.' That was his vision, his ethos: that things do break down. It's the natural cycle and then they rebuild again, and that's what our house was like as well, a little bit. But I am very grateful that it is still standing, and it's a new improved version, but the same as well.

Jeremy

How conscious were you of Rewi's job, and how much did he involve you in that as you grew up?

Lucy

I was quite involved in him being an architect pretty much my whole life. I used to spend a lot of time going to Dad's offices; whether it was after work or after school, I'd head there. When Mum became unwell, that prompted him to move his office into the house upstairs, to be closer to Mum and me. But because I was quite young, I just thought Dad was now working from home. And so it was quite cool because I would get home from school and Dad would be there working upstairs, and he'd go off for a couple of hours for clients, and then come back again. The top half of upstairs was Dad's office, the big, full bookshelves. I have one of his sets of bookshelves in my home now with his books on it, which is very nice. I would always be curious. 'What are you doing there, Dad?' And he'd explain things to me, and I'd be like, 'I can't see it!' And he'd turn things around, and then I'd be like, 'Oh, okay.' And yes, I loved the models he built, as well.

So from an early age, even though I didn't really understand the work he was doing, I was learning about the back stories to all these pieces which were models on the table, or drawings on a page. So yeah, I was super-involved, really lucky. But at the same time, Dad was just an architect. It was his job.

Jeremy

Did you go on site visits with him, too?

Lucy

Yes, definitely. What was nice is that the site visits were combined with family trips, which is why I have really fond memories associated with a lot of the projects that Dad was involved in. The Tūrangi township, that was great; we used to travel down to Tokaanu and Tūrangi.[2] And the trips up to the Hokianga while he was first working on the Wishart House. I have very fond memories of spending time up there. Dad used to say, 'Close your eyes and imagine something there and something there.' And I would be like, 'I can't, I can't.' He'd say, 'Just imagine, just imagine.'

Jeremy

Have you kept particular things that remind you of him?

Lucy

He had numerous notebooks which I'm in proud possession of. They are very special to me. He was never far from a little pocketbook, and he was a fan of the Artline 0.2 and 0.4 millimetre pens, which I am a fan of also. I'm still getting through his old stash of them. He was always drawing. He never stopped — not when we were out for dinner, or on the plane. We'd be sitting at a restaurant sometimes and he'd have left his pocketbook in the car, so he'd get the napkin out and he'd draw on it. He always had a pen on him. The notebooks are quite nice because they're the family memories that I get to take on. Looking through them they're just lines on paper, but they're coming from somewhere, which is cool.

---

2   In the mid-1990s Rewi designed, with Isthmus Group, a canopy for a shopping centre in Tūrangi.

The shape of the Thompson House from the street suggests a poutama pattern, an eloquent response to council-mandated height-to-boundary limits. This sheet has been cut, making it difficult to decipher the text at right. 'These were Rewi's original thoughts describing the concept or sense of the project: family, defence, placement,' says Pip Newman, who worked in Rewi's office at the time. 'Reflections to define or elucidate design significance and observations were often recorded during the design process.' *Architecture Archive, University of Auckland*

40 – 41

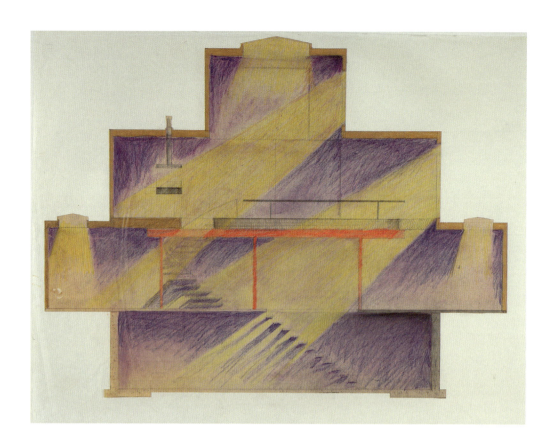

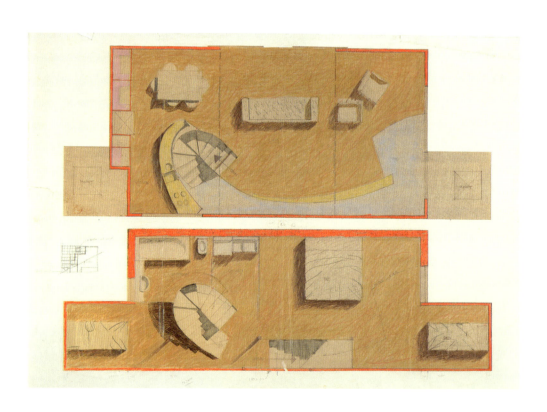

Homes

Drawings from Rewi's archives show early conceptions of the home's spatial arrangements. 'I always saw it as being on the marae,' says Rewi's friend and colleague Bill McKay of the house. 'You come on, you stand in the ātea, you wait until you're welcomed, then you're brought on.' *Architecture Archive, University of Auckland*

Jade

In his archives we've found some amazing ideas and process diagrams which are incredibly well articulated, and then other things where we're like, I don't know what that's about, but it looks really interesting.

Lucy

I think that's what's quite cool about creative people is that you don't always know what the idea is, and that's part of the wonder of it as well.

Jeremy

Are there projects of his that stand out in your memory?

Lucy

Growing up, I remember quite vividly going to the opening of Puukenga at Unitec. I remember him talking a lot about the Wishart House in Ōmāpere and visiting the site. I remember the children's museum and the City to Sea Bridge in Wellington. That stands out to me. And the giant fish canopy at the Ōtara Markets, because that model was particularly interesting for me as a child. There were always sculptures being built and drawings just being made and things like that. It was pretty special to be able to live and breathe that while we were living in our home together.

Jeremy

What were his connections like to home in Tolaga Bay? I know he grew up in Wellington. And Mike Barns talked about how his architecture was partly about him feeling his way into his Māoriness. What's your understanding of his relationship with all of that?

Lucy

It's something that I've come to have a better understanding of now, especially as I start my journey. I had thought it was something that was more important

in his later years, but now going through books and talking to people about the work he did, I see that it was super-important earlier. He was involved in the hapū and iwi and making sure the next generations had something, making sure that our children's children still can call places like Uawa home.

Jeremy

You've talked about all these experiences visiting sites and seeing projects being sketched. What do you think now as you look back on his legacy? It's probably hard to ask that of a daughter.

Lucy

I'm a very proud daughter. I always appreciated the work that he did. But it's not even necessarily the work that he's done, but the relationships that he built along the way are what I'm proudest of. How important his work has been with his students, with his clients, with his colleagues, with his friends, and with his whānau. It's really nice that he's remembered so fondly by so many people.

Jade

We've been blown away by that; listening to all these people and the outpourings of their emotion and their genuine feelings about your dad has been really touching. We felt privileged to be able to witness it.

Lucy

I think sometimes it's easy to forget. Part of the process of this book is connecting with people, and you speaking to other relationships that Dad had in his life, and me joining dots and making my own connections. It's a nice silver lining. I think it's never until someone is gone that you really see the true value of their influence and their work.

Pip Newman worked in Rewi's office in the mid-1980s with Nancy Couling and Mike McColl. One of the projects she contributed to was the Thompson House. Here, she recalls the collaborative atmosphere of the office and Rewi's deliberative design approach.

Jade Kake
What projects did you work on in the office with Rewi?

Pip Newman
We worked on the first drawings for his house. 'The Warrior.' That's what he called it.

Jade
Why was it called that? The Warrior?

Pip
Well, in the first image that we drew of it, of that ziggurat form, there was one sort of window that initially he imagined he might open up and that became a slit. The idea was, 'I can see out but no one can see in', and it was defensive, like in a medieval castle or a situation of defence. You can defend yourself, and no one can get in. It was about turning the back and defending and opening to the trees and the bush that was on the site.

Jade
I don't know what it was like for that project, but I know when we'd looked at the Wishart House in the archives, there were so many drawings of that same house, lots of concept drawings. He was drawing again and again and again. Was he like that with his own house?

Pip
Yeah. Little moves. Just changing it. Then thinking. Silence. Thinking. Silence. Meeting. Silence. Thinking. He had this way of … narrowing his eyes. I think it took a while for the design of the house to come about.

Jade
And what was that process of working collaboratively with him when he was going through his iterative process of small moves and changes? What was that like, going back and forth and being involved in that process?

Pip
Well, it taught me how to design how I design. I am committed to the architecture of small gestures. It's something that I feel very deeply. In Europe, where I worked for a long time, you don't do new projects very often. I was involved in a few, but, for the most part they're either retrofitting or repurposing. That overlaying and distilling. He was a distiller, like with whisky — in a barrel for 12, 24 months, and you wait. Something good is going to come out. But it's a process.

Jade
We've heard a lot from people about the way he would seem to move really, really slowly, but then move faster as it progressed. I heard from some people, 'Oh, it seems like nothing was moving.' And then he'd go away and come back the next day with a model.

Pip
Modelling is very important. Always model everything. I think his training in structure and engineering was so important because the mechanics of it were important. He knew how to do those things together, the tectonics and the structure. Those things were important, yes, but if you sorted out what it is, if you got that right, that was the distillation.

Jade
Do you have any thoughts on Rewi's legacy as an architect?

Pip
It's quite interesting. I've got a contradictory thought in my head about trust, how he trusted us as very young learners in his practice. Listening. That distillation. Looking and listening and pauses, the pace of what you do. That for me is really important. Really, really important. In our big commercial culture, that's crazy. Absolute craziness. Deciding to maybe do less, not more.

Jade
It takes a lot to resist that. It's easy to get caught up in the tide.

Pip
Absolutely. He'd take on the big projects, sure. But also he was open to smaller projects, like a papal stage or a piece of furniture or, I don't know, someone's stairs for their garden. Projects on a more human scale. It was that idea of it all being really important.

Rewi's early training in structural engineering was evident in the cantilevered edges of the Thompson House. 'It was defensive, like in a medieval castle,' says Pip Newman, who worked in Rewi's office in the 1980s and contributed to its design. 'You can defend yourself, and no one can get in.' A single slit in the street-facing exterior was the only way to see out in that direction. *David Straight*

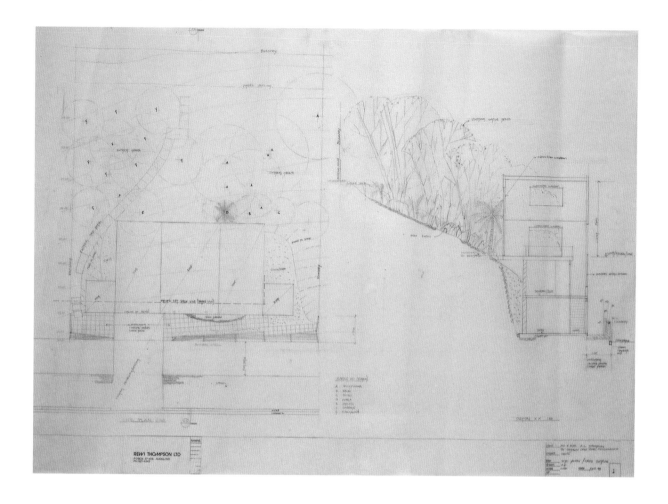

Above: Plans and elevations of the Thompson House from Rewi's archives. 'The house was an incredibly significant project for him personally,' says Rewi's friend Michael Thomson. *Architecture Archive, University of Auckland*

Opposite: Floor plans of the Thompson house as it was eventually realised.

Homes

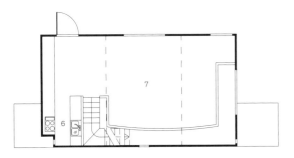

First floor plan

Ground floor plan

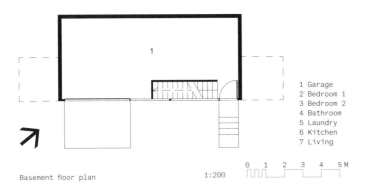

Basement floor plan 1:200

1 Garage
2 Bedroom 1
3 Bedroom 2
4 Bathroom
5 Laundry
6 Kitchen
7 Living

The Wishart House was designed for John and Pip Wishart and their children as a holiday home floating on poles amid the trees and overlooking the Hokianga Harbour. *David Straight*

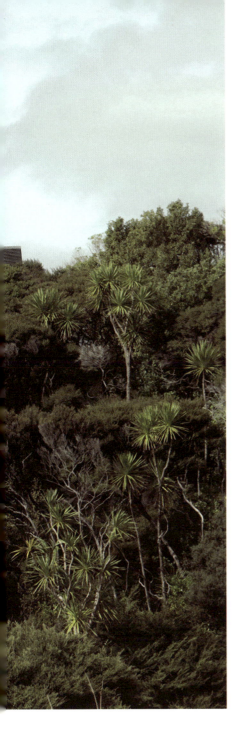

Wishart House

Ōmāpere
Hokianga

1989–98

John and Pip Wishart could be described as Rewi Thompson fans. Visit them at the holiday home overlooking the Hokianga Harbour that Rewi designed for them and they might suggest you watch an old VHS featuring the TV interview with Rewi that made them want to hire him in the first place. They also have a folder stuffed with printouts of articles in which Rewi appears, a loose-leaf summary of some of his career highlights. They're incredibly proud of their house and of the architect who designed it.

Rewi was proud of the home, too. It isn't unusual for the Wisharts to answer a knock at the door and find an architecture student or a visitor from abroad asking to see the place, requests that they're always happy to fulfil.

The house is perched on stilts like a long-legged seabird, looking across the harbour entrance towards the ever-changing play of light on the sand dunes at North Head. Its angled weatherboards echo the strata of the rocky cliffs that rise behind the house, zigzags that make it look as if the home is settling, gradually and unevenly, into the landscape.

John and Pip moved to Auckland from Christchurch soon after they married and became enchanted with Ōmāpere after holidaying there several times with their four children. Eventually, they managed to save enough to buy a piece of land on the hill just west of the main settlement. Soon afterwards, they saw Rewi interviewed about his work on the TV show *Koha*, and felt he was the ideal person to design their home.

They called Rewi and arranged a meeting. Rewi visited the site and asked them to write a letter explaining their aspirations for the house. Pip has kept a copy of the now-faded fax she wrote:

```
Dear Rewi,

Herewith an attempt to sum up the thoughts, feelings and
practical details tossed about on the visit to Omapere.

From our point of view the time you spent with us was of
enormous value, as by asking all the right questions, you
enabled us to focus on and follow up ideas which before had
been pretty vague and disconnected.

Firstly, the thing which to us is of special significance
and which seems right at the heart of the character of the
Hokianga is the play of light on the water and on the unique
landforms of the area as time of day, seasons and weather
change. You are right, there is a strength and power in
the landscape, but this is not something we find alien or
threatening, even in wild weather. Rather, the whole family
agrees that it is a place which produces feelings of both
```

elation and peace which, I suppose, is what a real feeling
of happiness often amounts to. We agree that the effect of
the environment is not to make us feel insignificant, but to
feel pleased to be there and become a part of it in response
to its power. There is a depth for us in the Maori meaning of
Hokianga — 'the returning place'.

Now, relating this response to building and living in that
environment — I'm sure your structural translation of
all those words like 'strong', 'simple', 'natural', which
we tossed about, will be a deeply satisfying expression
of our combined responses. The idea of floating out into
it very much seems to sum up the positive feelings we all
had towards that landscape and is a most exciting starting
point. Something else the family feels about the place is
that though the bar is so wild and the bush and hills so
mysterious, they are somehow protective of the harbour.
It always seems to us a safe place.

As for far more specific details, we are happy with the idea
that the house be sited against the ridge overlooking our
original 'house area', as the engineer suggested. I'm sure this
site could incorporate in the 'floating out' feeling, the best
views up the harbour, across to the sandhills and out to the
heads. The 'original' site, when drained, could be grassed and
slope away from the house as a natural extension of the living
space. We very much liked your ideas about this approach and
entrance, and are sure you'll come up with something exciting
there. We like the idea of one living area, open, but perhaps
irregularly shaped, to provide corners, as you suggested,
to experience the other elements of the environment, or to
isolate oneself a little from the main group (or the TV!), for
peaceful reading etc. A fireplace sounds a good idea — lots of
manuka wood, pinecones, driftwood — as we don't intend to use
the house only in summer.

Although the whole family won't always be there together,
we think three bedrooms, possibly with bunks in one of them,
would be about right, as our children might like to bring up
friends and we have friends we would like to ask to stay
from time to time (too far for day visits from Auckland!).
A bathroom and possibly an extra toilet and shower for sandy
bods and a laundry area would about fill the practical
requirements, with room for a couple of cars underneath.

Hope this all draws things together a little. You are most
welcome to come and have a bit more of a look at our tastes
at home. I think you were only in the kitchen when you
were here last. John often has a bit of time to spare on
a Thursday afternoon if you would like to come inside your
working hours.

Looking forward to a happy and interesting association.

Regards from all of us to yourself, Leona and Lucy,

Pippa Wishart

A few weeks after receiving this letter, Rewi asked the Wisharts to his studio to see a model he'd built. They were excited and decided to proceed, but almost a decade passed between their first call to Rewi in 1989 and enjoying their first holiday in the completed home. John and Pip initially paused the project to make sure they had enough money for the build, while Rewi worked through multiple iterations of the home that are now in his archives.

The first designs for the house had decks at either end, with another projecting from the centre of the house into the view. The drawings were submitted for approval by the Far North District Council in late 1992 or early 1993, but the home's unorthodox nature stirred opposition among some neighbours and resulted in a drawn-out consenting process. The gentle curve of the home's white, sail-like roof breached the site's height limit in places, and the council officers worried the unorthodox arrangement of weatherboards would leak (they never have). The decks at the front and side of the house were mostly removed during the consent process, but neither John nor Pip feel this has compromised the house in any way. If anything, the consenting obstacles made them even more determined to get the house built.

Visitors usually enter the home at its upper level across a bridge with palisade fencing that descends from the mezzanine (where the main bedroom and a bathroom are also located) into the dining area. The view across the harbour from here is mesmerising, but Rewi's design carefully rations it. While the kitchen and dining area have full-height glass that reveals the northern vista (as well as high southern windows that direct the gaze to the hilltop behind), the living room has only small slot windows looking into the mānuka at floor level on its northern elevation, something Pip says Rewi equated to the idea of lifting the bottom flap of a tent to peek outside. The ground-floor plan is flexible, with folding doors that can be pulled across to transform an eastern living space into a sleeping area when needed.

The home appears to sit lightly on the land, thanks to the slender poles that hold it aloft, but it is not a structure that wants to hide away. It is a gently assertive presence on the hill without being overbearing.

We met John and Pip at their Auckland home in mid-2022 and talked about many things, including their friendship with Rewi and the pleasure they still take in their remarkable house.

'It's pretty exhilarating in the morning just looking out,' says John Wishart of the home Rewi designed for him and his wife, Pip, and their children at Ōmāpere. The dining area offers views across the mouth of the Hokianga Harbour to North Head (above) and eastwards towards Rawene (below). The stained-glass panel is by Ralph Hotere.
David Straight

There are many iterations of the Wishart House in Rewi's archives, including this sketch showing the view towards North Head, a mezzanine area and an undulating roof.
Architecture Archive, University of Auckland

Homes

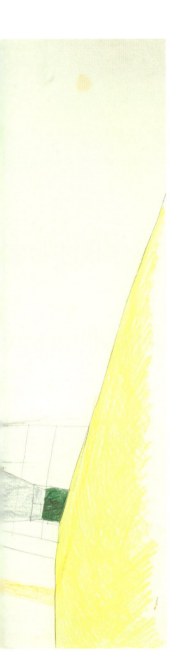

Jeremy Hansen
We're in this beautiful villa in Auckland. Your home in Ōmāpere is quite a contrast, and I wanted to ask you about how you came upon that. Was it Rewi that led that process or were you conscious of creating something that was very different to this experience?
Pip Wishart
Our first brief was for something entirely suitable for and expressive of that extraordinary site and Rewi's ideas were able to put these feelings into practice. When we first came back to Auckland, I would ideally have liked to have built, and we would've built something modern. When I lived in Christchurch, just before I married John, I lived in one of the Dorset Street Flats [designed in the mid-1950s by Miles Warren]. But we couldn't afford to build because we had four small children. So we looked for something big and old and we found this.
Jeremy
When and how did the Ōmāpere house come about for you?
Pip
When we first came to Auckland, I had never been to the far north. So when we'd settled in after a year or two, in 1982 we went and stayed in Dargaville and went on a sort of journey round from Dargaville to any places of interest.
John Wishart
We found our way up north to Ōmāpere. The beachfront was easy to get to, and we walked around and looked up as we went around the south and said, sort of speculatively, 'Wouldn't it be lovely to build a house up there?' Just dreaming at that point.
Pip
We were fascinated and wanted to come back, and so we came back several years running and stayed at the old hotel, which was just a great big villa-like farmhouse at the time with one funny little motel attached. We used to walk along the beach from there and fantasise about having a house up where ours is. And then the section came up for sale in 1988.
John
We bought it, and that was about as much as we could afford at the time.

Pip
We were thinking about what we would like up there, and then I saw Rewi walking along a beach somewhere being interviewed for *Koha*, and he was talking about a beach house that he'd built or designed. And I thought, that's the person for us: he'd be really sensitive to the area and I really like the look of his design.
John
The thing about him was that he was so fluent as he walked along and explained things. He was great. His manner, his approach just appealed.
Pip
I liked the way he explained his ideas.
Jeremy
So did you contact him soon afterwards?
John
We must have just rung him up. He was in the phone book, I suppose, under 'architect'.
Pip
He came around here, and we had a chat to him and we made a time to all go up and have a look at the site. Rewi and Leona and Lucy came up one weekend. Lucy was four.
John
They were very enthused.
Pip
We sat at a part of the section that's always called the lookout. I remember Rewi and I were sitting in the grass at the lookout, chatting about what we would like and our ideas coincided really well.
Jeremy
Is this when he asked you to write the letter?
Pip
Yeah. Rewi said, 'Go home and write me a letter. Put it all down on paper.' So I did. And he always kept it, didn't he? He called it 'the letter'. This was 1989.
John
It's such a very good letter and he responded beautifully to it.
Jeremy
How did he show his response to the letter to you? Was it a series of discussions?
Pip
We went to see him at his architecture studio and he'd built a model by then.

Jeremy

What was your reaction to that model when you saw it?

Pip

I thought, Wow, we'll be going on from here. This looks very much like something we can cooperate with.

Jeremy

You were excited?

Pip

Very excited. Mmm.

John

Leona said at times in the middle of the night Rewi would wake up and say, 'Aha, I'll do this.' He'd make a drawing. The model was very portable and turned up at various places.

Jeremy

Did it change much from that point?

Pip

It developed, didn't it?
He expanded it. More and more and more detail happened.

John

It was like a giant deck for a start, which curved around and was sheltered by the dug-out place above, which is really clever.

Pip

We had to change it a bit because we had a lot of opposition from the Far North District Council.

Jade Kake

What was the problem?

Pip

It was in one place slightly over height, and the original plans had a covered walkway from the garage to the house so that when we were unpacking in wet weather we wouldn't get drenched. They said that was too much site coverage.

John

There was also a six-metre height limit it was not supposed to be over. And, I don't know, 20 or 30 per cent of the roof was a bit over.

Pip

There were also to be decks on either end and a very small bit that you could walk out on the front where the big windows are. And they wouldn't allow that because of site coverage restrictions.

Jeremy

Do you mourn the loss of those things at all? As a visitor, it doesn't feel as if the building has lost elements.

John

We feel happy. We don't mourn it too much because what's left is so great.

Pip

I'm quite happy about that. The first time Rewi came up, he did a panoramic photograph of the harbour and the site where we wanted to build the house. And I remember him turning the model around so that it was in an optimum position to get the views and get the sun. He thought very carefully about siting that place and he made a wonderful job of it.

John

Yeah. It's facing exactly north, which is wonderful. And it just fitted into the slope so nicely. When it was just beginning, he was there as the digging out was going on. He said, 'Do it there and there and there.' He was very hands-on.

Pip

We stopped him for a bit while we organised finances.

Jeremy

How long was the process between meeting Rewi and occupying the house? Can you remember?

Pip

It was quite a long time, wasn't it, John? We met him in '89. And we stopped him for quite a while, while we were accumulating enough money. And then we had the battles with the council when it was notified. It didn't comply enough, so they had to have a hearing. But the majority of the people were extremely against it. I can't be bothered going into some of the reasons that they were against it.

Jeremy

When was it completed so you could move in?

John

It was early 1998.

Jeremy

And Rewi keep iterating over much of that time?

John

Oh. I think we had complete plans by '92 or '93.

Jade

I assume your intention from the beginning was that this wasn't a house to be permanently lived in. And given that, how did Rewi respond in being

able to pack it down, or any kind of maintenance issues related to the seasonal occupation?

John

I think he thought it was a practical place in all seasons, really. We and he actually quite liked the idea of wild weather. It is versatile from that point of view. Rewi said it was like a big deck with a central cooking and heating place, and then some sleeping at one end.

Pip

Yes. He said, 'You'll be here in all weathers, won't you?' It's not just a summer holiday house. Because of the north-facing windows, as soon as there's any sun, all that glass warms the house. And if there's no sun in the winter, you can light the fire. The big chimney runs right up through the centre of the house and it's like central heating. When you're going up the stairs to the mezzanine bedroom and you put your hand on there, it's warm.

John

It's like a nice warm column through the middle of the house. The house warms very quickly.

Pip

It's lovely being elevated. It's lovely being able to look right across the harbour and then out to the horizon.

Jeremy

You have this amazing panoramic view from the dining table, but the living area plays a different game, with a solid wall facing the view, with westerly windows into the bush and low windows to the north offering little downward glimpses of the site.

John

Rewi said at one stage, when we were talking about the contrast between the walls with little low windows where you were shielded from outside, that he didn't want to make it a glass house with absolutely no protection.

Pip

He wanted us to be able to escape to somewhere from the impact of the weather.

John

So you have beautiful views both north and south in the middle of the house. And then at the ends, you have more interesting views.

Right: Rewi 'didn't want to make it a glass house with absolutely no protection,' John Wishart says. So while the dining area offers expansive harbour views, the living room has a wall facing north with small slot windows at the bottom. Pip Wishart says the windows are an expression of 'the idea of peeping out under the tent'. David Straight

Below: High windows above the kitchen offer views back to the rocky hills behind the house, as well as the palisade-lined entry to the home, which descends from the mezzanine floor to the main living area. David Straight

Below: A view from the living area through the glassy dining room and kitchen towards a flexible sleeping/living space at the home's eastern end.
David Straight

Opposite: The main bedroom is located on the mezzanine floor above the living room in this photo. The living room also offers westerly views into the bush surrounding the home.
David Straight

Homes

Pip

He was quite good at explaining why it's got those funny little windows along the bottom. It's the idea of peeping out under the tent. And also he said, 'Sometimes it's very nice just to get glimpses of things as well as the great big, powerful view from the main window.'

Jeremy

How would you describe Rewi's process or way of working with you?

John

He was extremely adept and fluent and encouraging, and he was a positive force to have with you. We were already enthused, but he was such a good person at putting the whole philosophy to you.

Pip

The foreman on the site spoke of Rewi as if he was a very important person and a huge influence. He really respected him. Rewi was a good communicator with all sorts of people.

John

You can see why he was an excellent lecturer. He seemed be able to generate enthusiasm. The people around him loved him. We've talked to people who've been associated with him and they said it was a great experience. He was actually very modest, although there were some funny things that he had. In his office, he said, 'This is my skite board' on which the umpteen awards were stuck up that he had. He could laugh. He's just so missed.

Jeremy

How did he go about explaining the conceptual underpinnings of the house to you?

John

I suppose it was the really good drawings he had.

Pip

He was very fluent in communicating his ideas and then waiting for the feedback. [Architect] Hugh Tennent once came to the house and said, 'Why did you choose Rewi? He's an ideas architect.' And I said, 'Yes, because he is an ideas architect.' I'm a bit of an ideas person, too. I like ideas and I liked his ideas.

Jeremy

You mentioned the idea of the house being a large deck ostensibly looking at the view from its centre. I wonder

if you could talk through some of those specific anchors of the project. I was also thinking about the way the weatherboards are arranged and the curved roof. Where did aspects like that come from, and how did Rewi explain them to you?

Pip

The weatherboards are meant to reflect the strata of the land around the house, and particularly the big rock up behind us. The building inspectors from the council were worried about those weatherboards.

John

It's actually an important part of the structure, and it has never leaked, I might add, but they were very suspicious and kept on being suspicious of him. Rewi was a man who, if a curved line could be used, he would do it. He loved curves and shapes, and straight lines were not necessarily the default thing.

Jeremy

You mentioned earlier that the roof was derived from an idea of a sail.

John

That's how we saw it, wasn't it? Rewi explained that it's painted white, rather like a sail.

Pip

The roof is white because it is supposed to reflect the mānuka when it's in flower, Rewi told me. It's one of the colours that is quite dominant up there.

Jeremy

Did he ever talk to you about the decision to lift the house up on poles as it is?

Pip

Yes, because he wanted us to feel that when we came in, we were sort of floating out into the landscape. What he liked doing was coming in the upper door and then coming down into the body of the house and feeling that it carried you out into space.

John

And the palisading was so attractive as a sort of an entrance path to finding it.

Jeremy

Can you talk a little bit about the spatial organisation inside the house? Because there's a pleasing looseness to the way those spaces can be arranged and utilised.

Rewi arranged the weatherboards on the house and its separate garage (with mezzanine sleeping space for guests) to emulate the strata of the rocky hills behind the house; they make it look as if the buildings are settling gradually into the landscape. The entry ramp to the house arrives at the mezzanine level, where an interior stair leads to the dining and kitchen area.
David Straight

Below: The home is raised on poles because Rewi 'wanted us to feel that when we came in, we were sort of floating out into the landscape,' Pip Wishart says. *David Straight*

Opposite: The arrival sequence leads visitors on a path beside the separate garage towards the house, withholding the view until they arrive inside. The lower photograph shows the low slot windows of the eastern sleeping area. *David Straight*

Homes

Pip

That was sort of between me and Rewi, wasn't it?

John

The mezzanine came in early as a great idea for the upstairs. And then the fluidity was a great idea, wasn't it?

Pip

Yes. One of his ideas was that the big curved roof over it was like a tent, a tent over a deck. And the spaces inside should be adaptable, like they're in a tent — and they are. It depends who's at the house. You can shut bits off.

John

Yeah. You've got this sleeping area in the east, eating and looking in the middle, and then the west is about contemplating, reading, watching.

Pip

I love the space when it's all opened up and you can look from one end to the other.

Jeremy

Do you have favourite aspects of the house?

John

It's pretty exhilarating in the morning just looking out. Breakfast is looking north. And it's lovely in the afternoon if you're down the east end and looking towards the horizon as the sun sets. You look through the house, all three dimensions of it. It's very pleasing as you look through the palisades [leading to the mezzanine level and the entry bridge] and through the stairs. You're conscious that the sea's to the north, you're looking west, and the depth and the compartments of the house seem so right. It's fascinating.

Jeremy

What about you, Pip?

Pip

Different times of day are equally lovely in their own ways. And it's really beautiful at sunset. One of the things I really like about that house is that it's very unpretentious and it fits so well into the landscape.

John

One of the things council was on about was that you don't want to have structures infringing on the landscape. And Rewi said, 'Well, actually the structure can enhance the landscape.'

Jeremy

What did Rewi think of the house after it was complete? Was he pleased?

John

He was delighted, I think. And he kept mentioning it to all sorts of people who used to come and visit it. They would turn up and we'd say, 'Oh, it's lovely to see you. Yes, have a look around.' International people used to arrive and introduce themselves and say, 'We thought we should come here.'

Jade

He must have been proud of the outcome, telling all sorts of people to come and pop in. As we've been going through the archives, the sheer volume of drawings of your house is quite astonishing. You might not know the answer, but I just wanted to ask why you think he seemed to be so engrossed and obsessed by your house project?

John

I don't know, but it's something that really appealed to him. He got the message from Pip's letter and I think he really loved the whole idea. I'm not surprised to hear there were lots of drawings because I think he regarded the house as one of his highlights.

Jade

I was just speculating, but with the amazing location and attributes of the landscape, combined with yourselves as clients and your willingness to give him free rein with his ideas, it sounds like quite a generous and expansive relationship. It sounded as if you were receptive to his creative ideas and that's why you wanted him on board.

John

The whole thing just was a happy development. It really was.

Pip

He was such a dear person and so nice to communicate with. He was a good friend. He was doing this house when Leona became ill and gradually got worse and worse. And it was awful.

John

It's the unfairness of life. It was terrible.

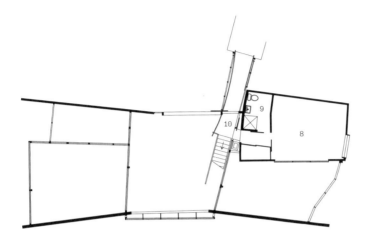

Mezzanine floor plan

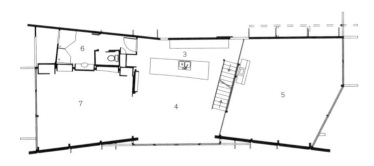

First floor plan

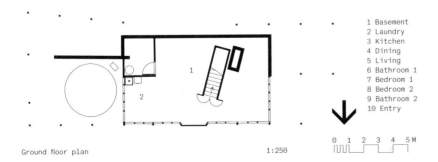

Ground floor plan   1:250

1 Basement
2 Laundry
3 Kitchen
4 Dining
5 Living
6 Bathroom 1
7 Bedroom 1
8 Bedroom 2
9 Bathroom 2
10 Entry

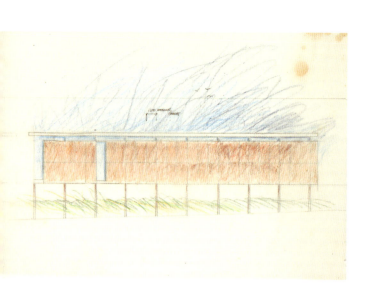

West Coast Studio

Tāmaki Makaurau Auckland

2015–19

Homes

'He was very, very interested in having a strong form in the land,' says artist Katharina Grosse of the studio that Rewi designed for her, and which was completed after his death. These drawings of the building are all from Rewi's archives. *Architecture Archive, University of Auckland*

Katharina Grosse is an artist whose work has received global acclaim. She is also one of Rewi's last clients. She sometimes makes domestic-sized paintings on canvas, but her most attention-grabbing creations are breathtakingly large-scale installations that feature bold swathes of brightly coloured paint applied with a spraygun to huge tree trunks, building exteriors, interior gallery walls, enormous drops of fabric, and piles of soil studded with glacier-like polystyrene chunks. She is represented by Gagosian, the global dealer gallery that sells the work of some of the contemporary art world's most revered practitioners. In an interview with Louise Neri on the Gagosian website, Katharina describes her spraygunned work this way: 'I can develop images of direct, nonlinear, and nonlogical energy that generate clusters of compressed emotions.'

The artist divides her time between Berlin and the coast west of Auckland, where her fascinating clifftop studio was designed by Rewi in 2015 and 2016 and completed after his death with the assistance of architect Graeme Burgess. Katharina agreed to the home and studio being part of this book but, to preserve her privacy, asked us not to feature photographs of it. She also shared many of Rewi's emails and early sketches and agreed to let us publish them.

Katharina's studio is high up a wild stretch of coastline prone to violent winds that blast up the cliffs from the sea. The building is a steel structure with dark brown aluminium cladding perched atop a cluster of tall wooden poles and tucked into the lee of the hill behind it. Its impassive northern face has a swooping inward curve that echoes the shape of the hill behind. The views here — steep, bush-clad hills tumbling down to a roaring ocean — are incredible, but the studio, with its almost-blank face punctuated only by a narrow horizontal slice of glass, all but ignores them.

There is no conventional entry sequence to the studio: we walked down the rough shingle driveway and around a deck at the rear before knocking on a tall metal door. Katharina's living quarters are just inside the door, a single long room that feels taller than it is wide. In here, the curve of the north-facing wall that we'd seen from outside traces inwards and compresses the space at the other end, where a door leads to Katharina's workspace.

There are minimal concessions to domesticity: the 'kitchen' consists only of a small, square island bench with a sink in it and some stools around it. There is also a bed, a couple of armchairs and a wood-burner. The space is daylit by clerestory windows. When you sit down you're at eye level with the narrow slot window on the building's northern side, through which you can see the hills dropping towards the sea.

At the end of the room, just past a slender bathroom, the building's workspace is a big white volume lit mostly by fluorescent tubes, although a slim vertical window on the western corner — something Katharina didn't want, but Rewi pushed for, and she's now pleased he did — reveals a glimpse of the water.

When she decided to build a studio, Katharina interviewed four or five New Zealand architects for the job. 'Rewi was one of the last people I met. Because there was no website, there was no way to contact him,' she told us. But once she discovered his university email address and sent him a message, he replied right away. 'I had the feeling he understood my artistic practice in relationship to the necessity to be here,' she says. 'He was a very inspiring man, generous in the way that he would bring bits and pieces to the table that I wasn't familiar with, but he did it in such a poetic way that it was very easy to deal with them.'

We spent over an hour talking with Katharina and walking around the building in early 2021. This is an edited version of our conversation.

Jeremy Hansen
What were you looking for with this building project?

Katharina Grosse
One of the basic ingredients was that it had to be off the grid, with water harvesting and solar power. It also needed to be low maintenance because I'm not here all the time. I didn't want to spend time when I'm here painting the house, repairing the house or whatever it takes sometimes on a bach. You could see very early on that Rewi came from a very engineering point of view: what the materials are, how they work. Is it going to be the steel structure that is clad? How does it meld into the landscape at the same time? He was very, very interested in having a strong form in the land.

We had this map of the contours and everything, [and] we made a little line and then said maybe that's an idea, and that's how we started the placing of the house. And also my site is really long, but very narrow, and goes down towards the beach. Out here [at her partner Judy Millar's house and studio, which is next door] I've witnessed amazing storms, where the whole house shakes. I found

it frightening and I wanted the inside of this house to be sheltered. We wanted to make a real contrast between indoor and outdoor.

Jeremy
Did you know what you wanted the house to look like?

Katharina
I didn't. I did think it could be slightly industrial. A lot of things were practical demands that I had listed. At the beginning, Rewi had an idea for a tower up on this tip here [she indicates the hill behind the house], and I didn't like the idea of having something to go up; I wanted everything on one plane.

Jade Kake
What were his thoughts around the tower?

Katharina
To view things — to dominate, I think maybe as well. To have a stand against the landscape. He thought, you can be very powerful here. You have to be, as the landscape is so powerful. So it wasn't like, oh, I have to be invisible; very, very different from the people's houses that are around here. Both approaches are very interesting. When

I built it, I was a little bit surprised also. I was wondering, did I do the right thing?

Jeremy

Once you'd decided against the tower, how did the building take shape?

Katharina

I think Rewi envisioned the form. He had it very early. But we were discussing things. The process of developing the design and the drawings was very good. He had an amazing ability to connect with you. I think you see that in the plans as well. It's very sculptural. I always think that it looks like you have a rectangular building that gives the impression of being turned in front of your eyes. I think it is a living, very animated form.

Jeremy

It feels unusual not to have glass everywhere. I say that because so many architects, when faced with a view like this, would open the building to it as much as possible.

Katharina

There was this discussion as well. I'm not a fan of a view in the sense that it is a feature of a house. But the window [in the combined living and bedroom] is quite big. It's a six-metre-long window. We had this thought — and that was also a very early thought of Rewi's — that you have the curve of the building and the curve corresponds to the horizontal line of the window. And also this idea of the slit that you watch but you're inside. We didn't want to make it like a multifunctional building, because I didn't want it. I'm happy living with very few things. And you don't need much out here. I don't live like that anyway. I was very old before I started to have, like, a house where I had a dinner table, for example.

My studios were always the main place, so the studios started to develop around other things, like there was a library or a place to write or a special place to read, but there's never been this idea of, *there* is the living room, and then there is *this* and *this* and *this* around it. So we had a lot of little things that we were contemplating, and then we did away with them to simplify it. And to give it a sense of proportion inside that suits the scale of the building.

Jade

The folded roof shape is really interesting.

Katharina

That was an important thought he had very early on. And also that it was going to be like a pavilion. So the idea of the light coming in under the roof through clerestory windows, which I don't think is very often done here. So the light is filtered and it's not so harsh.

Jeremy

The curve of this room also seems to narrow the space at the end.

Katharina

Yeah. It gets narrowed down and you have to go through like a little opening into the studio space. It's very dramatic. I did love that, that you are getting squeezed. It's like a secret little door or something.

Jeremy

It's hard to read the scale of the building from outside. And as we step into the studio, it's surprising how large this space is.

Katharina

It's a good studio size. I think it's a little bit industrial. But at the same time with this cut roof, it's a little like a pavilion, a little playful as well. Rewi thought it was like a belly of an albatross or something. And it's fantastic to open up here onto a rear deck because of this material difference in the white indoors and the ply outdoor.

Jeremy

Did you and Rewi talk much about your art practice and how that informed his design?

Katharina

He got it right away. In his first email he says, oh, your scale, your spray, your relationship to the work, I get it. Very early he said to me, 'I'm a Māori modernist', which his generation of course would be about, with Para Matchitt and Ralph Hotere; and all the people he was in touch with were probably influenced by John Scott, I guess.

Jeremy

Were there moments in the design process where you felt he was consciously inserting Māori design principles, or were they integrated into the whole process?

Katharina

For me it was of tremendous importance that he came from a Māori background. And he would always look at it with relative scepticism a little bit as well, even though it came back in the conversation all the time in the metaphors he used sometimes to describe something, and then he would also counteract them. When I, for example, was in Italy and I wrote to him about where I was and what I saw in terms of architecture, he said, 'Florence, such a surprise. One of my aunties was from Florence and there's a very strong relationship in our family with that place. So all these things mix in my head then at the same time.' He says, 'Well, you know I was an engineer before I was an architect and I came from a totally different background.'

So it was this interesting interweaving of things where you don't quite understand where you're coming from. I didn't grow up here; I'm not well-versed in it, of course. I only know about Māori culture from reading about it. He would point things out sometimes in emails, like when we go through the land, there are eyes watching us all the time, for example. He also thought that it was very important that you don't build for eternity. You build for a certain amount of time, you'll live here, you use it and then somebody else might come, as though you are the caretaker for somebody else who has been here before.

Jade

I do think that that really does reflect our cultural lens as Māori, both in our relationship with land and place and architectural tradition — it wasn't about permanent buildings, that's quite recent. I've heard Rewi has said things like that in a variety of settings and it's interesting to see that carried through, because everyone really wanted to preserve his house and some of us sort of thought, well, would he actually want that? Maybe not.

Katharina

Yeah. And also this reluctance to be documented. If you look up Māori architecture, for example, there is John Scott, with the chapel and the churches. He is such an icon. But I think Rewi really had a reluctance to have that done to his work. He did not want to be, I think, in the Pinterest world with this.

And that's why I'm also like this, and for other reasons as well, I would rather have the plans and the sketches and the thoughts about the work published rather than the building with photographs. I think he wouldn't have done that. It was very difficult for me to find out what he had built.

Jade
If that's what you feel is the best way to show the house, then that's great. How did you find Rewi?

Katharina
With the help of Judy, we had looked through a lot of different architects' houses and works and then I decided to visit or to write to five or four. And Rewi was one of the last people I met … The way we talked I had the feeling he understood my artistic practice in relationship to the necessity to be here. The delight he took in being part of it — he said, oh, what a surprise, let's meet. Let's see.

And the way that he came out here and looked at the site, I felt very comfortable. It was really about building this house and having an idea on a project that wasn't super-big, but was exciting. That was also something I really liked about him: that he never said, oh, that's just a small thing, but I'd like to do it because you're an artist. I think that Rewi was very careful and very clear about where he would engage his energy.

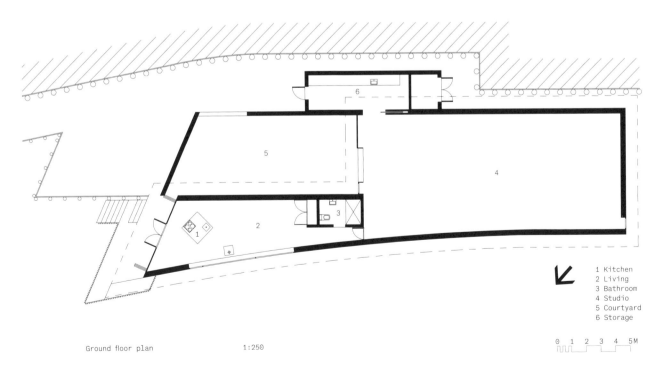

Ground floor plan   1:250

1 Kitchen
2 Living
3 Bathroom
4 Studio
5 Courtyard
6 Storage

70 – 71

Rewi and Katharina met on site in September 2015, just over a year before he died. Katharina shared Rewi's emails to her with us, and we've selected those that we feel illuminate his process the most.

We haven't edited the emails, leaving spelling and punctuation as we found them, although at Katharina's request we have taken out details that reveal the building's location. As above, the reference to Judy is to Katharina's partner, the New Zealand artist Judy Millar.

```
Von: Rewi Thompson <rm.thompson@auckland.ac.nz>
Betreff: new home
Datum: 7. September 2015 um 20:10:25 GMT+12

Kia ora Katharina,

Just a note to say how much I enjoyed our chat yesterday.

Lots of creative ideas and enjoyed the poetic-ness of our
chat.

My head at present is full of your dream, so I hope you
don't mind me sending you images of some of my thoughts, that
hopefully will progress development of your new studio.

In particular . . . the track that leads and beyond . . . it is
dark, the track bendy and narrow, deep in the bush almost
lost not knowing what is ahead.

Eyes watch us, for we are not alone.

The journey thru the native bush to [the studio] seems
a wonderful experience and expectation that hightens the
arrival from out of the bush and thrown out and greeted to
the wildness of the west coast and ocean.

Judys track leads us to a tall cave like 'split'.

It is narrow: as we enter: almost rubbing against the bark
like walls (textured play): the smell of the tree: The walls
seem to squeeze the urbanity out of us: to warn and tell us:
now that we are arriving at a beautiful and wonderful part
of the world.

We look up and see the clouds hurrying by: but we are in
no hurry! (glazed skylight over passageway also to light
mezzanine level). Refracted sun light dabbling/dancing/
exposing the textural qualities of the wood: like a beacon
guiding us leading us to what lies ahead.

Opening up to a clearing > a creative space

a space for performance and beyond the awesome power of the
ocean.
```

```
                I hope you have a safe trip back to Berlin.

                and just to say how wonderful to have meet you

                and thank you again to be able to be apart of your new home
                here in nz

                I keep in touch: probably towards the end of this week.

                arohanui / noho ora mai

                lots of kindness and stay well

                rewi
```

The email had two images attached, photos Rewi had taken of drawings in his sketchbook. The sketch plan is pretty close to what now exists, minus a few elements: there is no compressed entry, glazed passageway or mezzanine, for example. What followed this email was an international back-and-forth as Rewi tested a series of iterations.

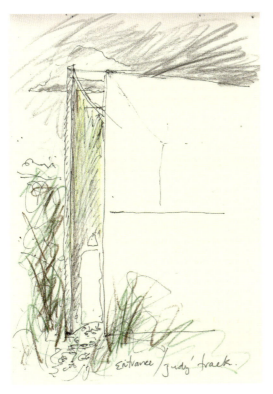

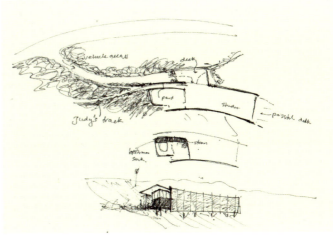

Rewi's emails with Katharina Grosse illuminate the way the building took shape. Some early concepts, such as the cave-like split at the entry shown in one drawing, were not realised in the building's final form. Its curved exterior was present in sketches from the start. *Courtesy of Katharina Grosse*

Less than a month later, Rewi sent this action plan.

```
ACTION PLAN: 14/10/2015

1. DEVELOPMENT OF BRIEF:

Previous emails and our meetings have provided a sound basis
for a brief, however you may wish to add to, alter or expand
in more detail.
    A simple response is just to tick or expand the lines and
hand write responses.

a. WORK STUDIO:

    • How do you typically work or are there a number of
      different work processes that you adopt or wish to
      develop?
    • What materials, equipment, supplies, other items do you
      need to execute your work.
    • Do these materials etc. need special storage, power,
      or other requirements like:
    • Storage system, tub, bench, etc.

Dimensions:

Height: 4.2M Is this a minimum dimension?
Width: 7.2M (I think) Is this a minimum dimension?
Length: 24M: This will depend on site coverage and how the
living space is located.
Shape: Capable to work with largish works on canvas.
Natural Daylight: South light
Contact with environment: Is it important to visually see
land or sea and or sky?
Is it important to hear the natural world.
Warm: I am assuming that the space would want to be warm in
winter and cool in the summer?
Ventilation: Good ventilation.
How important is acoustics?
Materials: What materials do you feel would be appropriate
for:

    Walls:
    Floor:
    Ceiling:
    Electrical: Do you require power at certain places in the
    studio.

b. WORK SPACE EXPANSION:

Do you require an adjacent 'external work space'
or alternative work space?

If you require this type of space, describe what type of
space it might be or used for.

What size does this need to be?
```

Homes

Will it need to connect to other areas like the entry/
delivery etc.

c. ARRIVAL / ENTRY:

In general would you arrive at your studio by car undercover
or shelter from rain and wind. Or would a car be lift at the
boundary and a link to the Studio via a walkway (similar to
Judys)

Do you require a garage for parking and storage? If so would
this want to be a part of the studio or separate.

Is it a wish to have a simple but exciting entrance to your
studio/living?

Delivery of Goods: I understand that packages / canvas rolls
would want to be delivered directly to the studio/storage.
I assume pick up the same.

d. LIVING SPACE:

How do you envisage this being located?

- Detached space form studio
- Spatially part of the studio
- Spatially separate but connected to the studio.
- On the same level as studio
- Elevated

Do you require separation between bed space and lounge?

Bed Size: What size do you require?
Wardrobe / Storage: What are your needs?

Lounge: How many people do you envisage the space is for?

Besides relaxing / reading what other activities would
the lounge area require?
Are there any special requirements?

- Ability to visually connect to studio, or any important
  landmarks
- Special technology / sound systems etc. to be
  accommodated?
- Would the lounge sofa say be a fold out bed for quests
  or
- Would there be stored somewhere a separate sleeping
  mattress?

Dining table: sufficient for how many people?

Small Kitchen: Describe your needs or how you wish to cook?

Do you have any preference for special equipment or
apparatus, items etc.

Do you have any preference for materials: ie stainless
steel for bench top.

Bathroom: Describe your needs? Do you have preference for
materials or fittings?

Describe what connections to the site do you perceive are
important. Visually, sound, other.

Do you require a deck?
Obviously good sun light / ventilation is important.
Warm in winter / cool in summer.
Any special power needs.

e. SERVICES:

Storm water: With filter system: will require storage tanks.

Power: Requires research: Obvious equipment are solar panels
combined with wind turbine.

Heating: Solid fuel burner

Waste Disposal: Twin tank system

Stormwater:

Telephone: From road frontage.

Are there any special requirements relating to services.

f. RESPONSE TO SITE:

You have expressed your personal, responses to the site.
Do you wish to expand on any other emotional values /
qualities that you feel I should be aware of or that might
influence the design.

External Materials
I know we have briefly touch on materials but do you have
any strong feelings relating to possible building form
and materials given the site and functional aspect of the
studio. ie

- Low maintenance
- sustainable approach
- engage with the forces of nature

OTHER: Please outline any other elements or considerations.

Ie: How often would you visiting or be staying at your
new studio?
Do you think you need to allow for expansion or future
additions?

Homes

Rewi experimented with the idea of the studio having different levels and a covered carport in early drawings he emailed to Katharina Grosse.
Courtesy of Katharina Grosse

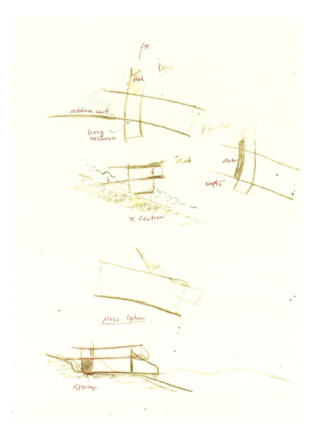

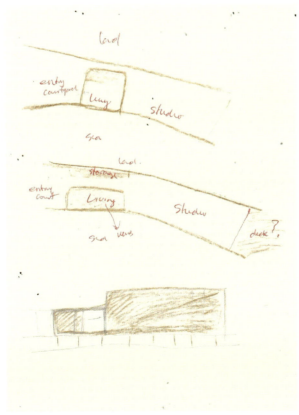

Concept:
The studio is created as a waharoa / gateway, a threshold that channels and captures the spiritual forces of land and sea. This energy is envisaged to engage with the human aspirations and spirit to ignite positive creativity.
The 'flute' like space is therefore open ended: both in a physical and metaphysical sense.

Presently there are 3 planning options but all are based on a common fluted concept.

Part Site Plan: The current studio location is determined by

- Driveway access to follow natural contouring to minimise excavation and fill, minimise length and gradient.
- I am anticipating that the driveway will be designed such that the excavation equals the amount of fill
- So that in principle no soil is removed from the site.
- Suggest that the studio / deck is suspended above ground and therefore minimise impact on ground and vegetation.
- Respond to 4.2M wall height and maximum building heights.
- Natural contouring.
- Views to beach and headland.

Option A:

The orientation of the studio suggests that the studio is a seem less work place between exterior and interior. Such that the work space is between to giant uninterrupted walls. Currently the back wall is straight and the seaward wall is slightly curved. This reinforcing the dynamic nature of the interior and a response or gesture of the power of the site.

South light is above the straight wall. This could be similar to the top of the curved wall if required. Another option of light is at the base of the walls. The end walls could be literally flexible. ie moveable screen like doors, such that they could used to mount art work or folded away to expose views etc. if desirable.

The internal space is 140M² as briefed (but could be larger if need be): the deck area is 55M² but could be any size. The deck / external courtyard is envisaged to be sheltered from the west wind, sunny and open to the bush. Effective work area is 190m².

The entrance requires more thought, although I have shown a corridor idea but not sure? I think the way the flute works is that the whole studio is the 'door'. *One is welcomed by the sea and the horizon beyond.*

The car parking and storage have been located to slide to the side of the studio and not destroy the 'flow' and openness.

The drawing indicates the cars parked within the set back distance to reduce driveway length (cost). Also indicated a possible location for water tanks / storage and compost w/c if required.

The bedroom and living space is provided as a mezzanine.

Cars parked in the setback and if you do not wish for a carport: would require a resource consent.

Option B:

This plan indicates the sleep / living is on the same level as the studio and located to be accessible to the deck.
The cars comply with the set back rules, however if there was no carport this would require a resource consent.

Option C:

Seem less work space between interior and exterior, except sleep and living is at west end.
The ensuite could be recessed so that the wall appears continuous. Literally the bed / living area is part of the seascape.
Cars are compliant.
Cross Section Garage: Car parks recessed as a cut into hill. (requires retaining wall)

Water tanks and septic tanks could be located under deck as an option. This would keep the area tidy.

Typical Cross Section Through Studio.

An 'elegant industrial' feel.

Envisaged simple / robust construction suspended above ground. At this stage structure envisage steel Portals with timber framing for walls, roof and floor. External cladding a suitable metal. Roofing still researching. Linings: walls gib as noted and floor timber ply or similar.

My current thinking relating to materials and construction is this:

Timber piles set in concrete. A steel frame I believe has 3 advantages. Firstly this will provide a structural sound primary Frame. It can be manufactured off site, and quickly erected on site. Given that the timber walls can be made off site, also this applies for the cladding and roofing and say aluminium windows. Therefore construction to achieve weather tightness could be very quick and cost effective.

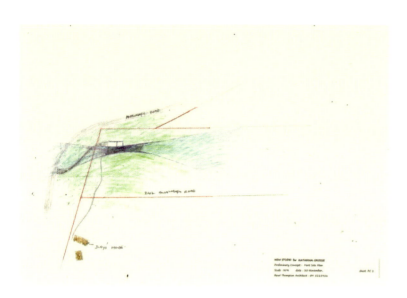

Homes

Opposite: 'The studio is created as a waharoa/ gateway, a threshold that challenges and captures the spiritual forces of land and sea,' Rewi wrote in the 2015 email to Katharina Grosse which contained these drawings. *Courtesy of Katharina Grosse*

Right: Rewi presented three possibilities for the studio's design to Katharina Grosse by email. The first created a large space with a large studio and a mezzanine bedroom and living area, while the second shows sleeping and living areas on the same level as the studio. A third option located sleeping and living areas at the building's western end. *Courtesy of Katharina Grosse*

Overleaf: A drawing from November 2015 shows the relationship of the studio to its terrain. Despite the spectacular outlook, views are limited to a long slot window in the living area. *Architecture Archive, University of Auckland*

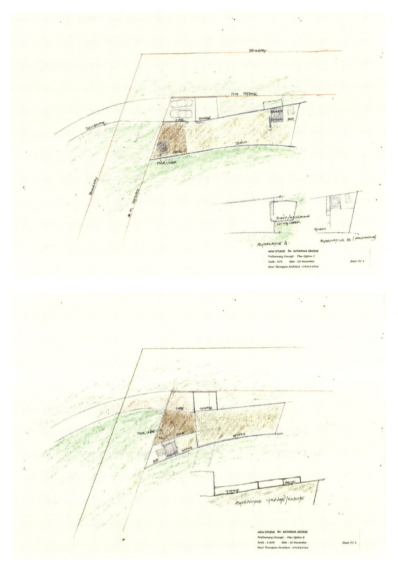

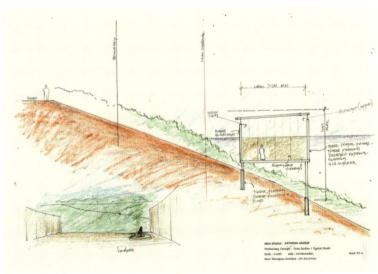

80 – 81

```
Anfang der weitergeleiteten Nachricht:
Von: Rewi Thompson <rm.thompson@auckland.ac.nz>
Betreff: photos
```

Datum: 11. November 2015 um 10:13:29 GMT+13

buckle; wall option: while much more dynamic does complicate and compromise the interior

I just though it might be interesting . . . not what you don't want rather than what you want!

deck 1: open deck facing the bush / protected from the sea winds and sunny.

interior 1: indicating spatial openness

paua: north wall treatment option like a mirror: paua shell . . . a reflection of the sea.

mezz: mezzanine option

plaster 1 and 2: form experiment: like a koauau or Maori flute: it was made of bone and sometimes stone.

makes a very chilling but beautiful sound. a instrument of the spirit of the wind . . . which the site has plenty of!

sleep 1 and 2: sleep / living adjacent to deck

steel 1 and 2: façade option using metal that weathers

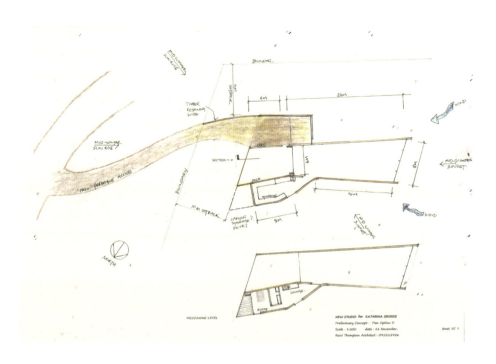

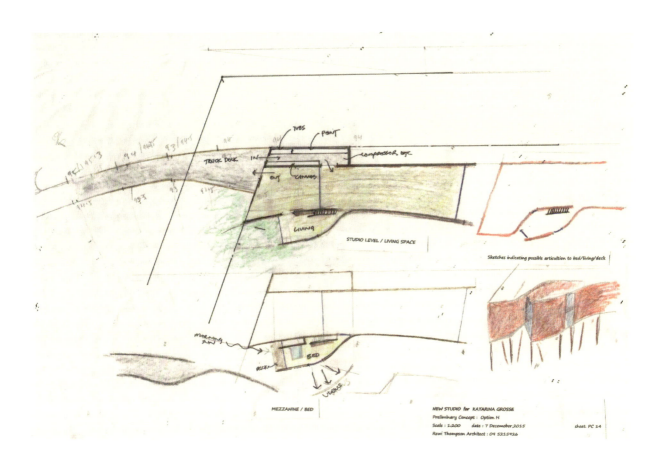

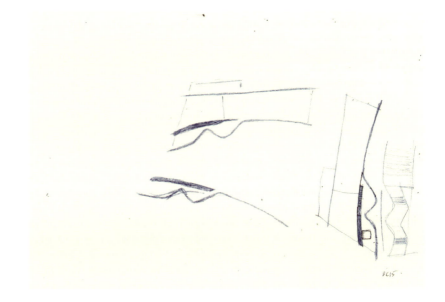

In late 2015, Rewi suggested other options to the curved exterior of the studio, while retaining the metaphorical anchor of the narrowing space that referenced the flute or koauau: 'an instrument of the spirit of the wind . . . which the site has plenty of!', as he wrote in his email. *Courtesy of Katharina Grosse*

Von: Rewi Thompson <rm.thompson@auckland.ac.nz>
Betreff: survey plan
Datum: 16. Dezember 2015 um 22:17:56 GMT+13

Kia ora Katharina,

Good news: you will see from the flurry of emails that we have the survey plan now.

I can now get back on to [the site] and fine tune the heights etc.

Should have something to show you end of this week end.

also just thinking about how 'views / sun etc can thought about relating to the living / bed space.

Please find attached an idea a simple cut or sliver: like a tattoo or moko a signature of identity:

this allowing a 'glimpse' from the deck area

all day sun / ventilation into the living / bed space etc.

also provides direct access between deck and living if needed.

just a thought

have a good week end.

nga mihi / greetings

rewi

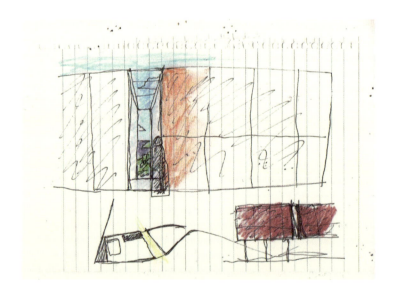

Homes

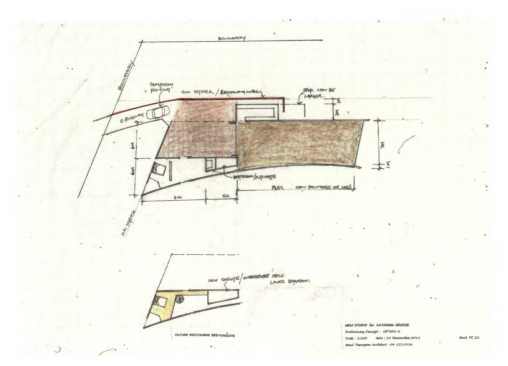

Opposite: As the studio plans developed, Rewi kept playing with notions of how to reveal the view without exposing the interior to too much of it: he attached sketches to one email which showed a 'split' in the building that allowed a glimpse of the sea from the rear deck. *Courtesy of Katharina Grosse*

Above: Rewi kept sketching different iterations of the studio's interior layout as he mulled over its design with Katharina Grosse via email. Sometimes, he built cardboard models which he photographed to explore these concepts further. *Courtesy of Katharina Grosse*

Graeme Burgess is an architect at Burgess Treep & Knight Architects and a tutor at the School of Architecture and Planning, University of Auckland. Graeme was a friend and a colleague of Rewi's and, unexpectedly, had the privilege of taking two of Rewi's last projects to completion after his death in 2016. Here he shares his memories of Rewi and discusses two projects: Katharina Grosse's west coast studio and a house in Titirangi that is currently under construction.

Homes

A model of Katharina Grosse's studio in the office of Graeme Burgess, who helped Katharina complete the building design after Rewi's death in 2016.
Samuel Hartnett

Jade Kake
I understand you started working with Katharina Grosse on her studio project after Rewi's passing. How did you come to be involved?

Graeme Burgess
Rewi was a very supportive person and beautifully enmeshed into all of our lives, and that year, 2016 — the year that he died — I was teaching in the same studio area as Rewi. He had his group and I had mine. We chatted a bit because we were in the same space and we were seeing one another. It was really nice.

I asked him if he would mind coming and giving . . . I can't even think what it was. It was more of an intuitive idea for the students and what they were looking at. They were supposed to be trying to find a way into their studio programme through something that was personal to them in their lives. He came in and did the most amazing thing. He just sat in the room. He'd got all these kids to give a pepeha without really realising that's what they were doing.

It was just magic, and he did it so beautifully because all he did was say 'Tell me about your mother and your father', and so it was opening those kinds of doors. What he did really beautifully was, in a very gentle way, open te ao Māori for us as Ngāti Pākehā without that way of understanding. He had this very gentle way of making te ao Māori enter into everyone's lives. It was so very beautiful. I was deeply shocked when he died later that year. I knew he was unwell, though. You could tell he was very unwell.

I got a phone call in December, not long after the funeral, from Judy Millar, who asked if she and Katharina could come to see us. They arrived and Katharina was feeling quite blown out because she and Rewi had been working for so long on that studio, and had created something amazing, which I feel demonstrates collaboration again — there's so much of that design that is absolutely Katharina as well. Katharina is also amazing. She has the most astonishing brain. Katharina played a big role in the design. She was fully engaged in the concept and had worked collaboratively with Rewi. Working with her to complete the project continued that collaborative process, with the underlying desire by us all to honour the kaupapa established by Rewi.

They had been turned down for resource consent. At that stage, all that Rewi had done was conceptual work up to resource consent stage and they just could not see what the pathway forward could be. How were they going to make it through? How could they get this thing to happen? I felt very touched to be approached, because it was a big thing, and connected so directly to wanting to honour Rewi, so that was the beginning of it.

Jade

How did it unfold after that?

Graeme

The key design that he'd come up with — this huge, long building with a folded roof and the curved wall to the exterior, and this crazy camping kind of living space — was bedded in already. What we had to do was try to work through a series of quite serious problems in terms of resource consent matters.

We had to get all of that resolved. It took a long time and it involved working through Rewi's design refining — or refining that sketch design — and turning it into something that could be constructed. His engineer, Grant Hudson, was involved as well. He had already been involved, but he hadn't completed his structural engineering design at that stage.

We had a list of materials and we had this concept, and we had to then try to turn that into a reality. There were a few changes along the way, some refinements that were made. And in fact, we did what we would ordinarily do, in that then Katharina was the client and we were trying — doing our best — to deliver what it was that she wanted as well.

Rewi's floor plan is not the same as our floor plan. There are very subtle shifts, nothing too serious. But a few things ended up changing, and you may not even notice them. One of the things is the crazy freestanding kitchen unit — that's not Rewi. But Rewi was always there as part of what we were doing. I would never design a building like that myself.

Jade

He's quite remarkable as a conceptual thinker. That's been brought up a lot in the various interviews. The way he approached concepts and the way he drove that concept forward is different to others, perhaps.

Graeme

I believe that Katharina interviewed other architects before she ended up working with Rewi. He wrote the most beautiful engagement letter that was filled with pūrākau and it was just a lovely, meandering, poetic thing.

Jade

Yeah, I've read it. It's really interesting, the way he communicates. It shows a lot about the way he thinks.

Graeme

Yeah. And it shows how he was definitely outside of the commercial structure of architecture. He was totally on level and more of a poet and an artist, but doing that through his architecture, through his teaching.

It took a long time to get that resource consent, and took even longer to get the construction drawings done because it was super difficult, and not because it wasn't straightforward. We had a team working on it. Initially, Rory Kofoed worked on taking the conceptual drawings through to something that could be built. For instance, he and I worked together on how that step deck operates outside her little living area so that you don't have the view out blocked by the rail of the deck. It may seem like a little thing, but it's important.

When Rory moved to work at Pac, Wade Southgate took on the challenge of completing the documentation. He was amazing, continuing the work to translate the concept into something that could be built. Wade has also been fully involved with the McCahon Place project. Without him that project would still be stuck as an idea and there would be no building.

Getting it through consent took a long time because it's a difficult site, a difficult situation. We had to do the most amazing number of ecological assessments, more than I've ever done. A herpetologist, Dylan the lizard man, came out and found a few

geckos on the site, which he was super excited by. But we were all thinking, oh no! It's a kāinga for the lizards. That's not good. We were very lucky with the contractor who we finally got to take on the project, too, because he was relatively young and very enthusiastic and wasn't put off by the idea of having to drive for an hour and a half every day to get to and from the site, which is mind-bending.

Jade

I understand there was another project of Rewi's that you worked on, after Katharina's?

Graeme

Yes. Grant, the engineer, said to me, 'Rewi was working with me on this other project, which is in McCahon Place in Titirangi.' He had designed this building and it was exactly the same situation — they had applied for resource consent and had been rejected. There were no construction drawings. There was nothing else. It was the same thing as Katharina's studio, and I thought, well, let's see if we can make this happen as well. Initially, I looked at it and thought it was just so stupidly complex that there's no way that I would want to even attempt to make anything of it.

I spoke with a colleague and he suggested another firm could do the work to complete the project. I spoke with them, and three months later they came back and said, 'No, we don't want to do it', by which time I'd been speaking with Alex and Dionne, the clients. I felt so strongly for their position. I really felt for them. They were not the usual architectural client either. Both Dionne and Alex are Māori. He has a business doing spouting and may have met Rewi through his work, but possibly not. They had bought this crazy site that's down an incredibly steep roadway. We documented that as well, got it through its consent processes, and it's being constructed right now. Probably no one really knows about it because it was likely Rewi's last project.

Jade

That's what we thought about Katharina's house. But there's another one.

Graeme

There's another one. There's another one that's being built. We've been answering questions, but we haven't been going onsite. But I know that it's probably getting quite close to completion. For me both were huge projects because of the time that went into them and wanting to honour Rewi, what he had done, and also to do the right thing for Katharina, and for Alex and Dionne.

At Katharina's, we made it a point that for the beginning of the project we had a whakatau out there as well, led by architect and artist Raukura Turei's dad, Pita Turei, who's very theatrical, lighting fires, and telling stories — some of which may or may not be true.

Jade
Love that.

Graeme
He also finished the process. We had it blessed at the beginning and at the end. The blessing at the beginning was really special because a lot of Rewi's students came out. Katharina attended the dawn ceremony, too, which was very special. We were standing on the site, which was still low scrub and bush, in the dawn. There were waiata and karakia and it was an incredibly beautiful, but transient, moment. But it also felt like the right way to make the project proceed and to have that connection, not to do it just as an ordinary building project, but rather as something which was part of that place, and which worked with the tikanga of te ao Māori.

Jade
Oh, what a privilege to have been a part of that.

Graeme
Yeah. A lot of Rewi's friends were there that morning, too — people who were very close to him, plus a lot of the students who'd been in that last studio programme that he had done. They were all there together, so it was a very moving moment.

Architect Graeme Burgess took Rewi's incomplete sketches of Katharina's Grosse's studio to create detailed final designs. This iteration shows tall west-facing windows that weren't included in the final design — although the narrow west-facing slot window was. 'Rewi was always there as part of what we were doing,' Graeme says of working on the project after Rewi's death in 2016.
Courtesy of Graeme Burgess

Multi-unit housing

Ngā kāinga nohoanga

Kia mau ki te tokanga nui ā-noho
There is no place like home

Laurelia Place state houses

Wiri
Tāmaki Makaurau
Auckland

1986–89

*With Pip Newman,
Michael McColl
and Nancy Couling*

Multi-unit housing

The residents of one of the Laurelia Place state homes designed by Rewi pose for a photograph. These slides are from Lucy Thompson's personal collection and some were published in *Architecture New Zealand*, but we've been unable to find the name of the original photographer.
Lucy Thompson collection

One of Rewi's most important early built projects, known as Rata Vine, was a group of more than 20 state houses in Laurelia Place in Wiri, South Auckland, of which little trace now remains. A story by Tommy Honey in the July/August 1989 issue of *Architecture New Zealand* says Rewi, with his colleagues Pip Newman, Michael McColl and Nancy Couling, 'arrived at the idea of the development as a "wilderness"; rows of houses are interleaved with native planting'.

The buildings were radical in their conception. One set of units (credited to McColl in Honey's article) high on the site was united under a single undulating roof. There were also, as Honey puts it, 'erratically arranged ... bach-like houses' hovering on poles under individual curved mono-pitch roofs (these homes are credited to Newman). Four additional stand-alone houses (credited to Couling) were more conventional in form. The material selection for all the homes was raw: exposed tanalised timber, plywood and metal. Somewhat ominously, in the *Architecture New Zealand* article Rewi says 'all the houses have natural finishes, they will weather and perhaps decay in time'.

Philippa (Pip) Newman is an architect and lecturer in the School of Architecture at Unitec Institute of Technology. After graduating from the University of Auckland in 1986, she worked alongside Rewi in his office as an architectural graduate until 1988. Here, she describes her experience working on the project:

It was the most intense and formative time. Probably the thing that's left the greatest impression on me was how demanding he was of us, but also how much he trusted us. It was a completely different way of working.

Nancy and I went to what was then called the Housing Corporation out in Manukau to ask them to fill us in on the brief for Rata Vine. Rewi didn't come. He sent us, one of numerous occasions when he made us responsible, and we reported back to him and we did things collaboratively. I imagine that often happens in offices, but as my first introduction it was very particular. We managed it all together. Of course [Rewi] had oversight, but all those design meetings, we took together.

One of the most critical components of the project was the landscaping and the notion that the spaces between were as important as the inside of the structures. I can't remember who the managing representative at the Housing Corp was, but they bought into that and there was a part of the budget to be set aside for it. But it never happened.

The landscaping was a really important part of the plan — breaking it down into the different roadways, selecting the plants, consulting with landscape people.

The relationship to land was important, and the way the buildings were arranged on the site was part of it. Whenever we worked with Rewi on any project, his approach was to ask the land first — about its form, and about what it would tell you about how you could occupy it.

I remember distinctly talking about the sociopolitical aspects of state housing and how in wealthier suburbs the house is a way of creating an identity for yourself as an individual. We often talked about it: how can you aspirationally do that in a lower socioeconomic neighbourhood? In the context of a social housing project, it was essentially about making distinctly different housing types to energise identity.

There is a sense in Tommy Honey's article that the houses might have been too experimental. Honey suggests that their daring was partly an effort on Rewi's part to reject the connotations of conventional state houses, but that this may inadvertently have resulted in some of their inhabitants feeling that they were being experimented on. It doesn't help, of course, that the landscaping — a fundamental element of the plan — was never completed. But from some angles, it looks as though Rewi's architectural aspirations for the homes somehow failed sufficiently to connect with or inspire their residents. This is something he seems to have seen as a calculated risk, telling Honey that 'the only way to raise the standard of architecture is to raise the level of criticism. A lot of these people don't see themselves in a position where they can make architectural comment, but they should be encouraged. Maybe it's time to really evaluate our housing position and get people involved with it.'

Bill McKay was at the School of Architecture at the University of Auckland at the same time as Rewi, and later taught alongside him there. He worked as a project architect on a neighbouring group of state houses in Wiri by Manning Mitchell at the same time that Rewi was designing nearby. In the following interview, Bill talks about his long friendship with Rewi, and why the state houses at Laurelia Place pleased architects but were less pleasing to the people who lived in them.

Above: The Laurelia Place houses were a collaborative effort in Rewi's studio: here, he is photographed with his team members Pip Newman, Michael McColl and Nancy Couling, all of whom worked on the project. *Lucy Thompson collection*

Opposite: The Laurelia Place houses were conceived of as a 'wilderness' in which rows of houses were interleaved with native planting, but the landscaping scheme was never carried out. The site plan shows some of what writer Tommy Honey described in an article in *Architecture New Zealand* as the 'erratically arranged' houses. *Architecture Archive, University of Auckland*

Jeremy Hansen
Tell us about how you first met Rewi.
Bill McKay
We were in Brick Studio. There were three different sub-studios at the School of Architecture in the late 1970s; Brick Studio was the radical one, and it had vertical integration — there was no separation between first years, second years and third years. We had Pete Bossley, Pip Cheshire, Rewi, the guys from Architectus, you name it: everyone who was anyone was in that studio. And that particular studio had a big culture of going to the pub across the road. Our lecturers were Kerry Morrow, Mike Austin, Nick Stanish, David Mitchell, and a few others. Rewi made an impression immediately. It was really interesting to come across someone like him. At the school he reached out a bit more to all of us. He seemed to radiate confidence. He was one of the students you'd look up to and go, 'Whoa. He's doing cool stuff.'
Jade Kake
This isn't really a question, but the more I hear about Rewi, the more he reminds me of my grandfather because he spent a lot of time in majority white spaces, in Australia in particular. And I was thinking it must have been so terribly racist. But actually, everyone loved him, I think because of the way he held himself in those spaces, and the way he could find common ground with anybody. So I think it's interesting, the way Rewi seemed to thrive and be comfortable in these environments that would have been challenging. And I think he would have been aware of that, because if nothing else, he would have stood out in these environments. I know that generation were, for the most part, told to go and learn how to be a Pākehā. And so that would have been an interesting time to live through.
Bill
It's not for me to say, but I do think it would have been difficult then. But I do perceive that his absolute kind of centredness in the Māori environment, and saying, 'This is what we are doing', became more apparent when he was teaching at the university than when he was a student.

Multi-unit housing

PERSPECTIVE

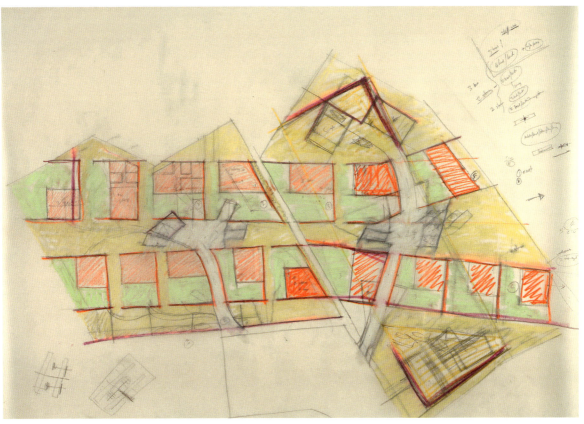

Many of the houses were clad in basic corrugated iron. In this photograph, some of the stand-alone houses, built on poles, are visible in front of multiple units located under the same undulating roof.
Lucy Thompson collection

The Laurelia Place houses under construction, and a completed interior.
Lucy Thompson collection

Multi-unit housing

Jeremy

You were working with Manning Mitchell on the design of a group of state houses in Wiri at the same time that Rewi was drawing a group of 20 homes that were being built next door for the Housing Corporation. Can you talk a bit about those projects? The Manning Mitchell houses are still there, but those designed by Rewi have been removed.

Bill

The buildings he did were very experimental, we felt. I agreed with Manning Mitchell's approach: the houses that they did — we did, because I was very involved in it — were fairly conventional with a few tweaks. My experience of social housing is that the people — having talked to a lot of them, being the project architect — just want what everyone else wants. They don't want to feel experimented on. And I really got that when I was going through it doing post-occupancy evaluations. I'd be hearing things like, 'Why has my neighbour got a garage and I've only got a carport?' Or, 'Why is our living-room wallpaper in their toilet?' That kind of thing.

We tend, as architects, to think of state housing as an opportunity to experiment. But the people in that area just wanted to be like everyone else; they don't want to live in experimental buildings. At the time, Rewi's buildings were highly thought of by the architectural community. They were attached houses, and if they'd been built in some beachside community for middle-class people, they'd be loved and still there. But I think that community felt, what are we walking into here?

It felt, to me, a lot like when the British started building social housing after the Second World War. All that modernism, streets in the sky, that kind of thing. It felt a little bit like that. I think it was just typical architectural thinking of the time: here's an opportunity to do something architectural.

Jeremy

Do you know why the homes he designed in Wiri are no longer there?

Bill

Well, I would presume that they didn't work, in design and perhaps in their material selection as well.

Jade

Rewi has often been described as a Māori modernist. I know you have a specific interest in modernism, and so I wondered: do you have a perspective on that, and on what Māori modernism is — and if Rewi was a Māori modernist?

Bill

One thing I know for certain is Rewi always said, 'I'm not a Māori architect. I'm an architect who happens to be Māori.' And certainly I wouldn't attach modernism to it as well. At the time, he certainly started off, as we all did, as kind of a humanist. Probably a New Zealand version of that, less concerned with aesthetics and a building looking as if it had been extruded from a machine, and more regional modernism with references to the vernacular, suited to the local climate, using local materials, that kind of thing. As opposed to the International Style: white, flat-roofed, lots of glass.

Jeremy

But Rewi was comfortable and consciously applying specifically Māori elements to some of his designs.

Bill

I think it was quite transitional between that kind of regional modernism and the International Style because also at the time we were at school, post-modernism was kicking the door down.

Jade

So it's almost like a confluence of modernist and post-modernist ideas.

Bill

Yeah. It was like an adolescence for architecture in New Zealand at the time, I feel. Things were a little bit mixed up. I hate trying to summarise or say what someone was doing, but I always got the sense that Rewi was looking for more of a Māori feeling, a spirit, rather than the tangible evidence.

Jeremy

His own home in Kohimarama is often cited as one of his best works. Do you think that building is important in the context of his other built work? What does the design of the house say about him?

Bill

I think it looks like nothing else. I adore everything about it. I just wish he had

Above: A drawing from Rewi's archives showing the arrangement of the Laurelia Place houses on the hillside.
Architecture Archive, University of Auckland

Opposite: An archival photograph of a model of the homes. They weren't to prove an enduring model of state housing: they have been demolished and replaced.
Architecture Archive, University of Auckland

Multi-unit housing

built it a bit better, but we were all building in a shitty manner at the time. I always saw it as a poutama pattern.

Jeremy
From everybody's descriptions of him and from my experience of him, he was a very open and accommodating person. Yet the front of that house seems very clear in its denial. Do you see it that way?

Bill
No. I always saw it as being on the marae. You come on, you stand in the ātea, you wait until you're welcomed, and then you're brought on. And then there's a series of challenges, a series of steps, and all that kind of thing. So it exists this way, but it also exists without knowing the protocol of the marae because you could look at the ground floor with its glass and go, well, it's a nice verandah, we'll go and stand in the shade there. It's like it's a challenge, but it's not saying fuck off. And then it opens up at the back, which is the thing everyone always forgets.

Jade
So, it's creating this kind of precision and putting in place these gates to pass or a structured welcome.

Bill
Yeah. It's a very linear experience, like on the marae. And the cup of tea.

Jade
That's an interesting perspective. I mean, we can't know because he didn't write much about why he did things, but I'm enjoying hearing people's interpretations. It's a bit like a work of literature: how people receive it is important, too.

Bill
Anything that's great attracts multiple interpretations.

Jeremy
Did you spend much time at Rewi's house?

Bill
Oh, yeah. When he was younger, they had parties there. Back in the day, you could just turn up. Life isn't like that now.

Jeremy
We've asked a lot of people this question, and had many different responses, but does it seem a shame to you that Rewi didn't get to complete more built projects, given the brilliance you're describing that was evident when he was a student and in his own home?

Bill
Talking to other people, many people say his own home is the outstanding work but then ask what else there is. And I don't agree with that because I don't think architecture is all about built outcomes. I think architecture is about the person you are, the politics that you've got, and the advocacy that you're doing, and the writing and being the person you are. It's not just a physical thing.

Jeremy
Were there particular reasons that you know of that meant he didn't get more work built?

Bill
I'd say the culture. There's not a conversation I have these days in which I don't end up saying 'fucking capitalism'.

Jeremy
And he didn't fit into that properly.

Bill
No. And it was also that when he was really operational, it was through the 1980s and the 1990s, and that was when Chase Corporation was rampant and all that kind of thing.

Jade
And I think he started practising before the Māori renaissance. He was certainly educated at that time, but the changes that that initiated in architecture didn't happen until quite a lot later.

Bill
Yeah. Totally. And it takes time for all that to filter through.

Jeremy
With that in mind, could I ask you to assess Rewi's legacy?

Bill
The other thing that we haven't mentioned is teaching. I taught with him a lot. And I could see his students being influenced by his presence. The second thing would be his being around his contemporaries and students. I would say he probably got called on a little bit too much to be the Māori person in the bunch of white people doing whatever project.

Jeremy
Do you think Rewi's influence or contribution was recognised or appreciated sufficiently at the time? I get the sense from looking through his archive that there were periods in his career where he struggled professionally — that it wasn't necessarily a linear path towards greatness.

Bill
Well, architecture's tough. If you're an artist you can get a job labouring or something and then come home and still produce your art. Whereas to produce architecture, you need clients and money.

Jade
Resources. And a whole army of consultants.

Bill
But his contribution was recognised by some of us. To me, he was one of the outstanding people of my generation. It doesn't matter whether you built anything or you're not in architecture: it's about who you are, what you think, what you say, what you teach. It's bigger than just, oh, what buildings did you leave?

Multi-unit housing

1 Living
2 Kitchen
3 Dining
4 Bed 1
5 Bed 2
6 Bed 3
7 Laundry
8 Bathroom
9 WC

Ground floor plan   1:200
Units 3,4,5,6,7,8,9,10

1 Kitchen   8 Laundry
2 Dining   9 Bathroom
3 Living   10 WC
4 Bed 1   11 Carport
5 Bed 2   12 Storage
6 Bed 3   13 Garage
7 Bed 4

Ground floor plan   1:200
Units 1&2

First floor plan

1 Kitchen
2 Dining
3 Living
4 Laundry
5 WC
6 Bathroom
7 Bedroom 1
8 Bedroom 2
9 Bedroom 3
10 Bedroom 4

Ground floor plan 1:200
Units 19,20

Multi-unit housing

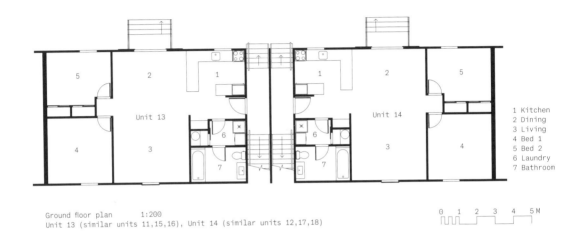

Ground floor plan 1:200
Unit 13 (similar units 11,15,16), Unit 14 (similar units 12,17,18)

1 Kitchen
2 Dining
3 Living
4 Bed 1
5 Bed 2
6 Laundry
7 Bathroom

Rewi attended almost 30 hui with Ngāti Whātua hapū members to help them develop a housing strategy for their papakāinga at Ōrākei. This photograph shows an unrealised cultural centre on part of the site, with housing scattered across the slopes. *Architecture Archive, University of Auckland*

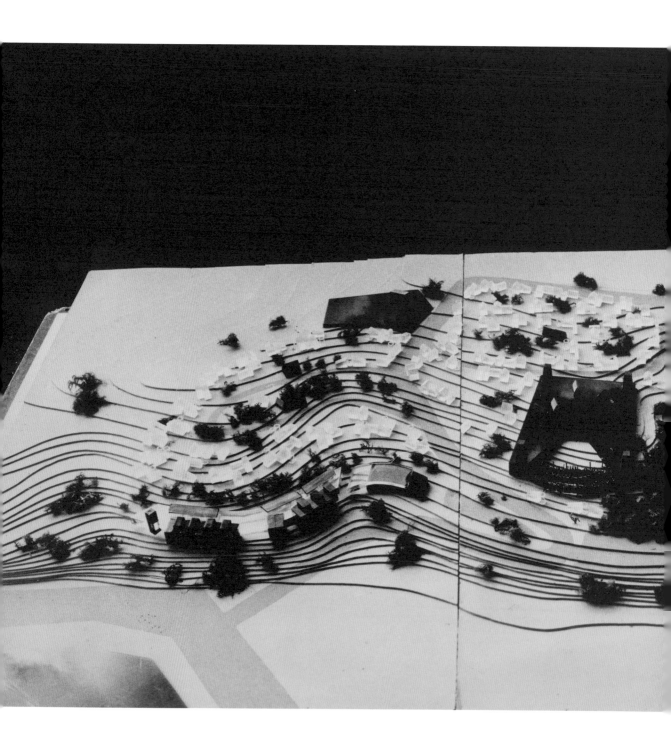

Multi-unit housing

Ngāti Whātua housing

Takaparawhau Tāmaki Makaurau Auckland

2000-04

Rewi Thompson wasn't Ngāti Whātua, but he was a vital part of that iwi developing a vision for its future at Takaparawhau, its kāinga in Tāmaki Makaurau. He was brought in to facilitate the creation of a housing plan at a tense time for the iwi, when banks were wanting their money back, and the next century of being able to develop their land looked to be slipping away.

Ngāti Whātua's Ngarimu Blair remembers Rewi talking to whānau 'like an uncle' at more than 20 hui held over a couple of years, putting them at such ease that groups who had their hearts set on stand-alone homes were soon enthusing over his sketches of medium-density housing with views of the Waitematā. While none of these visions were realised by Rewi himself, Ngarimu says Rewi's fingerprints are all over developments such as Kāinga Tuatahi, a group of medium-density townhouses that were designed by Stevens Lawson Architects (with whom Rewi had earlier collaborated on the 2006 competition-winning design for Auckland City Mission's HomeGround building, which was eventually realised in a modified form in 2022).

This is another way of saying that this series of hui, and the sketches Rewi developed from them, continue to drive the way Ngāti Whātua approaches housing on the kāinga today. And this, perhaps, is one of the best ways of measuring Rewi's influence — it is contained not only in his built works, but also in the way in which he was able to listen, calmly and patiently, and facilitate the development of a collaborative architectural vision. He was a person who, instead of imposing grand schemes on others, provided them with the vision and confidence to pursue them for themselves.

The friendship he established with Ngarimu Blair during this process extended into the duo working together on a 2007 design competition entry which proposed a bridge based on a hīnaki, or eel trap, to connect the city's Te Wero Island with Wynyard Quarter, as well as a 2009 competition entry for the redevelopment of Auckland's Queens Wharf.

'We had to tell whānau that we really didn't think they could have a stand-alone house, that we needed to go into multi-level apartments and townhouses,' says Ngāti Whātua's Ngarimu Blair. '[Rewi] started doing drawings of what the apartments and townhouses could look like . . . he'd just sketch something and whānau would be, Oh my god.' Although Rewi's plans weren't directly realised at Ōrākei, Ngarimu says his influence is evident in housing developments there today. *Architecture Archive, University of Auckland*

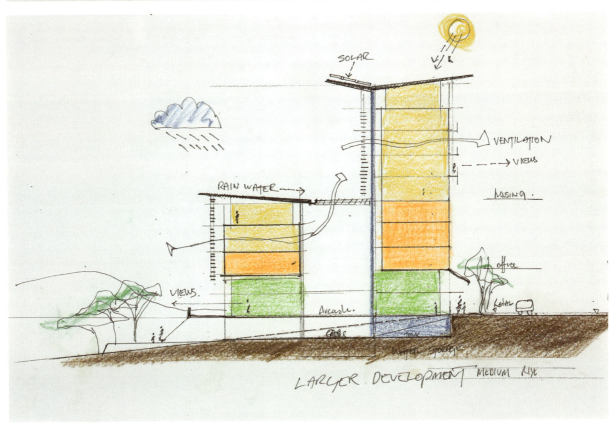

Jeremy Hansen
When did you first meet Rewi?
Ngarimu Blair
I can't even remember the year, but it must have been the early 2000s, if not the late 1990s. The context was, we were broke as an iwi. It's hard to believe right now — we have a $1.5 billion asset base — but back then the banks were calling in their loans because we had lost $12 million on a deal and we had borrowed $4 million to buy back 100 houses from Housing New Zealand on Kupe Street. The property market was going nowhere at that time, and so the banks obviously had absolutely zero faith in us.

To get out of that, our trust board of the day — my dear uncles and aunties, most of whom aren't here anymore — came up with a plan to lease Kupe Street for high-end housing, which then sparked an occupation by some of the whānau. A lot of them, rightly, were saying, 'Where's our housing? We need housing and you're going to lease this land for 100 years to rich people. Yes, we'll keep the land, but they'll have that for 100 years, and it'll end up like Paritai Drive [in Ōrākei].'

So that stopped those development plans in their tracks. Luckily the property market turned, and now we're getting invites to the cricket and rugby from the bank. But out of all of that, talking to the whānau who were occupying, it was clear we needed a housing plan. We didn't have one — we'd had one development that happened in the early 1990s, but there was actually no vision and no development plan moving forward.

So I asked who was the best Māori architect in the country and was told it was Rewi Thompson. I found his number and gave him a call. Here's this cool dude, Ngāti Raukawa, humble as. And we just went from there, trying to figure out how we would come up with a master plan for the whānau and get some kind of housing going.

Jade Kake
So did you immediately feel you'd found the right guy for what you needed at the time?
Ngarimu
Yeah. He was totally unassuming,

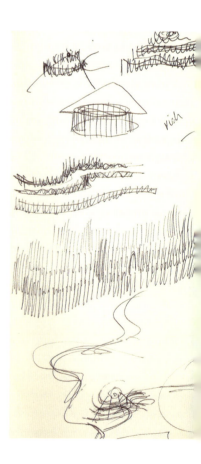

Multi-unit housing

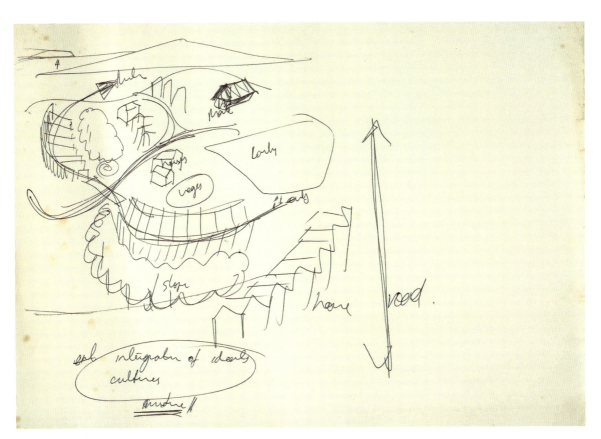

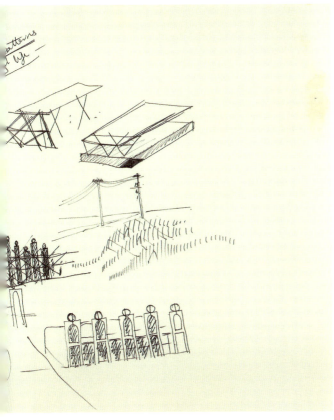

'Rewi put our whānau at ease,' Ngarimu Blair says of his work with Ngāti Whātua. 'He'd get big sheets of paper and just ask them how they would like to live.' *Architecture Archive, University of Auckland*

Some of Rewi's drawings show the entire Ngāti Whātua site at Ōrākei, with houses oriented towards the Waitematā and the view of Rangitoto. *Architecture Archive, University of Auckland*

Multi-unit housing

humble, but you could tell he had mana about him as well. I had no money, no budget, and he never really talked about money. He was cool to help out. We did get some research money because our project was around low-impact urban design and development.

Rewi put our whānau at ease. That was the main thing, because the politics of the village, coming out of the historic trauma, then the recent calamity of the banks foreclosing, high-end housing, occupation — tensions were really high. Not only that, we had to tell whānau that we didn't think they could have a stand-alone house, that we needed to go into multi-level apartments and terrace houses — most people still don't want that.

But Rewi could just cruise into the hui and talk like an uncle, do his thing and get people in a wānanga-type mode and thinking about the future in a really quiet, unassuming way. And that was what we did. We did at least 20 hui over a couple of years with whānau just talking about their future vision for the land.

Jade
So much of it is just building consensus.

Ngarimu
Yeah. And trust.

Jade
And giving people space to talk.

Jeremy
By the sounds of it Rewi wasn't presenting a design proposal at this stage.

Ngarimu
No, not at all. He'd get big sheets of paper and ask them how they would like to live. It got everyone in a good space to dream. And then he started doing drawings of what the apartments and townhouses could look like and how they could be laid out over the land. He'd just sketch something and whānau would be, 'Oh my God'.

And so it ended up with a housing strategy with some cool concept drawings done by Rewi and some good energy and momentum with whānau, who had come out of a pretty testing time in the community, to getting people thinking more positively.

We ended up with a housing vision and master plan, which then led to us doing the Kupe Street development, which wasn't in the end with Rewi but with Stevens Lawson. By then we had much more robust procurement processes than I had in my day, and I don't think Rewi, at that time, was really in a good space either. And I don't think he had those relationships with other architects that could get them to come in behind him.

Jade
You mean he wasn't set up to take on a project of that kind of volume and complexity?

Ngarimu
Yeah.

Jeremy
Was that ever awkward, the fact that it went ahead with somebody else?

Ngarimu
No. Well, he never said it was to me. When I look at that development, I see Rewi all through it anyway.

Jade
Something we've found a lot with Rewi's work is that he set the foundations for so many things that were taken forward by others. Sometimes he doesn't get the credit. It's amazing how many things we later find out he was involved with right at the beginning.

Ngarimu
That's because he never had a business development manager or a publicist.

Jade
I get the sense he wasn't really that invested in the business side of things; I think he just cared about architecture and designing.

Ngarimu
No, he was useless. Rewi, you're going to give me an invoice or what? But there were good lessons with him, about giving and not expecting anything in return. He was hugely generous with his time and his wisdom, and seeing that was pretty humbling. Yeah, that's probably the main thing, just a really generous guy.

Jeremy
You also worked on other projects with Rewi.

Ngarimu
Yeah. I'm not sure what the order was, whether it was the hīnaki bridge [connecting Te Wero Island to Wynyard Quarter] or Queens Wharf. The hīnaki

one, we wanted to enter that and be Māori entering it. We didn't win, but we should have. We were the only one on budget.

Jeremy
One of the interesting things about doing this book is that there's almost a sense of longing for the projects that Rewi didn't get to build, and this bridge could be one of those examples. I wondered if you had theories about why those opportunities didn't fall Rewi's way. There are a lot of reasons for the way those opportunities fall in architecture or other careers, but it sometimes feels like he never quite got the projects that he deserved. And the country would be richer for it if some more of those designs had been realised.

Ngarimu
Yeah. I don't know. By the time I met him, he was pretty much a one-man band. He had suffered some personal loss. Maybe he just didn't have the grunt around him to do this. I hope it's not because he was Māori, that people saw him as too much of a risk, and that he didn't have the flash office with the Audi and the black skivvy and black blazer. You still see that today, Māori professionals trying to win government contracts, contracts on anything really. The big agencies won't roll the dice on someone who is outwardly pretty brilliant but seems like a risk to them.

Multi-unit housing

Rewi's sessions with Ngāti Whātua hapū members included discussions about how to make their housing environmentally friendly. These drawings show detailed consideration of shared entryways and the thermal performance of the buildings.
Courtesy of Ngarimu Blair

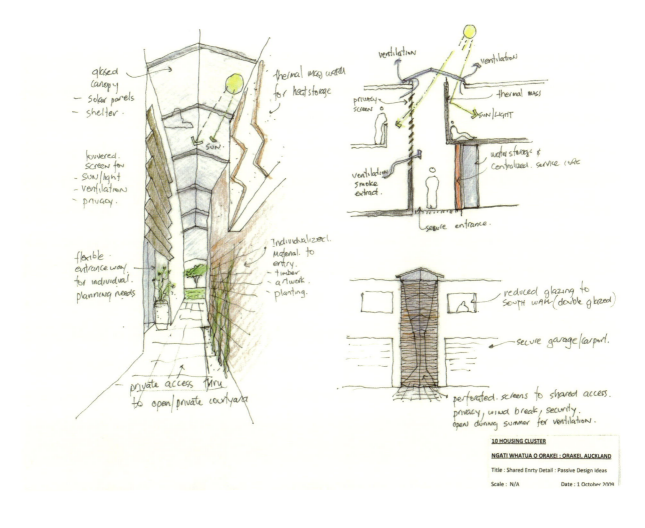

Everyday Homes

Northcote
Tāmaki Makaurau
Auckland

2015–16

With Isthmus Group

Multi-unit housing

Rewi designed over 50 state homes in Northcote in his role at Isthmus Group. *David St George*

One of the many sadnesses of Rewi Thompson's death in 2016 was that at the time he was entering a new and exciting phase of his professional life. He had worked with his old friend David Irwin at Isthmus Group previously — most notably in the mid-1990s on the canopy that covers some of the open space in Tūrangi town centre, at the southern end of Lake Taupō — but those jobs were conducted with Rewi in an associate or consulting role. But in early 2015 he left his teaching position in the School of Architecture and Planning at the University of Auckland and joined Isthmus's Auckland studio full-time.

The move meant he had the Isthmus studio to support him in his thinking, sketching and designing — as well as whole teams to inspire with his leadership. It had sometimes seemed as if Rewi didn't get to design the buildings he deserved; some of the people we spoke to suggested this might be partly because he never managed to build the apparatus of a fully-fledged studio around him, and therefore lacked the logistical capability to deliver larger, more complex projects. At Isthmus, these barriers melted away. His role at Isthmus wove together the previously separate strands of his career — teaching and designing — meaning he had arrived in the right place at the right time, free to lead the Isthmus team as they searched for the conceptual underpinnings of their landscape and architecture projects.

One of the biggest projects Rewi worked on at Isthmus Group was the design of Everyday Homes, a series of modular, compact, stand-alone houses, of which about 50 were built in the Auckland suburb of Northcote for HLC (Homes, Land, Community), then a division of Housing New Zealand. Kāinga Ora's current focus on greater density in public housing developments makes these stand-alone homes seem very much a product of their time. It was envisioned as a new type of state house, something Rewi infused with his own brand of ingenuity and humanity. His modular approach offered a variety of rooflines, window shapes and colours that lent a sense of individuality to each dwelling. He was excited about offering the families that moved into them a fresh start in a place that provided them enough comfort to grow old in.

Isthmus co-founder David Irwin knew Rewi from architecture school; many years later he enticed him to join him at the firm. 'He was loving it and people loved having him around,' David says. He later wrote, in a eulogy which he read out at Rewi's funeral, that 'it was like a dream come true, working side by side with someone I truly respected and admired — someone who lived and designed by their values, as solid in him as a rock'. Here, David talks about his work and friendship with Rewi.

Each of the Everyday Homes was designed in a modular fashion but with its own individual character expressed through methods including the roof pitch, window arrangement and material selection. *David St George*

Jeremy Hansen
David, how did you get to know Rewi?

David Irwin
I'll come back to that. I'm keen to sort of download to you some of the stuff that I've got, so I get it off my chest and then we can talk around it. I can answer that question easily, but I just need to get a few things out. It's quite hard, to be honest.

Jeremy
Sorry, David, take your time.

David
I probably met Rewi with Patrick [Clifford] and the Architectus guys at the pub, the Blue Falcon. Our practice was new, Architectus was new, Rewi was new. No one knew anything. Everyone was young and drinking on a Friday night at the Blue Falcon talking shit. Rewi and I went on to design and build stuff together; the classic one was designing the Tūrangi town centre glass canopy — that took two years and involved driving down [from Auckland] every two weeks and debating ideas philosophically for hours on end. That was an Isthmus contract, but the architecture is all Rewi. We basically drank our fee in the bar there. Over that period of time, I learnt heaps. To me that was my grounding in the philosophical position of where Rewi was coming from.

Jeremy
What did he teach you?

David
The value of the land, which is a bit ironic since I was a landscape architect.

Jeremy
And did you continue working together after that?

David
He worked with us on some early work on Manukau Square, then taught at uni and was sort of out of circulation in our world. So we didn't catch up as much over that period of time. But over the last few years, we got right back together again, and he was working inside the Isthmus studio, which was awesome.

Jeremy
So how did that later period of collaboration come about?

David
We were talking one day and Rewi was looking for some way to reconnect back in. I said, 'Oh, well, we've always got a space.' And we just got him back in — he was working in the studio on salary and it was great. And he was loving it and people loved having him around. The thing about Rewi was that he knew what he was doing, what his values were, from the very beginning. And he never moved off that and they were always right. And the rest of us were left scrounging around trying to work out what the hell we were doing. He worked it out a long, long time ago.

Jeremy
What would you say those values were?

David
Land. We developed an idea called 'land, people, culture'. Values which are what Isthmus is about. Rewi said, 'I'm coming back, but these values, if you go off them, I'm out.' So that was his proviso: he had the opportunity to walk out the door if we didn't fucking stick to what we said we were going to do. We needed someone around who knew what that really meant. Rewi Thompson was a manifestation of that idea, with a deep understanding of the value of the land, the people, the culture. That's what he knew from the beginning. And in the last period of time for Rewi, he wasn't well either. So he was working even though he wasn't a hundred per cent. I think none of us really knew how unwell he was until later.

Jeremy
Did it feel to you that the opportunity at Isthmus came along at the right time for him? It seemed like he wasn't interested in creating an architectural infrastructure around him, and you provided him with that, which allowed him to bring his best self to work.

David
Yeah, a hundred per cent. It was good for us, too. But there are some great stories [around Rewi's gaps in using technology]. Back in the day we were going to write a spec for this thing, so Rewi rocks up with it on a floppy disk. There's no computer in the world left that's got one of these bloody things except for Rewi's one. He was completely disconnected from all of that part of the world, like he just couldn't operate in there. And if you were a client and expecting these things, you weren't going to get them, so that could limit

Multi-unit housing

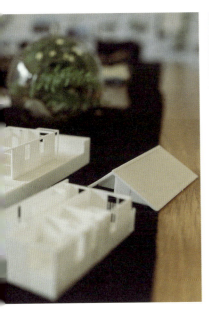

Models and drawings of the Everyday Homes in the Isthmus studio in Auckland. 'For Rewi, the architecture was incidental,' says his friend and Isthmus colleague David Irwin. 'It was the creation of these places, the simple things, that was what it was about.'
David St George

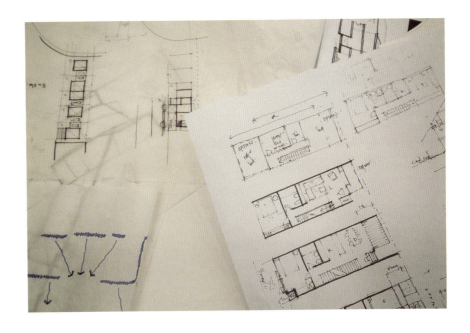

Residents of some of the Everyday Homes soon after they moved in. The residents at top left are Lopata, Aisea and Ola, but we haven't been able to find the names of the people in the lower photograph. *David St George*

Multi-unit housing

him. But if you put all that other stuff around him, then the depth and the talent could shine. It wasn't like he had a computer. I mean, I don't think he even used his laptop. But there were a lot of text conversations, a lot of drawings.

Jeremy

One of the projects he worked on at Isthmus was the creation of Everyday Homes, which were stand-alone homes designed in two-, three- and four-bedroom configurations to be built in large numbers by HLC. Can you talk a bit about that?

David

We'd seen the opportunity to create standardised housing like a new state home. It didn't quite eventuate like that due to some politics, but regardless, that's what we thought was needed and what we had the opportunity to do. So at one end of the spectrum, there's a thought that said they had to be affordable and simple and basically buildable by a builder with a ute and a dog. Rewi's answer to it was, 'We'll just stack Humes pipes and we'll make them into homes.' And I'm going, 'Rewi, we can't really put people in Humes pipes, are you serious?' And he goes, 'Yeah.' He was serious.

So at one end he was completely radical. Like, you know, we could do this. I'm going, 'Mate, we're never going to sell it to HLC. Trust me, it's not gonna happen. We're not even going to have that conversation, we're going to be chucked out the door.' And in the middle of all this, Rewi wrote a poem about it, about what was important about the everyday home. He came to me one Monday and said, 'I've written a poem.' I said, 'Brilliant.'

A Place Called Home

A place to meet, a place to greet
A place to laugh and a place to cry
A place to be happy and a place to
    be sad
A place to think and a place to sing
A place to rest and a place to eat
A place for my toys and a place to
    fix my bike
A place to hang my family photo
    and a place to grow my tomatoes
A place to rest and a place to sleep

A place to have friends and a place
    to share
A place that is friendly
A place to tell stories, a place to
    dream
A place to listen and a place to learn
A place to be merry and a place to
    make my cake
A place to keep me dry and a place
    to keep me warm
A place to study and a place to sew
A place to play and a place to dance
A place that is safe
A place where I am yelled at the
    most but a place where I am loved
    the most
A place called home

It's really good. It's everything, but not the architecture. It's perfect. For Rewi, the architecture was incidental. It was the creation of these places, the simple things, that was what it was about. It was, can you put your shoes at the front door and have them not get wet? For us as a practice, we have to hold on to that layer of thinking.

Jeremy

So in that sense, his involvement in the studio must have required learning to work with him in a pretty fluid manner.

David

Yeah, exactly. It's like a mentor, a philosophical mentor and a design mentor. Someone you use at the beginning to get the most out of them. He was excellent. That's just what he did.

Jeremy

It also makes him sound a bit like he lived on another planet, or is that a dumb way of saying it?

David

Yeah, he was in a different realm. There's a tendency in lots of design professions to look at an object and to worry about the beauty of the object. Rewi didn't. That wasn't the gig. Incredibly, not worrying about that — or not consciously that anyone could see — created an aesthetic that was actually beautiful.

When you watched Rewi draw a line on a page, it was always a beautiful line. Some people can put a line on the page with a beautiful proportion which seems completely effortless. And others of us put a line on the page and the line is not as nice. Rewi's lines were always nice. So he had an in-built aesthetic sense. Some of us might be quite good at philosophical ideas, less good at the aesthetics, but Rewi was really good at both. But other bits, like connecting to the internet or filling in a form or a time sheet, just forget it. That's cool, we didn't force him to do that. I could do that.

Jeremy

So he couldn't be described as erratic. It sounds like he came to work when you expected him to be there.

David

Oh, hell yeah. He was there every day: brought his lunch, did his stuff, drank bloody instant coffee every day, to my horror. He'd work seven days. If you let him.

Jeremy

How long did he work at Isthmus in this later period?

David

It wasn't that long. I think it was 18 months or something like that. It wasn't long enough. No, it was definitely ripped short.

Jeremy

It sounds like he was laying this amazing foundation for this next phase of his career, which he didn't get to have because of his death.

David

Exactly. He knew it, too.

Jeremy

What makes you say that?

David

Oh, he said it. He said, 'I've done my educational stuff, I want to go back. This is the way that I can go back. You've got land, people, culture; I need to be surrounded by this.' He was where I got that sort of thinking from, that idea of landscaping at the bottom and driving the architecture we're trying to do. He's the guru of it. It was exciting. I knew that if we could provide the environment for him, we could make some really special stuff.

Jeremy

You worked on Everyday Homes, but were there other projects that were in the works that you were excited about?

David

We were just starting on a couple. We started talking about master-planning of communities and things like that.

We were starting to play with taller buildings. I think Rewi knew that there was an opportunity that we had in front of us to make some good stuff, interesting stuff, and push those boundaries along a little bit. One day he said to me, 'David, over the years, I've become more landscape and you've become more architect.' And that was true. That's exactly true. That was sort of my wake-up call. He was right.

Jeremy

Was that Rewi being critical?

David

Oh, it was a fair statement. And that's how I took it. To forget the value of the land is not great, or to miss the hierarchy of that. If the whenua isn't healthy, then people can't be healthy. That underlying philosophical position that the health of the land is critical to everything — that's never going to leave me now.

Jeremy

It strikes me that he had a depth of security and/or self-belief in his own talent, but he probably didn't think that way.

David

Nah. I think the self-belief in his own talent is probably the wrong term, but I know what you mean. He's been grounded from the very beginning. He knew this way before any of us got it. He knew that this is what he brought to the table at the beginning.

Jeremy

There's not a lot of his built work. There's his house and there's Puukenga at Unitec, the City to Sea Bridge in Wellington and some other things. I wonder if there are a couple of those projects that stand out to you as demonstrating something fundamental about him?

David

If you're saying, is there something I can go around and see that's Rewi Thompson's, I think you can. His own home, for example. the spaces and the way it's arranged, it's radical. But that wasn't why he did it — because it was radical. He believed it was a building for his family to be a family.

Jeremy

He wasn't consciously provocative, you're saying.

David

No. But he was so incredibly radical.

Jeremy

One of the interesting things about being in his archive is that there are designs for little villa extensions mixed up with speculative drawings of prismatic buildings on water containing dinosaurs.

David

Yeah. He shouldn't have been doing villa extensions. His heart was never in that.

Jeremy

You can see little poetic gestures in the villa designs sometimes, but it also feels like he's slumming it on those gigs, like he's not a guy that should be working at that scale.

David

No. Here, we were working on a land-scape scale, but it was too late. That was the bummer. When we got back together again, I knew it was special. I just wish it could have lasted longer.

Multi-unit housing

'Some of us might be quite good at philosophical ideas, less good at the aesthetics,' says David Irwin. 'Rewi was really good at both.'
David St George

The Everyday Homes were envisaged as a new kind of state house, but their stand-alone approach now makes them look very much a product of their time, when medium-density options were still considered unpalatable.
David St George

Multi-unit housing

1 Kitchen
2 Dining
3 Lounge
4 Laundry
5 WC
6 Bathroom
7 Bedroom 1
8 Bedroom 2
9 Study

First floor plan

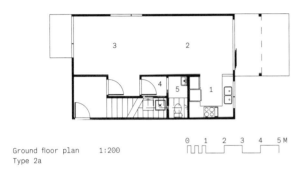

Ground floor plan   1:200
Type 2a

1 Entry
2 Lounge
3 Dining
4 Kitchen
5 WC
6 Laundry
7 Garage
8 Bedroom 1
9 Bedroom 2
10 Bedroom 3
11 Bathroom
12 Study

First floor plan

Ground floor plan   1:200
Type 3a

1 Entry
2 Lounge
3 Dining
4 Kitchen
5 Laundry
6 Garage
7 Bathroom
8 Bedroom 1
9 Bedroom 2
10 Bedroom 3
11 Bedroom 4
12 Study

First floor plan

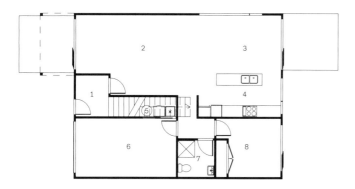

Ground floor plan   1:200
Type 4a

Multi-unit housing

Interviews — practice

Ngā uiuinga — mahi ngaio

Waiho mā te tangata e mihi
Let others sing your praises

Kevin O'Brien

Kevin O'Brien is a principal at Australian architects BVN. He met Rewi in 1999 and later asked him to become an external advisor for his postgraduate studies. They remained friends until Rewi's death in 2016. We spoke to Kevin about their friendship and their approach to place as a generator of architectural concepts.

Jade Kake
Hi Kevin. I thought it'd be good if you introduced yourself first.

Kevin O'Brien
Okay. My name is Kevin O'Brien. I'm a Brisbane-based architect, descendant of the Kaurareg and Meriam people from far north Queensland. I graduated from architecture school in 1995 and then did a postgraduate Master of Philosophy and finished that in 2006. And now I've had my own practice for about 11 or 12 years, and about four years ago I joined a practice called BVN as a partner.

Jade
Thank you. I've heard a little bit of this story, but could you tell us about when you first met Rewi and what your first impressions of him were?

Kevin
I first met Rewi in 1999 in Sydney. There was an international student conference at the University of New South Wales

and Rewi, Alison [Page] and Dillon [Kombumerri], who I used to work with in the Merrima Aboriginal Design Unit in Sydney, and I were all put on the same panel to show work, and I'd never heard of Rewi. And then he put up images of his house, and of Puukenga [the School of Māori Studies at Unitec]. Those two projects captured my imagination, and then we met afterwards and the two of us just hit it off. The next three days was walking, talking and a sort of promise to stay in touch. And we did. The following year I got a Churchill Fellowship, which is basically a travelling fellowship for citizens to go and bring back knowledge. I was looking at construction techniques and systems in Indigenous communities around the Pacific. My first port of call was Auckland, and I stayed for four weeks. I also went up to New Caledonia, Fiji, Hawai'i, Vancouver, and Anchorage, Alaska. Rewi and I really got to know

Interviews

each other through the course of that and stayed in touch pretty much onwards from there.

Jade
I've heard you talk before about Rewi's ways of thinking and the impact they've had on your philosophy and approach to architecture. Could you talk about that a little bit?

Kevin
I think they've had a massive impact. When I was going through the University of Queensland as an undergraduate, there was no one around me or in front of me. There was Dillon, who I didn't yet know was in Sydney. So it was quite isolating up here [in Queensland] and it was definitely isolating for Dillon in Sydney. When we all crossed paths eventually in the mid- to late 1990s and then with Rewi it was such a natural sort of engagement, because we were working and thinking on similar lines.

The great thing about Rewi was he had this ability to ask the right questions, as opposed to giving you the answers. After I'd seen the images of his house, in particular the section where it becomes evident that the whole house is actually looking into the rock behind, it just stuck with me. The little window to the main street was basically turning its back on the suburb and all the usual kind of affectations that architects get up to. It was focused on the rock as the origin. I didn't understand it at the time, but I thought, this is right up my alley. It took me a while to get it.

I'd spent a couple of years messing around in Ireland and came back in about 2003 and spent three years working for a practice called Donovan Hill while I was doing my postgraduate studies. The first year or two of my postgraduate degree were very anthropology-focused and I hated it. I ultimately came to reject the whole approach, and in the middle of it I was staying in touch with Rewi regularly. I found there was a loophole in the University of Queensland guidelines where you could appoint external advisors, so I asked Rewi if he could be an external advisor for my postgrad, which he agreed to, and then things went on from there.

Jade
What was Rewi like as an advisor and as an educator through that process?

Kevin
He was with me for about three years during that process. There were a couple of things I had to come to. One was this idea of culture being an origin of how you position yourself in the world. The second was, with that comes some kind of spiritual grounding. And if you've got that, then you need to make the right decisions. The conversations would start to get a little bit elliptical and I wouldn't be sure where they were going, but they kept coming back to those two things. And what was great about it is that we never once looked at work from some other country overseas. It was always what's here. What are you part of? What do you belong to? It wasn't about what you are.

In order to spend time together, we went across the ditch a lot to go to the rugby. We would get to the field an hour before the game and talk, have a few beers and watch the game, talk again at half-time, watch the game, and then have a few more beers and talk into the night. We were probably catching up in person two or three times a year, either in Auckland or Brisbane or Sydney, so it was fantastic to have that sort of engagement over three years. As you're doing postgraduate work, you're looking at all of these possibilities and you inevitably hit a wall because it's all overwhelming. Then you've got to let it settle and see what rises to the surface, I guess.

I was in two minds about whether to let my studies go and come back to it at another point. Rewi and I were in Sydney after a Bledisloe game sitting in a bar somewhere and talking and drawing, as he did. And then he asked me, where do you come from? If you come from somewhere, doesn't that mean the building's going to come from there as well? We were talking about that and I started doodling a section that goes through the water, up to the edge of an island and then does a half-arc for the sky. So you've got water, land, sky. It looks like a sector off a circle, but if you're inside of it, that's when you're physically present with other people and it's very spatial. And then when you're outside of it, it becomes more of a time thing and you're part of ancestral beliefs and all this sort of stuff. So that was the one big idea that allowed me to position all my postgraduate work around.

When you're doing postgraduate work, you end up with a bit of research about this, a bit about that, and you're looking to see what connects more. I had a heap of anthropological stuff and really classical research training over on the side, but it wasn't aligning with the way we'd go about the qualitative means of assessing built works. It was all over

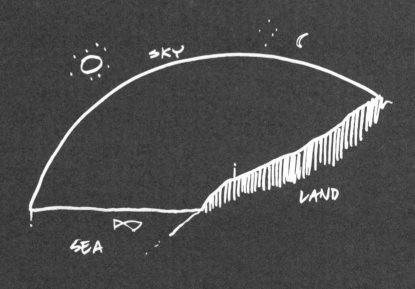

the place. So having this one idea that bound the whole thing and which came out of that diagram was great, because it became my version of space/time diagrams, rather than a time diagram being a straight line in a space. We don't have a word for time or space in either of our languages up north, so it sort of makes sense that I'd always struggled with those two concepts at university.

Jade

I wanted to ask what Rewi was like as a friend as well, because it seems like you guys spent a lot of time just hanging out.

Kevin

He was great, half-friend and half-mentor in a way. Knowing him meant a lot to me at the time and still does.

Jade

How would you assess Rewi's impact on other Indigenous architects? I know this is a tricky question in some ways because we've talked a bit about whether Indigenous architecture is valid as a concept to you.

Kevin

It's a really funny one and I've written heaps about why I think it's not a good category to use because I think it's a mercantile one. Now, that doesn't mean I'm right. I really came to hear the term more around 2010, and it was used primarily by non-Indigenous people to describe this other thing, and because of that anthropological training, all these sorts of words that have been arrived at — Aboriginal, Indigenous, all these things — were words to describe other conditions.

And I didn't think they were other conditions. They were still buildings and there's still this intent around architecture. That's the thing Rewi and I used to talk about: we'd separate that from culture. Our culture is this, and that helps us inform all sorts of things, but it's not the only thing that identifies us. So I sit really uneasily with that term. I still haven't got the answer to this, but there's a balance between being part of a minority and having a safe space within which to operate, which is how we all tend to connect and see each other. But how does that dissolve when you're trying to get to a bigger community of a nation? I don't know what the

answer is, but I know we need both. I've never described my work as Indigenous, and I don't believe Rewi described his in that way either.

Jade

I think I often describe the architectural work that we do as kaupapa Māori design, but the main reason I use the term Indigenous architecture is when I'm trying to think about how we connect with other Indigenous people practising in their own way, in their own context. So I kind of think of it more as a collective term.

Kevin

Yeah, I totally understand. My thesis was called something like 'Aboriginality and architecture'; I separated the two just to be clear that in my head they were separate.

Jeremy Hansen

I don't even know how to phrase this as a question, but it's really interesting to hear you talk about Indigenous architecture as a term and your reservations about using it. I guess I'm trying to find a way to ask you about the commonalities you and Rewi might have shared.

Kevin

What I came to understand we had in common was this innate respect for the ground you're standing on. That's where it started, and that's why I was fascinated when I saw his house. I didn't understand it at the time, and I'd grown up understanding this concept of country in Australia. There are over 300 tribal groups in Australia, and they're somewhat connected, but mostly very different. We've all got our own bit of Country with a capital C, and it has a ground condition, a water condition, plant conditions, all those sorts of things, and that has stories embedded into it.

If you peel off that bit of culture and you're just left with this geography of a thing, do you still feel something for it? Rewi was more along that path than I was, but had asked enough questions to kind of draw it out of me. That's where that sketch I mentioned earlier became important as a circuit breaker — I just called it the Country diagram because it's the way I understand the whole being of things now, or what I belong to

anyway. We talked a lot about that as an idea: what the thing is that you belong to. The conversation was never really about the architectural object. Even when we spoke about buildings, it wasn't in a way I'd talk about buildings with other architects. It'd be about what the feeling of the setting was or what it belonged to, what it connected you to. They were very different kinds of conversations.

Over time I think the conversation evolved so far that it drew me out and led to a big exhibition I did in Venice for the Biennale in 2012, the *Finding Country* exhibition. Rewi was highly influential in the way I thought about that. The other thing about it is that he put such a massive emphasis on this idea of the sense of intuition and the idea that there are other senses that you need to be connected to or aware of. I think that that sort of approach is not just about the individual. He didn't give you a set of rules. It was sort of more a set of questions. I've taught over the last decade in a similar way.

Jeremy

In a way, it sounds like the conversations you had with him were not conversations you even realised were available to you until you had those interactions. Is that a way you'd describe them?

Kevin

Yeah, I'd say so. They were never linear. We never said, right we're going to sit down and talk about architecture now. Like I said, we'd go to the rugby and talk about that particular player and in the middle of that conversation we'd talk about a project or problem I had. Sometimes whatever was happening on the field became a metaphor for what was happening in the conversation about architecture or culture or whatever it was we were doing or vice versa. They were the sorts of conversations that just incrementally build and build. We'd talk about what it was like when his wife passed away and bringing up Lucy by himself and all those sorts of things. We talked about everything.

Jeremy

Did he talk to you about how he got into architecture, but also how he existed in a space where he was so confident about facilitating the kinds of conversations you're talking about?

Kevin

That's a good question. We never had that chat. I think that the real conversation we were having was not about the discipline of architecture, but the idea that culture could inform the way you'd go about whatever it is you're doing. In a way, architecture was probably the last thing we talked about. These other things — culture, what you belong to, how you position yourself in that bit of Country, or how you'd stay connected to it — were more high-level things. Architecture is down there somewhere. We rarely showed each other work stuff. More often than not, the only time I'd get to see his work was if he was giving a talk and showing some of it.

Jeremy

Were you conscious of the lack of these kinds of conversations in both of your professional lives?

Kevin

I knew it was missing. I had a fantastic time socially in my undergrad studies, but intellectually I found it really challenging, and culturally I found it incredibly isolating. In about 1993 I was trying to work an idea through a cultural lens and it just fell flat in terms of the reception I got from people teaching at the time, so I just parked it. I imagine what it would have been like if I'd had someone like Rewi at that point in time. I think I would've got there a bit sooner.

Jeremy

Can I ask you for your assessment of what you think his impact or legacy is?

Kevin

I can only look at it from this side of the ditch. He's obviously been massively influential to me. If you keep asking the right questions and stay curious — I feel like that is the thing from him that I've passed on. So that is now coming up to another generation of younger graduates who have been teaching over the last decade. There's having a direct influence and having an indirect one, and he's indirectly influencing a whole other generation.

Jeremy

You talked earlier about giving a presentation as a student and how it fell flat because people who were assessing it didn't have the frame of reference to process it properly and respond to it in a useful way. Do you think those conversations are now easier for students?

Kevin

I'm not sure easy is the right word, but it's certainly different. The difference now is that there's an awareness. I think there are two sorts of extremes. One is experience-based in a way of making spatial settings that put you into the relationship with Country as an idea. And then at the other end, there's one that's purely symbols driven. I teach with the spatial one. The problem with the symbols is that they become sort of pseudo artworks and ways of claiming that something is receptive to Indigenous culture when it's not necessarily so.

Jeremy

Did you and Rewi ever talk about the responsibility, or the burden, of reshaping the education system to make it more receptive to students like you?

Kevin

I've had that exact conversation with others, but never with Rewi, because the focus was always, what's the next idea? What is it, how do you demonstrate it? How do you make it happen? Everything was an opportunity to figure something else out. That's what was great and why I'd look forward to those conversations. Some of his emails were slightly cryptic because of that.

I'm 50 next year, and there are about four of us now who are in our fifties in Australia, graduated and practising. Now there's this next layer of younger graduates probably kissing 30 now that are coming through; there's about four or five of them and they are incredibly skilled. I was so looking forward to seeing that happen because it means the load gets shared a bit.

Jeremy

We've talked about it from an educational perspective, but how does that work in a big machine like BVN, where you work?

Kevin

I've worked on and off with BVN for about 25 years. They're originally a Queensland practice, so there's a sort of culture and way of doing things.

It's people first, then you arrive at the architecture, which is what I like. But I think one of the main reasons I joined was that they were super-interested in all the *Finding Country* work that I'd been doing in presentations and at Venice. There's a real desire from the practice to engage better and understand what this idea of Country is and how that might influence the way we can do projects.

We've got a thing called the Designing with Country Framework, which has a series of layers: an Aboriginal layer, a colonial layer, a multicultural layer, then the project, then a technology layer and a global layer. The idea is that the strings from all of those layers intersect at the project. What we're saying with this is that there's a whole set of negative stories that touch all of these things, but if you could just find the positive things and weave through that, can you construct a narrative for a new argument?

Jeremy

So these layers you describe aren't necessarily in competition with one another.

Kevin

No, you're looking for the synthesis. I've just picked up a new project which I can't talk about yet, but it's essentially inside the ground, and it's totally turned all this stuff I've worked on for so long on its head. You had your feet on the ground and sky and stars were above you; with this project, it's literally in a cave. This would be the one I would've thrown at Rewi. And then it'd get kicked around for about a year. I find when I get stuck in certain things, I'll imagine the conversation with Rewi.

Pip Cheshire

Pip Cheshire is the founder of Auckland-based Cheshire Architects, the 2013 winner of the Te Kāhui Whaihanga New Zealand Institute of Architects Gold Medal for lifetime achievement. He is a former president of the institute and led the body on the signing of Te Kawenata o Rata, which detailed the institute's responsibilities under the Treaty of Waitangi and engagement in Māori design principles. He also attended architecture school with Rewi.

Here, he discusses his memories of their time as students, and his sense of Rewi's contribution to architecture in Aotearoa New Zealand.

Jeremy Hansen

Pip, how did you first meet Rewi?

Pip Cheshire

At architecture school. Word came up that there was an interesting project that a new guy had done, and I remember going down there to check it out. I can clearly remember it — a lovely black line drawing. I was a couple of years ahead of him, but I was an older student like him. People gravitated to something that was pretty hot, as they still do. The maturity of his vision made him stand out.

Jeremy

Speaking of university, he also invited you to provide feedback on some of the projects he was working on with his students when he was lecturing there. What was that like?

Pip

I was invited by Rewi to be a critic of a project he led students on in the Bay of Islands. These were kids from Korea and Africa and China working on this theoretical project and I was struck by the way that, under his leadership, they had fearlessly engaged in Māori mythology, Maori principles. These are subject areas most Pakehā approach with a fair bit of caution and nervousness about not wanting to tread on toes or whatever. But these guys, with Rewi's backing, just charged into it.

When we were talking about the project, Rewi made the point that New Zealand is a very new country — that there's only a few hundred years that separate the arrival of Māori here and the arrival of Europeans. His point was that both races and landforms were still making themselves, and that we had an awfully long way to go in terms of a long-term occupation of and identification with this place. It seemed to me that he was taking a very long and very generous reading of the situation. In some ways you could say that was an example of the endless grace and forbearance of Māori. But on the other hand, you could read it as a long-term vision of how things will be, perhaps in another 10 or 20 generations.

Jeremy

I know there are a lot of architects who end up in this position, but when you look back over Rewi's built work and the very promising start he had to

his career, it looks as though he didn't get the breaks later on that he might have deserved, and that New Zealand would've had a whole lot of really interesting buildings if he had. Do you have a sense of what factors might be behind that?

Pip

It's the implicit structural racism that happens in our society. People get incredibly conservative when it comes to shelling out the amounts of money that are involved in buildings. I think that's an enormous issue. I remember Pete Bossley saying something like, 'You get down on your knees when you see a half-decent building, because the world is awash with inspired students and others who can make beautiful drawings, beautiful models, beautiful form, but that's only about a tenth of the story.'

You then have to get that past the developers, and city hall and heritage. And that requires all of these political skills, and skills of speaking and presentation and lugubrious marketing. And I suspect that at each one of those steps, there is a wall of either explicit or implicit racism. Anyone who is successful at architecture is a highly gifted designer and maker of buildings, but that's only half of it.

Jeremy

You're saying there's an outlier quality to having the combination of those aspects to your personality, isn't there?

Pip

Yes. And when you get into that territory, people get very conservative. When I say people, I mean bankers and those types. It's just tough territory.

Jeremy

Is that changing?

Pip

I think so. I think the rise of the Māori economy, partly as a result of Treaty settlements and the inspired management of those settlements by a number of iwi, has really helped a lot of Māori architects. While I suspect all the constraints I've described that Rewi faced probably still exist, there is a much bigger path around them now through an alternative economy.

I mean, he was an endlessly gracious and charming man. But I can only feel his contribution in personal terms, really — and to me, he was an unconscious guide, a critical part of my educational transition from being a son of Christchurch to one of Tāmaki Makaurau. I think he was a critical element in that at a personal level for me, and I suspect for a number of other people, too, either knowingly or unknowingly. His Ngāti Pōneke Marae project has had a huge impact on that collision of modernity and Māoridom. He also seemed to be free of the decorative tendency of applying motifs to buildings. Through him, the protocols and values of Māoridom found an incredibly strong voice in contemporary modern architecture.

I've only been to two or three of his projects. I think the work at Ōtara, the fish canopy, is incredible. It's a relatively small bit of building, but I think it has a huge impact. And I think it's interesting that it's there and it's an integral part of Ōtara and its self-identity. And his own house, of course, has huge totemic value.

I also saw the Everyday Homes he did much later with Isthmus in Northcote. I thought they were really good, very clever. They were not 'Big Architecture', but they made moves that were sensitive to the way that people need to live, whether they be Māori or Pākehā or Chinese or whatever.

They made lovely allowances for intergenerational occupation through very small gestures: there was a lobby that opened into the house; there was also a bedroom down below; the bathroom was wheelchair accessible — all those basic and kind gestures.

Jeremy
Did you ever collaborate with Rewi on a project?

Pip
We made a run at a couple of things. I tried to get him involved in Britomart right at the beginning in 2004, when Cheshire Architects were involved in the master-planning of the precinct. I was very keen for him to share the studio there. But it just didn't pan out, for whatever reason.

Jeremy
What's your general feeling now as you look back on Rewi's contribution?

Pip
I think there's great sadness. He had huge architectural ability coupled with a very intelligent thoughtfulness. I tried to get him to be a spokesperson when I was involved in the Institute of Architects — I was leaning on the institute to formally engage with Māori design principles and I wanted Rewi to speak to that, to be the kaumātua for the institute, if you like.

But he was really reluctant to do that; I was never sure whether it was an issue with his health at the time, whether it was a personal reluctance to get involved in that more public politicking, or whether he thought it was irrelevant — that it was prioritising his Māoridom rather than his role as an architect. I had two or three conversations with him about it before I suddenly clicked that this was not something he wanted to do and I backed off. As a profession, we've got a huge amount to undo, to recalibrate and to reorient. It would be good if his voice was still around.

Patrick Clifford, Malcolm Bowes and Michael Thomson

Patrick Clifford, Malcolm Bowes and Michael Thomson are the co-founders of the Auckland-based firm Architectus. They attended architecture school with Rewi and became close friends. Here, they discuss university days, demolition jobs and helping Rewi build his house.

Jeremy Hansen
How did you all meet Rewi?
Patrick Clifford
Well, we'd probably been in the same places as each other before architecture school days — at least Malcolm and I would have, given Rewi was at Rongotai College in the late 1960s and early 1970s, and we were respectively at Wellington College and St Pat's Town, all in that Wellington world. My recollection of meeting Rewi is that he came to second year at architecture school at the University of Auckland. We'd been in the first year and he joined in the second year. Mike, you came back later, you'd had a year off or thereabouts.
Michael Thomson
Several years off. We met in our third year, and I think that's when I first was aware of Rewi as well.
Patrick
I vividly remember that when we met him he had arrived a bit late from the national surf life-saving champs with his Hawaiian shirt and his pink jandals. We must have met up in the studio.
Malcolm Bowes
The Brick Studio, as it was called.
Patrick
That's right. And the first project for the year was a performance piece that the studio put on. We did a little bit of lifting and backstage work and we got to know each other. And then we became not only fellow students, but friends. We began to spend more time together.
Malcolm
I think it's fair to say that, while he might have been a little bit late arriving, it didn't take him long to pick up the pace. And he made a mark very early in his time, through his energy and enthusiasm for the task.
Patrick
I can remember his first few projects. At that time architecture school wasn't as structured as I think it is now. There'd be a studio project every six weeks or so, but not everyone's work was discussed

when we had pinups or crits. The work needed to catch the eye of the tutors, and I remember Rewi's catching the eye. The first project, I think, was a little beach house out at Piha, which he'd used pink highlighters to illustrate. There was a graphical quality to his work that was very memorable. It was an approach that, to use the David Mitchell term, was really summary — not as in the season, but the ability to convey some interesting, powerful idea in an almost austere way.

Jeremy
Did he stand out from the crowd strongly at university or was he just a memorable character among a cast of them?

Michael
He couldn't really help but stand out, I think, not only because of his skills, also physically he stood out.

Malcolm
He wasn't an extrovert, though. He was actually a quiet and gentle person by comparison to others in the studio, who were a bit louder. Rewi really let his work speak for him, I think, most of the time. The other thing about him was that I don't recall him saying a bad word about anybody. He respected everybody and built good relationships, some stronger than others. Our relationship with him, I think, over the years that we worked in the studios together, grew enormously. He had a very strong relationship with Kerry Morrow at the time. They spent a lot of time in Monday Club across at the Kiwi Tavern.

Patrick
[laughs] The Monday, Tuesday, Wednesday and Thursday club.

Malcolm
Exactly. Monday, euphemistically. But yes, Rewi had a powerful presence, and it wasn't one that was forced.

Patrick
I think it's fair to say he had huge charisma. People liked him and he attracted people. Comparison is unnecessary, but certainly the studio was full of people who wanted to be heard. He was heard.

Jeremy
What happened after you finished architecture school?

Patrick
The summer before we graduated, we all worked together. We had an enterprise called The 380 Group: the three of us, Rewi and Tim Nees. And Lian Seng Ti, who is now in Singapore. Three dollars eighty was the hourly rate we were paid while we were doing some of our work. We did various jobs together.

Michael
The summer started with us stripping out the old building centre, including a kitset house that we somehow organised a contract to rebuild out at Patumāhoe. We used to pile into Rewi's Mini each morning and he would drive us down there.

Patrick
It was pretty intense, all working in this little enterprise, doing a bit of demo and some construction. I was staying with Rewi and Leona at their place in Logan Terrace. We'd be out building in the day; we'd probably pop into the Kiwi on the way home, and then get the fry-pan out a bit later in the evening. We didn't quite finish on time, so it dragged into our final year at university, which did cause a little bit of disruption, as we continued to drive out to work in Patumāhoe well into the first term. We sort of muddled our way through that, but it's probably fair to say that we'd all been at university for some time and were keen to start doing other things.

Subsequently, we did competitions and various other projects together, and we had built the foundations and the actuality of a strong relationship. After architecture school, Rewi initially went back to Structon Group and he did the project, among other things that I recall, for the Housing Corporation out at Wiri. Malcolm, you went to Cook Hitchcock Sargisson for a bit. Mike, you stayed on at university for a little while.

Michael
That's a euphemism for me. I was finishing off my thesis. But then I went and worked at Cook Hitchcock. Malcolm was there for about a year. And Cook Hitchcock had their office in this house in St Georges Bay Road which they'd split in half, and Rewi and Leona lived in the other half of it. And we all shared the bathroom, which got some amusing stories, but we won't go there.

Malcolm
His parents used to run the campground at Tolaga Bay, and he and Leona would go back there every summer for an extended period. And on a couple of occasions, we went and camped with them down there. And it was a very enjoyable time.

Patrick
We also helped him pour the floor slab for his house.

Jeremy
Could we talk about his house for a bit?

Malcolm
The house was an incredibly significant project for him, personally. I've always felt that. And it's probably the project I admire most of the work that he did. Rewi always talked about it as being the sanctuary for his family; the project sets itself up almost as a defensive mechanism for that. It sits in that suburb quite uncompromisingly, this very strong object sitting in its context. I've always admired it, but I can remember trying to square up some plywood sheets on the roof, unsuccessfully. And I've always felt sad, in some ways, that that project was never really … He just never had the wherewithal, I don't think, to complete it to the level that he would've wanted to.

Patrick
He referred to the house as 'The Warrior' — something that was defensive, safe and secure. I'm not sure if that's a term that's found in the archives. But it's certainly the way he described it to us. You look at that house as an object, but there are quite a lot of constraints and influences that sit in behind that: as 'warrior' implies and as Malcolm has talked about. And obviously it is also a planning diagram — the ziggurat shape is a response to the council-mandated recession planes, which he managed to comply with and subvert simultaneously.

Remember, he'd been at Structon Group for five or six years before he came to architecture school. And he had completed the Certificate in Engineering. He had significant knowledge about how you make things — structure and tectonics. You can see that in the base and the cantilevers of his house. The frameless glazing is quite particular and it was surprising — it's not

Interviews

domestic, and you didn't see that much at the time, especially right on the street.

Perhaps influenced by The Group and subsequent work from the 1970s, I think we all had a view about how we made things that were quite utilitarian, about using the bare minimum. We were trying to build houses as small as possible and, in our own terms, as affordable as possible, with quite spare means. That said, there was a desire to do something different and I think Rewi achieved that absolutely with his house.

Jeremy

I wanted to ask you what you make of the arc of his career. I'm interested in the way architectural opportunities come along. Some people have said that the financial crisis in '97 came at a time when it stunted the growth of the practice Rewi was building. Others have said he wasn't really interested in having the apparatus of a practice around him, which shut him out from some projects. But I wondered if you could talk about his contribution architecturally, or what you make of that generally?

Patrick

After we graduated, there wasn't much work around. But he was working on the Housing Corporation projects, and they were very significant and challenging, quite incredible projects for him to have at the time. I can assure you that for anybody practising architecture in the late 1980s, into the 1990s, into the 2000s, it was nothing like it is now. It was quite hard to get things to do.

Michael

I'd agree. His house and the Housing Corp project, and the one he did out at Unitec [Puukenga, the School of Maori Studies] are all significant. But the one I actually always liked was not built. It was a project for the Monier Awards, the Ngati Poneke Marae project. That was a really lovely project. I think that's probably one of my favourite projects of his.

Patrick

Jeremy, you asked about whether Rewi really wanted to have the infrastructure of practice. He seemed to in the early days because he had three people working with him. Those first few projects were big and demanding. What he did love most, I think, was the conceptual opportunity. So maybe there's some truth in that.

As time went on, he started to collaborate more. That would attest to the fact that he enjoyed the support of other people and other organisations, without having to create it in his own practice. We did a few other competitions together: a museum in Scotland, the Venice Gateway, and a number of others.

What seemed to me to increasingly interest Rewi was model-making and the physical representation of ideas. When he was in St Georges Bay Road, and then moved to his house, he was making models, big models, models of everything. And some were quite literal, but some were much more abstract and evocative. The most recent thing we did together was some work at the Manukau Courts, and I think we've still got a couple of those models.

Michael

We still do. He would turn up with these quite amazing models. They were very conceptual and had great ideas.

Jeremy

What do you miss about him?

Patrick

We used to get together pretty regularly, so friendship, a lot of shared history. There would always be some reminiscing on those occasions.

Michael

What you miss is, obviously, the comfort that you have with anybody you've known for a long time and have gone through those sorts of experiences with, like at university.

Patrick

Our respective families, we knew each other well. And yes, I think the relationships were very memorable. We really enjoyed getting together. Of course, we'd talk about architecture, but I suppose not so much in the abstract, probably more in relationship to our own experiences. I think it's interesting, the whole way in which he became more involved in teaching and so on, and that part of his life. I don't know whether he would have done more of that earlier, in a different time.

Nicholas Dalton

Nick Dalton (Te Arawa, Tūhoe) is the founder of TOA Architects and was taught by Rewi Thompson at the University of Auckland. Here, he remembers a pivotal moment from his architectural education, some of the challenges Rewi faced and how architecture has changed.

Jeremy Hansen
How did you meet Rewi?

Nick Dalton
I'd transferred to Auckland to do my architecture degree, and I think I bumped into Rewi in my first year, in 2000. He was incredible.

Jeremy
Did you know of him at that point?

Nick
Yes. There were very few Māori architects of that calibre, whose reputation was up there with the best architects in New Zealand, if not higher in some regards. He'd done that mahi for Pope John Paul II's visit, working with Frank Gehry, all those sorts of things. It was like, this guy's a superstar. We used to have barbecues on Fridays in the courtyard at architecture school. Dad came to one of them and was a total Rewi fanboy, but Rewi was so humble. He was quite amazing in that way.

Jeremy
What was it like to have him as a teacher at architecture school?

Nick
He was limitless in his blue-sky thinking. Nothing was too big a deal or out of reach. There were a number of moments at university that he really had my back. It was always effortless with both of us. He was always there. There was a moment which was quite pivotal to me: final assignments were due, and there'd been some personal stuff going on for me and I was still thinking about my project. A student came in and said he'd heard that a complaint about me being late with my project had gone up to Errol Haarhoff, head of school at the time.

Jade Kake
What was the substance of the complaint?

Nick
Who knows? This was small-time.

Anyway, it was the only time that I saw Rewi get quite heated. He said to the student, 'You tell Errol three words: Treaty of Waitangi.' Everyone kind of giggled, as you do. And Rewi was like, 'No, I'm serious. I'm here to protect the Māori students. So if he has a problem, he can come and see me.' At the time I didn't acknowledge the potency of that. But it is really important, particularly in this very Eurocentric kind of framework, from the School of Architecture through to practice, that that is said out loud: 'He's doing what he needs to do.' For someone like Rewi, who generally comes across as always being quite peaceful, this was a pivotal moment that I can't thank him enough for.

Jade
Did he ever talk to you about what the Treaty of Waitangi meant to him in architecture terms?

Nick

He said a couple of things which I thought were very profound. One of them was the idea of recontextualising tangata whenua, and what that means today and in the future. He was speaking about what it means to come from an activist perspective to asking what our future holds and what do we need to do to be great again, returning to be chiefs of our own law. He was taking away the deficit model and saying, 'If there are no limits, what does that look like?' When we're working with iwi groups who have come from a position of nothing, it's worth projecting to see what it might look like for them in 100 years.

Jade

It's always in my mind when you go to some marae because the quality of the infrastructure and the buildings means there are a lot of short-term problems people have just had to live with.

Nick

And they make do. So the biggest thing I continually think about Rewi is just, reach for the stars. Go for it. I was having a bit of a kōrero with Rewi once and he said he was at primary school when Neil Armstrong landed on the moon and he was like, 'Wow, this is so exciting.' He said when he was in the third form in high school his class was asked to write down what they wanted to be when they grew up. Rewi wrote 'astronaut'. He told me the Pākehā teacher replied, 'That's ridiculous, Maoris are plumbers,' and listed a few other menial jobs, then strapped Rewi in front of the whole class.

And when Rewi was telling me this, instead of being serious or feeling sorry for himself, he said, 'You know what? That old bastard was right — all my mates who are plumbers are millionaires.' He had this cheeky laugh. But for me, that story paints a whole lot of the journey he must have gone through and the challenges he met.

Jade

I was 20 before I knew there were any Māori architects at all, and it was so amazing to have them to look to. But I wonder what it was like for Rewi coming through, when there was hardly anybody and everyone was saying, 'Architecture isn't a thing for Māori.'

Nick

I met one of his bosses from Structon Group, Ross Brown. Rewi was working there as a structural draughtsman, but he would doodle all the time and his bosses were like, 'You're an architect, dude, we've got to get you to architecture school.' So there was a lot of support for and acknowledgement of his abilities. They recognised that he had a bigger role to play, which I'm so grateful for.

Jade

Rewi had a reputation for architecturally bold and sometimes contentious moves. Could you talk more about how that might have influenced your thinking and your approach to practice?

Nick

Architecturally, he didn't necessarily have a style. I think his work is very values-based, but also — it can seem like really cheesy terminology — some of his work was quite post-modernist, but not stereotypically. He had style, and effortlessness, and an ability to do something unpredictable. You're right about those bold moves, and I think I'm naturally inclined to do that anyway.

When I went into private practice I would ring him up, and he was just so available. He'd give me a big stack of books and publications. It makes me a bit upset to think back on it because I didn't realise what a big deal that was. It's hard to describe because he made everything look almost effortless, as if architecture had no boundaries. Now, whenever I hit a stumbling block, or let's say the vertical line of the poutama, I say to myself, 'You've got to find a way.' That's his influence.

At his tangi, a number of us caught up, and it was a real solidifier for us because I think we were all individually helped by Rewi and acknowledged ourselves as architectural mokopuna. In some ways we hadn't acknowledged how influential he was because he never went around and said, 'Oh I'm helping everywhere.' He just did it. Also at the tangi, his relations were explaining that he's from a tohunga line. So it's not by chance that he was a genius.

He was also the go-to guy whenever Māori input was required — I think he actually gave a lot, to a fault, supporting other people on that journey at the expense of his own work. And I guess we're realising that with the consultancy work we do, if we just keep being consultants we're not actually going to do buildings of our own.

This is probably the other piece — as a practice now, we're probably doing 90 per cent kaupapa Māori projects, which is phenomenal as a Māori architect. Twenty years ago, those opportunities didn't exist. So I feel for Rewi, and the fact that he was way ahead of his time, because if he was here now, there would be no limit. He'd be bigger than Jasmax, in my view. And our built environment would be way cooler.

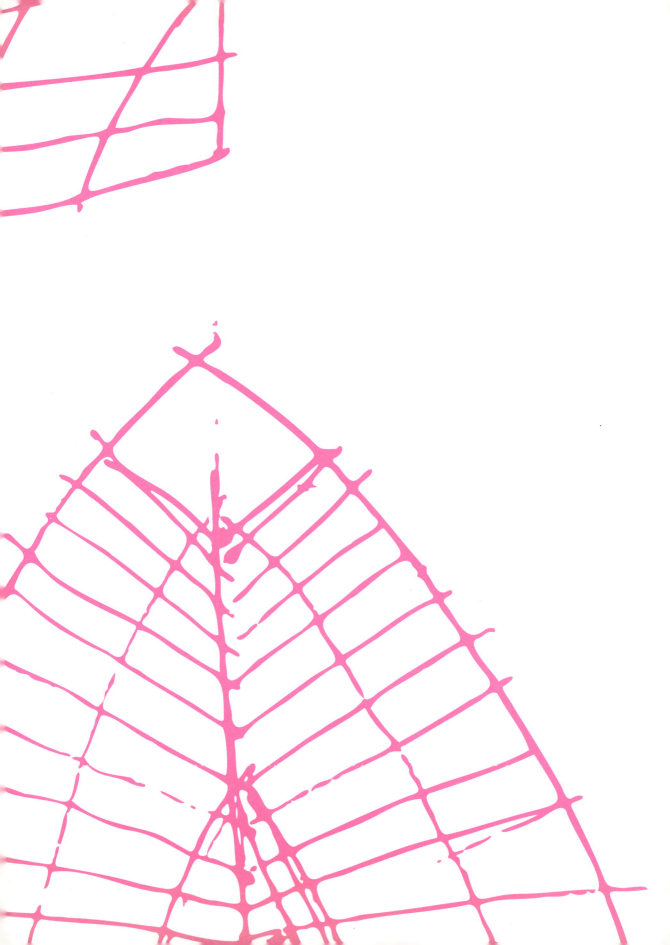

Civic and public realms

Whaitua tūmatanui

He whare i whakaarahia i roto i te pā tūwatawata o ngā tūmanako
A house that is erected within the fortress of desires (a building that is erected that fulfils the hopes and aspirations of the people)

Canopy, altar and Papal throne

Auckland Domain Tāmaki Makaurau

1986

Below: This tent-like canopy was one of two structures Rewi designed in the Auckland Domain for Pope John Paul II's 1986 visit to Auckland. It was here that the Pope was able to experience a Māori welcome. *Gil Hanly, Auckland War Memorial Museum Tāmaki Paenga Hira, PH-2015-2-GH1596-10*

Opposite: Rewi also designed a stage with cantilevered timber projections, where his Holiness conducted Mass. *Lucy Thompson collection*

Saturday 22 November 1986 was an auspicious day for Catholics in Aotearoa New Zealand: it marked the arrival of Pope John Paul II, the only supreme pontiff ever to visit the country. The Pope touched down at Auckland International Airport at 2pm; just over an hour later he was receiving a Māori welcome at the Auckland Domain, where more than 50,000 people had gathered to hear him speak.

The Pope circled the Domain in the 'Popemobile' — an adapted Mitsubishi L200 with an enclosed glass canopy — then ascended a temporary stage to hold the country's largest open-air Mass. 'I rejoice to be in your midst,' he said, before going on to express thanks for the Māori welcome. 'The strengths of Māori culture are often the very values which modern society is in danger of losing: an acknowledgment of the spiritual dimension in every aspect of life; a profound reverence for nature and the environment; a sense of community, assuring every individual that he or she belongs; loyalty to family and a great willingness to share; an acceptance of death as part of life and a capacity to grieve and mourn the dead in a human way.'

Rewi designed two structures for the Papal visit: a tent-like canopy and a temporary stage with wings of laminated timber cantilevered overhead. 'The canopy anticipates a strong figurative line in Thompson's work,' wrote architect and academic Ross Jenner in the journal *Lotus 105* in 2000. 'It evokes the kōtuku (white heron), a rare bird hailed as the bearer of good news, a theme common in myths and provided by the tribe from the . . . Thames region, who hosted the Pope and commissioned Thompson.'

Rewi also designed an altar — later donated to the Holy Trinity Cathedral in Parnell — as well as the Papal throne, chairs, a lectern and candlesticks, all of which were made from kauri by Father Theo Van Lieshout and four volunteer Thames and Coromandel parishioners. According to a newspaper clipping in Rewi's archive, Father Theo and his volunteers worked every night for weeks to finish the furniture on time.

Pip Newman worked on the project as a graduate in Rewi's office. Here, she shares some of her recollections of it.

Drawings from Rewi's archives show early renditions of the two structures he and his team designed for the Papal visit. *Architecture Archive, University of Auckland*

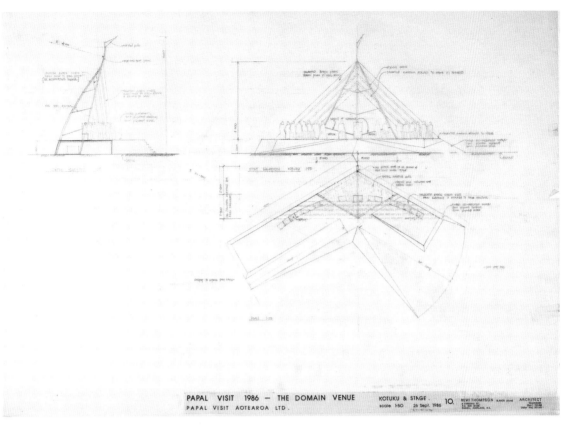

Jade Kake
What were your experiences working on this project?

Pip Newman
We did those drawings. We designed the furniture. The arms that supported the canopies had to be quite powerful. I remember thinking long and hard about the detailing for the glulam, because we had to have this really big cantilever. There were also components of that in the altar and the papal chair.

Jade
Why did the Pope come to New Zealand at that time? What was the significance of the event?

Pip
We did talk a lot about the fact that the Pope was coming to New Zealand. I don't think he'd ever come before and he's never come since. But on this one and only papal visit, a Māori bishop was going to be assigned to Aotearoa. So it was a significant event for the Māori Catholic community.

Jade
Do you remember what happened at the event?

Pip
We got tickets, and we went and saw the Pope. On the day, there was a full Mass. It was a long time ago, but what I do remember is that it was really hot that day, and we were all in this standing enclosure, like sheep in a pen.

Below: More than 50,000 people gathered in the Domain to hear Pope John Paul II speak. *Lucy Thompson collection*

Opposite: Rewi and his team designed the timber stage and canopy for the Pope's visit, as well as the furniture used on stage during Mass. *Lucy Thompson collection*

Civic and public realms

Ōtara Town Centre canopies

Ōtara Tāmaki Makaurau Auckland

1987

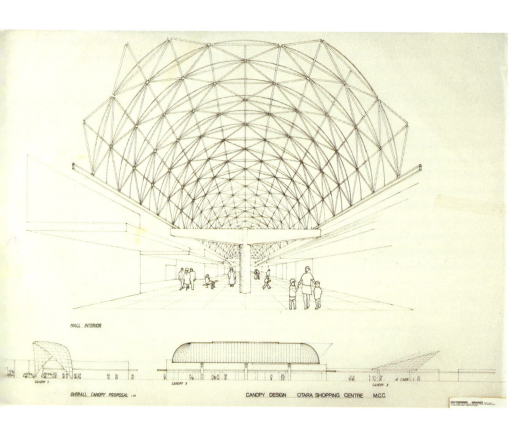

Left: A drawing from Rewi's archives showing the main section of the canopy at Ōtara Town Centre. *Architecture Archive, University of Auckland*

Opposite: Dancers of the Tangaroa College Cook Islands cultural group perform after the official unveiling of the first stage of the canopy, 1 November 1991. *Gerard Johnson, Auckland Libraries Heritage Collections, Footprints 03577, courtesy of Stuff Ltd*

The Ōtara Town Centre canopies were part of an amazing run of projects for Rewi in the 1980s, which included his own family home (1985), the temporary outdoor structures for the visit of Pope John Paul II (1986), a warehouse for Boehringer Ingelheim in Wiri (1986–89) and the state houses in Laurelia Place, Wiri (1986–89). He would also go on to create another shopping centre canopy, a less grandly scaled one in Tūrangi in collaboration with Isthmus Group.

The Ōtara canopies were commissioned by the Manukau City Council in an effort to revitalise and create a new sense of identity for the 1960s mall. Rewi selected the fish as a motif that suited the predominantly Māori and Polynesian character of the area: the canopies' glass panes are the fish's scales. The project is broken into three portions: the tall, arched central canopy; a smaller canopy at the entry to the mall that can be interpreted as the fish's head; and the tail near the community centre. The larger middle canopy shelters a stage for performances during market days.

The 'head' of the fish form, a separate canopy shown at right, is 'a beautifully detailed bit of architecture, like a pavilion,' says Albert Refiti.
Lucy Thompson collection

Civic and public realms

An elevation from Rewi's archives shows an earlier iteration of the canopies; the head and tail sections were to change substantially in its final form. *Architecture Archive, University of Auckland*

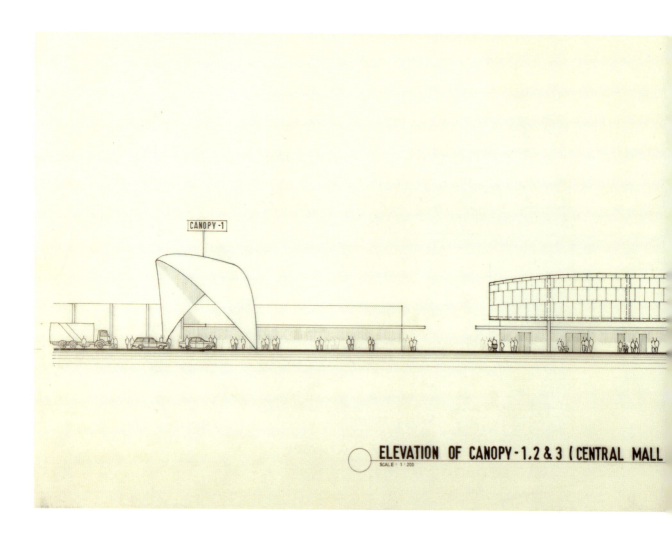

Civic and public realms

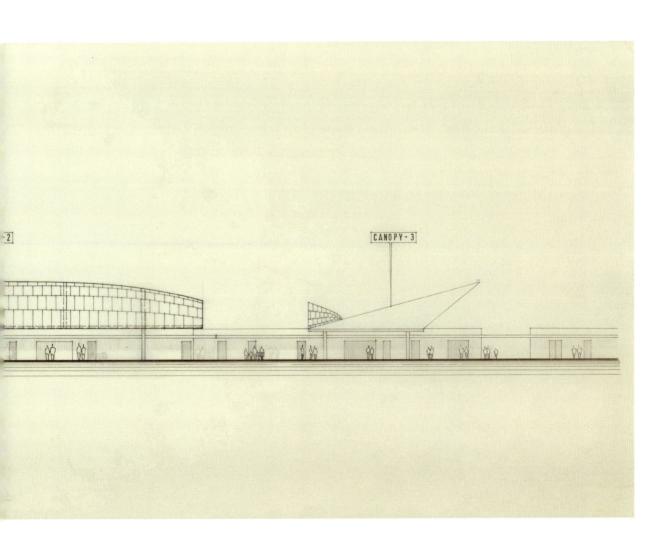

In 2002 Albert Refiti, associate professor in architecture, art and design at AUT, wrote about the canopy and other Polynesian architecture in Aotearoa New Zealand in the book *Art Niu Sila: The Pacific Dimension of Contemporary New Zealand Arts*. He described the Ōtara canopy as 'the most successful and contemporary adaptation of the fale form', going on to say:

> The Māori architect Rewi Thompson has created a structure that echoes the shape of a fale roof with an added twist. Thompson has avoided the simplistic adaptation of the fale form by not trying to imitate it directly. What he has done is introduce a narrative in the form of a fish to weave together references and connections to the Pacific. The fish as a metaphor is reminiscent of Maui's catch, and the large middle canopy looks like Maui's canoe hoisted by concrete pillars . . . The innovative canopy structure takes on the appearance of fish scales and is fabricated from glass panels attached to fine steel frames, giving it a woven quality.
>
> The large concrete columns supporting the canopies have been decorated by the local community with painted murals and woven panels. The complex is more popular now than when it was first opened. The local community, comprising mainly Pacific Islanders and Māori, seems to have embraced the design, which has become an icon for the Pacific community. This project suggests a new way to formulate an architecture that is enhanced by a Polynesian heritage, one that retains a creative interest in traditional forms without being limited by them.

In the interview on the following pages, Albert talks about his encounters with Rewi, his discovery of the Ōtara canopies, and their enduring architectural power.

Drawings from Rewi's archives show experiments in the arrangements of glass panels and colour in the canopy, helping them take on the appearance of fish scales. *Architecture Archive, University of Auckland*

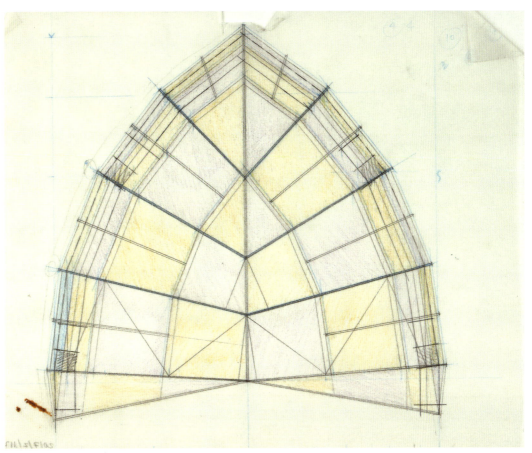

These images show the 'tail' section of the canopy, whose beams were painted by local artists. *Lucy Thompson collection*

Civic and public realms

Jeremy Hansen

When did you first become aware of the Ōtara Town Centre canopies?

Albert Refiti

When it actually opened because I would go regularly to the Ōtara flea market. When I saw it, I couldn't believe it. It was quite a futuristic and more expensive-looking set of buildings or canopies than what I'd become used to there. When that canopy went up, people would gather underneath it, there would be people playing music and it would draw a lot of people from the flea market in the car park to walk down and hang out around it. It weaves together that part of the town centre really well. It's quite an impressive high volume, but it's not overbearing. People use it, and it looks beautiful in the light.

I was at architecture school at the time, and one of my architecture school mates said, 'That canopy was done by Rewi Thompson.' I had known people who worked for Rewi at the time, such as Mike McColl and Nancy Couling, who I thought were really cool people at architecture school — now everyone was talking about their work and realising it was quite important.

Jeremy

Where did the fish as a concept driver come from?

Albert

I never really got to know Rewi until a bit later, and I spoke to him about the canopy. What I remember him telling me was the character of the building being a fish divided up into three, with the head facing the main entry, and then the big section in the middle, and the tail facing the library and community centre. One of the main things I remember Rewi talking about was this notion of the fish being Māui's catch — and that Māui being the demigod throughout the Pacific makes sense for us. In a way, the idea is that the fish is hung up on this portal structure that you see in the canopy's middle section as if it has been hung for the community to enjoy or be blessed by. I also remember him referring to the waterways around Ōtara — many of which had been covered over.

My friend Mike McColl, who was working for Rewi at the time, went out there for a site visit by himself early one morning when they were beginning the design of the project. A fishmonger arrived — Ōtara Town Centre was one of the main areas you went to buy fish — and he got him to hold up a fish and took a photograph. He took the photograph back to the office and Rewi developed sketches from there.

Jeremy

Do you feel Rewi was able to successfully combine Māori and Pacific motifs together in a building? And do you think that was a delicate balancing act for him?

Albert

I don't know. I mean, Rewi was a synthesiser. He was a drawer — the guy drew all the time. Drawing for him was the way to deal with complex ideas. Through drawings, you can narrativise symbolic things, cultural things, into the language of form and line. And then of course you have the tone and colour you can see in Rewi's beautiful drawings; that's what really sells the idea for me.

But I don't think the canopy is necessarily a Māori or Pacific building. I think the narrative that's built around that place is Māori or Pacific, though — I mean that underneath that canopy is a beautiful Polynesian space. It's a perfect ātea underneath the middle canopy, a proper Fale Afolau in a Tongan or Samoan sense, where people gather; a static space for people to sit. People tend to traverse around the edges, and then there are these lovely spaces where people gather around the columns. It's the characteristic of the form above you that creates that. It became a place for a lot of youth to gather after hours. Once the roller doors came down on the shops, there was nowhere for the young people to hang out.

Jeremy

From your description of first seeing it, it sounds as though people intuitively used it as Rewi intended.

Albert

Yeah, exactly. I remember having an argument with one of my colleagues at university at the time because there was an article in the paper that said the structure cost something like over a million dollars and it created nothing — they said there's no building here, as if it was a series of sculptures or something. And I said it's a beautiful

Auckland Council completed a refurbishment of the canopies in 2022; these photographs were taken after the scaffolding was lowered. Albert Refiti says the area under the central canopy is 'a beautiful Polynesian space. It's a perfect ātea . . . a proper Fale Afolau in a Tongan or Samoan sense, where people gather.' *Samuel Hartnett*

space, a beautiful Pacific space. I think people gather instinctively around the middle section of the canopy. They never go to the head of the fish, which I think is a beautifully detailed bit of architecture, like a pavilion. I don't think the tail is as successful as a piece of sculpture or a gathering place.

Jeremy
How would you sum up Rewi's legacy?
Albert
A group of us used to go through this exercise to think, who is the most important architect in the country? And I think most of us academics always thought that Rewi was the most important architect — the most creative, the most innovative, the one doing work that we think will stand up to international scrutiny. Not showing international people that we can make architecture that looks like international architecture, but showing people overseas how we make architecture in the context of Aotearoa, be it as a Māori or Pākehā or Pacific person. So I think he is probably our most important architect, from a particular modernist or post-modernist point of view.

Jeremy
How do you remember him as a person?
Albert
He was a complex person, but he was always good to me. He always felt like a mentor and spoke to me like a mentor. He always looked after me. When I was in my last years of university in the late 1980s or early 1990s, we used to go over to the corner bar at The Globe, and a group of older architects who were teaching at the school at the time would be there, including Rewi, and I always remember them being so generous to some of us young students and incorporating us into the culture of drinking and talking about architecture.

Jeremy
When you say Rewi was complex, what do you mean?
Albert
When he passed away, we found out that he had other parts of his life which had nothing to do with architecture. I never knew he coached rugby, for example. Rewi was very careful to not give away too much about his personal life; things were a bit more compartmentalised than we realised. And I think that was sad for a lot of us to realise in the end.

Rewi told Albert Refiti that the canopies were 'a fish divided up into three, with the head facing the main entry, and then the big section in the middle, and the tail facing the library and community centre.' This sketch over a photocopied panorama of the town centre from Rewi's archives shows an early iteration of that concept.
Architecture Archive, University of Auckland

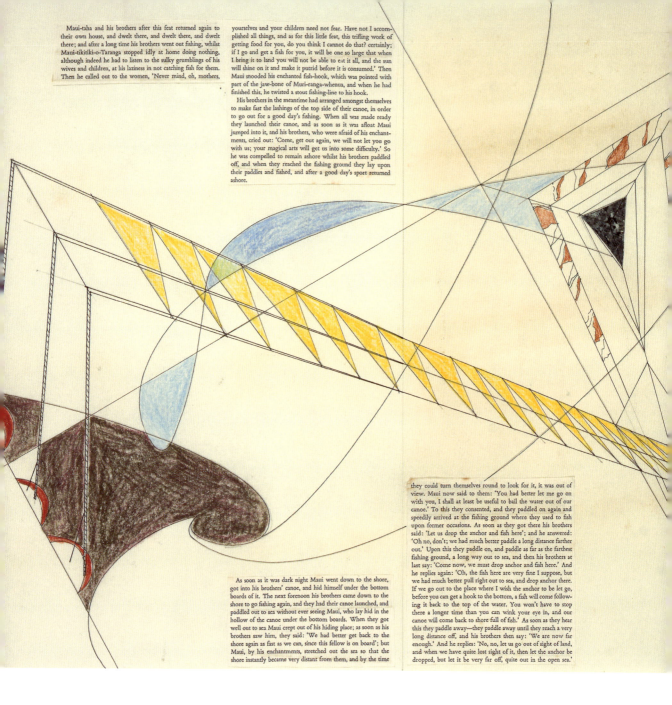

The conceptual basis of the Capital Discovery Place Te Aho a Māui children's museum comes from the story of Māui fishing up Te Ika a Māui, the North Island, after the hook he threw from Te Waipounamu, the South Island, lodged in Wellington Harbour. In Rewi's archives, a series of documents blend elements of collage and architectural drawings with the narrative. *Architecture Archive, University of Auckland*

Civic and public realms

Capital Discovery Place
Te Aho a Māui

Te Whanganui-a-Tara
Wellington

1988

With Athfield Architects

At first look, it was an unpromising space. In the late 1980s, the creation of Wellington's Te Ngākau Civic Square led the Roy McKenzie Trust to see an opportunity. Inspired by the Boston Children's Museum and San Francisco's Exploratorium, the trust's members dreamed of a Wellington institution dedicated to children's interactive learning. They formed a museum trust board, which lobbied the city council to allocate space for their venture in Civic Square. The challenge? The site was largely underground, tucked beneath the City to Sea Bridge as it stepped up from the square.

Philip Tremewan, the inaugural director of what would eventually open as Capital Discovery Place Te Aho a Māui, wasn't daunted. The trust engaged Ian Athfield as the architect for the project. Tremewan relished Athfield's creative vision and his desire for the design to emulate an Italian piazza, but sought a bicultural approach in its planning. He learned of an architect who he was confident could bring a powerful Māori perspective to the project. The board agreed and Rewi was brought onto the team as a consultant.

'We were continually discussing how we might shift people's thinking, and because this was a brand-new project it was wide open,' Tremewan remembers. But it wasn't as straightforward as it sounds. 'At first, Ian Athfield queried the need for another architect.' But Athfield didn't feel that way for long. Capital Discovery Place acquired a Māori name — Te Aho a Māui — and Rewi began to develop the motif of Māui's fishing line that would be embedded into the brick paving and pounamu-tipped pyramid on the bridge above.

Athfield's collaboration with Rewi on Capital Discovery Place also extended to the City to Sea Bridge — more on that later — and their entry to the design competition for Te Papa Tongarewa Museum of New Zealand with Canadian-American architect Frank Gehry.

At Capital Discovery Place, Rewi's work resulted in a showstopping treasure chest of an interior that included a red vertical slide visible through the window of the pyramid atop the bridge (the slide was included in *The Spinoff*'s list of 'Cursed Slides of Aotearoa' in 2021). Alas, the interior is no longer: after just three or four years, financial problems and earthquake safety issues meant Capital Discovery Place moved out and became Capital E in a new location nearby.

We spoke to Philip Tremewan to hear his recollections of the project and the then-radical act of insisting on a bicultural design approach.

Capital Discovery Place was located underneath part of Wellington's City to Sea Bridge. Its ebullient interior contained artwork by Paratene Matchitt, whose work also features on top of the bridge. The interior has long been demolished.
Grant Sheehan

Jade Kake
Can I start by asking, what do you remember of Rewi?
Philip Tremewan
He was a remarkable man, a magic guy. It's so sad that he died so early.
Jade
I'd love to hear about your experiences with Capital Discovery Place. Were you involved when Rewi was being commissioned? What was your role at the time?
Philip
The Roy McKenzie Trust decided that what the capital city needed was a children's museum. At that time, there were a lot of science centres being established: San Francisco has a very good science centre, and there was a lovely children's museum in Boston. That was kind of a reference point, the idea of children being able to go to a place and work with interactive learning. So the Roy McKenzie Trust set up a trust board and then said, 'We need someone to do this', and I got appointed director of the project early on, its first employee. At that stage the city council was saying they could offer space within the Civic Square project.

And so we sat down and started planning with Ian Athfield, because he was, as you know, designing the whole Civic Square. We had the space underneath the walkway across to the City to Sea Bridge. I went across to the States and did a big tour of various places and venues and got very excited about it all. But one of the things that was lacking early on — and that I pushed the board for — was a much more bicultural dimension for it. June Mead [the wife of Sid Mead, who was the first professor of Māori Studies at Victoria University] was on our board, and she was a supporter of this, and of having another dimension to it. I can't remember how we latched on to Rewi, but the board ended up agreeing to bring him into the design process. We already had a building shape, which was largely underground. And Ian Athfield, at first, was kind of, 'I don't want this.'

Initially Ath was very stretched designing the whole Civic Square project. I think that's one of the reasons he was a bit cautious about bringing another design person in, because it was very much his project. And so at first, he queried the need for another architect, but then he accepted that we wanted a bicultural input, and we wanted a Māori architect. Step by step, I think they just built their relationship from there. Rewi would come down from Auckland for a day and he'd sit and talk to me and to other people working on the project, and we'd have a meeting with Ath to talk about ideas. And Rewi would go away and do some drawings and some thinking, and feed them back in. And then went on to the Te Papa project.

Jeremy Hansen
Was it unusual at the time for you to specify a Māori architect? Because I don't imagine there would've been many public clients doing that.

Philip
It was unusual. It was around 1990 and 150 years since the Treaty of Waitangi's signing. A lot of us were thinking about how we might shift people's thinking, and because this was a brand-new project, it was wide open. There was no children's museum in New Zealand, there was nothing else to model us on. So how do we make it a bicultural place?

Jade
Where was the drive for this coming from?

Philip
Probably from me. I had a history. I worked with Oliver Sutherland [the Pākehā entomologist who was among the first to use the term 'institutional racism'] when I lived in Auckland on the Auckland Committee on Racism and Discrimination in the 1970s, and then I came to Wellington, where I worked on Project Waitangi. Both projects were Pākehā, working on Pākehā institutions. In Capital Discovery Place, people were very ready for that bicultural approach. It was a very new sort of place, and people got excited by the whole concept.

Jade
Now, when we do culturally based architecture, there's a strong drive to always involve mana whenua or whoever have mana whenua status there. Were mana whenua involved in this project?

Philip
There was consultation, especially among educationists, including Keri

Kaa. For instance, initially at the bottom of the steps, what Ian Athfield proposed was to put giant tuatara or lizards on each side, but he was told they can represent death. That was a Discovery Place-driven consultation. I don't know if Ath would've got that otherwise.

Jade
Were there other architects you considered to deliver that aspect of the project at the time, or was Rewi at the top of the list?

Philip
No, Rewi was way up there. He was the only person to turn to.

Jeremy
And how did you know about him?

Philip
I don't honestly remember how we found Rewi. I'm certainly not architecturally connected, but I would've asked around. We had a wide consultation with all sorts of people, from Moana Jackson to a number of artists. Someone must have said, 'Rewi Thompson's your man.'

Jeremy
Getting back to Civic Square for a minute, can you provide us with a bit more context about what was happening there before Capital Discovery Place became part of it?

Philip
Ath was designing the square very much with an Italian piazza in mind. Things were opening up in Wellington, that notion of a crowd of people coming into the city, and kids and families, and the sense of pleasure, enjoyment, excitement. Wellington's kept that, much more than Auckland has. Ath was very adept. He was a brilliant person at persuading people. I used to take him to meetings when we were enthusing about the project. And it's sad in a way, because now all the civic buildings are closed, the Town Hall is closed, and there's a slight sense of desolation about the place. It's just so, so sad after Ath's dreams of it being the central piazza for Wellington.

Jade
Did Rewi and Ian Athfield get on well when Rewi was brought into the Capital Discovery Place project?

Philip
I think for all sorts of reasons, Ath had the whole thing in his head, so he was a

bit reluctant to bring another designer into the process, but bit by bit, Rewi nudged things along. In a way, it ended up being slightly cosmetic. Discovery Place was just paying him as an extra consultant in the process because we wanted that bicultural input, but it did have a big impact on the exterior, and it did have a big impact on our name. We started off being named Capital Discovery Place, but then Rewi came up with the idea of Te Aho a Māui, Māui's fishing line for pulling up the North Island, and that's now embodied in the top walkway of Civic Square.

Jeremy
Did that big pyramidal architectural element exist in Ath's original plans?

Philip
No, I don't think so. Because that's where the braided ropes, Māui's fishing line, come together. The strands of Māui's rope are represented in the brickwork, and they come together in the pyramid, which is the South Island, which is topped with greenstone. Not many people know that it's actually pounamu on the top. I mean, it's thinly sliced, but there it is, sitting there. So it's as if Māui's rope is being thrown out from Te Waipounamu and, quite literally, the pounamu was there and rope strands diverge from there, the expanded strands of rope represented in the brickwork. The pyramid had big glass windows into the interior, and just inside was a vertical slide for kids. So you go off and you just drop vertically, and so you could look in and see kids go screaming and sort of disappearing down the slope.

Jeremy
What was Rewi like to work with?

Philip
Rewi was just a wonderful person to work with because he was nudging and pushing. He was very good at sitting down and working, working with clients, asking, 'Where are you coming from?' Listening, considering, working through ideas, and then he'd go away and think about it and come back, come back with some drawings, come back with some ideas. Paratene Matchitt was also with him. Para was working on those sculptures on the City to Sea Bridge, but he also did some work for

Civic and public realms

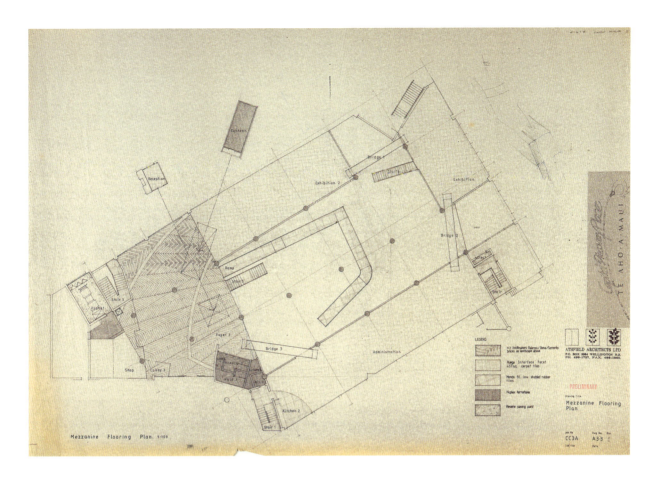

Above: A plan of Capital Discovery Place Te Aho a Māui's mezzanine floor from Rewi's archives. *Architecture Archive, University of Auckland*

Below: The museum's interior featured a bold red ramp and plenty of spaces to explore, including a slide that people either loved or hated, and a small stage. *Grant Sheehan*

Discovery Place inside, in the entryway to the slide area and in some installation work inside.

Jeremy

What do you think it says about Rewi's character or temperament that he was able to walk into this potentially volatile situation and end up, not only with Ath as a collaborator, but also creating this little jewel of a project?

Philip

I just think he was an incredibly centred person. He was quite confident of who he was and what he was doing. And I think he dealt with Ath's initial standoffishness; I don't think it worried him. He presumably had encountered that before. He knew what he was there for and he just carried right on. And I think that easy confidence and openness was quite remarkable. He had a wonderful sense of curiosity.

Jade

How long was Capital Discovery Place in operation?

Philip

Not very long. Three or four years, I think. The council decided not to support ongoing operational costs, there were engineering problems, and the whole thing became an earthquake risk. Which is a pity, because it was a great concept. For a while it became more of a performance space. And it transformed into Capital E, which is now a lot of children's theatre over by the TSB Arena, so it's gone on having a life. But that whole building was designed for kids. Now it's all been boarded up.

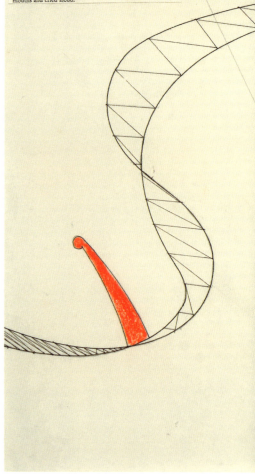

Civic and public realms

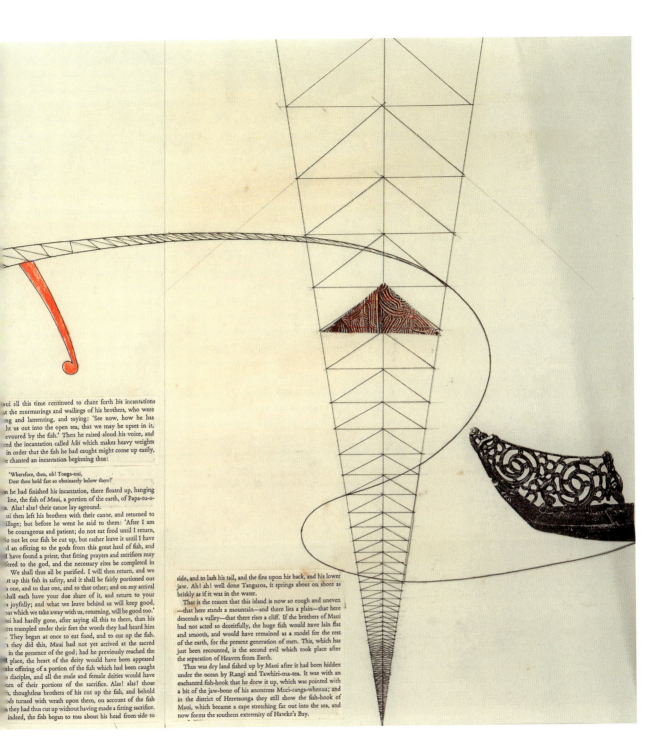

Another of Rewi's collages that combine the narrative of Te Aho a Māui with his own illustrations. *Architecture Archive, University of Auckland*

City to Sea Bridge

Te Whanganui-a-Tara Wellington

1990

With Athfield Architects, John Gray and Paratene Matchitt

Civic and public realms

Rewi designed a split pyramid form for the City to Sea bridge that is topped with pounamu; it is a representation of Te Waipounamu, the South Island, from where Māui threw his fishing line and lifted up Te Ika a Māui, the North Island, after his hook caught in the harbour mouth. The radiating brick patterns from the pyramid represent Māui's net, with the line and hook extending towards the harbour. Two of the Ian Athfield-designed nīkau forms rise from the edges of the bridge. *Paul McCredie*

Most beloved bridges are showcases of sleek engineering, but the City to Sea Bridge in Te Whanganui-a-Tara Wellington has an entirely different approach. It lumbers up from Civic Square past a split pyramid topped in pounamu, then invites visitors to take in the view from an almost ramshackle platform amid Paratene Matchitt's totemic sculptures. This platform tilts towards the vista, then collapses towards the harbour in a cacophony of stairs and concrete panels.

The excess of architectural stimulation is partly a result of the extensive collaboration that birthed the bridge. It is often credited to a single individual: Paratene Matchitt's sculptures are so prominent that some people believe the entire bridge is his work, while others single out Ian Athfield or Rewi Thompson for sole credit. The truth is that the lines are blurred because of the complicated nature of the commissioning of the bridge and of the organic collaboration that resulted from it.

The master planning of the Civic Centre project began as a collaboration between architects Gordon Moller, Maurice Tebbs and Ian Athfield before a decision to split the project into stages assigned individual structures to different architectural teams. Moller's recollection is that Rewi and John Gray were commissioned by Wellington City Council to design the City to Sea Bridge, and that they brought in Paratene Matchitt to work with them on the structure. Because the bridge was an integral part of Civic Square, Ian Athfield was also involved, particularly in the segment of the bridge leading from the square to the road edge above Jervois Quay.

Some of the bridge's design was evolutionary. An early 1980s proposal featured a bridge with a triangular wedge form and double splay, a shape that was echoed in a 1983 design competition for the Wellington Waterfront by a team including Bill Toomath, Derek Wilson and John Gray. When the design team charged with the creation of the Civic Centre started work in the late 1980s, 'they sort of inherited this idea of a large, elevated, triangular plaza that would bridge Jervois Quay and splay out to the north and southeast to the waterfront,' says Ken Davis. Ken was working for Athfield Architects when the Civic Square project got under way. Here, he talks about the complicated collaborative process that led to the creation of a Wellington landmark — and how Rewi's later proposal for Te Papa with Ian Athfield and Frank Gehry grew out of it.

A sketch from Rewi's archives shows an early arrangement of the bridge's pyramid form with the metaphorical net pattern and fishing line creating a complicated geometric composition on the bridge.
Architecture Archive, University of Auckland

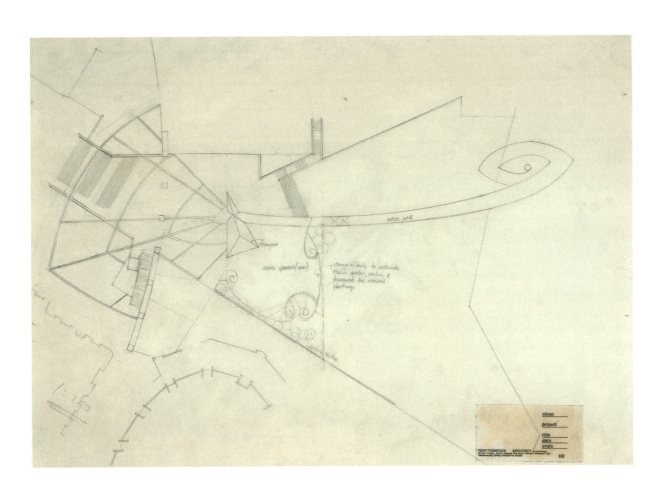

Jade Kake
When did you first meet Rewi?
Ken Davis
When I was at architecture school and he was a visiting tutor. He was in Brick Studio, which was kind of the groovy studio at architecture school. It's where all the 'cool' students went and all the cool tutors taught. I wasn't in that studio but I eventually navigated myself down there. I always remember Rewi driving his little mustard-coloured Alfa Romeo into the lower courtyard of the architecture school. I thought, wow, that's pretty impressive. But he was very grounded. I don't think he was captured by the trappings of success, whatever success is, other than his Alfa Romeo. So that's when I was first aware of him and then he must have tutored me a bit.

I remember his presence all the time at the architecture school. I served him large pints of beer at the university club when I was a barman and he would turn up at lunchtime with Kerry Morrow. They were just getting together, having a good old drink during the middle of the day. They certainly liked to imbibe, I seem to recall. I also had another connection with Rewi: before I finished my degree, I worked at Structon Group in Wellington, and that's where Rewi started his career with Ross Brown. Rewi wasn't there then, but there was still the sense that he'd left a mark in that practice.

And then after I graduated, I was offered a job at Athfield Architects, where I worked for six years. I was one of the project architects on the Wellington Civic Centre right from the get-go, from the site development master-planning through to working on the detailed design of the library interiors. I was there from the beginning at concept levels through to the final detail, and Rewi was involved because he got engaged by Lambton Harbour Management to help design the City to Sea Bridge. Rewi often came into our office at Ath's, and I got to know him a little bit more there.

When they realised that we needed to create a bridge that linked the whole Civic Square development with the sea, it resulted in a kind of subterranean space that they didn't know what to do

Civic and public realms

Opposite: Two of the many drawings in Rewi's archives that explore options for brick patterns atop the City to Sea Bridge. *Architecture Archive, University of Auckland*

Above: This drone photograph shows the bridge's three main sections: a wide plaza lifting up from Civic Square; a narrower central section; and a third section which opens (and slopes down) towards the harbour. *Paul McCredie*

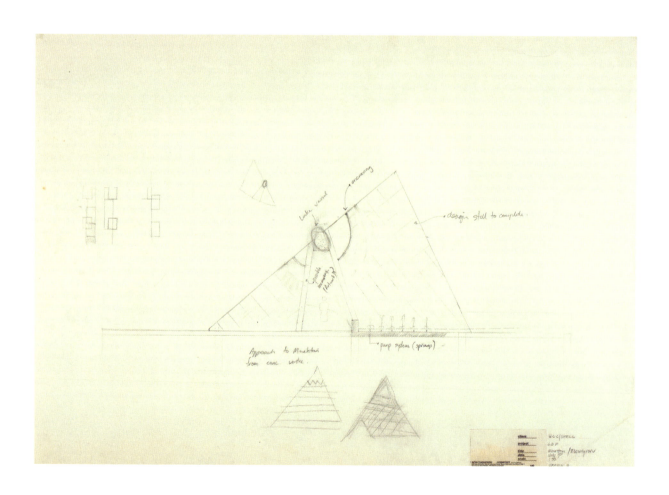

Civic and public realms

Opposite left: The pounamu-topped pyramid dominates the central section of the bridge, with poles by Para Matchitt occupying the central section. The Ōamaru stone sculptures on either side of the Civic Square entry to the bridge are by Matt Pine. *Paul McCredie*

Opposite below: 'I ended up having to work out how to detail the pyramid, and Rewi organised some greenstone from the South Island to go on the little peak,' says Ken Davis. This sketch of the pyramid is one of many from Rewi's archives. *Architecture Archive, University of Auckland*

with. That's what Capital Discovery Place became. As part of the design process that Ath and Rewi were busy working on and I kind of was engaged in on the periphery, they came up with the narrative around Māui and the creation story of New Zealand, and so a lot of the paving and the design and the pyramidal structure that you walked through was very much Rewi's idea.

Ath was quite happy to support that — a paving pattern that reflects a notion of a hook and a net — with the result being this stark pyramid that sat in among the palm trees. I ended up having to work out how to detail the pyramid, and Rewi organised some greenstone from the South Island to go on the little peak.

It was really complex because it's a steel frame that supports this oddly shaped pyramid with a slice in the middle. I had to work out the intersection of the grid lines in three dimensions. We're talking in the days when you just used a simple calculator; there was no sophisticated computing. I had to do a quadratic equation to work out the intersection points and I couldn't do it because it had been so long since I'd done them at school. I couldn't work out the intersection points, and I said to Paul Walker, who had a PhD and was working for us part-time, 'You were good at maths at school, weren't you?' And he said, 'Yeah, I got scholarship maths.' He sat down and did the quadratic equation and worked it out. So I had a very intimate association with Rewi's pyramid. I'm not sure that he ever thanked me for it because he didn't have to draw it up. He just came up with a big idea. But he was frequently in the office.

And then, of course, while we were doing the working drawings for the Civic Centre and the Public Library, Rewi and Ath teamed up with Frank Gehry and they disappeared to LA for 10 days and came up with their scheme for the Museum of New Zealand competition. I think the discussion about the assessment and adjudication around that project is probably worth an investigation in itself, actually. I've subsequently had discussions about it because supposedly the Gehry, Athfield, Thompson scheme was rejected

because there was some bad karma over the feather. It was just one Māori design advisor having a view on what the feather represented. I think what we've ended up with as a symbol of bicultural New Zealand is really one of the most disappointing pieces of public architecture we've produced in a long, long time, a lost opportunity in lots of ways. You can't really blame the architects; it's really just a lack of vision in those leading the project. I'm not sure Ath ever quite recovered from not winning that project. I don't know how it affected Rewi, but Ath was really, really crushed by it.

They came back in the middle of winter and we were busy working on the Wellington Public Library. And that's when Ath started scribbling on our elevations for the front of the library building. The building was designed to be supported on these big monolithic limestone columns, and Ath said, 'What do you think of the sketch I've just done?' He'd overlaid a bit of butter paper over the elevations and drawn these palm trees, the nīkau palms. So that's where that design element came from: his trip to LA with Rewi. It subsequently got quite widely adopted as a kind of an icon for Wellington.

Jeremy Hansen
Can I ask you about the City to Sea Bridge and Capital Discovery Place? There's some suggestion that it was a forced collaboration between Ath and Rewi, and Ath was supposedly not that happy at having to work with him, but then they got on quite well after that.

Ken
Ath would've known Rewi pretty well by then. Ath had a strong ego and wanted to lead design and stuff like that, but he was also a great listener, a great collaborator, and respected the views of his colleagues. So I don't think he would've had a problem. And he didn't have a problem collaborating with Rewi.

Jeremy
So could you say the City to Sea Bridge was Rewi's with some collaborative elements?

Ken
Well, yes and no. The problem was that you had two contracts. You had Lambton Harbour Management, who are a CCO

[council-controlled organisation] of the Wellington City Council, who are managing the development of the waterfront. They paid for the bridge, the link from the seaward side across the road where it connected onto the bit that we were building. Ath was always an architect to understand that you don't just consider what you're designing within the constraints of your boundary. Architecture is holistic, and urban design is a holistic thing that reaches beyond those artificial points of separation. That's why his house sprawls across three or four residential properties up in Khandallah, because he recognised that these are just abstract property lines that are meaningless in lots of ways, and often cause lots more problems than they're worth.

And he was always trying to break down those artificial barriers because he said he understood that architecture's more than that. Rewi was of the same view, and most good architects are. Ath was always a person to reach out and connect, and so was Rewi. So there was a high, high level of collaboration on that bridge. I think Ath utterly respected Rewi and saw him as a really important voice in New Zealand architecture. That linking of the Civic Square to the harbour was an important gesture. And the fact that we had Ath and Rewi as the two key creators of that is quite important, I think.

That's why that bridge is an important piece of landscape and architecture, because it's a reflection of the mutual respect of those two people. And it gave opportunities to integrate artworks with the Matt Pine newell posts [flanking the steps up to the bridge from Civic Square], and of course there's the Para Matchitt sculptures that were integrated into the design as well. Aesthetically, I'm not sure that I like it that much — it's a bit chaotic for me — but it was fantastic to be part of and help make.

Rewi played an important role in connecting these two parts of the city and architecturally leading this representation of the Māori creation story. Jade, you'd probably have a better view on that kind of modern, abstract interpretation of those narratives. Is that right?

Jade

I think there were a couple of Rewi's contemporaries who were similarly working to express Māori culture in the built environment in a contemporary way, but I think this was the kind of work that paved the way for what has become quite common and even expected these days.

Ken

There was a client body that was open and receptive to it. It was all about a growing acceptance of Māori as a key force in New Zealand's identity. It relates to language as well. As part of the Wellington Public Library project, I initiated the first use of bilingual signage on a public building in New Zealand. But I guess what I'm saying is that New Zealand was at this kind of tipping point. It was a few years after the '81 Springbok tour and Bastion Point; there was an acknowledgement that Māori was one of the national languages of New Zealand, and that here was an opportunity to physically represent that biculturalism in a public building. So I think in that milieu around which the Civic Centre was created, in which Ath and Rewi were critically involved as the creators, it's an important story in our cultural development as a nation.

Jeremy

When did you last see Rewi?

Ken

My next linkage with Rewi was many years later, when I'd moved to Auckland and had been asked to teach in one of Rewi's master's courses. I did that over a period of about a term and a half, and it was a wonderful experience to engage with him at that kind of level. This was not long before he died, and he seemed like his normal self, but maybe slightly more subdued. He was always a pretty chilled-out guy. He wasn't crazy and slightly manic like Ath. It was just a beautiful experience that I was honoured to have.

Jeremy

What was it that was so uplifting about that experience, Ken? I ask because there are quite a few people that have talked about Rewi in similarly emotional terms, that they've experienced something quite deep in collaborating with him.

Civic and public realms

The central section of the bridge is adorned with artworks by Paratene Matchitt that refer to celestial navigational guides and symbols associated with Te Kooti. The whale forms facing north to Jervois Quay represent the taniwha Ngake and Whātaitai, which are associated with the creation of Wellington Harbour. Pedestrians are funnelled down separate stairs and ramps towards the harbour.
Paul McCredie

Civic and public realms

Ken

I just think he was very special, a bit like Ath. I don't know what it is. You have a sense with some people who have a presence. Certainly with Ath I always had the sense that I was in the presence of greatness. And Rewi was of a similar ilk, really, a pioneer in his own way. It makes me quite tearful thinking about it because I've lost them both. And we're a poorer society for it. Why am I crying? I think it was his genius combined with his humility and his realness. I just respect it. Maybe because we all work in architecture and have that training and understanding of the difficult challenges in actually making stuff, we're drawn to try and do something better than what we already have. I think that's what links us all. Even though we might not agree on certain styles or approaches to things, there's a common sense that we're all trying to make a difference and make our environments better.

Jeremy

What made him a genius to you, Ken?

Ken

I think the fact that he had vision before his time. That's why he was like Ath, and that's why I know they got on. They were very much about the importance of architecture and urban design being a framework for humanity, for communities to exist and thrive. And they wanted to break some barriers. Rewi's work was quite out there, radical in a way, but he was very understated.

Going back to your question about genius, I don't know. I think these guys had a quality that was special. Ath was extraordinary in his capabilities, but also very aware of his vulnerabilities and frailties and imperfections, and Rewi was like that. They were truly human in a sense because they realised their capabilities and their limitations.

Opposite: The City to Sea Bridge's central section offers views of the harbour and back to the city, as well as a number of haphazard places to sit among Paratene Matchitt's artworks. On the harbour side, concrete panels appear to lean casually against ramps and stairs, as if they've been gradually eroded. *Paul McCredie*

Below: A photograph of a model from Rewi's archives shows an earlier iteration of the bridge with two separate curved sections leading to opposite sides of the lagoon, a journey Rewi's design echoes, albeit in a dramatically different form. *Architecture Archive, University of Auckland*

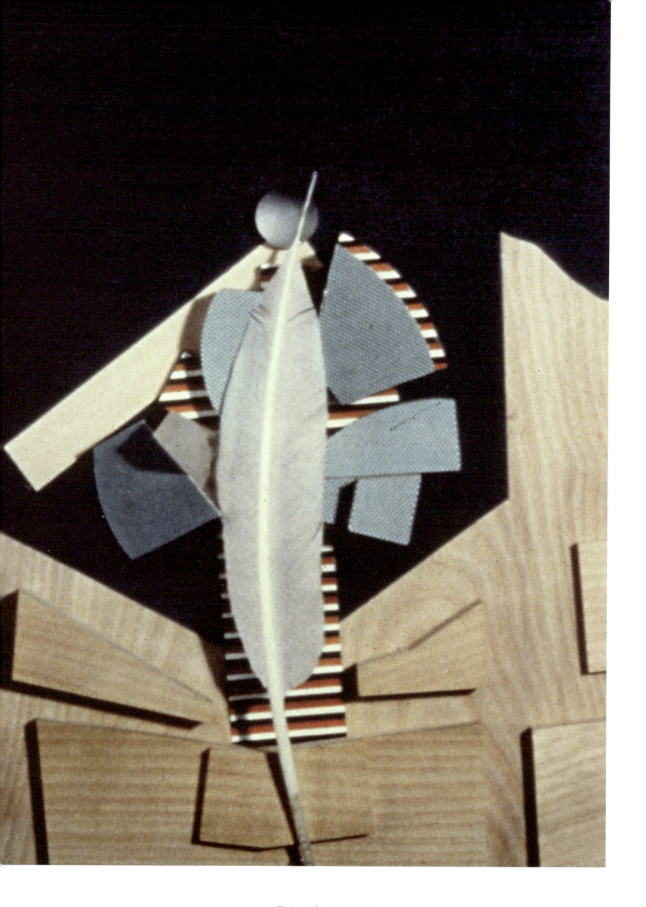

Civic and public realms

Museum of New Zealand Te Papa Tongarewa competition entry

Te Whanganui-a-Tara Wellington

1989

With Ian Athfield and Frank Gehry

A model of the proposal for Te Papa that Rewi designed with Ian Athfield and Frank Gehry. The scheme featured a feather as the key organisational element for an arrangement of museum boxes built on land reclaimed from the harbour.
Athfield Architects

It may be the country's most tantalising unrealised building: the proposal that Rewi Thompson, Ian Athfield and Canadian-American architect Frank Gehry created for Te Papa. Their design, dreamed up during a week at Gehry's office in Santa Monica, features a collection of boxy forms nestled below a translucent upturned feather projecting into Wellington Harbour. In the end, it didn't even make the top five in the design competition, perhaps partly because it ignored the requirement in the brief to leave a clear path for a V8 racetrack between the building and the harbour.

That the trio's Te Papa proposal was overlooked seems more fateful in hindsight: just two years later, Gehry won the commission to design the Guggenheim Museum Bilbao, a building that became a tourism magnet and catalysed extensive regeneration in the northern Spanish city. It also vaulted Gehry into architectural superstardom.

What was the Te Papa selection panel thinking? It's a question that makes many New Zealand architects who also entered the competition decidedly prickly — not necessarily because they think the Gehry/Thompson/Athfield proposal should have won, but because they see the 'New Zealand turned down Frank Gehry' headline as an overly reductive take on a competition process in which architectural outcomes were compromised from the beginning.

In 2011, journalist Gordon Campbell interviewed Ian Athfield about the Te Papa proposal for his website, *Werewolf*. It's a detailed chat with Athfield about the collaboration that produced the proposal. Campbell has allowed the piece to be reproduced in full here. The ellipses are his; the interview has not been edited for this book.

Frank Gehry and the lost vision for Te Papa

An interview with Wellington architect Ian Athfield about the other design for our national museum.

By Gordon Campbell

28 June 2011

Today, some thirteen years after Te Papa first opened, the arguments over its design seem a distant memory, and so very 1990s. The building is there. Many people use it, few people love it. This article isn't an attempt to rehash the ancient controversies. Instead, the aim is to treat one of the losing designs — the Ian Athfield/Frank Gehry design — as a parallel reality, a road not taken. It is (almost) amusing to think that New Zealand had the chance to have its biggest ever, most expensive public building designed by the man who went on soon afterwards to create what many critics now regard as the greatest building of the 20th century — namely, the Guggenheim Museum in Bilbao, Spain. In our wisdom, we not only turned Frank Gehry down. We also didn't think he was good enough to even make the shortlist of five.

That makes for a pretty interesting alternative reality: the Gehry we could have had, but refused to countenance. Of course, when New Zealand was casting around for designs for its national museum in the late 1980s, Gehry was not yet FRANK GEHRY, Architect Superstar. The Bilbao Guggenheim job was still a couple of years away. Yet given the time it takes for major works to be chosen and built . . . if New Zealand had gone with the Athfield/Gehry design the timing would have been absolutely perfect. When it opened in February 1998, Te Papa would have been Gehry's next major work after Bilbao. That alone would have made Te Papa a global event.

In fact, Te Papa would have slotted right in between Gehry's triumphs at Bilbao in 1997 and the Disney Concert Hall in Los Angeles in 2003. Leaving aside the aesthetic issues . . . if Bilbao's success story is anything to go by, the spin-off benefits to our tourism industry from such a building might well have dwarfed what we currently hope to receive from the Rugby World Cup this year.

As I say, the missing Gehry is one of the most tantalising 'what ifs' of this country's recent cultural and economic history. Such buildings can transform the cities that endorse them. We know that's true, from the Sydney Opera House example. Before the Guggenheim came to town, Bilbao had been a fading manufacturing city of 500,000 people, far off the tourism beaten track. That single building has transformed the city's economy and identity.

In the wake of what Gehry's building has done for the city, Bilbao has been able to build a new airport terminal, a new public transport system of trams and rapid transit, a major culture and leisure centre (designed by Philippe Starck) and has launched two massive projects of urban renewal, one adjacent to the same river Nervión that flows past the Guggenheim. Like its New York counterpart, the Guggenheim Bilbao is widely loved by critics and the general public alike. Meanwhile, Wellington has enjoyed some benefits from hosting Te Papa. Given the scale of the project it could hardly have done otherwise. Yet aesthetically and commercially, it has been something of a lost opportunity.

With time, other aspects of the museum become obvious. It becomes easier for instance, to see that Te Papa was from the outset, an explicitly ideological project. Functionally, the building has served as a $350 million storehouse for the nation's treasures. Yet Te Papa was also consciously intended to promote the beliefs about biculturalism held by the government of the day. The building was tasked with (literally) making those beliefs concrete. The architectural design, spatial layout, management structure and exhibitions were recruited into expressing and promoting that cause. Whatever its other virtues, biculturalism has proved to be a somewhat dubious road map for arriving at a good building design.

With all this in mind, *Werewolf* editor Gordon Campbell interviewed the Wellington architect Ian Athfield about how his working relationship with Gehry came about, and what official feedback (if any) he ever received as to why their suggested design was rejected.

The purpose of the Te Papa proposal developed with Rewi and Frank Gehry 'was really in exploring the relationship between the building and the harbour,' said Ian Athfield.
Athfield Architects

Civic and public realms

Gordon Campbell

To qualify for consideration for Te Papa, foreign architects had to be partnered in a joint venture with New Zealand architects. How did you come to team up with Frank Gehry — rather than, say, with Thom Mayne or Richard Meier?

Ian Athfield (Ath)

Right. There were three of us, with Rewi Thompson, who had a sole practice and was Māori . . . At that stage I was quite interested in Frank Gehry's work. I'd been doing a few talks in Australia and someone said how similar we were in our approaches to things, and they had Frank Gehry in Australia at that time. And I thought well, here's an opportunity of working with someone that we may have an affinity with.

Gordon

What was the basis of that perceived affinity?

Ath

Just that he tended to use sculptured forms, for instance. And would balance that against rather traditional building patterns. For a lot of his early works, he had employed a sculptor . . . His early work really fascinated me. And I felt the balance was appropriate, for something like Wellington.

Gordon

How do you go about buddying up with someone like that? Do you write them a fan note?

Ath

I think we contacted him, and said — would he be interested? We sent him some of the work we'd done at that stage. He said he was very interested. He was determined never to come to New Zealand again. He'd come to New Zealand, I think it was to Auckland, about ten years before and his wife — who was of Mexican descent — was not given a visa.[1] So he felt a little bit embittered by New Zealand, on the one hand. But then Rewi and I went across and we worked with him and they gave us very, very generous time. We probably worked for about six days together.

Gordon

What would you say were the main features of the design you eventually came up with?

Ath

The purpose was really in exploring the relationship between the building and the harbour. In developing a strong relationship — by dipping your feet in the harbour, rather than standing back from it. In doing so though, we were questioning the racetrack — and [retaining it] had been part of the requirement.

Gordon

Just to be clear on that. The sanctity of not infringing on Wellington's annual V8 racetrack around the harbour over-rode everything else?

Ath

It appeared to.

Gordon

That's quite amusing — given the deference shown to biculturalism in all other aspects of the brief. So the V8s over-rode the Treaty, to some extent?

Ath

Yes. It didn't take too long though for the racetrack requirement to be removed — *but* the relationship has still remained, as a wide boulevard [on the harbour side of the building] between the building and the harbour.

Gordon

And without the promised connection to the city centre on the other side, either.

Ath

Yes. Without that promised connection.

Gordon

Architects are perceived romantically — and maybe inaccurately — as solitary visionaries. How do they work co-operatively on a project such as this?

Ath

If you can talk about context rather than object, you have more chance of actually being able to work together. For me, it was very satisfying to have someone [in Gehry] who was as interested in context as he was in object. So I think it was a lot about collaboration. We talked a lot about the symbolism of Māori, and about the symbolism of New Zealand.

1   Berta Aguilera is of Panamian descent.

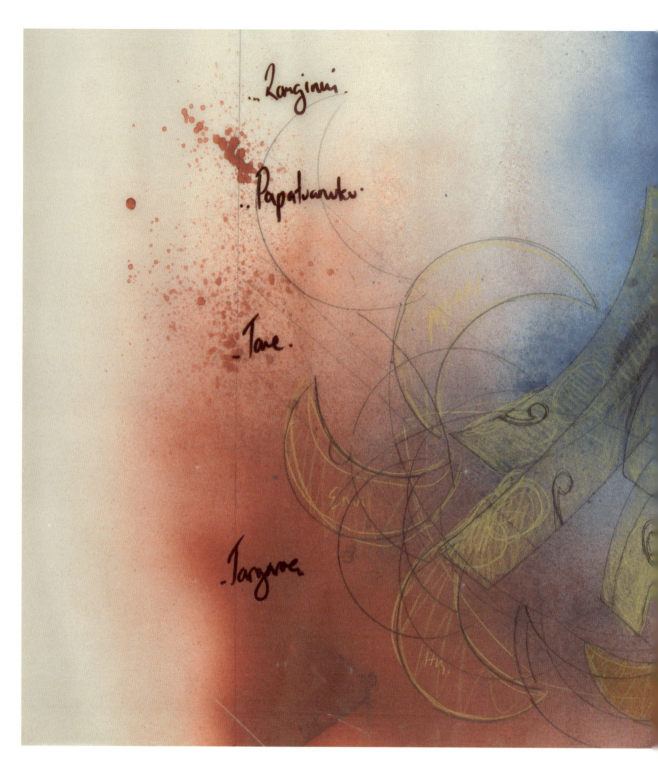

This drawing from Rewi's archives shows some of the conceptual anchors of the Te Papa proposal and its narrative links to te ao Māori. The longest element of the building connects to the city at its southern end, launching into the harbour at the other. *Architecture Archive, University of Auckland*

Civic and public realms

Gordon
What did he want to learn from you in that respect?

Ath
It was mostly historical. He did have a bit of knowledge about Māori. But also, with Rewi Thompson being Māori, it was quite helpful. He talked about the treasure-box which could have feathers, sitting in the rafters …

Gordon
So primarily, whose idea was the [steel and translucent glass] feather element in the final design?

Ath
I think it was discussed a number of times. We decided that was a very, very good ordering thing. Which would enable a series of objects to gather around. Something lightweight, while giving it quality of lighting, and I suppose something which represented Māori. And that's where it started and stopped. We realised it was a first step and you had to get into the first five — so you had to do something that was reasonably strong.

Gordon
Gehry had shown an interest in sail-like forms for some time. With the feather was there a meeting of minds over its Indigenous meaning and his fascination with that shape?

Ath
No … I just think he found it magnetic enough to embrace it.

Gordon
And from what you're saying it wasn't a purely decorative feature.

Ath
It certainly wasn't. I know Rewi and I went down to a hat shop — or a sort of game shop — and got a couple of feathers and started demonstrating how a feather might be an ordering [principle] around the spaces.

Gordon
When you say 'ordering' what do you mean?

Ath
An ordering, effectively, of the circulation space. We felt the galleries should work off circulation. The way the brief worked in that preliminary way, the principal space actually embraced land and sea, and this was really important.

Gordon

Gehry talks about the need to be democratic about how you circulate people through the internal space — as a way of coping with the museum fatigue that sets in once you've been inside for hours at a time. He believes the building should provide the opportunity of foraying out around the galleries and returning to a central space that will perhaps offer views of the city beyond, from a different perspective. Is that what you mean by circulation — or is it more external?

Ath

Circulation on this site seemed to be imperative given how the relationship between land and water was such a part of this [project] … [Our] whole concept allowed the building to go back right through that block of Cable St, Wakefield St … bringing it back into the city, one block further than it is now. So we were saying it was something which people passed through, vehicular traffic could pass through a [unintelligible] foyer, which was part of the space that went across the road. It was just a very generous gesture of interlocking [Te Papa] more into the fabric of the city.

Gordon

You didn't make the shortlist of five. Did you ever get any official feedback about the design?

Ath

Not that I remember. The five selected ones were put up in opposition. The authors had the opportunity of presenting them, and the also-rans had the opportunity of hearing that presentation.

Gordon

Given the strong bicultural emphasis in the brief, did you ever get any feedback about the feather?

Ath

I understand the Māori representatives at the judging level did take exception to it.

Gordon

On what grounds?

Ath

That it wasn't appropriate to have a feather above your head in a building. I think that was [from] Buddy Mikaere who finally I got to know quite well and who has personally always been

embarrassed about it. He was on the selection committee.

Gordon

Do you have a hunch that this might have been a convenient excuse — when they were really cost averse, or bothered by the daring of putting part of the building out onto the water?

Ath

We reclaimed part of the land … Yeah, like there always is, there was an agenda to get a building built within a political framework in which one had to be reasonably safe. There were concerns — for instance, that one of the judges was a Canadian — and he chose his favourite Canadian architect. A person who produced what was sort of over-organic stuff at the time. He was selected [for the shortlist], which everyone was surprised about.

Gordon

Was that the Cardinal–Tse design?

Ath

Yep, that's it. I think there was a general concern that how the hell did that project reach that level.

Gordon

Te Papa is a huge building [of 37,000 square feet] four times the size of the Sydney Opera House. The brief imposed some very ambitious and ambiguous demands about the inner space. Did all that somewhat dictate what the exterior would have to look like?

Ath

In part it may have. I can't recall when the decision to take on exhibition designers took place. I may be wrong, but I have a feeling that process was already going on when the architectural competition was held — to select the exhibition designers. And I think one of the main gripes of the [winning] Jasmax proposal was that they had exhibition designers who were selected separately from them. And who then seemed to work separately. So the integration of architecture and exhibition never ever came together.

Gordon

Yeah, but that's not an unknown situation is it? With the design of the Getty Center in Los Angeles for instance, Richard Meier had major problems with the landscape designer — who seemed to be a completely

autonomous addition to the project. And one that had been deliberately introduced perhaps, to stop the architect from being the sole arbiter of the project, on site.

Ath

Yes. But Richard Meier was an exceptional character. One of the people I met with Frank Gehry was Elizabeth McMillian, who was the editor of *Architectural Digest* … She had a long-term relationship with Richard Meier and I remember Gehry saying to her — 'Well, you know Elizabeth, he was always a prick.' As if … you got what you deserved by going out with him.

Gordon

Really? An architect with a colossal ego? That's unheard of.

Ath

Well … I still have problems with many of my fellow [architects] who are totally object-drawn, rather than condition-drawn.

Gordon

In the case of Te Papa, there was an argument put forward by [Museum of NZ Trust chairman] Bill Rowling that we can't have an iconic building because national museums just aren't that sort of beast. Take the Smithsonian, for instance. What's your rejoinder to that?

Ath

In some ways, I agree. Architecture is a background for history, for fashion, for many other things. It takes various forms. Quite often in cities where there are no strong, heritage type buildings, the over-dramatic building becomes passé. So Bilbao for instance in Wellington may not have been as appropriate …

Gordon

Really? But Bilbao wasn't exactly a centre of architectural ferment at the time. That museum became the gateway building for the renovation of the entire city, though. Beforehand, it was just an ageing, dying place.

Ath

That's right. And the pattern of the city and downtown was pretty well fixed. It was aged. And [the Guggenheim] pulled it out of that situation.

Gordon

What I'm saying is that *not* being in harmony is the whole point, sometimes.

Two drawings from Rewi's archives adhere closely to the arrangement of gallery volumes in the model of the building, with closer attention paid to the arrangement of the feather form atop it. *Architecture Archive, University of Auckland*

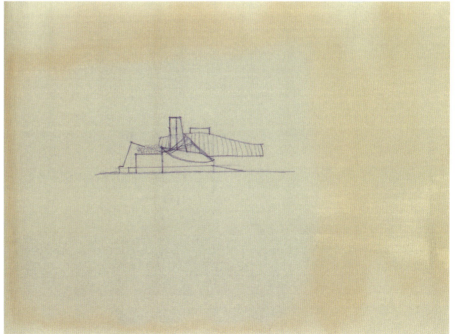

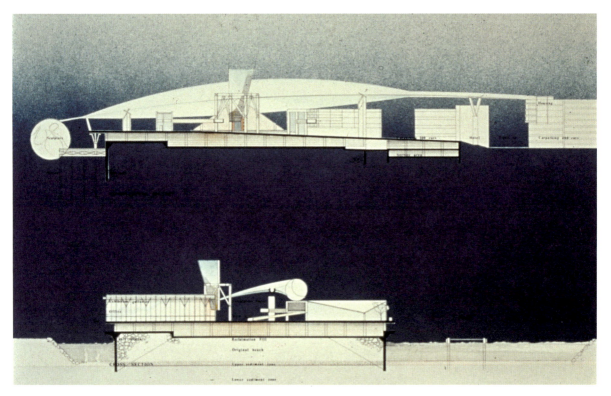
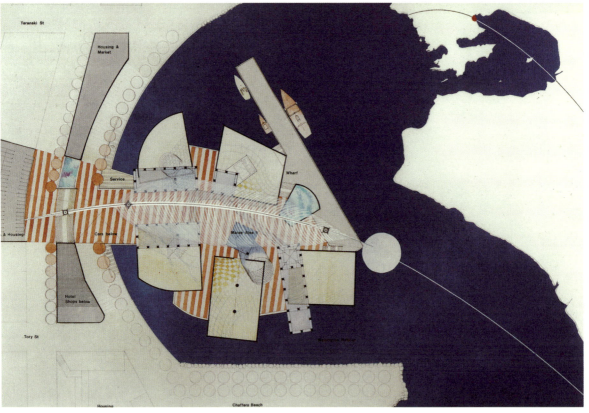

Civic and public realms

Ath

Right. It's a counterpoint. And that's a decision that has to be made fairly carefully.

Gordon

The real rejoinder to what Rowling was saying would be — if that's the case and national museums are inherently featureless and functional, why are you then demanding the best site in town for Te Papa?

Ath

That's right. We tend to want to put iconic buildings on iconic sites. Which this site is. I also think it's very much about landscaping. And landscape on this site is very much about water. It was also about light. The light moving in and out of the building.

Gordon

Yet in the brief, there seemed to be a demand for no natural light inside. In order to protect the dyes and pigments in the exhibitions.

Ath

In the exhibition spaces, that was true. We finished up in our diagram — and it still is only a diagram — with a number of enclosed boxes for that reason, within a free-flowing space. One of the things I've become aware of — even at this stage — is the threshold of museums, libraries and art galleries, and how that's [something] very, very difficult for people to move over. But if you make your circulation space a part of that threshold and don't even ask people to go into the galleries then you'll get more people in there. People, even by suggestion, will go there. So this really was a place to explore the relationship between water and land.

Gordon

Okay. But goodness me, some people would say — there are the national treasures. He was thinking of reclaiming more of the harbour to house them, and exposing them to the risk of earthquakes and tsunamis. Wasn't this always an impractical notion?

Ath

Not really. Christchurch is actually proving that well-built buildings will survive very well.

Gordon

So being on the water wasn't an intrinsic hazard?

Ath

I'd question that. I have a certain level of argument in Christchurch at present because I think that conservative engineers are tending to have their say.

Gordon

In what respect?

Ath

Well, the Dutch build below sea level. And always have for many years. Many Indigenous tribes build out into the sea. Each time, there's a different way of doing it. You can build a building like this like a boat — it could be, for instance, a concrete boat.

Gordon

Tell me more about what you mean by those 'conservative' engineers in Christchurch.

Ath

There's a tendency in the Christchurch context to say look, this land is no longer safe. You cannot build on it. But if you build in a different way ... if you build lightweight — and you don't accept the ground as bearing the structure, you will look at things quite differently.

Gordon

And you believe that from what we now know about the land in Christchurch this merely dictates a different type of building, rather than ruling out rebuilding altogether?

Ath

That's quite right. Yes.

Gordon

Back in the day when you were dealing with Gehry, he wasn't the so-called 'starchitect' that he is today. Did you see much sign of the fabled ego?

Ath

Not really. I found him very amicable. I saw his partners as actually being more aggressive, and protective of him ... Which is often the case.

Gordon

If cost considerations did finally play a role in the judges ruling out your Te Papa design wouldn't that have been ironic — given that Gehry has usually brought his projects in at, or below budget? As in Bilbao. And when cost overruns have occurred on his projects — with Disney Hall and Millennium Park in Chicago — they don't seem to have been his fault.

'We finished up in our diagram — and it still is only a diagram — with a number of enclosed boxes ... within a free-flowing space,' said Ian Athfield. *Athfield Architects*

Ath

He tended to know when to devise forms which were technically limited in the areas that demanded the greatest respect. In many of his buildings there was, you know, a repetitive element. Balanced against that repetitive element was the strong sculptured form. I didn't see the Te Papa design as being terribly much different. Certainly later, he's become more extroverted. That's just the way he's moved.

Gordon

If this design had been accepted it would have come in as the next major work by Gehry after Bilbao. There would have been vast international interest in it. Purely on that basis, for New Zealand and for Wellington, was there an opportunity missed here?

Ath

I've always thought there has been. Unfortunately, overseas architects have tended to be used poorly in New Zealand. Sir Basil Spence for instance. It is sort of an aeroplane opportunity quite often, other than [treating them] as serious contenders …

Gordon

Nearly 15 years on, there's not much sign of community affection for the Te Papa building. It gets used, but is not particularly loved. Given that the expressive role of the building was such a big element in the brief, surely on that score it has to be counted as a failure?

Ath

Um, yeah. It certainly became compromised and I believe that the architects found it quite hard work. Not necessarily to make it work, but I think that tension between exhibition and the architect … the landscaping requirements. It wasn't the most celebrated contract that Jasmax ever had. It just became hard work. The process was more tortuous than what they would have liked.

Gordon

Looking at the academic literature generated about Te Papa, it seems almost quaint to read the rationales put up at the time to justify the design. How, for example, the fault line motif that allegedly runs through the winning design was to be read as a metaphor for the geographic terrain while also being taken as expressive of the bifurcated-yet-unified Treaty partnership. All that seems somewhat ridiculous, especially since most of the public would be quite unaware of it while walking around the building.

Ath

Most architects would be, too. I would have thought.

Gordon

Was it the sort of language needed to get you onto the shortlist?

Ath

Yeah, there was a lot of talking at the time. I wasn't entirely convinced about it at the time, but then, I'm not terribly good at talking. I tend to draw lines rather than talk. So I'm not the best one to criticise things like that.

Gordon

This was our most expensive public building, ever. Do you think the nation got value for money, in any aesthetic sense?

Ath

I personally think they were short-changed. For various reasons [laughs]. But I do think they were short-changed … I still believe, though, that the building has the ability to break out of itself.

Gordon

What does that mean?

[In reply, Athfield gives a short account of a failed attempt during Dame Cheryll Sotheran's tenure as Te Papa CEO in an exercise funded by Denis Adam, to address problems related to the art displays.]

Ath

There are a couple of other absolutely critical mistakes. Like for instance, food should be available without the public being trapped in the gallery spaces. You should be able to move from the garden to the food and walk out again through the garden and really enjoy it without having to go in the front doors. These are basic things that I think are important. Those sorts of things should be addressed. Way-finding is also pretty abysmal around the space.

Gordon

You were involved with that last minute Mainzeal attempt to produce a cheap alternative to Te Papa, by revamping the Post Office building on Waterloo Quay.

Do you thank your lucky stars these days that nothing ever came of that?

Ath

Oh yeah, very much. I suppose that was a reaction to … I suppose I was getting rid of my frustration probably, more than anything. When the opportunity came up to deal with that particular building it seemed to be a way of breaking out of something that I'd become quite frustrated about. It never proceeded, but it just sort of gave us the opportunity to demonstrate that you go through a bit of a rough period, after thinking that what you'd done had a validity.

Gordon

That's interesting. A lot has been written about architects, and ageing. Frank Lloyd Wright has probably been a mixed blessing for the profession as a role model in that respect. Gehry once said something about how it takes until you're in your late 50s, early 60s to build a body of work and to learn the essentials of designing houses that don't leak etc — and then even if you gain prominence, it's all over so quickly. Unless you're Wright, and make it to 90 while still in full flight—

Ath

Or if you're Oscar Niemeyer. Who was once asked about the subject of women in architecture and said: 'That's the subject of a separate film.'

Gordon

Do you think you're managing to avoid the classic trap of ageing — where qualities seen as feisty and iconoclastic in your thirties and forties, can seem more like the attributes of a crank, say, in a 70-year-old?

Ath

I'm probably lucky in that I do have a fairly good supporting family and a fairly good supporting office here. With the exceptions of one or two things I've done reasonably well, I've never finished everything to a point where I've felt content about it. Which is good. So I will be around here hopefully [he gestures around his house-come-office] in the next two or three years, just to make it feel a little bit more complete. So that it sits here as a record of architectural influences over a period of time. But it's a bit more serious than that. It [the

Athfield house] challenges suburbia which is, I believe, one of the criminals of our built society. Architects aren't very good at dealing with suburbia. So if you want to break the back of suburbia, that's a lifelong challenge [laughs].

Gordon
Is that anything more than a disdain for the dreadful taste of the parvenus?

Ath
Not really. I just think that our pathways are quite often determined by things like risk, and safety. And the motorcar and roading, and by certain other disciplines.

Gordon
All of which have had certain liberating aspects as well.

Ath
They have had liberating aspects. But again, they also need to be placed in context. The biggest fight I've had in Christchurch was when I spoke out against traffic confluences … If I'd said something like the buildings should look like this, someone might have embraced me. But once you talk about one-way street systems, no one dares talk about traffic engineers … There are a number of subjects that are taboo, that you know you daren't do. One of the things that's important though is that everyone is now realising how their physical environment affects them. It is a lost educational subject I would have thought, and yet I'm always optimistic that we will move much quicker about thinking about our physical environment than we have done in the recent past, and about how much it affects us.

Gordon
Yet concern for the physical environment doesn't necessarily translate into an appreciation of good design, does it? It seems just as likely to mean people will think living in a tree-house would be dandy, because that's closer to nature.

Ath
There is that risk. But I think people are beyond that. They're starting to appreciate the quality of, for instance, detail design. They've got a lot better at that, at industrial design, and craft … People have become a lot more discerning at that sort of basic level. I think they've come to embrace architecture …

Gordon
Two last things: Bill Rowling once told me in one of his last interviews before he died that in his view, Te Papa was basically a tin shed and what was inside was what counted. With a client like that, are you glad you didn't have to be responsible for the Te Papa process?

Ath
I think that was part of the frustration of the architects who had to put the building together.

Gordon
Do you think there was an opportunity cost involved with what we eventually got, and which we're still paying?

Ath
Yes and no. Certainly Sydney has benefited from the Opera House. But the controversy about getting it built was absolutely huge. I know, people do forget it. I think that at the time, New Zealand did deserve a much stronger approach.

Gordon
You're right that it probably wouldn't have been a sustainable political cost — not given how say, the likes of Simon Upton were already gunning for the Te Papa project even when it had only a $250 million price tag. Is this another symptom of the short-term, limited horizon way in which New Zealand tends to do things? We certainly run the economy on that basis.

Ath
Unfortunately, that's what we do. Take the Queens Wharf fiasco, for instance … finally they're going to get an overseas terminal of some type, using some existing buildings. I think again — quite often — a competition is an excuse to get out of the problem [of risking a creative decision] fairly quickly.

Gordon
As an architect, was the building's role as a vehicle for expressing and promoting biculturalism ever likely to produce a good design?

Ath
I just don't worry about biculturalism per se. I think the world is a multi-cultural world, and biculturalism is a step in that multicultural awareness. And quite often it traps you. Although it is important for realisation and respect it will trap you, and it should not be embodied in a building per se. And if you do try to embody it, it will often not be seen. So then you have to talk about it. And if you have to talk about it being a bicultural building, then I think we've failed.

ME WHAKAURU KI ROTO I TENEI WHAKAATURANGA ETAHI WHAKAAHUA HEI WHAKAATUI NGA AHU A MOMO TAONGA HANGA TAPIRI ATU KI TETAHI TIKANGA ME NGA WHAKAMARAMA KAKANORUA MO TENEI WHAKAATURANGA. KO TE HAERENGA ATU KI TE PAPA TONGAREWA HE PIKITANGA NGAWARI I RARO I TETAHI TUANUI HEI MAIOHA ATU KI NGA MANUHIRI. KO TENEI KA PUTA KI TE MARAE. KO TE MARAE HE MEA TUTURU KI TENEI PIRINGA, A, KA TAEA KI TE WHAKAWHANUI. KO TENEI MARAE ME TAEA KI TE AWHI NGA AHUA MOMO TIKANGA. NA ROTO I TENEI KA TAEA AI E NGA MANUHIRI KE TE RONGO I TE AHUATANGA O TE WHENUA, ME NGA IWI, AHAKOA KEI ROTO RATOU I NGA WHAKAHAERE, KEI TE TAHA RANEI. KEI ROTO I TE MARAE KO TE MARAE ATEA, KOIANEI TE WAHI TAPU. ME HANGA TENEI KIA TAEA AI TE WHAKAHAERE I NGA KAUPAPA MO NGA MANUHIRI ME TE TANGATA WHENUA. ATU I TE MARAE ATEA KA HONO ATU KI TE WHARENUI ME TE HAU KI TURANGA. KEI TE MOHIO MATOU I RUNGA I TE TIKANGA MAORI ME WHAI WAHI KAI, WAHI MOE - KO ENEI E HANGAI ANA KI TE WAHI MAORI O TE PAPA TONGAREWA.

The approach to the Museum of New Zealand Te Papa Tongarewa consists of a gentle rise with a canopy, to welcome manuhiri (visitors). This opens onto the Marae. Which is an integral part of the total structure and is "expandible". The Marae space is flexible to allow varying rituals of encounter. This can mean that each visitor is aware of the presence of our land and people whether they be engaged physically or passively in this experience.

Within the marae is the Marae Atea, the sacred place. This is positioned to allow protocol too operate meaningfully for both hosts and visitors. The Marae Atea relates to the Wharenui and Te Hau Ki Turanga. Because of the uniqueness of the Te Marae Atea, a special enclosure may be included for Te Wahi Tapu (sacred ground). We acknowledge a place for Te Wahi Tapu as a major consideration for Maoridom. We also recognise that Maori protocol may require catering and accommodation facilities and these that relate to the Maori component of the Museum.

By the use of a central public space, the Marae is connected to the various departments. These are arranged around this central space and articulated so that they acknowledge each other and, by virtue of their respective forms, colour, texture, stance, etc. will come together in dialogue or debate. This is also expressed externally, so that the "conversation" is experienced both towards the city, harbour and the greater surroundings.

Each department will have its entry/foyer skylit, to welcome the visitor as if on a Marae. The quality of light will be controlled so that the various activities and dialogue can operate within a harmonic atmosphere.

Separation of each department provides identification and highlights its uniqueness and entity. The space generated by this separation becomes equally important, and an integral part of the total experience. This area allows the visitor to "take time out", reflect, relax, talk; a "release" space. They will be able to relate and capture views back to the city, hills and sea.

In a more philosophical and cultural sense, these areas connect us with our natural worlds; the wind, the rain, the stars. This is reinforced by articulating landscaping so that our experience links us with each other - the land, past, present and future - can be fully appreciated.

The functional/administration spaces will relate to the public areas through landscaped voids so that people feel connected as one entity. Alighting the museum is a canopy symbolised as a "feather". The significance is our connections with the larger world and universe.

"...I have descended to share a message, to draw together and shelter our people, hold me here; don't let me depart."

The interpretation of all the elements will be subjective and passionate to achieve a bi-cultural meaning. This visual impact will thread together a richly woven journey of our cultural heritage past, present and future - and provide an appropriate symbol of national identity and symbolism.

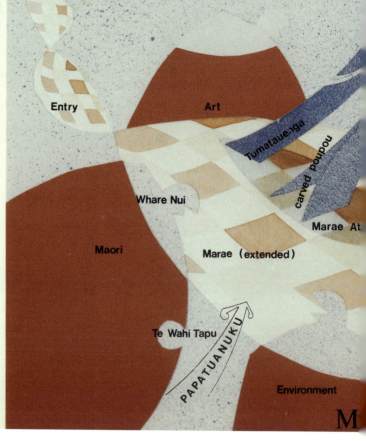

Civic and public realms

A drawing from Rewi's archives illustrating the Te Papa proposal's conceptual layers and material references. *Architecture Archive, University of Auckland*

MATE WHAKAURU I TETAHI IHONUI MO TE KATOA, KA HONO ATU TE MARAE KI ERA ATU O NGA WEHENGA O TE PAPA TONGAREWA. KO ENEI WEHENGA KEI TE MOOWAHO O TE IHONUI, KA HANGA KIA HANGAI TIKA TETAHI KI TETAHI, A, RA RUNGA I NGA AHUA, I NGA KARA, I NGA KAKANO ME NGA TU KA PIRI AI. HE PERA TONU TE AHAU MO WAHO KAI PIRI AI KI TE TAONE, KI TE MOANA ME ERA ATU KEI WAHO. I IA KUHUNGA ATU KI NGA WEHENGA ME RANGI MARAMA, HEI MAIOHA ATU I NGA MANUHIRI, ANO KEI RUNGA I TE MARAE. KO TE MARAMATANGA KA TAEA KI TE WHAKATIKA KIA TAEA AI TE WHAKAHAERE I NGA KAUPAPA I ROTO I TE WAIRUA WHAKAKOTAHI. KO TE WEHEWEHENGA O IA WEHENGA KA TAEA AI TE WHAKAURA I TONA AKE AHUATANGA KIA TUTURU AI TONA AKE MANA. KO NGA WAHI KA WHAKAWATEATIA I TENEI WHAKAWEHEHENGA KA TU MOTUHAKE KI ROTO I TE KATOA. KO ENEI WAHI HE WAHI WHAKATA MO NGA MANUHIRI, HEI WHAKAAROTANGA, HEI KOREROTANGA, HE WAHI TAANGA MANAWA, TAANGA WAIRUA. I KONEI KA KITEA ATU TE TAONE, NGA PUKE ME TE MOANA. I TETAHI TIKANGA KO ENEI WAHI HONO TATOU KI TE TAIAO; KI NGA HAU, KI TE UA, KI NGA WHETU. MA RUNGA I TE WHAKATAKOTO I TE WHENUA KIA HONO ATU TATOU KI A TATOU – TE WHENUA, NGA WA O MUA, NGA WA O NAIANEI ME NGA WA KEI TE HAERE MAI, KA WHAKAARONUITIA. KO NGA WAHI WHAKAHAERE/WHAKAMAHI KO ERA WAHI MO TE KATOA KA HANGAA KIA WHAKAPIRI AI TE KATOA. KO TE TUANUI ME WHAKAAHUA KI TE RAUKURA. KO TENEI KO TO TATOU HONONGA ATU KI TE AO WHANUI ME TE AO KATOA:

"...KUA TAU IHO AHAU KI TE WHAKAATU I ETAHI KUPU, KI TE HONO ME TE WHAKAMARUMARU I TO TATOU IWI. PURITIA AHAU, KAUA AHAU E TUKUA KIA HAERE....."

KO NGA WHAKAPIRITANGA O ENEI MEA KATOA ME HANGA KIA PUTA TE WHAKAMARAMATANGA KAKANORUA. MA ROTO I TENEI KO TA TE TIROHANGA KANOHI HE TUITUI HAERE I O TATOU TIKANGA O MUA, O NAIANEI, O ANGA WA KEI TE HAERE MAI – HEI WHAKATAKOTO TETAHI TAUIRA WHAKAKOTAHI MO TE MOTU.

Health and corrections

Ngā whare whakaora

He hauora te taonga
Health is a treasure

Tiaho Mai Acute Mental Health Facility, Middlemore Hospital

Ōtāhuhu
Tāmaki Makaurau
Auckland

1995-96

With Worley Architects

Health and corrections

A sketch of the new proposed Tiaho Mai entry. *Courtesy of Grant Bulley*

Although it has since been demolished and replaced by the new Tiaho Mai facility designed by Klein Architects (stage one opened in 2018, and stage two in 2020), the original Tiaho Mai project, which opened in 1996, was perhaps the first healthcare project to involve mana whenua and Māori cultural input. As an outcome of those processes, a wharenui was included in the project and located towards the front, alongside the main entry. This approach is now common in healthcare projects, but the original Tiaho Mai project was the first of its kind to achieve this.

This project represented the beginning of Rewi's involvement in health projects, and was followed by the Mason Clinic Extension (1999), Tāne Whakapiripiri at the Mason Clinic (2003–06), and Kaitāia Hospital (2006). Grant Bulley was the project architect on both Tiaho Mai and the Mason Clinic Extension, and Wally Fitness worked with Rewi on Tiaho Mai, Tāne Whakapiripiri and Kaitāia Hospital. Both briefly touch on and provide greater context to this project in their interviews.

The pare or carved lintel over the door of Tiaho Mai.
Courtesy of Grant Bulley

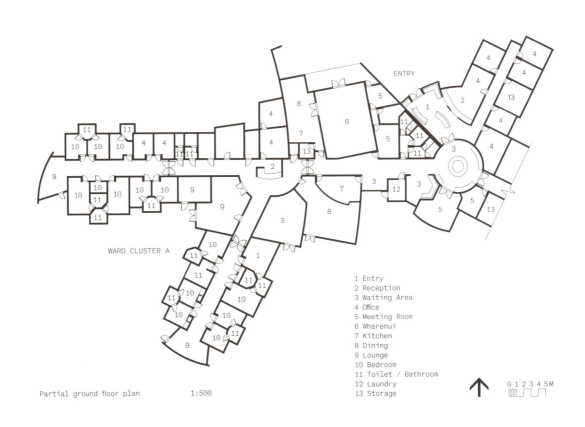

Partial ground floor plan 1:500

1 Entry
2 Reception
3 Waiting Area
4 Office
5 Meeting Room
6 Wharenui
7 Kitchen
8 Dining
9 Lounge
10 Bedroom
11 Toilet / Bathroom
12 Laundry
13 Storage

'The idea was based on a marae concept,' says Melanie Mason of Tāne Whakapiripiri, the forensic mental health unit at the Mason Clinic on which she and Rewi worked together.
Jamie Cobel

Health and corrections

Mason Clinic

Point Chevalier
Tāmaki Makaurau
Auckland

Extension
1999

With Worley Architects

Te Papakāinga o
Tāne Whakapiripiri
2003–06

With Maunsell

Conceived in the wake of the publication of the Mason report, the Mason Clinic Extension project on the Mason Clinic campus in Point Chevalier incorporated a wharenui and considered te ao Māori perspectives in forensic mental health design. It is believed to be among the first of its kind in Aotearoa to do so.

About the project, Professor Deidre Brown (Ngāpuhi, Ngāti Kahu) has written that 'ideas of encounter, based on the architecture of the marae and its meeting house, influenced the entrance to the building, as well as other healthcare facilities that Thompson has worked on, since the initial approach forms the users' first and most profound impression of their treatment'.[1]

Grant Bulley was the project architect on both Tiaho Mai (1995–96) and the Mason Clinic Extension (1998–99). He is a registered architect with more than 25 years' experience, including 14 years leading teams in a wide range and scale of commercial, retail, industrial, healthcare and residential projects in New Zealand and internationally. Grant was also a student of Rewi's at the School of Architecture at the University of Auckland in the early to mid-1990s. He currently works as a project manager and registered architect for TOA Architects. We spoke with Grant about his collaboration with Rewi on the Mason Clinic Extension project.

1   Deidre Brown, *Māori Architecture: From fale to wharenui and beyond* (Auckland: Penguin, 2009), p. 154.

Jade Kake
When did you first meet Rewi?

Grant Bulley
I had Rewi as a lecturer and also as a tutor in studios and various other things at uni, so I knew him well. Obviously Deidre [Grant's wife, architect and academic Professor Deidre Brown] was at uni with me and she was part of the te ao Māori world, so we were both quite involved and interested in that.

Jade
I understand you later worked together on the Mason Clinic Extension in Point Chevalier. How did that come about?

Grant
After I graduated in 1993 I ended up working at Worley, which was a big engineering company, and that's where I met Wally Fitness. We worked under the structural engineering department because there wasn't an architecture department — at the time it was only Wally and me. Wally had come from Stephenson & Turner so he had some experience with hospitals.

Waitematā Health put out a request for proposals for a new mental health centre at the Mason Clinic. In their request they asked, 'What's your proposal for honouring Treaty obligations, and also what's your proposal for bringing some te ao Māori into the mental health system in alignment with the Mason Report?' Judge Mick Mason had written that report in 1988, and it was pretty critical of the whole system and especially around Māori mental health, in which, as you know, there's massive, disproportional representation. This is going back to around 1994, so they were probably cutting edge at that time.

I said, 'Look, I know Rewi Thompson, we should get Rewi involved in this.' Worley was a conservative engineering company, so there was perhaps a bit of reluctance and they asked, 'Oh, do we really need to?' Then I pointed to the proposal and of course, being typical engineers, they would want to tick the box on everything, so they said, 'Okay, we'll go and have a talk with Rewi.'

I phoned Rewi very tentatively because I didn't know if he was going to be involved, and he said to me, 'Yes,

Grant. Okay, well let's do this, but as long as we don't just put tukutuku or a pattern on the walls. We're finished with that, we don't want to do that.' I said to him, 'Okay, no, we'll make a concerted effort to do something different.'

So Rewi joined the team. He was engaging in the background with mana whenua, and I was working on the concept. Rewi would come back and we'd talk through how these ideas could be incorporated into the overall concept. At that time, we were just trying to get basic things in there — such as, how do you approach the unit, how do you interact with people? Which is very much looking at it from a te ao Māori point of view, where you had whānau and family coming in to support or reconnect to people who have been disconnected for years and have got to that point where they have been admitted. Forensic mental health is an escalating thing. In that situation, the important thing is to try to get some support mechanisms around them to reinforce the care that's happening inside. That's the way forward.

Jade
What were some of the key concepts Rewi brought to or championed through the project?

Grant
We were talking about having connections and entranceways and various other things, and I remember Rewi saying, 'Oh, we should put a marae in the unit.' In response the forensic people at the unit were saying, 'Oh, my God, we can't do that. There's all these security issues and the police and all that sort of stuff.' But Rewi was clear: 'We need a marae. We need somewhere for people to come and stay. We need a space for them to interact with, and to go through.'

So, at the end of the day we came up with a compromise. It wasn't a marae but we did manage to get a small budget on the project to put a whare in there. People, if they were well enough, would be escorted to the whare and meet with whānau. In fact, it was also the other way around as well, whānau would come in and meet with them, and we had meeting rooms for them to use.

There's a lot more engagement nowadays, but for that time, it was

groundbreaking. It came about through Rewi constantly saying things like, 'Look, this is kind of all or nothing. You can't just put a tukutuku on the wall. This is not just about putting a colour on the wall.' So he was giving us guidance around that. That was the first time we had had hui with mana whenua and with other interested parties. I guess it was the first meeting house, not a marae but a whare, that we put inside a forensic mental health unit, and it was perhaps a token thing but it made ripples.

Jade
That might've been the first project of its kind, or among the first?

Grant
Yes, I think it was. It took a lot of effort and a lot of pushing, a lot of convincing, to get budget to put those kinds of things in there and do it well — including for things like carving. Even the name of the units, which we gave te ao Māori names, such as Kauri, E Tū Tanekaha and Kahikatea, that was a first as well. Up until then they had been named things like 'Mason unit' or some other unit, and we said, 'No, we want the units to have te ao Māori names.' We had mana whenua at the opening, and it was great because we had, for the first time, people actually engaging with and coming to the unit.

At the same time, mental health practice was undergoing major changes. They'd gone away from the uniforms and keys. They wanted to make it more personal. And they also had kaumātua come in and they had kaumātua on staff, not only for te ao Māori world but also for Pasifika, and they made a huge difference.

I can remember going there one time and there was a big guy, very agitated and quite violent, and the Pacific Island kaumātua just went in there and said, 'Oh, come on, boy, we'll have a cup of tea now', and 10 minutes later they were having a cup of tea together. It was just wonderful to see that kind of de-escalation, when you have people who can understand and empathise with your culture and your language.

After that I went on to work on other projects around the country. I worked on another project in Porirua, and we included a small whare in that project. We also did another one for Southern Health. People started to recognise that there was real value in these approaches. Then we did step-down facilities (or transitional units), and again we had mana whenua come in and help. So there was a real ripple effect from that, and I think that made a huge difference to the whole approach to mental health architecture.

Jade

What do you think is Rewi's ongoing influence and legacy?

Grant

My experience was really over a number of years, and of course I also knew him personally. He was always good to talk to because he'd often say things to me like, 'Oh, it's all or nothing', and 'Let's not compromise it, let's try to get something that's meaningful in there.' I always remember that, even in the work that I'm now doing at TOA. I'm always saying to Nick [TOA director Nick Dalton], 'Either you have it or you don't. If we're going to go for something, let's make it special.'

We recently opened the new Taumata o Kupe education centre at Te Mahurehure marae in Point Chevalier. That project's also pretty groundbreaking. But I created a lot of that with Rewi's influence and with Rewi's words in my ears. I guess that's the influence that he had on not only me, but also on many different architects in New Zealand, including Nick. I think that's his biggest legacy for me. He was always a very quiet man, very unassuming, beautifully humble about everything. Just a really nice soul.

I remember talking to him about projects, where he was talking about the whenua, and digging the dirt up and he used to say to me, 'Oh, Grant, we've got to leave the dirt here. Don't take the whenua away. Leave it here. Let's put a mound or make some landscape around it.' That was always important. Everything for him was about the whenua, land and location, and that's informed a lot of what we do now at TOA, with cultural mapping and that sort of stuff. It makes some beautiful stories and it'll make a backbone for a project, and it's beautiful to see that type of stuff. That all started with him.

Jade

I felt that, too. I think, especially for my generation of architects and designers coming through, we are privileged in the kind of careers that we're able to have and the way society has moved on in a positive way. Rewi laid the foundation for the kind of careers we're able to have and the kind of meaningful work that we're able to do.

Grant

Absolutely. When we were at uni I talked to him many times about his house and what it was, the unusual shape and the ideas behind it. It was a beautiful house. I always remember him in connection to his house. It was just so brave, so bold. That whole house was fantastic. I remember he also spoke about the mauri of a space and how the materials were used. He used the plywood from packing cases to clad it. People used to say to me, 'Oh, it looks like concrete,' and I would say, 'No, it's packing cases. It's plywood.' The whole idea was that it was supposed to be this temporary thing.

After he passed, there was a discussion with Nick about what's happening with the house and whether somebody should save it. I said, 'Look, I don't know, but for me, a lot of the time when I was talking to Rewi about it, he was talking about the mauri of a space, and a building is no different. It lives and dies. And maybe we should let it die because that's part of it.' It had that temporary quality and was intended for temporary construction. That was just my take on it. It was wonderful to have those different thoughts and different thought processes, and to be able to explore some of those things. That was his strength, I think, and his magic.

Jade

Did you ever work on any other projects together?

Grant

No. We always talked about doing something, but he was always on one thing and then I was on something else. We would talk about different projects when I caught up with him and had a beer or a cup of tea, and he came around to the house for lunch a couple of times. I feel in the later years that he had some tough times. When I look back on it now,

I think we were all so busy that we didn't realise that as much. And I think, 'Wow, we should have really reached out and been a bit more in touch with him.'

Jade

A lot of people felt that way.

Grant

Rewi was that kind of person. He was really stoic and he was his own person, and he was very calm about things and he didn't let things phase him. But I don't know — we, both Deidre and I, just feel bad that, at that time, we didn't reach out enough to him.

Jade

Did you have anything else you wanted to say before we wrap up?

Grant

No, except to say that I can't really think of another architect in New Zealand who had more influence on me and, I guess, on my generation, than Rewi. It started off at university and in being brave and also so proud of te ao Māori, and so eager to share the good about it. That got me into the work that I'm doing at the moment.

He always talked about an architecture of Aotearoa, rather than focusing on the stuff coming from Europe. It's that kind of legacy of recognising what we've got in Aotearoa, and that we've got something special. We don't need to look to classical architecture, to Italy or elsewhere. We've got so much richness here that we can use.

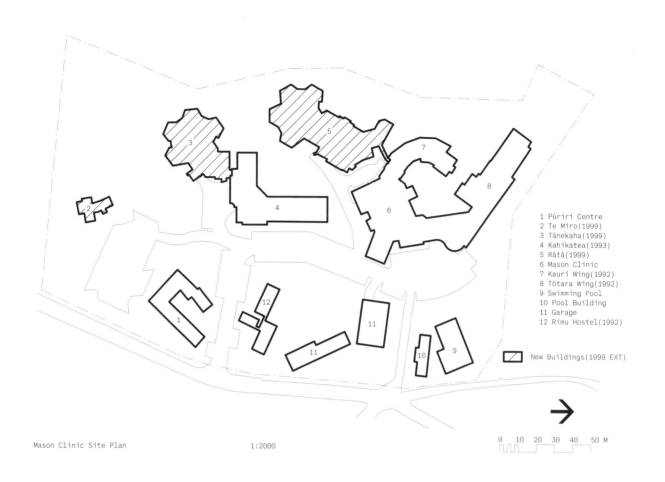

Mason Clinic Site Plan 1:2000

1 Pūriri Centre
2 Te Miro(1999)
3 Tānekaha(1999)
4 Kahikatea(1993)
5 Rātā(1999)
6 Mason Clinic
7 Kauri Wing(1992)
8 Tōtara Wing(1992)
9 Swimming Pool
10 Pool Building
11 Garage
12 Rimu Hostel(1992)

New Buildings(1999 EXT)

Te Miro Ground floor plan 1:200

1 Marae
2 Fale
3 Kitchen
4 Office
5 Store
6 Hall
7 Toilet

Tāne Whakapiripiri was Rewi's third healthcare project (in collaboration with larger firms and specialist health planners and architects), and his second project on the Mason Clinic campus. Extending on previous projects, and in an approach that has since become commonplace, Rewi advocated for the inclusion of a wharenui within the complex. In a break from previous schemes, the buildings were organised in a kāinga arrangement, with a courtyard stitching the elements together. For this reason, Tāne Whakapiripiri could be considered an early example of a courtyard concept, pre-empting much of what would later become best practice in mental health architecture but derived from a cultural basis and philosophy of hauora.

Melanie Mason is a principal registered architect and health planner at Jasmax, with close to 20 years' experience in the health sector. As a newly registered architect, she worked alongside Rewi as the project architect for Te Papakāinga o Tāne Whakapiripiri. She has since gone on to work on several other major mental health projects, including Te Aka Forensic Mental Health Unit on the Mason Clinic campus, and the second Tiaho Mai Acute Mental Health Unit at Middlemore Hospital. Here she reflects on the project, working with Rewi, and the enduring legacy of this project on healthcare architecture in New Zealand.

'It's such a huge part of the healing process: to be welcomed through the wharenui, via the ātea space, to be greeted by that familiar face,' says Matt Fleming, who worked with Rewi on the design of Tāne Whakapiripiri.
Jamie Cobel

Health and corrections

Jade Kake
When did you first meet Rewi?
Melanie Mason
It was 2004. I was a relatively young, just-registered architect at the time. I had just joined Maunsell (formerly Maritec), which was a multidisciplinary company that had a small architecture section but was mostly engineers. Wally Fitness was the leader of the architects within Maunsell at the time and they were doing a lot of health projects. I was launched straight into the Tāne Whakapiripiri project at the preliminary design stage, and met Rewi almost immediately after starting there. I'd worked on retail design and a bit of commercial and multi-unit residential, but I hadn't worked on a project that had any cultural input at all, prior to that. I'd registered about six months before, and launched straight into this project which was forensic mental health, with a significant cultural element.

Jade
Wow. Deep end.
Melanie
It was completely in the deep end. But the client was amazing. Rewi was an inspiration, and so it was a dream project, really. And the building is still fairly highly regarded on that site. I've worked on the site more recently, including two other buildings, and one of them is the adjoining building to this, which is the other part of the Kaupapa Māori forensic stream, which is about eight years old. So it was nice to come back 10 years later and work on the site again.

Jade
So that we can understand this project within its context, can you give me a bit of background on the history of mental health architecture in New Zealand?
Melanie
Mental health architecture in New Zealand, and more widely in the world, typically was large Victorian-style sanatorium buildings on sections of land. Like the old Carrington, which Mason Clinic is now in a corner of, also like Kingseat in Auckland, Sunnyside in Christchurch, or Seaview in Hokitika. Then there was this whole trend in the 1980s where those all got shut down. There were people who had been

institutionalised for a long time and now were pushed back into the community.

There were a whole lot of things that went wrong with this approach and the result was lots of units being built on healthcare and hospital campuses, including most of the Mason Clinic buildings, which were built in the late 1980s and early 1990s. The Mason Clinic is a forensic facility, but there are a number of other acute units built on hospital campuses — like Middlemore, for example, with Tiaho Mai, and Hillmorton in Christchurch. Hillmorton is part of the old Sunnyside campus, which had a large Victorian building but, unlike Carrington, has since been demolished and a large portion of the campus sold for other uses.

The length of stay for acute units is many weeks, possibly months; however, the stay for a forensic patient at the Mason Clinic may be much longer and extend to years. There are people in the Mason Clinic who have been there for 20 years or more. Acute units on hospital campuses are for those acutely unwell; the difference for forensic units is that the patients are connected to the justice system, and could be serving a sentence while being cared for in the forensic mental health setting.

Both acute and forensic units built during the 1980s and 1990s generally used a hub-and-spoke-style plan, with radiating wings and very much a 'command and control' model. So, the staff are in the centre and they look out down the patient wings.

There's since been a change, and I've worked on some of the more recent units which turned that around and put the patient at the centre. The first unit to really do this recently is Tiaho Mai, a 76-bed acute unit at Middlemore Hospital. I was the architectural lead on this project, which was completed in 2020. Everything looks inwards to a retreat space in the middle; everything wraps around. It doesn't put the staff at the centre like the older units. It puts the outdoor and living spaces in the centre and takes a salutogenic design approach, which is an approach to health design that focuses on factors that promote health and well-being (rather than on factors that cause disease or illness).

Jade
Can you tell me a bit about the Tāne Whakapiripiri project?
Melanie
Tāne Whakapiripiri is a 10-bed forensic mental health unit. 'Forensic' means that the people who are admitted to these units, as at the Mason Clinic generally, have been referred from the judicial system. A person may be at the Mason Clinic to be assessed for their mental health in relation to being fit to stand trial or suitability to be housed in a prison versus a mental health unit. The Mason Clinic campus has a number of different types of unit to suit different patient groups. Some people are at the Mason Clinic to be rehabilitated, and Tāne Whakapiripiri is one of the rehabilitation and minimum secure units on the campus.

It's a challenging place to be working in as an architect because you have to understand a bit about mental health. The building is in a health setting, but it has got the overlay of the Corrections and judicial requirements. From a containment point of view it's like a prison, but it has to be therapeutic and put well-being and recovery at the centre. You have to find the balance of both.

I am unaware of how the vision for this unit came about, but certainly there was an acknowledgement that Māori are horribly over-represented in the forensic mental health space, and that a more culturally appropriate building was needed to address this.

It was very much focused on providing something different to what they already had on the site, which was a more Western programme around how they were treating people for mental health. It also provides a wharenui space for the whole of the site. The wharenui faces back into the rest of the site very deliberately, and it gets used externally by other groups. It gets used for tangi, for example, and various other uses. Anyone who is associated with the site in some way can come and use this building. The wharenui also has an important function in the therapeutic environment of the unit.

One of the key things I remember about Rewi's influence is that he was a fount of knowledge in terms of working in this cultural space, which I'd never done before. So, he was a bit of a teacher, definitely in terms of upskilling me on something I had not a lot of knowledge on. And he also was, I guess, a translator between the architectural team and the cultural advisory team that were already part of the fabric of the Mason Clinic. The team included a kaumātua, as well as quite a few other embedded Māori staff members.

I acknowledge at that point — and this is the early 2000s, remember, and the environment has changed a lot since then — that this was probably quite innovative at the time. Truly embedded cultural design was in its infancy in New Zealand at that time, especially in the institutional health space or other similar big institutional buildings.

Rewi was able to shed light on it and take some of the information that we were hearing and authentically translate that into the design. He didn't spend a lot of time on the design, he let us do that, but he was very much the conduit or the translator. The idea with the building was that it was based on a marae concept. A marae has a strong meeting house and a wharekai towards the front. There's tikanga around how those buildings are placed. The buildings behind that serve different purposes are quite village-like and spread out and placed more organically. That was the original concept for the building, which Rewi was integral in developing.

This provided for an organic-shaped courtyard between the village-style building arrangement. We couldn't have all these separate buildings from a staffing and observation perspective, and with all of the other requirements around mental health, we had to join them up. But we still tried to keep that quite organic courtyard in the middle.

Jade

That's so interesting. I did wonder because you've worked on a few other projects on the site as well as other projects elsewhere. I'd love to hear your thoughts about the impact of what was done here, and then what impact that's

had on future projects on the campus and on other sites.

Melanie

I've been back more recently; the building has changed a bit but it's still a really nice space. Three-quarters of the courtyard is bordered by buildings, and there are some fences that fill in the gaps to provide the secure perimeter. It was before New Zealand — before a lot of the world — was doing courtyard-concept mental health buildings. If you look at some more recent ones, they are often designed around this architectural concept of internal courtyards, retreat spaces, that all of the various interior spaces face into. The Tāne Whakapiripiri project was an early version of a courtyard concept, which I didn't realise until later.

Then when I had the opportunity to work in mental health again, I realised it was really innovative at the time but it wasn't necessarily deliberately so. It was because it came from the marae concept as the organising element. It came from the right place, and because it was responding to cultural aspects and themes — rather than a Western architectural programme — it was innovative in terms of the way that mental health is now being designed.

That was the context; and I look back now and think, there's a whole lot that was done in this unit that I think is still super-relevant now. I think that was largely driven by the dialogue between the cultural team at the Mason Clinic, Rewi being right in the centre, and with the Maunsell team, being supposedly the mental health experts having done a lot of mental health — but more traditional, Western-style mental health — in the past.

So, this unit almost accidentally pre-empted a lot of what we are now doing in terms of mental health unit design. It was driven by cultural principles of the marae and came from a totally different mindset in terms of concept; it turned all of that on its head.

I'd like to be able to design a unit again that's a bit more organic, like this one. Some of the more recent units, they're quite rigid, even though they have got nice internal courtyards. This unit feels a bit more relaxed than a

formal rectilinear plan. I keep thinking, if I could have the opportunity to design something in the future of the right size I would definitely look back at this design for inspiration. Units such as Tiaho Mai, with its 76 beds, are on an entirely different scale. It's hard to apply the same principles.

Jade

I think of our role as synthesising a lot of different complex opportunities and constraints, and I think it would've been such an interesting experience to be at that intersection of Corrections and mental health as well as these cultural drivers and how you are trying to bring them all together in a sensitive and meaningful way.

Melanie

Absolutely. Security is priority, but how do you do that in a way that doesn't feel like you're in a cage? How do you make it a healthcare setting and not a prison setting? The design aim is to make it a healthcare, therapeutic care environment, quite different to a prison. Then you overlay the cultural drivers on top of that as well. As I said, I was pretty naive when I went into this one, particularly in the cultural space, but I was also learning all about healthcare design at the same time, this being my first taste of the healthcare sector. Rewi was instrumental in achieving this intersection of all these aspects successfully, and educating me along the way.

Jade

I've been finding it interesting learning about healthcare architecture. One of the things I've been finding most challenging is in the strictly cultural spaces. You've got a lot of control in that the tikanga will dictate what happens in those spaces. But when it comes to the clinical spaces, there are so many constraints on how medicine is practised currently, and it's hard to understand how changing Māori models of health and care can then influence changes in design. That change has to happen first before you can design differently. So, I found that to be an interesting challenge.

Melanie

Yes, definitely. What I'm enjoying at Jasmax is that because we have our

Many mental health facilities are now designed around courtyards, but Tāne Whakapiripiri's approach was considered radical for the time. *Jamie Cobel*

Waka Māia team here[1] I get a lot more exposure and lots of support and first-hand ability to gain more insight into what we're doing to make a change in this space. Hopefully leading to more meaningful outcomes that make a difference.

Jade

You'd be well positioned because you understand the healthcare stuff really, really well. Something I've found challenging is that I understand the cultural stuff, but I'm still getting to grips with the health stuff, which I think will take a long time. It's hard to know which things are fixed and which things can be challenged.

Melanie

I totally get that. But I think health will definitely benefit from people like yourself starting to challenge things more, like Rewi was doing. We can design operating theatres, for example, the way that we've always designed them, or we can ask, is there a different way? There are certain things you have to achieve around infection control and all those practical and technical aspects, but is there a different way you enter, or a different way to experience it? What is it like before and after surgery? How can things be less stressful and people be made to feel comfortable? It's interesting to be working in that space and to see what we can do with the design to increase equitable outcomes, which clearly New Zealand needs to grapple with and hasn't done enough of yet.

But now's our chance with the Māori health authority Te Aka Whai Ora and changes in the environment. The Mason Clinic, I understand, is about 60 per cent Māori in terms of patient numbers. Obviously the vision for this unit came from a real driver that the existing campus wasn't addressing with their old units … because they weren't achieving positive outcomes. That was an early version of an acknowledgement that something had to change, and hopefully this continues to gain momentum; Rewi had a real part to play with this project to start changing the way we approach the design.

As I said, I had a relatively brief time working with Rewi, but it's had a lasting influence. And it's something that I've thought back to quite a few times when in more recent years I've been working in the mental health space, and more generally, in any healthcare project. The acknowledgement of trying to increase equitable outcomes for Māori that was happening with this project at the time was ahead of what we are more consciously doing now.

---

1   Waka Māia is a Māori cultural design and advisory team founded in 2015 within New Zealand architectural firm Jasmax.

Health and corrections

Matt Fleming is a registered architect and director of Thema. In the early 2000s, he worked alongside Rewi, Wally Fitness and Melanie Mason during the concept design of Tāne Whakapiripiri. Here he reflects on working alongside Rewi on this project and on its impact on healthcare and mental health architecture in Aotearoa.

Jade Kake
Could you start by explaining how you knew Rewi? I understand that you were a student at the university when he was teaching, and maybe you didn't have a lot of exposure to him, but did you meet him or get to know him a little bit in that time?

Matt Fleming
Yes, that's right. Rewi was a lecturer and tutor when I attended university from 1994 to 1999. Though not always in the design papers I chose, but he was always present. I had spoken to him a few times at various events and had heard a lot of good things about him. As a student and as a young graduate, it felt to me as if he was already well known and quite established. He had a way about him that felt down to earth and personable in terms of how he approached design and how he dealt with people. Rewi seemed to get down on our level and would try to make us feel the design rather than simply observe it. He approached design with a warmth.

As a consequence of meeting Rewi, I ended up doing a design paper with Tony Ward, and, as part of that process, we went down to Parihaka together for a hui. Rewi opened my eyes, and after that experience I wanted to learn more about another side of New Zealand.

Jade
And that you might not have been exposed to that much through your studies at that point?

Matt
Or even in my upbringing. Rewi definitely brought a holistic perspective to the table.

Jade
When did you get the opportunity to work together? How did that come about?

Matt
When I graduated, I ended up working for a couple of firms. It was after the financial crash so there wasn't much work around, and many of my colleagues left the country or entered other career paths away from architecture. I spent a year working for a very small company because I couldn't afford to travel overseas and had to support myself. The firm took what it could get, which was not much. After that year, I ended up working for a larger firm, which still did not have much work on, and then in about my third year of working I landed a job in the architectural department for Maunsell, a large New Zealand engineering firm with a small but growing contingent of architects.

Jade
When was this?

Matt
In 2001. The Maunsell architecture department was run by Wally Fitness, who had a track record in public health and, in particular, in-patient mental health. At that time, he had won a contract for the company to do two psychiatric units at the Mason Clinic in Point Chevalier. One of them was a kaupapa Māori unit, and Wally had the foresight to engage Rewi. I was introduced to Rewi at the beginning of the project. I was excited to be in a work situation with him where we were both working on a job together as colleagues rather than as a student and lecturer.

Jade
What do you remember about working with Rewi at that time?

Matt
I just remember him being very softly spoken. He was very quiet, but also very ... It's hard to describe ... He was

Opposite left: Tāne Whakapiripiri's design included interiors with gentle curves, natural light and views to the courtyard. *Jamie Cobel*

Opposite right: 'Rewi could understand fundamentally, even then, that there could be a more humanistic approach,' says Matt Fleming. *Jamie Cobel*

very authoritative, but I don't think that he necessarily sought to command attention. I think his approach to leadership was to do rather than say, if that makes sense? In my view, he wasn't after fame or glory, and maybe that's why he got along with Wally because Wally was the same kind of character. These guys weren't flashy, they were just quietly there in the background.

Jade

Getting on with it.

Matt

And that was Rewi. I perceived him to be contemplative and quiet, but he was also very assertive in a quiet way. People listened. And maybe it's because if someone's very quiet and they just say what they mean to say, you're going to listen to that person.

Jade

What was the design process like?

Matt

I remember him turning up to one of the meetings and he had this corrugated cardboard model of the village, and with this he was able to explain a lot of things in it. He was also able to shift between two cultures — Māori and Pākehā — quite quickly, and overlay the language and culture of building and design.

He moved easily between those various parameters. Then on top of that the layer of healthcare and, on top of that, mental health as well. That's a lot of layers that Rewi was able to effortlessly and convincingly shift between. He had this concept, and I think he really sold the concept, and then we worked through the documentation of that in a broader sense.

Jade

What were some of the key concepts for this building?

Matt

One of the key concepts was the courtyard arrangement. Within the complex there was a communal pod, the men's whare, the women's whare, the whare kai, the whare hui, and a very small staff hub right in the middle. And then around it was this courtyard. The primary feature was that it was a village with the marae ātea space at the front. And coming into that village, being received into that village, there would

be karakia and that familiar face of the whare, so to someone coming into an institution there was the ability to feel warmth and belonging.

Jade

The courtyard arrangement is really intriguing because it seems the approach that Rewi and the team were introducing with this project was being mirrored internationally and what was emerging as best practice, but perhaps in this case coming from these cultural drivers, as opposed to what is best practice internationally around mental health architecture.

Matt

When I look back at Tāne Whakapiripiri, that was one of the first of the courtyard approaches, where although it did have acentral nurse station building, it was all around the courtyard and you could see through the courtyard to all the other buildings. I think that set the scene.

Under the Mental Health Act, you can be sectioned into the forensics unit if you have been unlawful and have a mental health ailment. The decision is made for you, and you can be forced into taking medications. In contrast, if you've got a physical ailment such as a stomach ulcer, you're never forced to go and take medication for that stomach ulcer, you're only advised to.

If you're trying to treat mental illness the same way you would treat any other illness, and normalise mental illness as if it were on the same path, then forcing someone into it is not entirely appropriate. It's horrendous for anyone. But if you've been battling a mental health ailment and come from a rural environment, and maybe you've had limited interaction within the Pākehā world up to this point, and you are suddenly fronting up to a foreign institutional building, it's especially horrendous.

At least now for Māori the intention is that they have this familiar face, this familiar space that they can come into, that they feel is not foreign. I think that's such a huge part of the healing process: to be welcomed through the wharenui, via the ātea space, to be greeted by that familiar face.

Jade

It's not quite on the same level, but it's

similar to the conversation about prisons. Do we abolish prisons, or is there this interim step where prisons are made more culturally fit for purpose? I was impressed when I went to Ngāwhā and saw the work Rewi had contributed to. We went through a pōwhiri and met the carvers who were working in the studio, and it was an interesting experience, because on the one hand I think prisons shouldn't exist, but actually I think what they have done there is really positive.

Matt

Yeah, I agree it's very similar. At Tāne Whakapiripiri Rewi introduced this whole concept which helped with that. People were able to enter a building that would be able to support some cultural elements that they would be familiar with and find comfortable, and that gave them a certain amount of dignity and familiarity when placed in that situation. It was not necessarily only for Māori: it acknowledged that even Pākehā might not really want an institutional and clinical approach.

It's just another approach that may be more holistic. And I think that — even within the courtyard — allowing crying, allowing yelling, allowing all the human emotions to be expressed and let out is a different approach to the typical hub-and-spoke arrangement. The courtyard approach also opens up other possibilities: you can have planting and teachings and special support for all sorts of different things within that courtyard, within that safe environment. This can also foster younger clinicians who have interests in traditional rongoā to develop.

I remember Bruce Talbot, who was one of the senior executives of the Mason Clinic, saying that they had a waiting list of people who wanted to get into that facility by choice. There was a mana to the facility and there was respect, and as a consequence there has not needed to be a lot of interior maintenance carried out in comparison to some of the other buildings on the site.

There was something about it — an intrinsic value you probably can't quite put your finger on — that encouraged healing and had a really lovely feeling. I'm sure it's the case if you went back into it today. Nothing's been damaged because a lot of people have gone through and hopefully healed. And the building's been a facilitator of that process. And so, in my opinion, that ought to be a tribute to someone who started the entire conceptual idea and got it right.

Rewi could understand fundamentally, even then, that there could be a much more humanistic approach than was then the status quo. He brought a fresh perspective to us, probably a real perspective. It wasn't even likely that this was a novel idea; more likely, it was one that many people agreed with but lacked the power to express in a way that would be taken seriously and would grant them access to a building that was used by a significant portion of society.

Rewi was successful in encouraging at the conceptual level taking into account a different design strategy, which is now becoming widely supported. This earlier design philosophy has served as support for more contemporary psychiatric facilities.

Rewi didn't necessarily have a background in psychiatry, but his skills as an architect as well as his cultural background gave him an ability to address or respond to a cultural need in mental health. Hopefully, this served as the catalyst or the seed for much of the contemporary thinking about mental health, among Māori and even Pākehā.

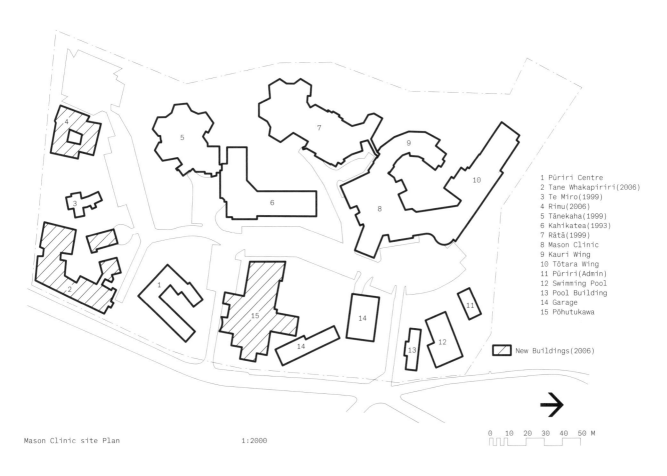

Mason Clinic site Plan   1:2000

1 Pūriri Centre
2 Tane Whakapiriri (2006)
3 Te Miro (1999)
4 Rimu (2006)
5 Tānekaha (1999)
6 Kahikatea (1993)
7 Rātā (1999)
8 Mason Clinic
9 Kauri Wing
10 Tōtara Wing
11 Pūriri (Admin)
12 Swimming Pool
13 Pool Building
14 Garage
15 Pōhutukawa

New Buildings (2006)

A sketch of the entry to Kaitāia Hospital, where a new design was developed in response to an assessment of crucial health services and a reorganisation of the interior.

Health and corrections

Kaitāia Hospital redevelopment

Kaitāia
Te Hiku o Te Ika

2005

With AECOM

Wally Fitness is an architect and health planner. In the early 1990s he worked at Worley Architects, which later became Meritec, Maunsell and then AECOM. As an architect specialising in health from the 1970s through to the mid-2000s, Wally has been involved in a number of significant projects and has seen profound shifts in the industry. He worked with Rewi on multiple health projects from the mid-1990s to the mid-2000s, including the original Tiaho Mai Acute Mental Health Unit at Middlemore Hospital, the Mason Clinic's Tāne Whakapiripiri, and Kaitāia Hospital.

We spoke with Wally about his recollections of working alongside Rewi, as well as the ongoing legacy of their collaborative work within mental health architecture.

Rewi's work at Kaitāia Hospital included decisions such as placing a wharehui at the front of the facility and bringing the community in to create carvings and tukutuku panels for it. *Courtesy of Wally Fitness*

Jade

How did you know Rewi?

Wally

It was through working on Tiaho Mai, the Middlemore psychiatric unit. Peter Wootton, the director of architecture at the time, engaged Rewi to provide cultural advice and cultural design services on that project.

Jade

What was the scope of that project?

Wally

We were decanting Kingseat Hospital, which was of the old style of mental health institution with about 600 patients in multi-storey dorm-type facilities. The whole approach to mental health was changing and Middlemore was only going to be 40 or 50 beds. Middlemore would take the acute mental health unit patients for only two to three weeks, treat them and then send them back out into the community.

To do that, they had to have a huge number of consultation meetings with clinical staff, mana whenua and the community. Before then I had never known health projects being briefed to reflect on cultural input, and for that to be included in the design process. It would've been the first project in healthcare. As an outcome of that process, and Rewi's involvement, a wharehui was included in the project and located towards the front, which to my knowledge hadn't been done before. Rewi was brought on board for the Middlemore project, and then when we did several other mental health units it just followed that he should be the one we called upon to provide continued cultural advice and support.

Jade

Did you work together on the Tāne Whakapiripiri project?

Wally

Yes, we did. We did an initial concept, which was very rectilinear in approach with bedrooms off corridors and things like that and wasn't what they were looking for. Then Rewi came along to the next meeting and massaged things along. After that, we went away and came up with something that was a little bit more communal. The bedrooms were off a communal space, and it was totally irregular in form except for the rooms themselves, which were regular in form but leading into open spaces. Rewi facilitated that and we got the show on the road. It proved to be a pretty successful project, I believe.

Jade

Did you work together again after that?

Wally

Yes. In 2005, around the time when I was leaving AECOM, I worked with Rewi on Kaitāia Hospital. That was the last project we worked on together. At the time they were going to close Kaitāia Hospital and there was a lot of animosity in the community about that. There were protests and all sorts of things happening up there, and it became very political. A team was sent in to assess what health services should be provided at Kaitāia.

We were working on a project with a couple of Australian health planners at Whangārei Hospital at the time and we were asked to go up to Kaitāia to a meeting, a workshop, to help them to decide what was going to happen at the hospital. I recall one of the Australian architects standing up and talking, in an Australian accent, about the 'cultural aspects of the Indigenous people'. That's a word that we don't use much in New Zealand. You could see the reaction on the people's faces. Their heads went down and their eyes looked at the floor and they thought, 'Oh, another Australian'.

It was totally different when we were actually appointed to the project. We went up and Rewi was there with us. We introduced him in the meeting and Rewi, in his usual way, was very quiet, subdued, respectful, got the trust of the people and engaged with them so well. Sue Wyeth, the service manager up there at that time, was most impressed by Rewi's contribution, which was mainly in those meetings with the local community, getting them on board with the project. In particular, I remember his use of simple models, which he used to engage extremely successfully with people.

The reality was that we saved Kaitāia Hospital by reducing it in size, matching what they really needed and reorganising everything. Rewi's approach to talking to the community and getting them on board was very much appreciated by the people up there.

Jade

What was the scope of that project?

Wally

It was only a small project in reality, but we reorganised the hospital so that the main entrance went directly into the outpatient department and off it were departments co-located all together on one floor level. The maternity, accident and emergency and outpatient departments were all together so that they could run it very efficiently and not spread around the campus.

And at night, which is the tough time for running those sorts of places, they could shut down all the non-24/7 components and just have the 24/7 parts operating; the emergency department and the ward right next to each other. One doctor in ED could cover the ward or maternity because the volumes going through the place are very small. You needed that clinical expertise there all the time and not scattered all over the campus, so we just moved things around.

Jade

Aside from playing a critical part in that community engagement, what was Rewi's role in the project?

Wally

It was really putting in that cultural overview, making sure that what we did there was culturally appropriate and supportive. The wharehui was placed at the front of the facility and given equal rights to the main entrance to the hospital so that people could enter through there if the occasion warranted it. Rewi also assisted the people up there to organise the carvings and the tukutuku panels for the wharehui. That was all done locally and voluntarily to a large extent.

Jade

How was it received when the project was completed?

Wally

It was received really well. We went up there for the opening and there was a big marquee outside and the whole community there. Shane Jones was one of the speakers and that was the first time I'd heard him speak in person, as an orator. That was quite a buzz.

The facility itself is working really well for the community.

Jade

Having worked with Rewi to varying degrees across a variety of health projects, would you consider that this way of working (and Rewi's role within it) has changed some of these things around how we design health spaces, to be more culturally fit for purpose?

Wally

Oh yes, definitely. And it all started off with the Middlemore project. Middlemore was in 1995. But I'd been working in healthcare since the 1970s. In those days the architect was the key person. There weren't any project managers around, and we were given a very concise brief. I worked with Stephenson & Turner to start with, and that's where I was trained in healthcare, working on Auckland Hospital and various hospitals. We didn't even have user groups. Every project has that element in it now, or every healthcare project normally comes out with the requirement to have cultural input in some manner.

Jade

It sounds like Rewi was a critical person in terms of ushering in that change. Obviously not him alone, but being involved with some of those early projects.

Wally

Yes, absolutely. I would say it also reflected what was happening in society at the time, too.

Health and corrections

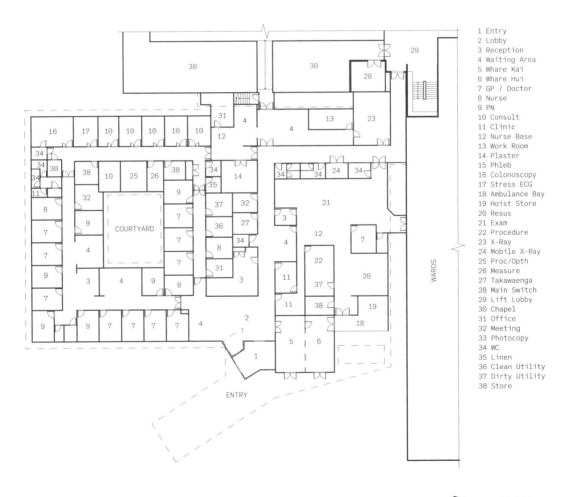

Ground floor plan 1:500

Northland Region Corrections Facility

Ngāwhā Te Tai Tokerau

1999–2005

With Mike Barns, Stephenson & Turner and Cox Group

Health and corrections

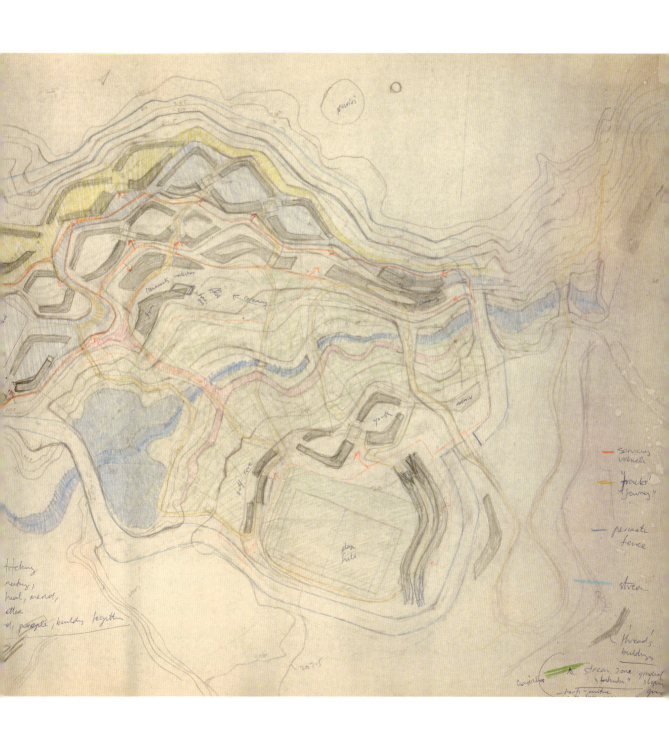

A sketch from Rewi's archives by Rewi and Mike Barns showing a conceptual layout for buildings at the Northland Region Corrections Facility.
Architecture Archive, University of Auckland

Designing a prison could get you cancelled nowadays. Rewi Thompson helped design two, not with the intention of supporting a carceral state but in the hope that they could be places of genuine rehabilitation. The first of these was the Northland Region Corrections Facility at Ngāwhā, near Kaikohe. He knew that Māori were imprisoned in greater numbers than others and believed that a prison that promoted a greater connection to the whenua could help those inmates 'be their own chiefs', as John Walsh noted in a 2005 *Architecture New Zealand* feature on the prison.

At Ngāwhā, this resulted in Corrections abandoning its initial intention to bulldoze the prison site into a single flat area and instead embracing the design possibilities offered by the natural terraces and stream running through it. A village-like compound with a sense of openness was designed, where buildings were curved and possessed generous overhangs. 'In case Corrections wondered at the point of all these design elements,' John Walsh writes in his article, 'the architects noted that "the employment of traditional design values" would be "critical to the management of the behaviour and in the reduction of the internal 'temperature' of the facility".'

Ross Brown was a colleague of Rewi's at Wellington's Structon Group in the early 1970s. At that time, Rewi was a structural draughtsman and starting to ponder the possibilities of studying architecture and making it a career. The duo continued to work together during Rewi's studies and, much later, when Ross was working for Stephenson Turner, teamed up to work on the Northland Region Corrections Facility and, subsequently, the Spring Hill Corrections Facility near Meremere in Waikato.

Here, Ross talks about those projects and his long friendship with Rewi.

Above: The entry portal building at Northland Region Corrections Facility was designed with deep overhangs for shelter. *Courtesy of Ross Brown*

Below: A typical porch detail at the facility, with clerestory windows allowing natural light into the central corridor systems. *Courtesy of Ross Brown*

Right: The wharehui entrance faces an ātea and welcoming space. 'We had to break the cycle; the prison had to be about rejuvenation, not about incarceration,' says Mike Barns.
Courtesy of Ross Brown

Below: Rewi drew over an early site plan for the facility, showing an area with an open stream as an alternative to the large culvert that was originally proposed.
Architecture Archive, University of Auckland

Health and corrections

Jeremy Hansen

Ross, one of the things that drew us to do this book was that we felt in some ways that Rewi might have not got the projects that he deserved. Not that this doesn't happen to other architects — but it would've been great to see him work on something on a significant scale, and the country might be richer for that.

Ross Brown

His potential was to achieve more, and there are various reasons for all of that. There were two major, major setbacks for all architects during his working life: the crash in 1987 and the Asian financial crisis — which also affected New Zealand — in 1997. And then of course, the financial meltdown of 2008.

He was also a bit of a newbie going down the direction he was headed in. You had John Scott and he'd done a fantastic body of work, and Bill Royal, and a few other people on the fringes bringing Māori cultural awareness into New Zealand design. But this wasn't an accepted norm at the point when he was forging out. In fact, the area where we were able to do that mostly together on major projects was the work we did for the Department of Corrections.

Jade Kake

I'd like to hear more about that.

Ross

Rewi and I were both in the same firm [Structon Group], and then went on and did various other things. He came to Auckland and I ended up working in Auckland from 1994 to 1998 on the Sky Tower and the casino, then I took this job back in Wellington. The Department of Corrections was putting together a policy to rethink and rebuild, to relook at the whole basis for incarcerating people. They advertised for teams to be put together to design for this new approach. They were going to build four new 'correctional campuses' around New Zealand. I spoke to Rewi really early in the piece — this was 1999. Of course, the statistic that was mentioned frequently was that more than 50 per cent of prisoners in New Zealand were Māori.

Jade

And incredibly, that's still true.

Ross

It's an unbelievable statistic. The first of these new facilities was going to be in Northland. Have you ever been there?

Jade

Yes, because we were working on a project in 2019 that meant we had a couple of hours there. It was amazing.

Ross

So you've seen what turned out. Anyhow, to cut a long story short, we put together a team that included Cox Group, specialist prison designers from Australia who had done a few supposedly new-age prisons in Western Australia, although they kept trying to design things when Rewi and I were trying to design them a different way, but that's all right. We got through it all in the end.

Jade

So you called Rewi to be a part of the team?

Ross

Yeah. We had a yarn and said, 'If we can really show that we care about redressing this terrible imbalance in the prison population, then maybe we've got a chance of getting some of this work.'

Jade

Had you done a design at this stage?

Ross

No. But we put in a major pilot to do with Māori, with the aspects that we thought were going to be important if Corrections were serious about it. Anyhow, the key thing was that Rewi and I went to the interview. Corrections were serious about it because they had a whole line-up of local people there — they'd picked the site by then. They were pretty pleased to see that we had our Māori representative with us, because I don't think the other groups even thought that was particularly important. They were enormously impressed with our describing how we were going to try and approach the whole problem in terms of bringing some humanity into prison design. And we weren't just saying it — it was a serious thing on both my and Rewi's parts.

Rewi said, 'I'll need somebody else to help me', and he got Mike Barns. The minute we knew we had the job, we roped in Mike as part of the group. We'd obviously put up a good coherent case for trying to do this seriously, that rehabilitation was going to be possible.

I must say that Corrections had put together fantastic briefs, in which they were finally saying these prisons would have proper facilities to learn, with classrooms and technical training workshops.

It turned out to be an absolutely marvellous experience. The Labour government took great interest in it and followed it closely. We did a lot of consultation — I was going up to Kaikohe at least once a month, and Rewi came with me on almost all those trips. Corrections said it was the perfect site — just outside of Kaikohe near Ngāwhā hot springs, with hot water running through the middle of the site in a very pretty stream with tangled greenery around it. Corrections suggested putting a culvert right across the site and filling the stream in. Rewi was particularly unhappy about this. I was, too. It wasn't a very natural way to be dealing with the environment. But Rewi carried the day by saying that the waters of Ngāwhā were symbolic and healing if you wanted to go bathing in them every day. Now the stream is fairly obvious through the middle. And we arranged the buildings to follow the lie of the stream.

Jade

Could you summarise what the key concepts were?

Ross

We expanded on the notion that whatever we were going to do on the land was going to be inscribed into it carefully rather than excavated and filled. The land was going to be treated as sensitively as we could. Rewi did some absolutely beautiful drawings that were magic. And then we had all these sketches that showed buildings that were attempting to do the right things with regard to the landscape. We tried to use low-pitched roofs rolling through the landscape around the compounds. It's all low-key architecture, definitely recessive, except for the whare, which we went to a bit of trouble to make, as it is an important place.

Corrections came to us with the idea of a big square for each of the compounds there, which had to have an internal courtyard. So we pushed and pulled to get them running on the contours.

Rewi was hugely involved with the landscaping as well. He had particular things that he wanted to see happen in terms of placement. He'd come up for a visit and drive around the community and come back with very large rocks. I don't think he was carrying them himself, but somebody had managed to get them on a trailer. And they'd be placed in specific locations that he wanted them to be in. When we subsequently worked on Spring Hill Prison in the Waikato he did the same thing, driving all over the Waikato finding these amazing old rocks. He loved rocks.

While we were working in Northland, Rewi was also working on the Wishart House at Ōmāpere. I think we made that part of our story — the fact that Rewi was already involved in work in the area. He knew the landscape, he knew the people . . . Corrections wanted to hear all that sort of stuff, however tenuous it was. Rewi was a major part of our success in getting that job.

Jeremy
Jade and I were talking earlier about the ethical tangle that working on a prison project can involve, and I wondered if you could characterise the approach the two of you had to that. Did you believe you could create a net positive outcome?

Ross
Yes. I read an interview once with [American architect] Richard Meier and he said, 'I would never ever design a prison.' It was as if that would be the lowest job that you could possibly imagine. There'd be a lot of architects who would go along with that. But after Rewi and I read this Request for Proposal document from the Department of Corrections, we said, 'This is not the normal stuff that you might be asked to do to just put people in boxes' — which it all turned back to again, after the National government came in.

Anyway, Rewi and I both thought this was something that could be done properly, rightly or wrongly, and that it could make a difference to the people who were going to live there. When we got the job, the first thing Corrections do is they take you around the other

Above: The iwi services and visitors building sits just outside the facility's secure perimeter at the main access point to the site. *Courtesy of Ross Brown*

Below: The facility's education block is sited to follow a curved pathway along the main axis of the site and overlook the stream bed below. Rewi told the Department of Corrections that 'the waters of Ngāwhā were symbolic and healing', Ross Brown says, and he persuaded them to retain the stream on the site. *Courtesy of Ross Brown*

Health and corrections

correctional facilities or prisons in New Zealand. They were all utterly dreadful places. You don't realise that these things could be as bad as they are until you've been shown around. There are all these metal doors clanging, hard surfaces everywhere, with the prisoners making noise in them just to be heard. We said that we could design buildings that could lower the temperature.

On one level, all this can sound very self-serving, I suppose, and can make it sound like we were simply justifying the fact that we wanted a job. But the people at Corrections wanted it to be done properly. And Rewi and I were genuinely serious about getting these jobs and making not just the best of them but making them something unique and special.

Jeremy

Can you remember your first meetings with Rewi?

Ross

Yes. I brought a picture that reminds me of a lot. It's one I've always had handy for some reason. It tends to sum up what he was like then. He was larger than life. We'd gone away for a weekend and Rewi put down a hāngī in the lawn and it was the most amazing evening. I was working at Structon Group in mid-1972, after I'd been in Europe for four or five years, and Rewi joined in the beginning of 1973. I met him for the first time at his interview for the job. He was a structural draughtsman. I do remember him being interviewed and being a seriously earnest and convincing guy. He got a job just like that.

He started to get to know us down the other end of the office, the architectural end; he was gravitating down there all time. He could draw well, and he'd come down at lunchtime and hang about everybody's boards and show much more interest in our end of the office. We said, 'Well, if you're interested in this, you don't have to be a structural draughty. You can be in our part of the world.' He got serious on that, and told us that he was serious, and went to Auckland University. He didn't need any encouragement, but we gave him all the extra encouragement that was possible. We wrote messages of support for his application because he was a terrific

worker in the office. Everybody thought he was just the ticket in terms of being a top-calibre guy. He was also a great sportsman at the time. He was playing rugby and he was surfing at Worser Bay Surf Club. He threw everything into everything.

Jeremy

So you stayed in touch through this period when he was at the University of Auckland.

Ross

Yeah. And I gave him a job in the Auckland office to work on stuff that I was working on in Auckland for the Housing Corporation, in the Manukau City Centre and an office building in Ōtara Town Centre. He and I worked a lot together on that and on a building on the corner of Beach Road and Emily Place, a little one with an outside lift.

Jeremy

Was he explicitly using Māori design principles on those early projects you worked on together?

Ross

Yeah. He wanted to talk about that for the Emily Place building, but it was bloody hard — the client was Brierley and they weren't exactly conducive to those notions.

Jeremy

What do you think gave Rewi the confidence to introduce Māori design principles to clients like that when they may not have been interested?

Ross

I honestly think he always wanted to do it. He always knew that there was something there. He talked about it a lot. There was no real discourse about it at the time. He was biding his time, I suppose, and he probably didn't feel he was getting enough of an opportunity to explain what he really wanted to see happen in those jobs — although he did try to at every opportunity. When we worked together again a few years later, this is where he said, we're going to really get an opportunity to do these things. By then he knew a lot more about what he thought was important.

Jeremy

You mentioned you were on a design awards jury with Rewi and John Scott in the late 1980s. Did Rewi and John Scott have a good relationship?

Ross

They did. I remember we spent a night in Kuratau. John Scott had only just finished designing a house in the same subdivision down the road. In fact, he ended up doing two there in Te Pohue Street in Omori Heights. Aussie architect John Andrews was also there as a judge, and very impressed with the food for the evening being hoisted from a hole in the ground — the hāngī that Rewi put down on the front lawn, with a little help from me. And the big discussion that night became about front doors and thresholds, that sort of thing.

Jeremy

What did you think of Rewi's own house in Kohimarama?

Ross

The building's on a difficult site that he was able to get really inexpensively because it sits in the lee of a steep bank behind. It's also difficult from a sun point of view — the site was oriented really badly for the sun. The front of the house was completely closed off to the street. I used to press Rewi on the subject of whether the front being as blank a façade as it is, a really interesting form, was a rejection of the suburb that he'd found himself in and the values of the various people who might be living close by. And he'd agree with the fact that it looked like that, and that suggestion might be true.

I don't think he'd ever say anything like that was exactly what he was doing, but that was definitely allowed as an interpretation of what might be going on. I don't know how well he got to know people there. They all found it, I think, pretty mysterious. It's an amazingly impassive house, an enigmatic house. The back, which is more open, gave a chance to relax in the environment a bit more. Maybe I'm reading too much into it all, but yeah, we definitely had those conversations at the time he was building it.

A roof detail on the facility's gymnasium. The prison at Ngāwhā, Mike Barns says, was Rewi's 'opportunity to change Māori incarceration for the future'. *Courtesy of Ross Brown*

Mike Barns (Tūwharetoa ki Kawerau) is an old friend and colleague of Rewi's who worked with Rewi and Ross on the Northland Region Corrections Facility. He first got to know Rewi when they were at Wellington Polytechnic together — two of very few Māori in the architectural field at that time, as Mike says. Here, he remembers early days in Wellington with Rewi and their later collaborations, including the prison at Ngāwhā.

Jade Kake

Hello Mike.

Mike Barns

Hello. I'm happy you guys have taken the initiative to do this book. Rewi was such a humble guy and he was never one to promote himself. And I think that was part of his charm. He was very recognised in a lot of architectural circles, but not beyond that, and I think there's a requirement to record people like Rewi for posterity and for history's sake, otherwise stories just come and go.

Jade

We're interested in understanding Rewi as a person, understanding his work, locating him within his time and context, but also thinking about his enduring legacy because I do think he's had a real impact on the way we practise architecture, particularly for us as Māori practitioners.

Mike

Sure, okay. This might help point towards those topics you want to bring out. I first met Rewi in Wellington when we were at Wellington Polytechnic training to be draughtsmen together, probably two of the few Māori in the architectural field at the time. So this is 1971, 1972. Rewi was doing his structural NZCSE, New Zealand Certificate in Structural Engineering. And I was doing my New Zealand Certificate in Architectural Draughting (NZCAD). He was employed by Structon Group, where he met Ross Brown. He hadn't met Leona at that stage. So we were a couple of young bucks. His family was from Tolaga Bay, but he grew up in the city and Strathmore out by the airport. His mum and dad were both quite strong influences on him. I think his dad drove one of the Wellington City Council buses. So we sort of grew up together. He was a lovely guy, so soft and fun, loving, not outspoken, he just kind of kept to himself.

We got to know each other because a girlfriend of mine at the time worked for Structon Group, and she'd tell me, 'Oh, we got this Māori guy working for us.' But we never really made the time to get together until we met at a party at Structon Group. We just hit it off. He reminded me of all my bros or my cousins. We were a similar age and at about the same stage in our studies. And we didn't actually search each other out, but we just kind of bumped into each other every now and then. We were a couple of young Māori boys in the city. I was fresh down from the Bay of Plenty doing my cadetship in the Ministry of Works architectural team, and he was doing his young Māori boy thing at Structon. And so we'd meet, we'd have a few jokes and get a little drunk and then I'd send him off home or he'd send me off home.

And it got to a stage where we were getting quite close, as you do along the way. So we were probably 18, 19 years old, something like that. Then I tried to get him into music. I'd joined a rock band. Every young Māori boy joined a rock band at some time. I didn't know, but Rewi at the time was learning to play guitar. I was in a group with two other Māori guys. We played a lot of Santana-type music and Black Sabbath and Jimi Hendrix, all that stuff. We got a gig in Lower Hutt, a spot. But Rewi never really had the confidence in himself to play. He got himself an electric guitar and he was teaching himself. I tried to get him to join a band, our band. He said, 'No, no, no, I'm not good enough. Not good enough.' And I said, 'It doesn't matter. You know, you learn as you go, you pick it up. It's just the guys, we're okay, they'll embrace you.' No, no, no. He taught himself how to play a lot of the songs that we were playing, but he wasn't really good. Well, that's not fair. He wasn't as good as he wanted to be just because he didn't give himself the confidence. So, anyway, we hung out together.

We graduated with what they call diplomas these days, from Wellington Polytech, and after contracting for a couple of years as a draughtsman I decided I was going to go on and study architecture. Rewi didn't want to leave Structon. He really enjoyed it there. He loved working with Ross. He and Ross had a great relationship, but Rewi wasn't pivoting into architecture at that time. He was still pretty well in the structural space. It wasn't until, I guess, '75, '76, that his mind started turning to architecture. He was definitely creative, but not as creative as he was later when he really got into architecture.

I went up to Auckland Uni — I was approved for a place there. They used to have a place for guys that had done the Certificate in Architectural Draughting to go into the second professional year on the architectural degree course. It was a five-year course in those days. So I went to uni and Rewi started to get interested in architecture. He was in touch with me and he said, 'Oh, I'm thinking of doing architecture, switching from structural engineering.' I said, 'Go for it, you'll be a great architect.' He still wasn't very confident. And then suddenly he just switched. He said, 'No, bugger it, I'll do it.'

So this is now '77, '78. He had met Leona at that stage. I said, 'Come on up, you'd be great in the architecture school.' He was offered a place in the school, which he accepted. He stayed with my wife and me in Parnell for maybe six months. I kind of helped mentor him through those early years of architecture school. But man, he picked it up and he just went for it. He had a great sense of humour. He poked fun at everything. He was a bit like Athfield in that regard, he poked fun at himself.

He never took things too seriously, but he was in love with architecture as a discipline. He actually struggled in his first year. He wasn't doing very well because that step from polytech to the university is quite a big step. But towards the end of his studies, he put in a submission for the Monier Awards, which was a set of architecture awards. Rewi put up this brilliant scheme for the Ngāti Pōneke Marae.

It was very detached. It wasn't realistic — it wasn't supposed to be, it was just a schematic. It was that design you've probably seen where there is this large canoe coming out of Pōneke Harbour that went up and rested on Mount Vic.

I think Kerry Morrow was a judge, and I was a judge. And I think John Scott was a judge. I talked to Kerry as we were walking around, looking at the schemes up on the wall. I said, 'We need to give an award for this, this is beautiful. It's brilliant.' So then we pulled John Scott over and said, 'John, what do you think about this?' 'Bloody amazing, really.' So we talked John into it, basically.

Everybody else who entered was so serious about their architecture. Then you had this entry by Rewi, this kind of outer space thing that just arrived. It was totally not practical, but it answered a lot of stories that were floating around in Rewi's head. To be honest, he wasn't really enshrined in his Māoriness at that point. He went back to Tolaga every now and then — but it was his mum and dad who were really attached to Tolaga Bay, Rewi wasn't so much. And I think he felt, 'I'm in the city, but I don't really understand my roots.' And it was at the same time that there was quite a bit of stuff going on in Wellington — a lot of identity stuff, not just with Māori, but also with Pasifika.

So I think that first project that he won the Monier Design Award for was him trying to understand his identity as a Māori growing up in the city with no real roots there. He was like a lot of Māori at the time, just kind of drifting around the cities. That first project that he did helped him start to define his Māoriness. When he won the award, I think it confirmed his validity as a Māori commentator, and probably gave him a lot more confidence in those early days around his architectural capability.

I think I was the second or third Māori student architect in the school up until that point in time in New Zealand. We had about 90 students in the intake per year, so there were not a lot of brown faces around, and you had all that stuff we were trying to work out as cultural identity. Rewi was coming into an academic programme and wondering, is this appropriate for me? Then boom, he gets an endorsement through his design award. He never showed off about it. He was always humble. But I think it gave him an endorsement that made him feel he had a hope. He just got stronger and stronger. Always modest, always humble, always joking about himself and his inadequacies, but a strong, believable person. A lovely person, actually.

Jeremy Hansen
You mentioned that there were very few Māori students at the architecture school. What was it like for you and for him being Māori at architecture school? Was it okay, or was it weird at times?

Mike
I mean, it was fine. When you were inside a professional architectural company, there were no Māori there as well. When I was at the Ministry of Works, I was the only Māori inside the architectural team at that time. Rewi was the only Māori inside Structon Group. But I don't think it worked against us. I got treated like anyone else. I didn't feel disadvantaged. And in architectural school we were embraced by the other students as much as anyone else. And I don't think either of us felt out of place there.

All the cultural politics were quite different then; I know Ngā Tama Toa was just starting to take off at the engineering school right next door. And there was some stuff starting to happen at the student union and some of the other degrees, but in architecture, I didn't feel disenfranchised. In fact, because of my draughting background, I felt a bit surer in the degree than a lot of the other students at the time. I had knowledge that was industry-based; it wasn't theoretical architecture, but it afforded me some credibility. I didn't feel competent intellectually or academically, but you kind of build that up over time. So I don't think Rewi ever felt out of place there as a Māori. I think he belonged.

Jade
How did he develop his architectural approach after he finished architecture school?

Mike
Well, I went to the US and did a master's in architecture at the East–West Center in Hawai'i and got tied up with the [Indigenous] renaissance thing. When I got back in '85, Rewi and Leona had [their daughter] Lucy; Leona was working and Rewi was working. He was just about to build his house in Kohimarama, and they were living in Parnell. Rewi was so committed to his practice, to his architecture. He would take hours: he'd think about something and draw it, wasn't happy with that and would keep scratching away. All of his stuff was very, very considered — over-considered at times, I thought. But that was his passion, that was who he was. He thought deeply about things.

We would still catch up on Fridays for a beer. I went on to lecture full-time at Auckland Uni; Rewi never took that path at that time. I don't know whether he was necessarily unconfident about his Māoriness at that stage, or if he just saw that there was a more appropriate pathway to traverse inside the Pākehā camp. I don't mean he was part of the camp. I mean, he found it very easy to talk with people like Ross Brown and Marsh Cook, Roger Walker and the noteworthy people in the field, whom he knew personally. And they respected him as well.

It was out of respect that he chose that methodology, but his work was always very highly informed by Māori and not just his Māoriness. He was learning about being Māori at the time and that came out in his work. He was running his practice full-time. He had quite a wide clientele. He really found his feet, and he was an identity in architecture at that stage with a lot of respect for him.

Jeremy
Did you also work together?

Mike
Yeah. In about 1999 Ross Brown came to both of us and said, 'Hey, we'd really like you guys to think about coming onto our team to be part of this prison up north.' We both knew Ross and liked and respected him. We said, 'We've got a kaupapa of our own, Ross, are you cool with it?' It wasn't a political statement. It's just where our hearts were at. He said, 'That's why I'm talking to you guys.'

The prison was going to go into Ngāwhā, which is a Māori community. Ross thought we needed to provide an appropriate design for Ngāwhā that had to be embedded in Māoriness. And we said, 'Hey man, that's us.' So Rewi and I got together and decided to do that project together. He had his office, I had my office, and we would meet and talk about things and just scribble and write up key principles. I think we got to a stage where we'd mapped out a lot of the kaupapa that we wanted to explore with the project. We agreed that I would write up the design language, and Rewi would start doing some of the design work and

Health and corrections

that the design work would be distilled from the design language.

I was still lecturing full-time at Auckland Uni at the time, and I said to Rewi, 'A lot of this stuff is just in our head — this is untested, and we need to test a lot of the stuff.' He agreed, so I ran the programme as a design studio at the School of Architecture. We got approval from the Department of Corrections to do that. And we ran it as a vertically integrated 10-week design programme with years two to five in our design studio.

And with assistance from Corrections, we ran focus groups with previous Māori inmates from Pāremoremo prison to test some of the ideas. The challenge for the students was to go and research incarceration, how First Nations people have been incarcerated around the world. We knew we had to talk about this. This was an issue for this prison.

When we started out on Ngāwhā, we brought Māori Marsden into the conversation. We asked him to be our kaitiaki on the project. He initially said, 'What the hell are you doing? Building a prison for Māori? You're fucking Māori architects, what are you doing?' And we said, 'Yeah, that's why we're doing it: because we're Māori architects. We don't want other people doing this work.' We won him over. We wanted to speak to the bros on the ground, and Māori Marsden helped us do that. We had focus groups with different groups, with gangs.

Some mana whenua were very anti. They said, 'There's no way this prison is going to house our people on our land. This is just crazy. This is the biggest injustice.' And we said to them, 'These boys in prison are your nephews and your sons, and isn't it more appropriate that they are housed here on your land? You guys are providing the awhi for these kids. Isn't it better that we actually build this right here in the rohe? And then you guys will have a role not only in awhi-ing them, and management, but also in the design of the facility.'

When we presented that, half of them said, 'Yep, it makes sense to us.' The other half were still anti. Māori Marsden got up and spoke to them and called them out: 'You guys, take responsibility for your people!' he said. We probably convinced 90 per cent of mana whenua to get involved and stay involved, but it wasn't just the design. The design still had some way to go at that point. It was the conviction of people like Māori Marsden asking them to support us.

In the meantime, Rewi and I were back at the office, scratching away and talking about what the students had come up with. They decided we weren't going to call it a prison: it was a university, a place where Māori could learn how to be Māori. They'd gone into the criminal justice system, they'd been dealt a sentence, and this was kind of multigenerational. We had to break the cycle; the prison had to be about rejuvenation, not about incarceration. I think that Ngāwhā prison was probably years ahead of its time. It got built. About a third of what we intended was finally incorporated into the project, but that alone was amazing. It was the first prison of its kind.

Jeremy
It's interesting to hear about the satisfaction you and Rewi got from the Ngāwhā project, because one of the things I've been thinking as we go through this is how, for many reasons, Rewi didn't get the projects he seemed to deserve later in life, and New Zealand would be much richer for him having been given greater opportunities. And I just wondered if you had any thoughts about why those opportunities may not have come his way.

Mike
I think Ngāwhā was at a stage in Rewi's life where he had made a whole lot of contributions to New Zealand architecture, but it was small-scale stuff until then. And this was his opportunity to design an institutional facility that was going to have an impact. You know, this was going to change Māori incarceration for the future. He saw that his work was really valuable at a national level, but the neat thing was, he never changed. He was still the humble guy and he was just doing little sketches and the concepts were amazing, so simple. On Ngāwhā, he got to see that it was going to affect generations of Māori. He went on to do a second prison with Ross, Spring Hill. I wasn't involved in that as I had moved to the US. I think he was kind of disappointed in Spring Hill that he couldn't get as far as we got with Ngāwhā.

Anyway, there was a lot of respect for Rewi in architectural circles. Everyone knew him, everyone loved him. He was Rewi, he wasn't pretentious. He didn't always dress the flashiest. He was just very approachable. But the public works projects were kind of lined up beforehand and the clients didn't have a vision for Māoriness in there. I don't think the cultural politics were at that stage at that point in time. With the public projects, the government wasn't courageous enough to involve Rewi in those things.

I don't think that'd be the case today. It certainly had nothing to do with Rewi's capability. He struggled approaching large-scale projects until he just elevated himself and treated it as a piece of art, or a highly informed piece of architecture where he wasn't frightened at the scale. Yeah, it's sad that we lost him at the time we did because I think today there would be a lot of projects open to him.

I know he enjoyed the partnerships that he had with Ath [Ian Athfield]. Ath was a perfectionist, he was a deep thinker and he loved Rewi. He and Rewi would laugh all day, they'd drink beer and they'd poke fun at everyone, just laugh their heads off. They had a groove, their own groove, and I think Ath brought Rewi into projects because he wanted that different insight, not necessarily just a cultural insight, but a different insight.

Jade
So how did his career progress without those sorts of projects?

Mike
When I came back from Hawai'i, I got busy trying to rebuild my own company and Rewi was busy on his works. Some of his projects didn't come off. I remember he was struggling financially, as many young architects do. I don't know whether all of his clients were paying or not. And then he got offered the job at Auckland University, which was really a lifeline for him. His diabetes was also starting to kick in

quite a bit. I think he had just lost Leona, Lucy's mum. He wasn't depressed, but he wasn't his usual bubbly self.

He was lecturing but he was still practising architecture as well, and I got him to share some space with me in Mount Eden. It was fantastic. There were a couple of projects we were bidding against each other on. So we'd both turn up to the interview and he'd be sitting in the waiting room and I'd come in. He'd say, 'Oh, that's what you've been working on for the last month.' I said, 'Yeah, you dickhead, why didn't you tell me you're working on this?'

We'd be sitting out there cracking jokes between us. If he got the job, he would hire me and my draughtsman; if I got the job, I would hire him and Jane [Baldwin, who worked with Rewi for years] to support us. So it didn't matter who won the job, we were both going to get the work. That was pretty cool. We did that a few times.

Jeremy
You talked before about how public entities during Rewi's career may not have thought to include Māori design principles or Māori architects in their projects. But from the way you've described Rewi it seems unlikely that he would position himself as the sole arbiter of Māori design values on those types of projects.

Mike
Rewi never claimed to be a Māori architect, never claimed to be *the* Māori architect. He assumed that position without any boasting, without any claiming, without professing to be an expert on Māori architecture or Māori architectural drivers or Māori kaupapa. He was given that status, but he would never have said, 'I'm the expert. I have done all this work in Māori architecture.' And he was actually unconfident throughout his whole life, I know this as a close friend. And even though he was very successful as an architect, let alone a Māori architect, I think if you got him in a room, he would admit, 'Yeah, I've got a lot to learn about my Māoriness.'

When he did the canopy at the Ōtara Town Centre, he did that beautiful archway, and that was quite early in his career — he was still discovering himself and linking with

other Polynesian cultures. He learned a lot from that; he learned what he didn't know. He was finding his Māoriness through his architecture, but he never claimed to be an expert in tikanga or Māori architecture. He expressed what he knew and it was unfolding as he grew in life.

His architecture was his own personal journey and his Māoriness was becoming more and more evident. If I was to be candid, I think he may have been a little afraid of it. It may be unfair to say that. There was a wealth of knowledge from Ngāti Porou. Just last night I was listening to some tapes from Sir Tamati Reedy, and Api Mahuika, some old tapes. All these strong, strong guys, from Ngāti Porou, that Rewi either didn't want to or was afraid to seek guidance from.

But to be honest, in his architectural world he didn't need to. He had enough to do, he had enough in his head bringing together concepts and expressing them in a beautiful way. Perhaps his biggest legitimacy was not only that he didn't claim to be an expert in tikanga and in expressing that tikanga through architecture, but also that he was almost tangential to that whole expression of Māoriness. I think the distance in his relationship with his Māoriness was not out of fear. It was out of respect, actually: he respected Māoriness so much that he didn't want to dally with it. He didn't want to play with it. It was almost like he thought, 'If I play with it, I'm doing a disservice, I'm reducing it.'

I think in a lot of our Māori architects' work, we feel the importance of the work we are doing and we want to state the principles we're trying to pursue in our architecture in quite strong terms. Rewi felt those principles, but he never felt he was the expert orator explaining it. He said, 'This is my rendition, I'm not claiming to be the expert. Anyone can come along and shoot me down and you'll be right, but this is what I'm presenting you.' And his work was beautiful. It was light. It wasn't heavy overstatement in my mind — there was always a lightness around it, which I loved. I think that's what turned him on to a lot of people.

He was quite a complicated thinker, but he was also a very simple thinker. He thought in very clear, simple terms and he layered those meanings on top of each other. And you could see that in his work, the layers of meaning, but essentially his thinking was very pure, simple thinking. He wasn't like Ath, who was quite a complicated thinker. And Roger Walker was an even more complicated thinker; but Rewi was just very pure, simple.

He lived his life through simple principles. He wasn't a complicated person. He was a simple, honest person. I never knew him to lie in all the time that I knew him, 45 years, longer than that. And we were close for a lot of that time. He was such an honest guy, and his architecture was honest. It was his perception of how he saw things.

Jeremy
Did you ever talk about this?

Mike
I never challenged him about his Māoriness. I just respected that he was at wherever he was at on his journey. I mean, we are all at our own place on our Māori journey. But whatever he produced, I loved it.

Above: In front of the visitor centre is a landscaped area leading to the stream that runs through the site. *Courtesy of Ross Brown*

Right: The central courtyard of the accommodation block features stepped sections to follow the contours of the site. *Courtesy of Ross Brown*

Education

Ngā whare wānanga

Kāore he mutunga o tēnei mea, te ako
Learning never ends

Sketches from Rewi's archives show his experimentation with the curved form that is the organising principle of Puukenga.

Education

Puukenga, Unitec Institute of Technology

Ōwairaka Tāmaki Makaurau Auckland

1993

With Southcombe, McLean and Co.

The first Māori studies buildings began appearing on university campuses from the late 1980s in response to expanded tertiary courses in Māori studies and increasing demand for spaces that could meet the cultural needs of both staff and students. Puukenga is the School of Māori Studies at Unitec Institute of Technology Te Whare Wānanga o Wairaka in Tāmaki Makaurau Auckland, a place where hundreds of students each year immerse themselves in te reo Māori in classrooms Rewi designed. The Puukenga project combines critical cultural and academic functions: the building operates as a learning space, but is structured conceptually by ideas of tapu and noa, and the roles of tāne and wāhine in te ao Māori.

Whaea Lynda Toki (Ngāti Maniapoto — Ngāti Kinohaku, Ngāti Te Kanawa, Ngāti Pēhi) is a kaiāwhina (student support) and kuia/rūruhi for Te Noho Kotahitanga Marae there. The campus also contains Ngākau Māhaki, a wharenui designed and built by Te Arawa tohunga whakairo Lyonel Grant, which opened in 2009. Here, Lynda reflects on her experiences of the whare and the whenua over the past three decades.

Opposite left: Visitors to Puukenga follow its dramatic curve to a central gathering space with a pouihi carved by Blaine Te Rito. *Samuel Hartnett*

Opposite right: A glass screen containing loosely arranged timber offcuts separates the office space from the central gathering area. *Samuel Hartnett*

Jade Kake

Would you mind starting with who you are? And then we can start looking through the building and the site.

Lynda Toki

Kia ora mai tātou. He uri āhau nō Maniapoto, nō Te Nehenehenui. Mōkau ki runga, Tāmaki ki raro, Mangatoatoa ki waenganui, he mihi ki Te Arikinui, hau pai mārire ki a rātou. Ko Ngāti Kinohaku, ko Ngāti Te Kanawa, ko Ngāti Pēhi ngā hapū. Ko Whareōrino rāua ko Maungaroa ngā maunga. Ko Te Puke Hōkioi te whare hōkioi. Ko Tawapiko te papakāinga. Ko Mirumiru ki Marokopa me Oparure ngā marae. Ko Lynda Toki ahau. Nō te whānau Kete mai i Marokopa. Kia ora.

Ko te whenua nei ko Rangimatarau. Koinā taku tino tū, i te tuatahi. He aha ai? Mō taku tamāhine. This is back when Carrington Tech was around. My girl had come in for an interview — she had applied to come here for tertiary learning, was accepted, and then came home. She had gone down to Taranaki, to Mōkau, and was staying with my grandmother. She wanted to spend time with her great-grandmother before coming into tertiary.

Jade

He tino taonga.

Lynda

She had come back, had her interview and then come home and said, 'I don't think I could go there.' She said that the energy of the whenua was too much for her. At that point I said, 'Well, you focus on your studies and you leave the whenua to me.' That was October 1991.

In November I thought, right, I'm going to come and look for this place where my girl is going to come to for her tertiary learning. I had no idea that it was so big. There were four gates, and I had no idea where she was going to be doing her learning within these four gates. I just drove up and down the road looking, and then in the end I went down to the beach—

Jade

To Point Chev?

Lynda

Ki Taiaharau.

Jade

Koinā te ingoa tūturu?

Lynda

Āe. I had a karakia there and asked for one gate. I drove back up and gate three, gate three welcomed me in. It's a carpark now, but I stood at the top of the hill and looked down and I thought, okay. I have no idea where my daughter is going to do her studies within these four gates, but I needed to know that whatever I did that day was going to reach her.

So, I did mahi ā-whenua from gate one, the extremities of gate one, the boundaries, all the way to gate four. I had no idea what was over the back, and so again, it was to do with the extreme boundaries on that side, which ended up being Te Auaunga. I just stood there and did mahi ā-whenua until I reached the water. Over the water, my mahi was able to spread right across all four gates and to the back.

And that was . . . the first session. Then I came in December and did the exact same thing. And then again in January of 1992, so that my daughter could be here, and start her studies in February 1992. At that time, this whenua, here, right here, was the bull paddock.

Jade

Karekau he whare?

Lynda

Kāhore ngā whare i konei. The bulls were the only things I saw moving.

I didn't know any of it at that time, but years later I would come in and I would learn the history of this whenua. So I'm not surprised that this whare is here, that Puukenga is here on this site, on this whenua.

But what is so special about this whare Puukenga? I could not put my finger on it for years. And then I realised that this is the only whare Māori that I have been to that actually reminded me of the whare Te Miringa Te Kakara [built by Te Rā Karepe and Rangawhenua, leaders of the Pao Mīere movement, in the shape of a cross, with four entrances]. Because of all the doors.

Jade

Auē. Pērā i tērā wānanga whānau.

Lynda

Well, not exactly, engari, pārā a roto. You know? As a mokopuna, I was taken there with my koroua, with my tūpuna, and I sat alongside them in that whare. It would be years until I figured it out.

To the left of Blaine Te Rito's pouihi, the tāhuhu (ridge beam) at Puukenga represents a division between the northern and southern skies, with four spotlights over the informal student informal space referring to the Southern Cross. *Samuel Hartnett*

Education

248 - 249

A sketch from Rewi's archives shows the irregular weatherboard patterns on the exterior of Puukenga's main volume, with part of the rectilinear classroom block at one end. *Architecture Archive, University of Auckland*

Education

It was to do with the ramp here. If you've never spent time within that whare, you wouldn't know. And if anyone went back and looked, that whare would seem tiny. But it was actually huge on the inside because you walked up a ramp and then you sat back under the eaves.

That is what is so special about Puukenga to me. It reminded me of that whare. All the doors within this whare, the astrology on the ceiling — it's one of the first things I noticed about this whare.

Like I said, I found this whare in 2003. I had been upset. I was doing a science course to do with health and well-being, and a staff member had just said Māori didn't have a science. I was horrified that in 2003 this was what they were saying. And it upset me so much that I wandered off, and ended up walking out here.

A staff member, Susan Watene, found me and brought me into this whare. And I didn't realise it at the time, but I was greeted by a wahine nō Maniapoto, Whaea Beryl Woolford-Roa, and she brought me into Puukenga.

And one of the first things I noticed was that all the lighting was not in straight lines. Interesting that I would notice that first? Well, no, because at Miringa Te Kakara, as mokopuna, that's where we were put. I runga i ngā karakia tawhito o ngā tohunga i reira. Karere ō mātou wairua ki a Ranginui. Ahakoa ka moe taku tinana ki te papa, karere pai te wairua. And then you start to recognise the star systems, and the familiarity grows. And then I ended up coming here and being a student here and just never left.

I guess that is because of this whare. Eventually I realised, although I was thinking about astrology, our maramataka, that the beam running through the middle of the house divides the northern and southern skies. Okay, this is about left brain, right brain, North Pole, South Pole. And so more and more of this house was revealing itself to me.

Jade
He maha ngā whakaaro i poupoua ai i roto i te whare.

Lynda
Mīharo kē tēnei whare.

Jade
Pai te roa o tō noho? Pai te pōturi o te whakamārama o tēnā mea, o tēnā mea?

Lynda
Āe. Well, because I came here and became a tauira here, and then I got to hear the kōrero about it, but there was still this familiarity that I knew was something innately within me. It wasn't until years later that I realised — all the doors, the exit doors of this whare, the ramp within this whare — the connection to Te Miringa Te Kakara. Which is interesting, because at the end of 2001, because I had returned to education, into tertiary, into higher learning, I went back to Miringa Te Kakara. Seeing the whakapapa of all those different rooms, they all had their own name. Of our pou out there, the first thing I saw was a wahine holding up all the men.

Jade
He tohu.

Lynda
He tino tohu. Koinā te āhua o Papa. Always holding us all up. Yeah. And I guess, recognising ngā kete o te wānanga on the wall, hanging on the wall. During the 2020 lockdown, I had this moemoeā that I spent time with Koro John Turei. We were sitting on a log, up by gate four, and he told me that is where he wanted the marae to be.

At the top of the puna. I thought, wow. How amazing is that? And then he said to me, 'So, what did you do?' And I thought, what did I do? What are you talking about? What did I do? And he said to me that during their karakia it didn't matter what they did or how many people were brought in. There was already a karakia in place that they couldn't break through. And then I remembered, of course. I did that for my daughter.

Jade
Ko koe te kaikarakia tuatahi.

Lynda
And I said, oh āe. I did do that. Because I didn't know whether my daughter would be able to come here, because she was too sensitive to this whenua.

Jade
Nā konā, kua huri te wāhi o te marae, mai i korā, ki konei.

Lynda
I'm not sure why it ended up being here.

But when he said that about the mahi that had already been set in place, to do with Puukenga being here, to do with the marae being here, that's when I said it was because this was a bull paddock and the bulls were the only things moving on the whenua when I was doing that mahi. They held my attention.

Jade
Koinā te wāhi.

Lynda
They held my attention. Is this the right place for the marae? Maybe, because this is where the marae is. I heard that when Lyonel started his work on the marae he had a bird's eye view of the whenua, and I guess he chose to put his whare here as well.

Jade
Tata ki Puukenga.

Lynda
Āe. I just acknowledge the architecture of this whare Puukenga, for building this whare here. For incorporating our taonga within its walls. For the sake of our tauira Māori.

Jade
He āhuru mōwai tēnei whare.

Lynda
Āe. With the puna running through it.

Jade
He aha ōu whakaaro e pā ana ki te wai?

Lynda
Te wai unu roa o Rakataura. Te wai unu roa o Wairaka hoki.

Jade
Ērā momo wai.

Lynda
Āe. Koinā. He hokinga mahara mō mātou, ka rere te wai i roto i ō mātou tinana. He taonga hauora. Ki ahau nei, koinā te āhua o tēnei whare. He taonga hauora.

Jade
He aha ōu whakaaro e pā ana ki te tātai arorangi? I tīmata koe ki te kōrero e pā ana ki tērā, engari, he āhua kūare ahau e pā ana ki ngā kāhui whetū, he aha te hononga ki ērā?

Lynda
I woke up this morning and all I could think about was he mihi atu ki a Meremere, te whetū o te rangi, ki a Pūtara, te whetū o tēnei marama, ki a Rēhua, te wānanga.

Jade
Ko Rēhua te tohu o te mutunga o te wānanga.

Lynda
I roto i tēnei whare, ka hoki ngā mahara.

Jade
Āe, he maha ngā tohu o te hokinga mahara. Koinā te take o ētahi o ngā mea.

Lynda
He whare wānanga tēnei.

Jade
Koinā te whakamahia o te whare i te nuinga o te wā, nē?

Lynda
Āe.

Jade
Ia wā ka haere au ki konei, ka wānanga.

Lynda
Me te ingoa, Puukenga. Koinā te akiaki i ngā pūkenga o ngā tauira. He whare manaaki, i ērā momo taonga i roto, i ngā tauira.

Jade
Āe, ko ngā tauira ngā taonga.

Lynda
Kāhore au i mōhio ki a Rewi, engari, he mihi tēnei ki a ia. He tino mihi ki a ia.

Jade
Āe, nā te mea, kei te mōhio koe ki ngā hua o tāna mahi. Tērā pea, koinei te whare Māori tuatahi o tēnei wāhi, o tēnei whare wānanga.

Lynda
And so I'm not surprised that Te Pūkenga, the integration of all the Institutes of Technology and Polytechnic, puta noa i te motu, chose the name Te Pūkenga. Ki ahau nei, koinā.

Jade
Koinā te ingoa.

Lynda
Ka tū tēnei whare.

Jade
Āe, i te tuatahi.

Lynda
I akiaki taua ingoa i ērā momo taonga i roto i ngā tauira katoa.

Jade
He ātaahua ēnā whakaaro.

Lynda
Koinā te māringanui, ki ahau, e pā ana ki tēnei whare pūkenga.

Jade
Karekau aku pātai e toe ana. Ko te mea matua ki a au, ko te whakarongo ki ōu whakaaro e pā ana ki tēnei whare ātaahua.

Lynda
Āe. Koinā. He whare ātaahua. He whenua ātaahua tēnei. He whenua rongoā. He whare rongoā tēnei, he whenua rongoā.

Jade
Ngā mihi i te takoha o ōu whakaaro e pā ana ki tēnei whare. Mīharo ki a au te tātai ki Te Miringa Te Kakara. Kua kite au i ētahi whakaahua o tērā whare, kua whakaaro au e pā ana ki tērā whare i ngā wā maha. Ko taku hiahia, ā tōna wā, ko te whakatū i ētahi atu whare pērā i tērā, hei whakatū anō i ngā wānanga tawhito.

Lynda
He kōrero anō tērā.

Jade
Āe. Engari e pā ana ki te hoahoanga, he mea mīharo ki a au tērā whare. E hiahia ana au ki te ako tonu.

Lynda
Mō ngā tamariki mokopuna o taua whare, he whare mō ngā tamariki mokopuna. Ki ahau. Magic happens. And so, koinā ngā whakaaro i roto i ahau e pā ana ki tēnei whare, to do with the room. To do with all the external doors. Of course, the shape is nothing like Te Miringa Te Kakara. But you know there are āhua in here.

Jade
Āe, he maha ngā āhuatanga i roto i tēnei whare e pērā anai ō tērā whare.

Lynda
Ngā mea i roto i tēnei whare i kitea i tērā whare.

Jade
E hāngai ana ki tērā.

Lynda
Me te whanaungatanga ki a Rakataura.

Jade
Rakataura?

Lynda
Ko Rakataura te tino tohunga o Tainui waka.

Jade
Nē? Ka pai. Āhua mōhio.

Lynda
Familiarity, ki ahau. Ērā momo. Familiar. Familiar. Not quite understanding what, but definitely a familiarity. Āe. Koinā te whakaaro. Whanaungatanga i tēnei whare ki te whenua nei, ki a Rakataura, ki Te Miringa Te Kakara. Ki taku mahi ā-whenua ki Rangimatarau 1991 hoki. Āe. Mauri ora.

Puukenga nestles among the trees near a stream that runs through the Unitec site. The metal-clad classrooms have concealed spouting behind the roofline that breaks through the exterior walls in elegant spouts. *Samuel Hartnett*

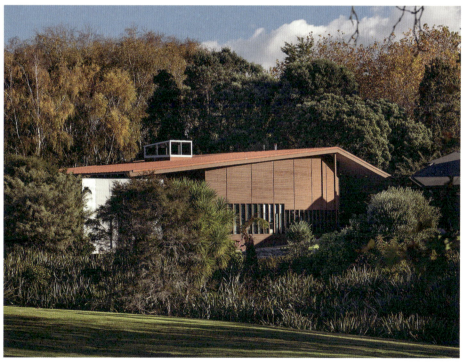

The following is an edited excerpt from an article by Rewi Thompson, published in 1995, in which he discusses aspects of the design concept for Puukenga.[1]

Design Process

The puukenga symbol designed by Kahu Te Kanawa became a 'communication tool' to initiate discussions, provoking thought, organising a broad range of topics, and developing the kaupapa (brief).

This symbol was adopted as the basis for generating two- and three-dimensional (models) design techniques that were comprehensible and sensitive to concerns, and the ways in which these concerns were resolved.

Tikanga / Cultural Protocols

Kaumātua John Turei reflected the knowledge, leadership and wairua (spiritual) wisdom of the project. This was incorporated into the building by traditional rituals such as karakia (blessing of the site), the placing and lifting of tapu, and guidance to all those involved.

Protocols such as the pōwhiri (welcoming ceremony) for the ancestors were observed as part of the construction stage. Such traditions were not exclusive, allowing all people, including students, construction workers, polytechnic hierarchy etc. to be involved.

Ngā Rama

The lighting design for the auditorium refers to the night sky. The tāhuhu (ridge beam) defines the Northern and Southern skies. The primary celestial bodies (light fittings) were positioned within the space, just as they appear in the night sky.

For example, the fluorescent fittings refer to the large and small Magellanic clouds, and four spotlights over the student informal space refer to the Southern Cross etc. The positioning of light fittings in a more practical sense identify task areas and highlight spaces for artwork.

1   Rewi Thompson, 'Rewi Thompson architect' [collection of two articles on two projects, the Puukenga Māori Education Centre at Carrington Polytechnic and the housing complex at Rata Vine, Wiri, for the Housing Corporation of New Zealand], *Transition* 47, 1995: 20–31.

Education

Whakapapa — The Creation

Wāhine Toa (Women)

Papatūānuku (Earth mother) connects to the environment, in this case as 'life giving water'. Women in this sense symbolise preservation, continuity of life (birth), and the umbilical link child, mother and the gods.

The threshold (point between physical outside world, and spiritual inside world), is experienced and expressed by the woven puukenga panels (doors), and the entrance 'journey'. The entry signifies the entering into the domain of women or womb.

The water element as a spring, the visitor guided between diverging walls (to accentuate the 'journey between outside/ inside or physical/spiritual' etc.), defined by Haare Williams as 'walls of discovery'.

The entry is completed as the visitors emerge (from walls), descend (steps), and are met by Hine (pouihi). The karanga (call) is reflected in the shape of the walls and screens. These walls are embellished with artwork and concave, as to clothe, protect and nurture the occupiers.

Tāne (Men)

The classrooms are arranged as three sets of twin rooms. Ngā kete o te mātauranga (the baskets of knowledge). These rooms are portrayed as the male influence in Puukenga to protect and complement the female influence. For this reason, the classroom design expresses the male principle (rational and pragmatic).

The external appearance reflects an ordered and formal format. The interiors are practical and focused. This relates to good natural lighting and ventilation, soft wall linings and earthy colours. The traditional male role as teacher is reflected by the spatial relationship of the pouihi (staffing area), kaumātua (portraits on walls) and students (classrooms).

Ngā Whakairo

The Puukenga building incorporated artwork as a necessary and integral part of the design. The carving, by carver Blaine Te Rito, represented the primary ancestors of the Māori.

The pouihi is the focus of the building. It is positioned so that all visitors are welcomed, and its presence is felt throughout the building. The pouihi emerges from the 'underworld' surrounded in water (the spiritual umbilical link). Hine emerges as the representative of Women. Kupe, Māui and Tāne are symbolic of many human principles.

Tāne is inverted, his feet pushing against the sky (separation from his primaeval parents). The skylight dramatises this act. When it rains, the 'tears' of Ranginui are seen to fall upon Papatūānuku and 'his family' (the act of Aroha).

Whakapapa (carving)

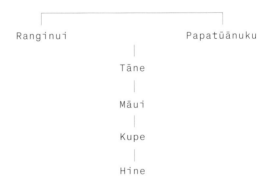

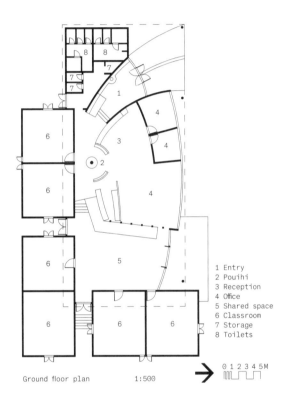

Ground floor plan 1:500

1 Entry
2 Pouihi
3 Reception
4 Office
5 Shared space
6 Classroom
7 Storage
8 Toilets

Waikato-Tainui College for Research and Development

Hopuhopu
Ngāruawāhia

2000

With Chow:Hill Architects

Education

Rewi 'absolutely understood the magnitude of the project', says Sarah-Jane Tiakiwai of his contribution to the design of the Waikato-Tainui College at Ngāruawāhia. *Erica Sinclair for Waikato-Tainui College for Research and Development*

The Waikato-Tainui College for Research and Development was Rewi's second major education project. In many ways, it was a fundamentally different project to Puukenga. Waikato-Tainui was the client, and the college represented the bold vision of Sir Robert Mahuta, Waikato-Tainui leader and principal negotiator of the Waikato Raupatu Claim, the first historical Treaty of Waitangi grievance settled with the Crown, for a contemporary, tribal wānanga, drawing on the best of old and new knowledge to create a site for the production and transfer of knowledge for the benefit of Waikato-Tainui uri.

In this project, Rewi's facilitation skills and ability to grapple with tribal whakapapa, stories and histories and interpret these architecturally were especially valued, and his connections to the Kīngitanga through Ngāti Raukawa acknowledged.

Rewi worked on the college project in collaboration with Chien Chow and Richard Hill, as part of a Chow:Hill-led team that won a design competition for the college.

Dr Sarah-Jane Tiakiwai (Waikato-Tainui, Te Rarawa), now Deputy Vice-Chancellor Māori at Te Whare Wānanga o Waikato University of Waikato, was the college's inaugural academic director and a member of its development steering committee. Here she reflects on the development of the college, her experiences working with Rewi and the college's ongoing legacy.

The main pou, carved by the late Wikuki Kingi senior and his whānau, is the focal point of the building. The pou is 18.2 metres in height and spans two storeys within the void adjacent to the main stair. *Erica Sinclair for Waikato-Tainui College for Research and Development*

Education

Jade Kake

Could you start by sharing a bit about Sir Robert's vision for the college as a contemporary form of whare wānanga that also drew on what he'd learnt and experienced internationally?

Sarah-Jane Tiakiwai

The college is first and foremost a memorial to the raupatu, and a memorial to all that was disrupted. Considering our traditional whare wānanga was an opportunity to really think about what a modern construct could look like for us. In the context of the other wānanga that we have, which have different purposes, what does it mean for the tribe? In the context of raupatu, the confiscation of land, it was the loss of opportunity to continue those sorts of practices. Certainly, it wasn't about trying to replicate what had happened, but to remember and to never forget.

Clearly Sir Robert had a vision of what it meant to imbue these qualities and to hark back to the traditions of our own wānanga and the idea of noho wānanga, and to recreate that in a modern context. But equally he drew on his own experience of being at Oxford, which he felt was similar in the sense of wānanga and the concept of wānanga — colonial constructs aside. Because of those experiences, he thought that the physical manifestation of that could be achieved at the college.

I think it was really an opportunity for him to provide a physical space for us as a tribe, to think about that legacy of our tūpuna. To remember that we were always learned people, we were always interested and had expertise in different areas of knowledge and specialisations that existed across our whare wānanga — not just in Waikato-Tainui but across the motu — principles of valuing knowledge, valuing learning, the whole process and importance of learning. Yes, the college was one such space for learning, but he was also clear that for some of our cultural practices you don't come to the college; you go back to the marae. He was clear that the college wasn't to replicate or replace our marae.

Jade

Different context.

Sarah-Jane

Different purpose. For some people it might be the entry space to go back to marae, but primarily it was that these knowledge centres are important. They were important then, and they continue to be important now and should remain important into the future.

Jade

Wow. What a long-ranging vision.

Sarah-Jane

Very much so. I think at the time people just thought it was crazy.

Jade

Bit ahead of his time. They didn't get it, but maybe they got it later.

Sarah-Jane

I think so. I think the legacy is where mātauranga Māori is now, which wasn't really even being considered back when the college was first being built. Although we've come a long way, we've still got a long way to go. I think it's also about, in the traditional whare wānanga, honouring the different forms of knowledge, which includes cultural arts, design and all of the knowledge and thinking that comes into the design process. So, without it being really obvious, the college pays tribute to that. The physical building is really a manifestation of our knowledge, but in that design space.

Jade

You were on the steering committee for the project, but did you also have a day job? What was your role at that time?

Sarah-Jane

I was doing my PhD. I was employed as a research fellow by the Centre for Māori Studies and Research, which was contracted by the tribe. I was based out at Hopuhopu, near Ngāruawāhia, with Sir Robert, so he was technically my boss. I was part-time while I was doing my PhD. I kind of waxed and waned between going part- and full-time, but I worked full-time on the college project.

A team of project managers looked after the design and construction, and a committee oversaw the project. My role on the committee was secretary. Denese Henare was the chair of the working party, which was what you would call a project governance group. I oversaw all the monthly reporting and made sure that Sir Robert was briefed.

I was also the liaison with the project team. When they needed to talk to somebody in the tribe, I would go and find out if they needed a kaumātua, a decision from Sir Robert, or somebody else. At points, part of my role was to liaise with, and bring together, our kaumātua so that the designers could talk to them about certain things.

Jade

What were your experiences working with Rewi?

Sarah-Jane

I engaged with him on the project from when it was up and running through to its completion. Chow:Hill were the architects for the college. There was a design competition, and it was an opportunity for different groups to put forward their whakaaro about what it was that they thought the college could be or could look like.

When Sir Robert gave the brief for the college, it was as an eclectic range of sayings. He talked about 'Māku anō e hanga i tōku nei whare, ko ngā poupou he māhoe, he patatē, ko te tāhūhū he hīnau', Kīngi Tāwhiao's tongi. He also talked about 'Kotahi te kōhao o te ngira e kuhuna ai te miro mā, te miro pango, te miro whero', Kīngi Potatau Te Wherowhero's tongi, as well. But then he took phrases from the Bible, Exodus 3:5: 'Nā ka mea ia, kaua e whakatata mai ki konei; wetekina ōu hū i ōu waewae, ko te wāhi hoki e tū nā koe, he wāhi tapu.' So when you come into the space, you take off your shoes as an acknowledgement of the sacredness of the space. Then, because he really liked English literature, Sir Robert had — I think it's Wordsworth? — 'Earth has not anything to show more fair . . .'

Chow:Hill brought Rewi into their design mix because they — Richard Hill being English and Chien Chow Chinese — thought it would, given the kaupapa of the project, be helpful to have somebody who was Māori on the team. The Chow:Hill and Rewi Thompson design wasn't obviously Māori, in the sense that it didn't evoke a waka or some other discernible Māori shape. I think part of why it resonated was that it was seen to have an international focus, but also as very grounded in a kaupapa that was uniquely Māori.

Education

Opposite: The entry to the college. 'My recollections of Rewi throughout [the design] process was that the relationship wasn't one where he was only speaking to the Māori aspects of the project,' Sarah-Jane Tiakiwai says. 'He was more, I think, the expert advisor and he came in at the points he was really interested in. *Erica Sinclair for Waikato-Tainui College for Research and Development*

Below: 'The physical building is really a manifestation of our knowledge,' says Sarah-Jane Tiakiwai, who was on the steering committee for the development of the Waikato-Tainui College. The design, she says, 'wasn't obviously Māori, in the sense that it didn't evoke a waka or some other discernible Māori shape. I think part of why it resonated was that it was seen to have an international focus, but it's also very grounded in a kaupapa that was uniquely Māori.' The residential components of the building are contained in the three wings at right. *Erica Sinclair for Waikato-Tainui College for Research and Development*

One of the things that I do remember, particularly with the old people associated with the project, was that people resonated with Rewi because he was Raukawa. They felt that those Kīngitanga connections were really important, and they were comfortable with that link between Raukawa and Waikato. It wasn't as though that was the thing that got the project over the line, but because of that relational and whakapapa connection — and the relationships between Raukawa and Waikato, specifically — some of the old people felt a level of comfort, knowing that he was from there.

At the time that the college was being built, it was such a new concept for us as a tribe. He absolutely understood the magnitude of the project, and guided us through it, in terms of subtleties in design, things that we didn't necessarily think of but that he had imbued into the design. For example, when we started to think about the naming of each of the three settlements or residential wings, we talked about them as māhoe, patatē and hīnau. Rewi suggested we slightly change the finishing on the doors of each of those settlements to represent the different woods. He got that. For us, it was an opportunity to work with somebody who we wouldn't necessarily have to explain those things to.

He understood what kinds of things would be important to the tribe and had already put those into some of the design elements. He was a very humble person from what I recall. Obviously he knew his stuff, but he worked in a way that was unassuming. I have dealt with people before who come across as, 'Well, this is who I am, and I know this, and I know that, and you listen to me.' But he came across as, 'Well, this is what we're here to do, and how do we bring this to life?' The old people really resonated with that. He understood what was important implicitly and that was reflected in the way that he worked and in the way that he approached the project. I think he understood the magnitude of it without making a big deal about it.

Jade

A lot of people have shared that same kind of kōrero — that he was very humble, he didn't come in all flashy and trying to be, 'This is me.' A few people have said that he was authoritative, but without trying to be authoritative; it was just that he was quiet. When he did speak, people listened.

Sarah-Jane

When you're in these design meetings, you've got things such as budget constraints and so on. But we always had our kaumātua in those meetings as well. I would like to think that he took his cue from them in terms of how they were feeling. What was it that they were talking about? What was it that they were sharing that was important to them? Obviously when Sir Robert was in those meetings, everybody would listen to what he had to say, but Rewi just seemed to navigate his way through that. It wasn't a big challenge.

The other thing I remember is that he created a space for Chow:Hill. There were times when we had meetings with Chow:Hill without him. I think that they understood enough about the cultural considerations, and we got to a point where they were really comfortable with the old people, and the old people likewise were comfortable in those discussions. My recollections of Rewi throughout that process was that the relationship wasn't one where he was only speaking to the Māori aspects of the project. He was very much part of the team, although Chow:Hill were the lead. He was more, I think, the expert advisor and he came in at the points he was really interested in.

I don't think they ever relied on Rewi to be that Māori māngai for them. I think they were clear. I think it was probably due to his mana that he was able to assert, 'That's not my role. I am here because I have this expertise and I'll bring that expertise to the project, but I'm not going to do . . .', what we now call now cultural loading. 'That's not me, that's not my role.' It never came across that way. He was never kind of trotted out as the Māori architect who will answer our questions if we didn't know what the Pākehā or the Chinese person had to say. I certainly felt that he was there under his own mana and not there to try to appease us as Māori or to represent Māori.

Jade

Yeah, it was more of a genuine collaboration, but with Rewi bringing certain expertise and certain things like his whakapapa with him.

Sarah-Jane

Yep, absolutely. I think the end product captures exactly Sir Robert's vision. It is an international college, but when you arrive, you know that you've arrived in the heart of the Kīngitanga and the heart of Waikato, and then it's complemented by all the other artworks around it. This is effectively the tribe's whare wānanga. The most modern construct was Fred Graham's pieces coming up the hill in reference to the traditional whare wānanga that used to exist, reinforcing that message that we've always been like this as a people. We will continue to be like this as a people. Continue to wānanga, continue to value knowledge, and continue to come together and produce knowledge, and new knowledge.

Jade

What can you tell me about the artists who also worked on the project?

Sarah-Jane

We had some great artists. Fred Graham did the pou coming up the hill. The two pou at the side were designed by his son Brett and supported by Eugene Kara. They tell stories of the Pai Mārire and also the raupatu. Inside the building, the main carvings were by Īnia Te Wīata, and the Rawiri whānau did the piece about coming from Hawaiki. Warren McGrath did the piece on Māui. Then around the corner you've got Tāwhirimatea, Tangaroa . . . that piece was done by the Ngākete whānau from Ngāti Tamaoho. The big main pou was carved by the late Wikuki Kingi senior and his whānau. So, a collection of both contemporary and traditional artists. I initially thought, 'How would this work?' But it does.

Jade

It all comes together. I was struck by the carving that goes over the double-height space. I'd never seen anything like it, and when I first went there I was amazed.

Sarah-Jane

The installation of that was something. They had to drop it in using a vertical crane. The roof had been installed already, and it was down to the millimetres in terms of the parts of the roof that they'd left open to drop the pou in. The glass was in place, so you can imagine a lot of navigating to get that in.

Jade

Did you have anything else you wanted to share?

Sarah-Jane

Just to re-emphasise the importance, reflecting back now and talking to some of the old people who were a part of the project, of Rewi being from Raukawa. Like I said, it wasn't why he was involved in the project, but it almost seemed as if it was a natural thing that he'd be involved because of his connection. I don't know how you can explain it, but some things are meant to be. Because the intent of the college was to be for the motu, and to have an international focus, it made sense to have somebody who wasn't from the tribe to have such a critical input. The fact that he was from Raukawa, and had that critical input at the design phase, I don't think was an accident.

When I think, 'What's the legacy?', it's Sir Robert's building and vision and legacy, but Rewi's contribution, in a very small way, cements the importance of those connections of whakapapa, connection to kaupapa. The way in which the college has come about underlines the importance of those things. I'm not a design person, but that's what I take from it every time I go back to the college. I think of those relationships, connection, the contribution that people have made to the kaupapa of the tribe, of the Kīngitanga, but in the context of the building I always reflect on people like Rewi, Richard Hill, Chien Chow, all of the team who contributed, all of our artists who contributed. The project was of its time, and he was the right person to be a part of bringing that vision to life.

Drawings from Rewi's archive featuring elevations of the college. Architecture Archive, University of Auckland

Education

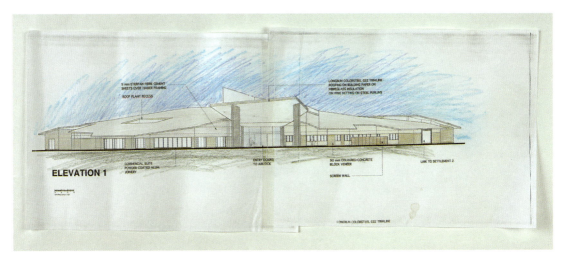

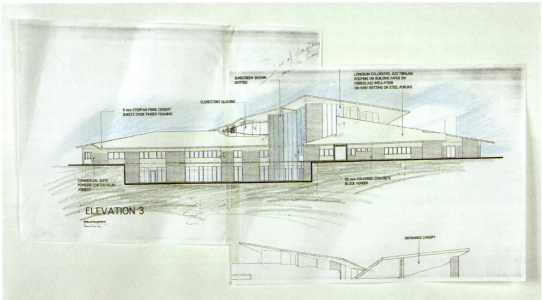

WAIKATO ENDOWED POST GRADUATE COLLEGE
Developed Concept Design   98018 / DD / 14B SEPT. 1998

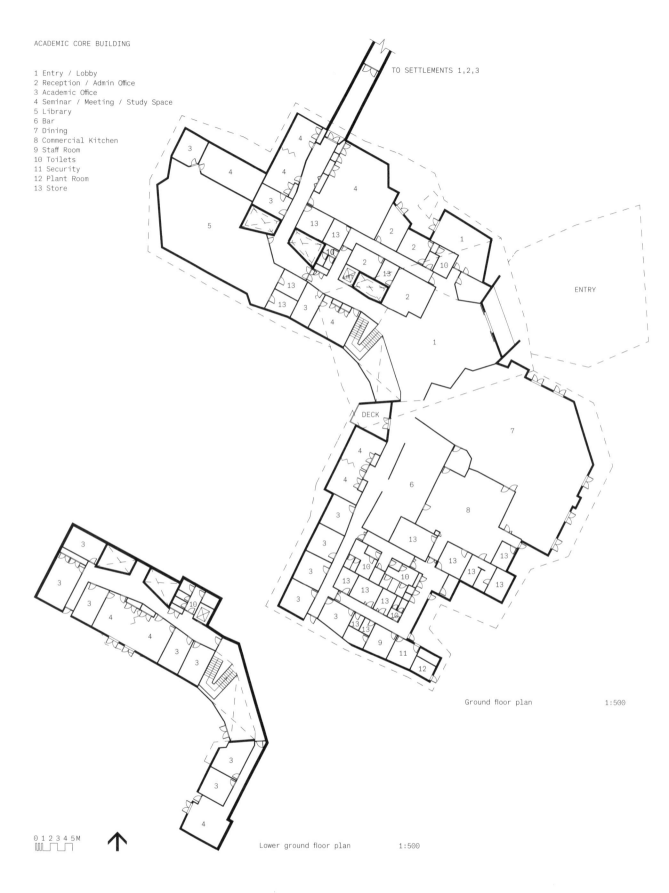

Interviews
— pedagogy

Ngā uiuinga
— mahi ako

Ki te kore e whai hua ētahi atu i tō whai
mātauranga, moumou te whai
If others don't benefit from your pursuit of
knowledge, it's wasted

Deidre Brown

In 2002 Rewi Thompson was appointed an adjunct professor at the University of Auckland's School of Architecture and Planning, where he taught and worked with colleagues to develop a more culturally responsive curriculum until he moved full-time to Isthmus Group in 2015.

During this time he introduced hundreds of students to the principles of Māori design, encouraging Māori, Pākehā and Tauiwi to utilise them with confidence and respect. His friend and colleague Professor Deidre Brown (Ngāpuhi, Ngāti Kahu) told us he championed the contribution of women, Pākehā and Pasifika students as co-tutors and practitioners.

Jade Kake

Deidre, I'm really interested in where Rewi fits within the broader tradition and trajectory of Māori art and architecture. I know you've written quite a bit about this, but I'd like to understand him at a certain point in time: how he's built on what's happened previously, but also how he's influenced what's happened since.

Deidre Brown

I'd regard him as a bit of a visionary. You've got John Scott and also Bill Royal, Wiremu Royal, going through the architecture school just after the war, and very much working in the modernist tradition of architecture. So, Rewi came to it, but with a completely other way of seeing the world, and seeing the relationship between building and the natural environment. It must have been informed by his own upbringing because he brought it with him.

The little bit that I know about his sister, who taught Māori art history at the University of Canterbury and was also an accomplished music composer when she was at secondary school, means it sounded like they were both gifted children and that they had this other insight into not just the Māori world but the Pākehā world as well, and were able to bring it together intellectually. This is the kete of knowledge that he brought with him to the school, where he had a very strong understanding of the conceptual basis of architecture. And he had no worries upending what was considered the standard way of working.

Word got around that there was this new person in the school, and everyone should come and watch him crit because he had this whole other way of seeing the world. He was moving towards a post-modernist way of thinking. He had this ability to think about the outside formalism of a building and how it related to the wider landscape around it, how it fitted into Aotearoa New Zealand, how it fitted into the city, the idea of the building as a symbol or a tohu that speaks out to people who are moving past it and not just moving through it.

If I was using strict historical architectural terminology, he's beyond the modernist period. He moves into this other period of working in New Zealand architecture and he was very, very good at it.

When we look at his work, he had that period of working which was just before the stock market crash. He went on a tour of North America, I think, with other architects. There was money around and he was able to work on projects. Then as we move through the stock market crash, architects had to think about working in other ways. There seemed to be what some regard as a fallow period in Rewi's work, where he wasn't designing a lot of houses or buildings. I think the intersection of the stock market crash probably put the hold on what was emerging as a very promising practice that he had established at the time. Of course, some people came out of that better than others. I suspect he was of the group of people that didn't come out of that so well.

But actually, when we look into his archive and you talk to people who were working with him, what he did was what others did later on, like Rau Hoskins. He was doing a lot of consultancy on much larger projects.

So we see him working, for example, on the Mason Clinic, the forensic mental health secure facility for people who have committed quite serious crimes, but they're subject to the Mental Health Act so they're not treated like regular prisoners. They live in that facility for the rest of their lives. That was just after the Mason Report had come out. Rewi was able to interpret those ideas within the Mason Report into this space.

They wanted to move beyond just 'Māorifying' a building by putting up great artworks — which is what we see, for example, at the Auckland High Court, which was about the same time — but actually thinking about the spaces and how they worked in terms of kawa and tikanga Māori so that families visiting could enter in with mihi whakatau, or pōwhiri, and that would not interrupt the facility and others would not interrupt the flow of the passage of those people into those buildings. There were going to be kaumātua rooms, because the Mason Report said that people will get better if whānau are involved in their care. Rewi's design really embedded that in. He worked on Ngāwhā prison as well, as a consultant, and so there were probably a series of these consultancies.

Jeremy Hansen

You worked with him for many years. What was that like?

Deidre

I began to engage with him when I returned to the school to teach and we got paired up for teaching. I think it was partly because I was such a straight up and down academic. They thought that I could do the paperwork better than Rewi could and that he was so creative and that we were both Māori, so we should naturally be together. So we formed this supervision team, teaching in the studio but also co-supervising the master's thesis students as well. I got to see his teaching up close.

When we taught studio, the thing that really struck me was that he never gave up on a student. He and I, particularly him leading, would spend a lot of time with those struggling students to find something within their work. He never gave up on them and he always found something. Some of them just made this rocket progression from where they were when they began and where they were at the end because of that.

The concepts that we were dealing with, which were really fundamental Māori concepts, he was able to talk to them about. He also brought out things within their own cultures. I remember there was a young woman who was an exchange student, I think she was from Scandinavia, and he managed to connect with her over the idea of the long, dark night, when they have those long, dark winters. You could see that instantly clicked with her and her project moved to being set in a night-time space and he was able to work with her to develop that.

Another one was a student who was of Chinese descent who was very interested in the fundamental things that underlay the physical environment. So he brought her down into this metaphorical space of darkness and she was able to work with ideas of the dark to be able to develop her work. They were really creative, fundamental concepts that he was able to make a connection to with the students' own background.

He was interested in the studio projects, particularly around the idea of extended family living and how that might be demonstrated through housing. He would use other works of art — he was very interested in Robyn Kahukiwa, whom he described as a cousin, so we'd often start with images of Robyn Kahukiwa. He told me many times that the way that she depicted the world was the way that he saw it. Of course, she in her early works depicted the idea of people living in the city but having Māori ancestry and how those two worlds came together.

Jeremy

One of the most tantalising projects in his career is the one he worked on with Ian Athfield and Frank Gehry: the unsuccessful design for Te Papa. What do you know about that?

Deidre

His concept for Te Papa — and I suspect it came from him — was based on the idea of a feather. But one of the kaumātua on the advisory committee said that the feather was a sign of defeat. Once he said that, the whole thing was off. Whether or not the feather is a symbol of defeat, I'm not sure. It can be a symbol of identity. Feathers can mean different things in different rohe, but that, I believe, signalled the end of that project progressing any further.

Had he gotten that project, that would have been transformative. Obviously there was a lot of work with the Te Papa project for the people that did win. To have that overarching concept of the feather and the recognition of that work, you can imagine the publicity that would have followed on from that. That must have been incredibly disappointing for him, particularly when his tikanga and his kawa was quite strong in itself. That would have struck at a cultural nerve as well, because from his perspective, I don't think he would have seen that as a mistake or read it in that way. Otherwise, why would he have done it? That was really the big project as we came out of the stock market crash.

Jade

Can you think of examples that characterise his approach to some projects? There are some outlandish visions in his archive. We've become so accustomed to this narrative of blending into the land, but he wasn't always interested in that.

Deidre

There was one design studio where I offered a site which was from our whānau, which was up north at the Rangihoua pā site. It was a site with tremendous history because it was also the site of the first organised mission station, the first Pākehā settlement in Aotearoa. Rewi loved it. We walked the land with the local kaumātua who's one of my relatives. It was this great rolling landscape, this big, epic open space. Rewi said a big landscape deserved big architecture. It could have been so easy to dig in and make little hobbit versions of buildings and things. No, Rewi wanted the students building skyscrapers and into the ocean.

It was this idea that big landscapes deserve big architecture. That was really important to him and it opened my eyes to a way of working with landscape. Some of the students that we worked with in our teaching worked within the school themselves as design tutors; you can see that Rewi kind of thinking coming through in the way that they teach.

Jeremy

If we're talking about his built work, which projects do you think were most significant to him?

Deidre

I think the fish canopy [at the Otara Town Centre] meant a lot to him. When Royal Associates were designing the marae and Māori studies complex at MIT nearby, they designed the complex as a hook, so it could be the hook for Rewi's fish. The community came and decorated the columns afterwards.

There was his own house. And there was a house up north on the Hokianga. And the Sumich house, which was a townhouse he did for a rugby friend. And there was the studio out west. We often talked about the Mason Clinic. I see that as a bit of a breakthrough project when it came to institutional

design because that was when he, and other architects, too, were pushing to raise the question, can you have a marae in a secure facility? They were pushing for kaumātua space as well. I know that these are difficult spaces, but he wasn't shy of working in them.

And there was the Ngāwhā prison, which was highly polemical for the Māori community there. Rewi did a talk about what they were doing. I think he said that because there was a degree of excavation involved, he described it as putting a moko on the landscape. I think he was proud with the work that he did at Ngāwhā in terms of that connection out to the landscape.

Jade

I found the Ngāwhā prison particularly interesting because there are so many issues around it. Just from a general perspective, there's a lot of ethical issues around whether we should even *have* prisons. But then we're still trying to mitigate harm and create good outcomes in the situation we're in currently. We went there, my first thought was to walk through the grounds, and it felt very different to how I expected. Then we arrived at the whare and went through a pōwhiri. The prisoners welcomed us. Then we had an amazing cup of tea.

It did seem like a lot of the prisoners were engaged in meaningful and restorative work while they're incarcerated. I was struck by the cultural connectedness that was embodied in the programmes but also in the buildings. I'd love to hear more of your thoughts.

Deidre

Yes, those understandings of well-being, of tikanga, from a Māori perspective pervaded that work. It was this idea that every dwelling, because they have their own dwellings there, would have a maho, which looked out to the landscape.

The idea of containment, partial openness and then going out into a wider landscape, he connected that with the idea of healing and the passage of people from where they were going out into the world. He felt that if people could see the land, it would heal them. He had this strong idea of whenua being something that could heal people.

Interviews

Karamia Müller

Rewi taught Dr Karamia Müller, a lecturer at the School of Architecture and Planning at the University of Auckland, when she was studying for her bachelor's degree. It was a time when, she says, 'there weren't many people I knew of who were brown' among the students or the teachers at the school. Later, she worked alongside Rewi as his teaching assistant for a studio design project.

Here, she looks back on those experiences and the pathways Rewi opened for her and other students from Māori and Pasifika backgrounds.

Jade Kake
Thanks for meeting us, Karamia. In the book we're talking to people about Rewi as a family member, as an educator, as a friend, as an architect, as a colleague. And we're doing it in a pretty organic way, but it seems important to try to get a well-rounded view of him.

Karamia Müller
I'm happy to help.

Jeremy Hansen
How did you meet Rewi, and what were your first impressions of him?

Karamia
I would've met him the way he was part of the educator landscape when I was first at university. I'm going to carbon-date myself now, because my undergraduate degree was in the early 2000s — so make of that timeline what you will — and I guess at that time he was known as a professor and specialist in Māori design principles.

We're in a different time now, where Indigenous creative practices are being more recognised. But at that time there weren't many people there that I knew of who were brown, and were designing in a radical way that drew on Indigenous concepts. I knew of scholars, architectural historians and people working in the space from a traditional perspective, but there were almost no Indigenous architects I knew that had a fully-fledged career and had iconic buildings behind them. In a way, he was kind of this master. And I was always a bit nervous, actually, to throw myself into his orbit. I was a bit intimidated. I guess I was trying to find my own way.

So I first encountered him in the early 2000s when he was one of the teaching staff; where I came to really grow that relationship was in, I think, maybe 2014 or '15, when I was invited by the school to become his teaching assistant for a fourth-year studio design project. The project had this beautiful brief Rewi had created about dreams for the sea, and about that threshold and that connection between this urban space and the ocean.

The one thing that really stands out for me is his humble, generous openness to other people's perspectives and a willingness to consider them. It felt like if you were to enter into a kōrero with Rewi that everything was on the table. And everything was respectfully on the table: his way of facilitating was a bubbling up of ideas.

He had a respect for ideas and an exceptional talent for making ideas spatial. I've been in this industry for a while and I've never seen somebody take an idea and put pencil to paper and refine that idea with an instantaneous kind of creativity. It was incredible, and something I was lucky enough to witness as a teaching assistant to his paper.

He'd often facilitate what turned out to be an overflow of ideas. To me, it felt like the next phase of that teaching would be taking the intangible into the tangible world by sketching and really drawing out ideas for students and helping them find this architectural language. He did it with such grace and such openness and humility.

Jeremy
I don't want to label it necessarily, but it sounds like you're talking about someone who seems inherently gifted.

Karamia
I think so. There are a lot of stories about his gift. You know, people talk about him taking to paper with highlighters and deconstructing design expectations through his own natural talent. There are lots of stories about him pinning up papers at architecture school and having these incredible structures coming out of the ground, and imploding people's ideas of what architecture could be or should be. And coming from a place of te ao Māori. My experience definitely aligns with that narrative. He had a phenomenal talent that was nurtured through genuine curiosity.

Jade
I love that. I feel like it's a real talent to be able to translate cultural intangibles into something tangible; but of course, he wasn't just relying on designing it intuitively because he was also teaching students. So what did you see of how he taught students to think and practice in that way?

Karamia
I think he also had the technical know-how to back up some pretty radical design proposals. I remember a student talking about a way to mechanise parts of the waterfront, intentionally designing them underwater so they disappeared, to be submerged. And all three of us were working at this idea when Rewi produced a pencil and said, 'I think what you could do is this,' and you could see that for every junction that he drew, he sort of drew in section how it would work.

And for me, as an educator, to think that you might be able to teach a student how to submerge a city ... I mean, you want to be able to technically transfer that kind of possibility to students within the studio spaces. It's also uplifting and inspiring for them to be working in that way.

To see it done, that memory still sticks with me: sitting down and watching this section being drawn of how to sink a city. And the intention was to prioritise the ocean over capitalism. It was this kind of wild idea that suddenly through this drawing had given that aspiration materiality in a way that makes it fly. For students, and for me as a fellow educator, it's incredible.

I don't want to project onto him, but for me, it felt like a gift of transformation. That it's always possible, with design as the engine. That was one of the most incredible gifts I got from him. But I don't think he saw things as gifting, because he's actually way too low-key. His humility exceeds that kind of thing. It was who he was. He was quite a special person to work with.

Jeremy
You make it sound as if his work was underpinned by optimism as well.

Karamia
I think his general outlook was a positive one on students' work. I don't think I really saw anything negatively interpreted by him. It was always like an open interpretation where he spoke to the strength of work. He saw the potential of students' work, which is very easy not to when you've been there for a long time. The cycles of teaching can sometimes make you feel a bit cynical about students, but he seemed very positive in a great way.

Sometimes he wasn't so well, and he'd have to carefully manage his sugar levels. But even in spite of that, Rewi was always curious in a way that was bigger than our studio, bigger than the moment.

I think that's really powerful. I'm not sure how students thought about it, but that's definitely how I experienced it.

Jade
Something that really strikes me is the fact that a lot of people have described him as a philosopher. He has a philosophical way of thinking. And I think that he was able to blend that kind of utopian, transformative thinking with the pragmatic and the buildable and everything in between. Which I think shouldn't be unusual for architecture, but sometimes I think it is because often now, academics get to play in that philosophical space and people in practice are doing house alterations. Maybe it's because he was in practice and working as an educator that he was able to span that breadth.

Karamia
He definitely did for me. The way he opened conversations up — his generosity was very much about making space. He was very difficult to rush, really. I think that also gave a lot of permission to be philosophical. You felt that the right thing to do was to think deeply on something with him because he made that space possible. I like to think that he was intentional with the tempo and rhythm of things. There was a special philosophical pace to his practice.

Jade
When did you have Rewi as a teacher when you were studying?

Karamia
I took a paper on biculturalism that he taught with someone else. I suspect it was a period of time where I was socialising quite a lot. I didn't hand in the most detailed assignment.

Jade
But you did have him as a teacher, and then, when you returned as an educator, he was there as a colleague. Maybe the impact of that first part might not have been huge, from what you were just saying, but I'm curious to know how he influenced you across that trajectory, both in practice and then as an educator?

Karamia
I think just in being the kind of practitioner I was more familiar with. The people who made my built world,

and that of my family and communities, they looked like Rewi. Just seeing him in the school was comforting. I didn't quite grapple with what that meant at the time. But it was comforting to see him within the landscape of the school and also to see him actively teaching Indigenous principles, because my education was, for the most part, largely Eurocentric. The paper I took with him, the paper on biculturalism, was the first architectural paper that I remember being engaged with the politics of the country.

Later, when I felt more comfortable in my own skin and returned and did my master's and knew the sorts of things I was interested in and the values I wanted to teach by, seeing someone so themselves within a space that really demands a kind of Eurocentrism, seeing somebody so comfortably themselves, was very profound. Because it's very difficult, I think, within the ways different systems layer themselves and can make Indigenous designers not feel completely able to be themselves.

To see Rewi there as an educator gave me confidence to be my own version, to take up my own standpoint and feel at least confident to test ideas, and to feel confident that things happened over a long period of time — you don't need to get things perfect. He was very much, 'Speak from the heart and the rest comes,' and I took a lot of security from that: if you are genuinely yourself, you'll figure things out. That's not really something you get in studio papers or history or theory, so to hear that from someone so respected, so genuinely talented and open and curious, is valuable.

I was looking forward to more time with him. But in a way, he had taught me the things that I needed to know. And now working with archives, I feel, in a way, is another kind of relationship that I'm continuing with him and his practice.

Jeremy
How do you feel about the way he handled this potentially fraught area in which he's an Indigenous architect and teacher in a school that, as you said, has its own Eurocentric way of doing things, but he was able to make Pākehā and Tauiwi feel quite comfortable working

with Māori design concepts themselves? I wonder how you felt he pulled that off, because it's potentially quite tricky.

Karamia
I mean, he's Māori, so that's a big deal. I think he also focused on meaningful engagements with the material, with the problem at hand or the issue at hand. He took people where they were in terms of their cultural competency and respectfully challenged them to be better and to deepen their understanding in a meaningful way. It may have seemed intuitive, but I think he was very careful with his pedagogy.

I also think he made spaces safe. I know that 'safe' is a word that is thrown around, but when I say safe, I mean that ideas could be respectfully broached and challenged in a way that people felt as if they could keep progressing rather than being reprimanded around lack of awareness. In the biculturalism paper that I took with Rewi, you could immediately see the breadth. And even at that time, we had people from different backgrounds and the way we came to a bicultural model was challenged.

I think it was something that he thought about deeply, all the time, philosophically and practically, and he spent a lot of time working at it. He worked at making spaces safe for people to bring their ideas to the table, and then safe to accept the challenges that were made of them. He'd been working at that for a long time in a way that no other educator I've ever seen has done. Well, very few educators have worked at it for that length of time with that context.

Jade
I have a related question, which is around the idea of Rewi as a Māori modernist and how you bring modernism into a cultural context and create ways of working together. I think I'm on a long journey of trying to understand that, but I'd love to hear your perspective.

Karamia
That's a really interesting question because Deidre [Brown] made a case that modernism was to the detriment of aspects of Māori architecture, taking away ornamentation, and that had its own kind of impact.

Jade

Rewi's work reconciles these seemingly at-odds things.

Karamia

That's true.

Jade

I don't think there's a simple answer.

Karamia

I don't think so either. One point to consider when reconciling these things is how he thought all buildings had a lifespan. That probably sits in contrast to a modernist perspective on what buildings ought to do. So perhaps one of the ways he reconciled this was understanding that all buildings come to an end and they are returned to the earth. Maybe it doesn't make sense when we take into account a smaller period of time, but once we think of an expanded model that's more cosmological, maybe the way he reconciles it makes perfect sense.

I think he was somebody who had core beliefs and values and lived them out through his practice and his teaching. He was gently assertive, which to me is a very Pacific way of doing things as well. That struck a chord with me.

Jeremy

I wondered if you had a way of characterising the ongoing influence he has on the school, and perhaps on architectural education in general.

Karamia

I think if we didn't have a Rewi, there'd be a real gap to pick up or to think through. In the discipline we think through precedence as one way of developing a design method and validating a design methodology. So, in a very physical way, his buildings are that.

I think bringing practice to and enlivening a foundation of kaupapa Māori, animating it in the way he did, meant that we are not starting from zero. Thanks to him, we've got an archive, we have buildings, we have a pedagogy: a canon, in a way. I'm using a Western term, but for the purposes of a Eurocentric kind of degree, we do have a canon. So in terms of being able to transmit knowledge, Rewi's work is really helpful within the context of teaching.

Lama Tone

Peseta Faʻamatuainu Toʻotoʻoleʻaava Lama Tone is a sole architecture practitioner based in South Auckland, and a lecturer in the School of Architecture and Planning at the University of Auckland. He is New Zealand-born Samoan, with whakapapa and family chiefly titles to Lufilufi, Vaimaso and Faʻasitʻo Uta on the island of Upolu and Puʻapuʻa on the island of Sāvaiʻi. He also has ancestral links to Lapaha (Muʻa) in Tongatapu, in the Kingdom of Tonga, and Mecklenburg, Germany.

Lama had a previous career in professional rugby, and met Rewi as a mature student. Rewi was one of Lama's lecturers, and they later worked together. Here, Lama reflects on Rewi's philosophical approach to architecture, and on our spatial and genealogical connections across the Pacific.

Jade Kake

Rewi was one of your lecturers when you were studying, and then you were later colleagues. How was that for you as a student, to be exposed to his way of thinking?

Lama Tone

I came in as a mature student. I had stuffed up my neck playing rugby, so it was at a time of my life where I started asking, 'Who am I?' And going through university, especially architecture, made you think outside of the square. It was a brand-new world for me and I didn't miss rugby because architecture made you think, not worldly, it just made you think more about things in an internalised way.

But there were no Pacific lecturers at the university at that time. I had only come across the writings of Albert Refiti — which I loved — who was an academic across the road at AUT at that time. Then I also started hearing that Rewi Thompson was around; I knew who he was, and I loved what he'd done and his ideas around architecture. And so I started applying to be a student under Rewi. I know Pasifika and Māori people are very similar. Well, we have the same DNA, the same ancestry.

Just hearing Rewi speak made me feel at ease and comfortable, because he wasn't there in a flash suit or anything; he rocked up in his jeans and looked like he didn't wash his face most of the time. But that's what I love about it: he was a very genuine person. And easy to relate to. A Tongan brother who I went through the school with and I easily related to him because he was almost like one of the kaumātua in our cultures; he talked about shelling mussels and taking them to your relatives. Rewi had that and I appreciated that about him. He was really easy to chat to. And the words that came out of his mouth — because our culture is all about listening to the kaumātua and their stories and then them passing those on to you — that's what I appreciated about Rewi as well.

Jade

Obviously he had a real impact on you as a student, but how did you feel that dynamic change when you became

colleagues and you started working together more?

Lama

As an undergrad student I had met Rewi multiple times and I was a student of his as well, going through the school. And then I had the humble privilege and honour to co-teach a fourth-year paper with him, to do with papakāinga and his thoughts around that, working with a brief from Ngāti Whātua. It was a nice relationship that we formed over the years.

I got to see Rewi teaching students about the appreciation of things like whenua, moana and maunga. It was quite a powerful imprint that he left on the students, because all the students see is the glamour of an object, things that look like they've been dropped out of space but they have no context and no relationship to the environment.

Jade

I had that kind of education, that kind of traditional classic architectural education where it's very focused on the object. And I really struggled with that because I couldn't quite reconcile what I thought architecture was for, and how I wanted to practise, with what I was learning at architecture school; and it took meeting Māori and Pasifika architects who thought the way that I did, but were already doing it, to realise that there was a place for me in architecture and the kind of things that I was wanting to achieve could be done through architecture. That was the big thing that kept me in the profession. I think it might have made a difference for me if I had had a lecturer like Rewi when I was in my undergrad studies.

Lama

Yeah, it was nice to be on the other side of the table, on the other side of the fence, with Rewi when we did become colleagues. But to me, I was always a student to Rewi.

Jade

That doesn't change.

Lama

Everybody was. It didn't change whether we sat at the front of the class; I was always a student of Rewi Thompson right up until he passed; his views and his approach to architecture had a profound impact on my life.

Jade

How did that culturally based and philosophical approach impact the way you approach practice as a designer?

Lama

I drew a lot of parallels with Rewi's approach and it made me view the world and life a little bit more sensitively because Rewi had that kind of real sensitive outlook about stuff. He reminded me that the little streams and the awa were the life or the bloodlines of Papatūānuku. I had never come across an architect who actually talked like that, that appreciated the earth as a living being, as an earth mother. It was really nice to hear. It was philosophical. It really was.

That's the way I'm teaching my students now: I've passed that on because I truly believe in it. It took Rewi to tap into that for me and appreciate that that's what architecture should be, how people who have lived in this region for hundreds and thousands of years actually view Le Moana and the islands. Rewi reached in and pulled that out of me and many other students who have since gone on to do other things.

Jade

Something I appreciate about that kind of approach is that obviously it's very relevant for Māori and Pasifika students, but even students from other cultural backgrounds; it encourages them to tap into their own cultural context and bring that into their architecture and their perspective. That positionality is really important.

Lama

Yeah. I went through the school with Tongans and there weren't many of us. I mean, you can count how many Pasifika and Māori as well: when we went through the school, there were about ten of us. About four Pacific Islanders and the rest were Māori. There's mutual respect in the Pacific; when we come to New Zealand we understand the views of Māori. We had to respect that.

Jade

Yeah, everything should be under the korowai of mana whenua, and I feel that strongly, too, because I grew up in Australia. I was born and raised on Bundjalung country and I later lived in Turrbal territory and in a few other places. But I was mindful that the way that I would work there is very different to the way that I would work in Whangārei, and different again to how I'd work in Tāmaki Makaurau. But I think once you've been introduced to that way of thinking then you carry that wherever you go. And I think that's important irrespective of your cultural context because otherwise you risk recolonising through architecture. And you can do that as Māori or Pasifika people; we can if we're not mindful.

Lama

During that phase of me finding out who I was, I remember one conversation we had as colleagues. Rewi asked me, 'How far are the limits where you think you can design?' And I said, 'Look, wherever the Pacific Ocean touches, that's where.' And then I asked him, 'What about yourself?' And he said, 'Well, obviously design in Aotearoa. And then Cook Islands.' I think, because of the whakapapa connections.

So those are the kind of things that stuck in my mind, too. He talked a lot about Australian architecture in terms of the Aboriginal view. He said on one of those trips over to Australia with some students, they went to see some of the Indigenous people there and spoke about their philosophy on the world. He said it was beautiful. It was almost like you were a centre but you had a dome over you and this was the way that you viewed the world.

It was really nice and it made you feel safe, I think, especially as a young Pacific architecture student. It made you feel safe with Rewi because you knew that you were going to tap into something that you probably kind of already knew, but he made you feel that this is something you should know. Deidre Brown was another person who had a huge impact on me. She was my master's supervisor. She encouraged me to pursue a master's and PhD. It was great to have those leaders at the university. Especially for Pacific students.

Jade

I like those questions, 'Where do you feel like you can design?', 'Where do you feel you can go?' I think everybody should ask themselves that.

Lama

Yeah. I think it was interesting for me being a young colleague with Rewi teaching some of the Asian students and wondering how Rewi was going to tackle that, supporting those students to design here in Aotearoa with this Māori world view. It wasn't easy, but I think the students fell in love with just looking at things through a different lens. They were probably taught right up till third year about this Pākehā world view.

And then they went to fourth year and everything kind of shifts and Rewi's right in the centre, trying to bridge things between these students and what it's like here. But I do always remember Rewi saying, 'This is your home now. You come from that place: what do you bring here?'

Jade

That's so important. I think you get the best out of Tauiwi students when you relate it to their own cultural context because I've seen some of them show up thinking they have to leave that all at the door and be like Pākehā.

Lama

I've been blessed to teach third-year papers at uni, including third-year design in second semesters, which is the last design paper for the Bachelor of Architectural Studies. For that paper, I've taken them across to the islands probably five times in a row. We form a brief then, and we come back and they design something cool. In a lot of the ideas that we use, I try to draw on some views that Māori have that are the same as what Tongans and Samoans have. This idea of the extraction of Papatūānuku and Ranginui pulled together; and then you've got this offspring of light. There are similar stories over in Sāmoa.

We approach it in another way where we dig up a lot of the concepts, Pacific or Samoan, and try to create something that uses these ideas to approach the brief a little bit differently, so that we get another sense of identity within the building, but maybe something that's more relative to the people and the way they live. Some of the students have done really well. They find things interesting. Some students love how you approach a design problem with these beautiful ideas and out of it

comes a beautiful piece of architecture that relates to land and sea. So that's been a success, I think.

Jade

Being trained in New Zealand and also having Rewi among your lecturers: how did that kind of education influence the work that you've since done in the islands, but also for Pasifika communities in Aotearoa, and what are the differences?

Lama

The work that I do is not fancy visually or aesthetically. It's more about spatial responses. Creating spaces that are able to fit intergenerational living — for example, the older kids want to come back home and save money, yes, but they also want to live at home so that they can look after Mum and Dad. That's always been the case. I look at the Samoan clients that say, 'Look, our house is too small. When we have funerals or celebrations we have to hire a hall, or we put out a tarpaulin in front of the house.' They never complain; they're quite resilient.

They're always trying to make things work, but some of our people try to extend their houses just so that they can accommodate functions like that. In Aotearoa, there's been a shift, and the garage spaces have now become more the utility space for these multifunctional things to happen. Meanwhile, the living room in the back's not used much except by the elders, while the main family is in the garage space, or you've got a tangi that's there or somebody's twenty-first birthday.

My community, they're living in the diaspora. There are not many Samoans or Pacific Islanders doing what I do. So it's really nice when people connect with you in your own language or to know that another brown person can understand what it's like to live here in New Zealand. Another thing, too, is how our people don't understand council regulations and things like that. So it's nice for them to have a brown person that can explain it to them. And that has helped to some degree in trying to help some of our people here in South Auckland.

The only thing that they get a little bit iffy about is the cost of things.

Because they expect things to cost not as much as it actually does, and price is going up with materials and then there are RFIs (requests for information) from the council, and you drew the house today but why aren't we hearing the hammer tomorrow? I'm still broke as, being a solo practitioner here in Māngere, because there are not a lot of people who like the fancy stuff or can afford it; they just want four walls to go up to extend the back of their house so that they're able to function.

Jade

I feel like a lot of our Māori and Pasifika architects don't necessarily do the hero architecture but they do a lot of the smaller stuff that makes a tangible difference to people's lives. One of the things we've been talking about, Jeremy and I, is that maybe Rewi didn't quite get his dues in his time. He did do some of the big hero stuff, like the Te Papa proposal that didn't go ahead, and some public space stuff like the Ōtara fish canopy that's well known. But I think that doesn't get the flashy magazine articles, when you're doing these little alterations and things like that, which might be very meaningful for that whānau or make a big difference in that community but it's not hero architecture.

Lama

But thank God for those works now. For example, the fish canopy in Ōtara. It's mandatory for me to put that in my briefs every year. Not just that, but also Puukenga, and his house at Southern Cross Road. He had a few projects that are informing the next generation.

Jade

What do you feel is the enduring legacy and ongoing influence of some of these built projects?

Lama

I think Rewi is somebody I would call a tautai or highly skilful fisherman who can float in both waters, the deep end and the shallow end, bridging modernist and cultural values. He would self-identify as such: 'Look, I'm a modernist architect and I'm Māori.' So it was always something interesting in the two kinds of worlds.

Jade

How do you reconcile the two? Because

I always found that hard to understand. Rewi was doing it, but I don't think I have a full understanding of it because what I learnt about modernism at uni, a lot of it was removing ornamentation and anything cultural was seen as ornament. How do you bring those two things together?

Lama

I think the answer will be that only Rewi could do that and do it really well. I love the way he spoke about the projects. It's almost like you cannot have a building in front of you without the words to go with it. It's almost like his words became the aesthetics of the building. Rather than those physical things, the visual things that were removed, it's the words that came with it that really created mana for the building. I don't have any models or drawings of Rewi's, I only have his words. And those words are firmly implanted in my psyche and my thinking towards architecture. And about life.

I distinctly remember these conversations we had because I knew, just like with an older statesman in the village or an elder or a kaumātua, you always remember the words. A proverb that comes out of our culture in Sāmoa is 'E pala ma'a 'ae lē pala upu', which means, 'The stones may rot long before your words do.'

And this is my approach around Rewi. Even just watching him with students and trying to teach them about architecture, it was way more than just a building or a space, it was always about people. I distinctly remember waiting for the rain to stop when we finished the session on the ground floor at uni before we walked back to our cars. And he said to me — and I've never stopped thinking about this — 'Lama, my mum always told me to look after my people.'

Although we were talking about architecture and what it meant, what Rewi was trying to say was that it was about people and phenomena and all those beautiful ideas around family and communities.

Rewi knew who he was but he also had a very big interest in modern architecture. It was almost as though he was the custodian between the two — te ao Māori and modernist architecture.

He was almost bridging the two through words and simple sketches. He was a modernist architect, but his thinking was way beyond.

Amber Ruckes

Amber Ruckes (Ngāi Tūhoe) is a PhD candidate and teaching fellow at the University of Auckland School of Architecture and Planning. During her architectural studies, Rewi was Amber's lecturer for several design studio papers, and co-supervisor for her master's thesis. Here, she reflects on her experiences with Rewi as a teacher, mentor and guide, and his 'gentle navigation' approach to teaching.

Jade Kake

Do you want to talk about when you first met Rewi and what that experience was like?

Amber Ruckes

When I came back to Auckland Uni, Rewi's paper was the first one I took, and in some ways it was quite jarring, in challenging me to be more comfortable in te ao Māori. At that time, obviously, I knew about Māori architecture, though I wasn't especially familiar with Rewi's work. But I did know that I was interested in contemporary approaches to architecture as well as understanding the traditional processes. Now that I know more about what he gave to the community, particularly in the Māori and Pasifika context, I realise his manner was very soft. There were no formalities. When I meet some international architects that are coming in, they have great work. But it's a lot—

Jade

Flashier?

Amber

Yeah, a lot flashier. And his was just a gentle, very humble energy. There was this feeling that he wanted to be a part of this journey with you as opposed to directing you. So he would make space for you—

Jade

To grow and learn?

Amber

Yeah.

Jade

And it sounds like he was really present.

Amber

Yeah, even with his eyes closed. He wouldn't ask questions directly. He would—

Jade

Tell it like a story?

Amber

Yeah. He would tell it like a story. And after he left, you'd be sitting there going—

Jade

'So what was he trying to tell me?'

Amber

And then you'd just have to sit there for a while. So I had him in Design 5, and then Advanced Design 2, and then he was my thesis supervisor along with

Dr Deidre Brown. And definitely by Advanced Design 2, my friends knew that after I had my meeting they should leave me, because I'd be sitting there and staring at the ceiling and saying, 'He said this. Yes. Okay.' I just had to marinate in what he said. And then I'd come back for the next session, and it was different … I wasn't necessarily looking for a seal of approval in the same way as I would with other tutors.

I'm thinking back to when I was growing up, because I was living with my nan and koro for a bit, and they would show me how to do something, but then they wouldn't necessarily show me how to do it perfectly; they would say, 'Think about what you're trying to achieve and then create a path to get there.' And they would just watch and observe. If I was heading towards danger, they would voice up and bring me back a little bit. But I think that way of teaching was very much how I experienced Rewi's way of teaching. Particularly in academia, there's this thing where it's meant to be challenging—

Jade

But he didn't have that adversarial approach.

Amber

And he would subtly … I guess he was more empowering than challenging because he'd still (since I can't find another word) challenge you, but it would be in a different way that would allow you to—

Jade

Have a more expansive way of thinking, maybe.

Amber

Yeah. I guess he wouldn't challenge you for the sake of challenging. There'd be no ego. I've seen him in meetings — for example, when he did the Venice Biennale, and I was working at a practice at a time when they were involved as well. And he'd come and just listen, and I'd be doing my work and hearing other people talking. He would maybe contribute to 2 per cent of the conversation, but it would be a very rich 2 per cent. And he observed what everyone was saying and took on people's opinions. So when he said something, it had quite a lot of weight to it.

Jade

And people listened.

Amber

Yeah. I remember when he was teaching, he'd close his eyes—

Jade

So that he could listen better?

Amber

Yeah. Well, the first time I experienced it, I was like, 'Are you asleep?' But then he'd come back and he'd be like, 'You said this,' and we'd realise, okay, he is listening.

Jade

It's like those kaumātua on the marae.

Amber

Yeah, it's exactly like that. And they're just taking in everything.

Jade

A lot of people commented on how, especially as a teacher, even as a practitioner, he never seemed to be in a rush. Obviously, he always had heaps on, but didn't give that impression.

Amber

Yeah. For example, in Advanced Design 2, which was second semester fourth year, the way the brief was structured compared to the other briefs: by the time that mid-semester crit came, everyone else had building forms and stuff—

Jade

Like a scheme?

Amber

Like a scheme, or least a draft version of it. And he was like, 'Nope. Nope. Just keep exploring a site, keep exploring your concept, that experience.' He'd encouraged us to go out to talk to people in the community. I'd spoken to Te Puea Marae. And when I had my mid crit, I started crying when I was reciting the kōrero that I had learned on that visit. And I had no idea why. And Rewi simply said, 'Kei te pai, it's because you are actually feeling their mamae.'

And he always pushed those things to the point where he wouldn't let us, in that instance, do a building until three weeks until hand-in, but he wanted us to really dive into that wairua and massage those qualities, and to understand those aspects before we make those big design moves, so that, essentially, we didn't lose that.

Jade

I think that's such an important lesson, because even in practice now, I'm always banging on about process being more important than outcome, and holding back on having design ideas; even when you feel them starting to spill out, just consciously pulling yourself back so you take that time to listen and really understand the site and the people and the history, the opportunities, constraints. And then, only then, are you in an informed position to weave those together.

Amber

Yeah. And I remember a lot of us were quite—

Jade

Impatient maybe to get into the building?

Amber

Yeah, and maybe quite anxious because you'd see your peers with their beautiful drawings. And they'd started their renders and they were on track, and you'd still be—

Jade

You've got a cardboard model and some sketches.

Amber

Yeah. You've got sketches and they've got these interesting qualities that you've explored. But I think, too, because of that, that was probably the fastest design translation I'd ever made. One thing I say to students is, sometimes with architecture, you have to know when to stop designing, because you don't want to overcook it. But oddly, even though we were working quite slowly, the translation was quite seamless.

Jade

I'm sure there's a whakataukī about that idea of 'going slow to go fast'. Āta haere kia tere?

Amber

I think literally, even though there's a photo of Rewi in the staff room, every time I think about when I have conversations with my PhD supervisors around 'make this form', I'm like, 'Yes, I'll start making'. But often, I don't feel as if I have that information yet. And yes, I can keep making, but I'm conscious that I want to be quite intentional with what I do in this because of that influence from Rewi.

Jade

Yeah, and because you had those experiences with him and saw the outcomes of that way of working, you were able to stay true to your kaupapa and push back if there's pressure to keep making and producing objects and things.

Amber

One thing I tell students, there are so many different types of pretty, and Rewi's work was relatively raw. He definitely had lovely models. But going back to the conversation around process, those sketch models were just as precious as the final ones, and sometimes even had more weight, because of the formality of those ideas being translated into architecture, I think particularly acknowledging the architecture being practised in a largely Pākehā environment, you needed to make space for that broadness that was always welcomed in Rewi's briefs.

Jade

I don't know if you've seen many of them, but he had a massive collection of drawings when he passed, and his daughter, Lucy, donated them to the Architecture Library. We've been working our way through the archives. His drawings are really expressive, and we keep hearing from people that he was just drawing all the time.

Amber

Yeah, definitely drawing a lot. But, at least in my experience, he'd be drawing — he wouldn't draw the exact thing, if that makes sense, going back to your point about being expressive. It'd be just enough for you to say, 'I get it … wait, no, actually I don't.'

Jade

It's a little bit cryptic.

Amber

And you're thinking, 'Okay.' And it was definitely more than just 'What is architecture?' but rather, 'What could it be?'

Jade

And maybe to create those questions in your own mind as someone who's experiencing it.

Amber

I think even though he had that complexity, his ability to knuckle down and find the purest way to articulate all these complex elements is something I myself try to do.

Jade

Or that ability to distil complex ideas?

Amber

Yeah. And going back to the processes and holding back, that is just from observing what you've made, and more so, observing what you've made but just giving it more time to mature in its own way.

Jade

What was he like as a thesis supervisor? Because obviously, you'd had those experiences with some of his classes; but did you have quite a lot of one-on-one time while you were developing a thesis?

Amber

He was my co-supervisor, along with Dr Deidre Brown, but they always came together. By that time, I was confident with that team. At the same time, I was always conscious of thinking, when you've been exposed to someone for so long, does it still have that same newness? But I think his holistic way of allowing you to sit in those spaces, he didn't have that same — or he never expressed it anyway — urgency. It'd be like, 'It's fine.'

Jade

The pace you need to do this is fine.

Amber

Yeah.

Jade

Follow the process, go on the journey.

Amber

Yeah. And in a lot of ways, I didn't see too much transition. It was just building on the person I got to know in design studio. But it was almost like he did give that space … it made me stronger in holding myself in those spaces.

Jade

And he didn't have that expectation that you do things his way?

Amber

No. And gosh, even though in the back of my mind, he does remind me of my koro. I remember going to my koro and asking him questions and he would give me five different examples and let me sort it out. And so in some ways, indirectly directing, but not forcefully … I'm sure he knew what he was doing.

Jade

I think that's such a Māori way of teaching.

Amber

Exactly. He just gave you the space to figure it out—

Jade

On your own terms?

Amber

Yeah. He was very empowering. While developing my skills, I didn't actually realise how much of his way influenced or still influences me, particularly now as a teacher. And with this PhD now, there are so many times I wish he was here, because there's stuff that I wouldn't have had to explain.

Jade

He would just understand?

Amber

Yeah. And even those small nuances, small elements of support, are like a slow confidence building. It's like he's slowly placing little blocks to help you, help your foundation get stronger. I think particularly in that te ao Māori way, there was a strength that he gave you and he still had plenty of strength for himself. I don't know how else to explain it.

Jade

Did you ever teach alongside him?

Amber

No, unfortunately I didn't get to teach with him. But I do know that a lot of my processes, like when I'm writing design briefs now, are very much based on my briefs that I did with him.

Jade

So you've carried a lot of those lessons into your work as an educator, as well as research.

Amber

Yeah. Also, I think Rewi's lessons weren't necessarily just in architecture. But he wouldn't push things. When he was my supervisor or my tutor, and in his interactions with other people, he wouldn't push things unless he knew you were ready. And the pushing was a very soft push. When I look at teaching today, I try to model it based on his gentle navigation.

Mike Austin

Dr Mike Austin (Pākehā) is an architect and retired academic. Mike was instrumental in driving mainstream acceptance within academia and practice of Māori and Pasifika architecture as legitimate forms at a time when these were largely considered through an anthropological lens. Through his foundational work he has paved the way for the many Māori and Pasifika architects and architectural scholars who have followed.

Mike was a lecturer at the University of Auckland in the 1970s when Rewi joined the School of Architecture, and shares some of his memories and reflections on Rewi as a student, as well as his enduring legacy.

Jade Kake
I thought I'd start by asking you about when you first met Rewi. I was particularly interested in your perspective because you were championing Māori and Pasifika architecture as a thing back when people were saying it wasn't. And so I was quite interested to hear how that academic work and the advocacy work intersected with Rewi's work as a practitioner, and as an educator.

Mike Austin
I don't know what year he arrived at the School of Architecture. I don't remember the date. But certainly, he arrived. He'd been working at the Structon Group office, and his first-year project was an international airport in Auckland. He just wanted to get his teeth into some architecture, and, well, he did it. This was terribly impressive. I think I said at the time it would've got an A in third year. So he arrived as an extremely competent student. After this happened, I was really worried that he would a) get bored and b) be a loss to the school.

Jade
Could you just go work in architecture at that time?

Mike
Yeah. I just thought, oh, he can go back to Structon Group and say, 'Yeah, I've tried that.' And he wasn't the person to care about an academic qualification. So I suggested to the dean of the school, Allan Wild at that time, that he be allowed to skip a year so he could get through the course quickly. So that happened. I don't think that'd happen these days, but that's what happened then. And we worked out a way that he just . . . The main problem was how did he get through the subjects in that time? So he had to do a bit of extra work in the subject, but he was churning out architecture non-stop.

Jade
Yeah, I keep hearing he was drawing all the time as well.

Mike
Yeah. And so, when you have somebody like that, they're precious. Not that institutions always realise they're precious.

Jade
What was your role at the time?

Mike
I was just a teacher at the school. And the other thing that happened was that I started to become interested in Indigenous architecture. I was approached by a man who said he had a marae up north called Kenana Marae near Mangonui. He wanted us to go to this marae and do some designs for them, and I said, yes, okay. So I set up a studio, and Rewi came. I don't know what year he was in; it might have been first year, but I think it was more likely second or third year. But we went up there, and we were welcomed, and then we spent a couple of days in the house. The first night, Rewi was right down the end of the house, almost hiding. And the women were up the front knitting and talking and chatting. Then at one stage, one of them said, 'Well, this Māori boy down there, he'll know all this.' And everybody sort of looked at Rewi and he said, 'Who are you calling a Māori?'

Jade
Aue.

Mike
And he didn't want to be identified in that way.

Jade
At that time.

Mike
No. And he did a big drawing, which I can still remember, of the place. It was all whimsical and had sheep wandering in with the design. But it also had all sorts of other qualities. And he actually said it had been good, the experience, but he gave the impression he'd never been on a marae before. Now, I don't know whether that was true or not.

Jade
Yeah, it's difficult. That's actually been the trickiest thread to untangle throughout all of the stories of Rewi's life because you hear such conflicting but coexisting . . . It feels like it was a tension that was there throughout his life.

Mike
Yep. So that's my first contact with that. And then, I don't know that he came on any other trips . . . I wasn't really competent to take a group to a marae,

but we were getting requests. Because in those days, people didn't have dining halls and their marae were—

Jade
Oh, a lot of marae in the north were just halls; they just had the hall as the main building and nothing else.

Mike
Yeah. So we'd go to these marae, and it was an education for me, and the students were tagging along. There were two other students who were peers of Rewi at that time whose names were Mike Barns and Tere Insley, and the three of them were mutually supportive. I don't think Rewi came on any other marae trips, but Mike and Tere did, and they would often be our leaders by then. Sometimes they'd get a hard time from some of the elders. The elders would say, 'Quiet, tamariki.' I felt for them. I had started writing a thesis at that point because I think these marae experiences, I was thinking, this is really significant stuff that I want to try to understand. In some ways, what we were doing wasn't regarded as architecture.

Jade
At that time?

Mike
There was a general feeling that there was no such thing as Māori architecture and the idea of going out to a marae wasn't really architecture. So that was the context. A crucial moment for me was in his final year. And Rewi and I were at the Kiwi, which was the pub opposite the School of Architecture.

Jade
I've heard a lot about that. They went to the pub a lot.

Mike
It was very memorable for me. I was with Rewi one night, and I said, 'Rewi, you need to start taking this Māori architecture seriously.' And he said, 'No, I don't want to do that.' I think I said, 'Why don't you involve yourself in this?' Because he wasn't involving himself. And he said very clearly to me, 'I don't want to be a Māori architect, Mike. I want to be an architect.' And I thought, 'Yeah, okay.' He knew I respected him a great deal. So that was the agreement, that I wasn't going to try to force him to become a token. So I said to him at the

time, 'Well, good. You want to be a really important architect.'

Jade

I wonder if at that time, too, and maybe even still, the idea of being a Māori architect is seen as kind of lesser than being an architect, which is, implicitly, a Pākehā architect. But everyone's journey is different. And I think it seems that through the work that Rewi did do, he came to that work eventually, but in his own time.

Mike

Yeah, absolutely. And I respect him for that a great deal.

Jade

Did you have any reflections on the impact that Rewi might have had on New Zealand architecture or this idea of Māori architecture?

Mike

Well, I think it's quite important. It's because he was respected as an architect, but people didn't see his being Māori as taking away from that, anyway, but rather adding to it. So he had a lot of status in the school as an educator and so on. Always. Because he had a great architectural mind. He would always think of the other point of view.

Jade

Yeah. Something I've heard a lot is that the way he thought was interesting and different to other people.

Mike

Yeah. So he's interesting from that point of view. But that's his legacy, and everybody who came in touch with him felt this. He sort of lifted architecture in people's minds. He was always the architect. He was never anything else.

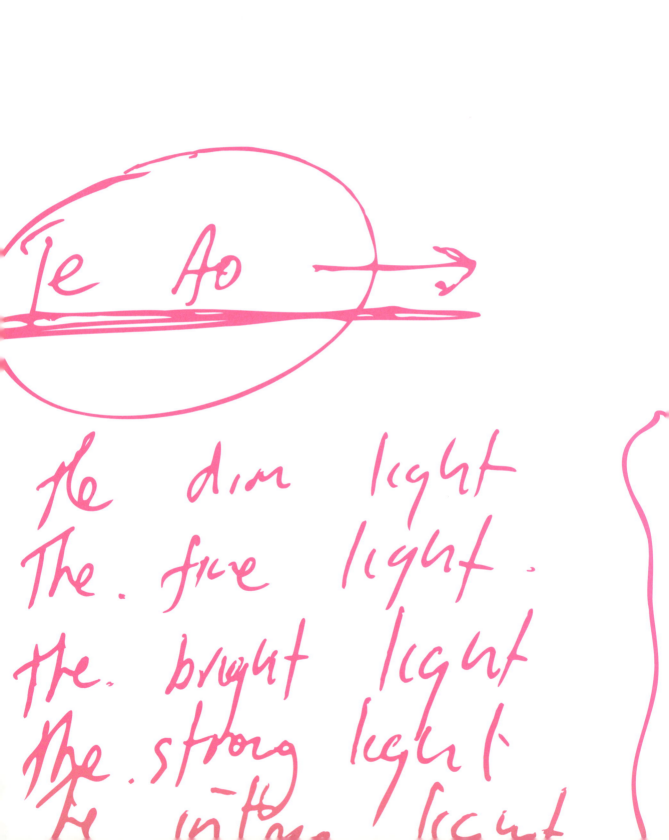

Te Ao

the dim light
The fire light
the bright light
the strong light
the intense light

Exhibitions

Ngā whakaatu-ranga

Haere ki wīwī, ki wāwā
To go here, to go there

Triennale di Milano

Milan
Italy

1996

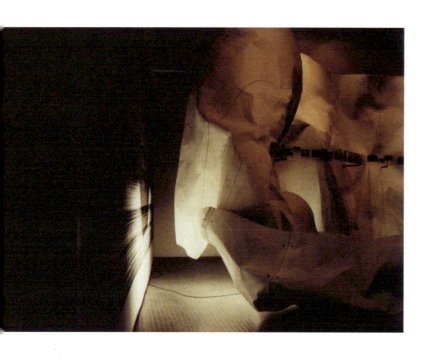

The Triennale di Milano installation was created by Ross Jenner, Simon Twose and Rewi, and was a paper 'treaty document' about 2 metres high and hand-made, designed to look as if it had blown into the gallery. *Courtesy of Simon Twose*

Exhibitions

The Milan Triennial was Rewi's first major exhibition. The exhibition explored overtly political ideas on the world stage — a large paper sculpture representing Te Tiriti o Waitangi was constructed and paired with a large toki form positioned as a challenge to both the Treaty and the architectural images inscribed on its surface.

Simon Twose is an architect and associate professor at Victoria University of Wellington Te Herenga Waka School of Architecture. He and Rewi collaborated on the exhibition for the Triennale Di Milano/Milan Triennial 1996, and then on a range of built projects when the two shared an office in the late 1990s. Here, Simon shares his experiences and memories of Rewi and their working relationship.

The timber framework for the Triennale installation was made in pieces and assembled as a flush surface about 12 metres long. *Courtesy of Simon Twose*

Jade Kake

Do you want to start at the beginning? How did you and Rewi first meet?

Simon Twose

The beginning. It would've been when I was a student — 30 years ago. I knew Rewi then. I asked him for a job after I graduated from school because he was one of the architects I admired the most. When you're a student, you think, 'Oh, I only like these guys who are really radically rethinking things,' and he was one of those architects. I thought he would be a great person to work for and learn from. That was in the late '80s. Rewi was doing lots of projects then but he didn't have enough work for me at that time. I ended up getting a job at Warren & Mahoney in Christchurch for a year, then went overseas, and when I came back to New Zealand we were both involved in projects and teaching at Auckland University.

We ended up collaborating on competitions and architecture school projects through mutual friends at the Auckland school, like Kerry Morrow, Ross Jenner, Sarah Treadwell . . . people who taught me and also were friends with Rewi. We were both part of the school's contribution to the 1996 Milan Triennale, which the School of Architecture was invited to contribute to after the success of the 1991 Venice Biennale entry. And after that, we had quite a bit to do with each other. We did several competitions — like one for the Gallipoli memorial — then I helped Rewi out now and then on various design proposals, such as the Waikato Museum extension, student housing schemes at Unitec, and a few others.

In 1996, Rewi, Mahendra Daji and I looked around for office space, because I'd just started a new practice with Mahendra. And so, his practice and my practice ended up sharing an office just by Grafton Bridge for four years. That's when we collaborated on a few projects, such as the Hopuhopu project for Tainui, and we were also able to review and crit the work each of us were doing, which was great. I moved to Wellington after

2000 and Rewi stayed in the Grafton office. I saw him only occasionally after that, mainly at Auckland Uni when we were both examining or reviewing work, that sort of thing. He was a great mentor to me when we were at Grafton and it was fantastic to share the day-to-day office life with him and Des; it was a lot of fun.

Jade

Tell me about the Milan Triennial project.

Simon

The Milan project was a group show of 29 countries that were invited to exhibit work in the Palazzo dell' Arte as part of the Milan Triennale. The theme of that year was 'Identità e differenza' (Identity and difference), which was about 'plurality in forms and cultures'. Ross Jenner was the commissioner and our approach addressed the theme from the angle of biculturalism. The architecture school got invited on the basis of the exhibition at the Venice Biennale in 1991 that won the Venice Prize. So this was in 1996.

Rewi, Ross and I worked on the exhibition and it ended up being this huge, sculptural, paper 'treaty document' which filled the gallery space, almost like it had been blown into the room from afar. The document acted as a landscape for works of New Zealand architecture that were exhibited in images — and these hovered over its surface, in a deliberately ambiguous relationship to the 'treaty landscape'. I worked on the big treaty piece, which was a representation of Te Tiriti o Waitangi, but also a kind of contested landscape, and a space of dialogue for the represented architectural work. The treaty document was around two metres high. Rewi made this big toki form on the other side of the exhibition, which was challenging the treaty surface (and the images of architectural work) and had models of his and other buildings inside it.

The drawings of New Zealand architecture were exhibited on trans-parent panels in front of the treaty

structure, and then lit so that they cast shadows on it, and so there was a separation between the work, the drawings and the landscape — as though their marking of the land was contested, rather than being rooted to the land. Light was projected through the architectural work onto the treaty document, and there were also drawings on the document itself that interacted with the cast images and drawings.

One wall was covered with lines of black powder, which I thought was a really good idea at the time. You know the string lines you use in construction, the chalk lines that you stretch tight and ping to make a line? We used black bone dust, and pinged one whole wall with loads of these lines. The idea was, these were 'lines to be drawn', future architectural marks on the treaty landscape. But it also became a wall that people could draw on . . . and then all that dust got transferred to all of the other things in the exhibition and through the rest of the Triennial. It was actually kind of hilarious. New Zealand spread through, marking everything.

Jade

How was it made?

Simon

The paper sculptural element was made by hand. Andrew Barrie, along with a whole bunch of others, put it together as a complex series of pieces that could fit in the belly of an aircraft. The project was the result of many people in both the design and construction.[1] I built a little model of the gallery space and made a model of the treaty document out of crumpled paper. I made a little tool and then measured the crumpled contours at several stations and transferred the shape into 2D hand drawings. It was very analogue and old-school. The scaled-up sections and plans of the crumpled form were then fabricated in timber and cardboard by Andrew's team. So it was a pre-digital process where that shape was just literally a scaled-up crumpled document, based on our initial concept sketch drawings, which we turned into the finished built form. The treaty

---

1 Andrew Barrie, Romilly Blackburn, Sean McMahon, Justin Marler, Glen Watt, Roberta Johnson, Nicola Kovacevich, James Mooney, Bianca Pohio, John Haydn, Srdja Hrisafović, Nigel Ryan.

sculpture was made in pieces using a series of wiggly-shaped timber frames, at stations around the form, and clad in a cardboard skin that was distressed to reflect the crumpled nature of the document. The pieces were all cunningly clipped together with flush connectors so they could be put together as one seamless surface, but also be able to come apart and stack one on top of each other in an aircraft cargo container. The final installation piece ended up being around two metres high and about 12 metres long.

Jade

As someone who was collaborating with him on various things, what are some of your reflections on Rewi's way of thinking and his way of designing?

Simon

He's the most amazing conceptual thinker. Architects consider themselves conceptual thinkers, but it's not necessarily always the case. With Rewi, the concept was always the absolute strong thing that would be carried through the whole project. He would pursue what appeared, on the surface, to be quite simple concepts, but he would pursue them so doggedly and artfully, and that would develop an amazing richness through the project.

Often with architecture the conceptual stuff just dribbles away as it turns into a project. With Rewi it was always there. He would always start a project by looking at the very widest perspective he could, from the point of view of the whenua. He would look at a project and he'd go, 'Oh, here's the site, we need a section all the way through the hill, through the sea, right out into the distance.' He'd always start with that kind of world view and the wider orientations or implications of a project. One of the projects I can remember was all about the koru, but also the cosmos, the sort of spiralling cosmos that came out of that, both at a human and a world scale.

That conceptual approach is quite rare. But also — and it's really hard to define — his talent was in successfully realising simple concepts in architecture. When he did something very strongly conceptual, like the Ōtara project, which was a representation of a fish, Rewi took it to another level where it was at the level of art, rather than just being symbolic representation on its own. It's hard to define, but he had that ability … an amazing talent to be able to bring the concept right through until it's at that level of being really significant in terms of architectural artwork.

Jade

Yeah, I think the differentiation is really important. Something I found when I was a student is the way they taught was really focused, and maybe this wasn't the intention, but the output of the students was this obsession with crude metaphors applied to buildings.

Simon

They're always disappointing because it's kind of simplistic, although it's really hard to articulate. But only Rewi could take those things and turn them into absolute works of art. When they're done the way you were describing it, they are quite disappointing. And it's almost like they diminish the objects that they're meant to be representing or the metaphors they're meant to be taking. They don't do them justice, in a way. But Rewi had a way of doing them justice.

Jade

A big part seemed to be his ability to listen carefully, and for a long time, before he made any design moves.

Simon

Definitely. He was hilarious in the office. He had this really, really crap old wooden chair that I was always worried was going to break. He would lean back on it and it would flex and creak. And I would turn around and see him and he'd be leaning back on this creaky old chair with his head down, and I'd be thinking, 'Oh God, he's asleep.' Sitting there in front of his drawing board asleep, wasn't touching it. He'd be like that for ages and then he'd sort of grunt and slowly move forward and draw a few lines. He'd take his time and he'd be thinking deeply about what he was about to draw.

Jade

As an educator yourself, what impact has learning from and working alongside Rewi had on the way that you teach and the way that you practise?

Simon

Oh, heaps. Heaps. Often, it's very indirect. He was a great mentor

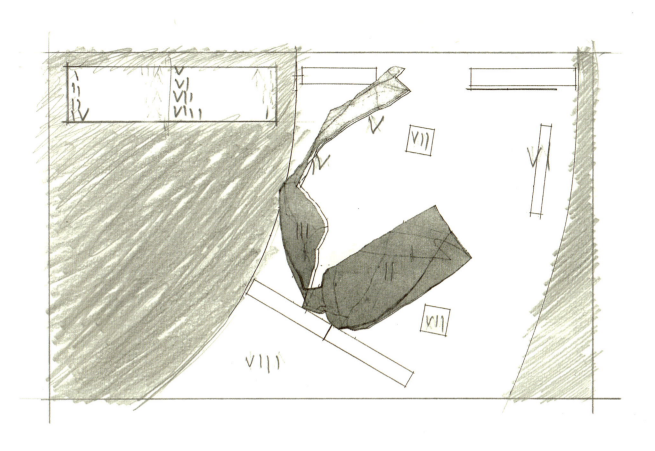

A sketch plan of the Milan installation from above. 'With Rewi, the concept was always the absolute strong thing that would be carried through the project,' Simon Twose says.
Courtesy of Simon Twose

to me, and because I went through the University of Auckland School of Architecture, I was very interested in conceptual work. But he was that transition into practice, and his conceptual approach to practice comes through in my teaching, especially when trying to get students to take into account mātauranga Māori. I'm in no position to teach them that, but having that background of talking and working with Rewi, I have sort of a window into that world and am able to tell people how they need to consider these things, and how to even approach thinking in a conceptual and cultural way — and how it might intersect with other ways of thinking. It's really that way of thinking, his way of thinking, that I use on a daily basis in the studio.

Obviously Rewi is so important in terms of how he connects to a whole bunch of conceptual thinking on architecture in practice, and teaching and research, and how he has influenced that. His conceptual approach, particularly driven by a te ao Māori kind of approach, was influential on me as well. He had a real impact — and part of it was through us collaborating on things like the Milan Triennial.

Early sketches of the Milan installation. The paper that filled the gallery space had transparent panels in front of it that displayed New Zealand works of architecture that were lit so they cast shadows on the paper. 'There was a separation between the work, the drawings and the landscape — as thought their marking of the land was contested,' Simon Twose says.
Courtesy of Simon Twose

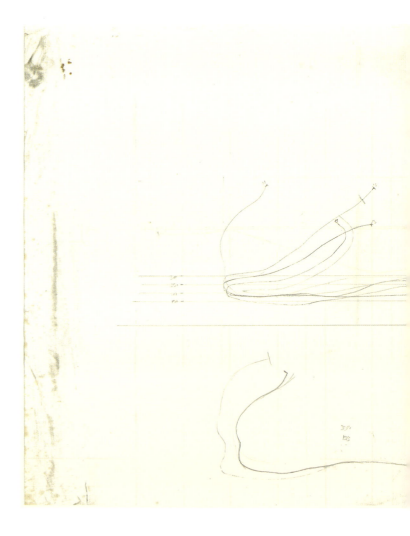

Exhibitions

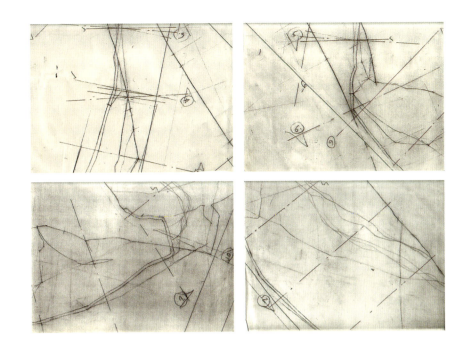
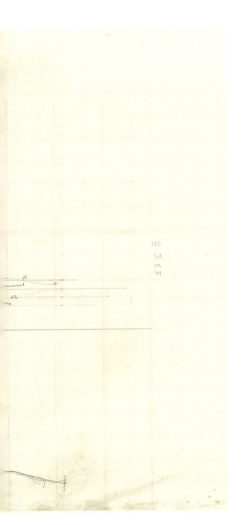

Future Islands, Venice Architecture Biennale

Venice
Italy

2016

A model of Rewi's house floats above one of the exhibition's suspended islands. *David St George*

Exhibitions

Future Islands, New Zealand's exhibition at the 15th International Architecture Exhibition (Biennale Architettura 2016), held from 28 May to 27 November 2016 in Venice, Italy, was one of Rewi's last projects. *Future Islands*, which was about potential, about speculation, and which sought to interrogate the architectural culture of New Zealand, was another opportunity to engage critically with architecture and explore philosophical and political ideas on a world stage. A model of Rewi's house sat on one of the exhibition's suspended islands and captured the imagination of architects and non-architects alike, presenting a re-imagining of a way of being and existing in the contested landscape of Tāmaki Makaurau, Aotearoa.

Charles Walker, a professor of architecture and the head of school at Huri te Ao, School of Future Environments at AUT Te Wānanga Aronui o Tāmaki Makaurau, was the creative director of *Future Islands*. Here he shares his reflections on the project and Rewi's contributions to it.

Jade Kake
How did this collaboration come about?

Charles Walker
I'd known Rewi for years off and on and we used to go drinking together on a Monday night. And, you know, we just had a conversation, and then there was a call for expressions of interest for the Biennale project that the NZIA put out and I thought, this could be interesting.

Jade
The theme for 2016 was 'Reporting from the Front', which was about 'sharing with a broader audience the work of people that are scrutinising the horizon looking for new fields of action'. I was interested in why you responded to that theme the way you did, because the themes are always quite high-level and loose and there's lots of room for interpretation.

Charles
Originally it was supposed to be all about unbuilt work, about potential. So the whole *Future Islands* idea came about through ideas that were emerging, but had not perhaps become fully formed — that idea of futurity, and what could be. Things that architects were thinking about, but hadn't necessarily been able to build.

Jade
Right. And to quote the curator, Alejandro Aravena, the provocation was twofold: 'On the one hand we would like to widen the range of issues to which architecture is expected to respond, adding explicitly to the cultural and artistic dimensions that already belong to our scope, those that are on the social, political, economical and environmental end of the spectrum. On the other hand, we would like to highlight the fact that architecture is called to respond to more than one dimension at a time, integrating a variety of fields instead of choosing one or another.'[1]

Charles
Yes. So, the idea was this speculative thing and I didn't want it to be too didactic. I'm interested in the history of ideas, architectural ideas, in New Zealand. We don't do a lot of speculative projects in the profession. I think architects here are busy doing real things. They don't have time to work on speculative projects, whereas I've got lots of friends in Europe who, if they're working in Berlin and they've got no work this year, they'll think, 'Well, let's just redesign Berlin.'

Jade
Do you think part of it is that when you are working in Europe, so much of it is additions, alterations. There's not a lot of new work, especially in a lot of those older cities, whereas here we have an environment where we've got heaps of new work — we're demolishing things all the time, and there's heaps of vacant land.

Charles
Also, young architects here build a lot. Typically, all architects build things for their family, and so early in their careers they typically can build a few things, and then once you've built things for all of your family you're kind of finished. It's very hard to make the

1   Alejandro Aravena, 'Biennale Architettura 2016', labiennale.org/en/architecture/2016.

Above: Of the exhibition's suspended islands, Charles Walker says: 'We just wanted them to float very gently in this space.' *David St George*

Right: The entry stair to the first-floor palazzo space in Venice where *Future Islands* was first exhibited. *David St George*

Overleaf: Of the palazzo space in Venice and temporal aspects of the exhibition, Charles Walker recalls: 'We wanted people to come in and be in Venice and smell the canal and hear the noise from the courtyard and then also appreciate how the light changed during the day.' *David St George*

Exhibitions

Above: The haka pōwhiri at the opening of *Future Islands* in Venice. *David St George*

Below: 'Some students came with us to the opening, and they did a haka in the piazza outside the exhibition to open it,' says Charles Walker. 'It was just sensational, and people really loved it. People were hanging out the windows watching it.' *David St George*

Exhibitions

leap into the next stage because there are big commercial firms that sweep up that larger work. There was this idea of unbuilt speculative things and possibilities for what it could be. I knew Rewi was interested in these things as well. A lot of his projects were quite speculative, and he didn't see himself bound by any rules, really. He would use any medium and play around with ideas. And he always came at things slightly laterally, with interesting conversations around what he might do. I knew that he'd worked on other exhibitions before — the Milan Triennial in 1996 and the Venice Biennale in 1991. When I started to put a team together for the Biennale, Rewi seemed like a logical partner.

Jade

How was the exhibition mounted in the space in Venice?

Charles

We ended up with a big palazzo space in Venice. It was difficult to get into. It was on the first floor of a building, and you had to come up a kind of dog-leg stair to get into it. It had big windows on both the east and the west, big windows on both sides. On one side was a courtyard, and on the other side was a canal.

We just wanted it to float very gently in this space. These things were just hung from the ceiling, and with quite a complicated system because we were not allowed to make any holes. We had to design clamps to suspend the islands in some other way. We spent a couple of weeks installing it. We got a lot of advice from people, including the NZIA, recommending that we should darken the space, that we should block it all out and illuminate the islands, which probably made sense from an exhibition design perspective. But as the creative team, we just wanted people to come into the exhibition, and to be in Venice, not in a black box.

Jade

So you didn't want to block out Venice? Those temporal qualities.

Charles

That's right. We wanted people to come in and be in Venice and smell the canal and hear the noise from the courtyard and then also appreciate how the light changed during the day. Depending

on the time of day that you came into the exhibition, it was quite a different experience. The other thing I really liked about it was that the audience was also part of the exhibition. Depending on how many people were in the room or what they were doing, that was also part of it. The experience of being there with other people and these floating objects: I think it worked really well.

Jade

Who made the models?

Charles

Minka Ip was in charge. He's a former student of mine at Auckland Uni who's now a professional architectural model maker. He made a lot of the models and coordinated other people making them — sometimes students made them, sometimes architects made or supplied their own.

Jade

How did you activate the space?

Charles

We had some digital projections. Bruce Ferguson, who specialises in that kind of work, projecting onto buildings, was on the team. And we had some sound. We played it on the stairway, so as you came up the stair there was this kind of wiretap and a bird sound, as a transition from the Italian piazza into the dark space up the stair, where you came into this other one.

Jade

A space to prepare your thoughts. A transitional space.

Charles

It was very subtle. Some students came with us to do the opening, and they did a haka in the piazza outside the exhibition to open it. It was just sensational, and people really loved it. People were hanging out the windows watching it.

Jade

How was the exhibition received?

Charles

We received really good feedback. I think people were surprised because they didn't know what to expect. New Zealand didn't have an official pavilion, we had this other palazzo, so people had to find it and, when they came up into it, I think it was quite different perhaps from what they had somehow expected. Rewi's house was a bit of a hit. A couple of projects, because of the way we'd built them, the way they were presented, because of their unusual formal qualities, were always remarked on. Rewi's house had a strangeness about it, a kind of sculptural, almost archetypal quality. We also had a model of Ian Athfield's house. We had it stepping down, fixed on the wall, like a piece of sculpture. I think those two were among the most photographed. *Future Islands* was probably Rewi's last project. His final project — and he never saw it.

Jade
That's really sad.

Charles
He didn't go to Venice because he was ill. He passed away before we brought it back to New Zealand to tour. When we brought the exhibition back, in honour of his memory we sprayed the model of Rewi's house black, and the island Rewi's house was on was pink, that shocking pink that he was very fond of. This one island that was pink with Rewi's black house on it just kind of floated in the space.

Jade
Did you approach it differently when you brought the exhibition back to New Zealand?

Charles
That first exhibition of the New Zealand tour of *Future Islands* was also the first exhibition held at the new Objectspace gallery in Ponsonby. That was a real thrill. Objectspace is essentially a black box. So we did black out and illuminate it, and it looked fantastic. It looked really good, but it was a different kind of experience. I'm quite glad we didn't black it out in Venice, but I'm really glad that we saw it in this illuminated black box space.

Jade
Yeah, and Objectspace is very inward focused. It's not supposed to be looking out and experiencing the street.

Charles
Yeah, that's right. We emphasised the blackness of the black box in there. Then when we took it to other places, we just had to adapt it to the shape of the space. Next, we took it to the Adam Art Gallery in Wellington, which is a very high, long and narrow space, so that was a completely different kind of experience.

Then we took it to Hamilton to the Waikato Museum, which has really low 2.4-metre-high ceilings. It's like a domestic scale. That was really challenging. And then to Christchurch, where we put it in the Ara Institute of Canterbury's exhibition space, which is essentially a glass box with one wall of glass. That was very bright, and very challenging. They were all very different. In developing the concept, we wanted it to be different at different times of the day and to be immersed in the different sounds of different contexts.

Jade
In terms of Rewi's contribution, was that mostly working with you on the overall concept?

Charles
Yeah, the idea and how we put it together. We had this basic idea and really we just threw ideas around. 'What do you think?' 'What do *you* think?' We had quite a big team. There were 10 people, and every person contributed in a slightly different way. So it was almost a conceptual provocation. What are we? What are we trying to do? How are we doing? Is this a good way? Everyone had a different contribution to make.

Rewi would never say, 'You must do this.' No. He would always come at things and casually voice his ideas, as if it was just something floating past, and that was why I liked working with him, because I'm also a bit floaty and I'm not really practical. I think the idea of these floating future islands, and the possibilities of things that were unbuilt appealed to us both.

Jade
Obviously there's a collaborative process, but something I've heard from others is a lot about Rewi's approach being like a gentle navigation, asking prompting questions and leading people to follow their own path.

Charles
I think that's right. He wasn't forceful. He wasn't didactic. I always thought his work was very poetic, and the way that he thought and spoke was poetic, too. But he was also quite a straightforward man. Few words, but always carefully chosen words.

Rewi passed away in November 2016 without having seen the exhibition. 'When we brought the exhibition back, in honour of his memory we sprayed the model of Rewi's house black, and the island that Rewi's house was on was pink,' says Charles Walker. *David St George*

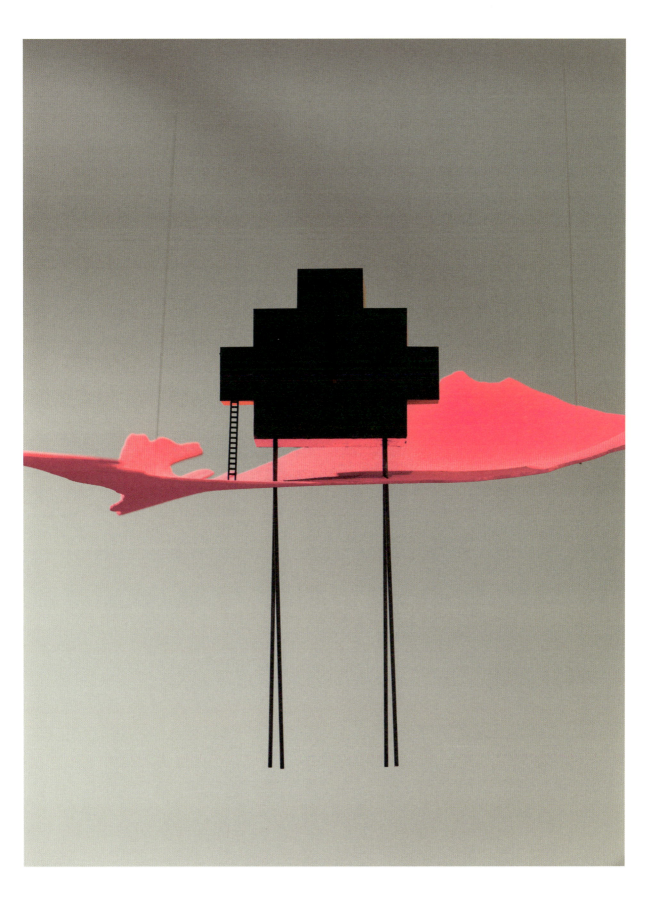

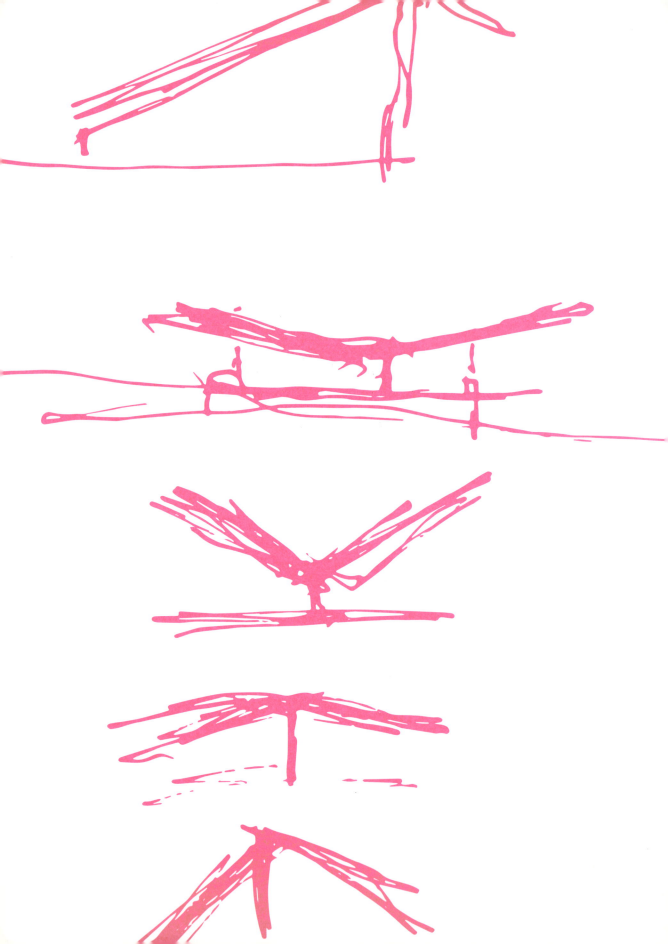

Speculative and unbuilt

Ngā kaupapa kore hanga

Mā te pohewa mā te auaha hoki,
ka whakapuaki ngā kura e huna ana
*Through imagination and creativity hidden
treasures are expressed*

Ngāti Pōneke Marae/ Hometown Museum

Te Whanganui-a-Tara Wellington

1980

One of Rewi's most arresting projects, the Ngāti Pōneke Marae (described as the 'Hometown Museum' in some documents) is an abstracted waka form dragged partly from the harbour and lying on the slopes of Tangi-te-keo Mount Victoria. Devised while Rewi was still an architecture student, it is a breathtaking form which displays both his conceptual clarity and sense of daring.

Rewi wrote briefly about the project (along with some of his other work) in a 1988 article in *The Landscape*, the journal of the New Zealand Institute of Landscape Architects Tuia Pito Ora. In the article, he uses the following quote (the ellipsis is his):

Tired and hungry we hauled
our canoe
high onto the beach
Within its hull contained our culture
We had arrived ... home

He goes on to write: 'This is a vision rather than a building. A cultural statement symbolising the question of relationships between modern/ traditional, land/sea/building, natural/ built. The functional aspect of the museum is based on Marae protocol and Maoritanga. Visitors arrive by sea (base) and ascend into the "hull" to experience various associated functions.'

In sections, the various associated functions ascend from a Ngāti Pōneke display on the lowest level (labelled 'Welcome' on the plan), through a craft workshop, dining hall with kitchen (labelled 'Eat'), sleeping accommodation, members' entry and changing rooms, a stage (labelled 'Entertain/Participate'), a lobby, a meeting house and a lookout tower at the top. The structure is designed to straddle Oriental Bay Road, and the plan suggests its future form is extendable up the hill.

The project won the AAA Monier Tile Award in 1980. Rewi's friend Mike

Leaning dramatically against the slopes of Wellington's Tangi-te-keo Mount Victoria, the award-winning Ngāti Pōneke Marae was dreamed up by Rewi in his final year of university.
Lucy Thompson collection

Speculative and unbuilt

Barns remembers being on the judging panel with Kerry Morrow and John Scott, and says the Ngāti Pōneke Marae project effortlessly stood out from the crowd.

'Everybody else who entered was so serious about their architecture,' Barns remembers. 'Then you had this entry by Rewi, this kind of outer space thing that just arrived. It was totally not practical, but it answered a lot of stories that were floating around in Rewi's head.'

Barns says designing this project and subsequently winning the Monier award was a boost for Rewi. 'That first project that he did helped him start to define his Māoriness. When he won the award, that really helped. I think it confirmed his validity as a Māori commentator, and probably gave him a lot more confidence in those early days around his architectural capability.

'There were not a lot of brown faces around [at architecture school], and you had all that stuff we were trying to work out as cultural identity. Rewi was coming into an academic programme and wondering, is this appropriate for me? Then, boom, he gets an endorsement through his design award. He never showed off about it. He was always humble. But I think it made him feel he had a hope. He just got stronger and stronger.'

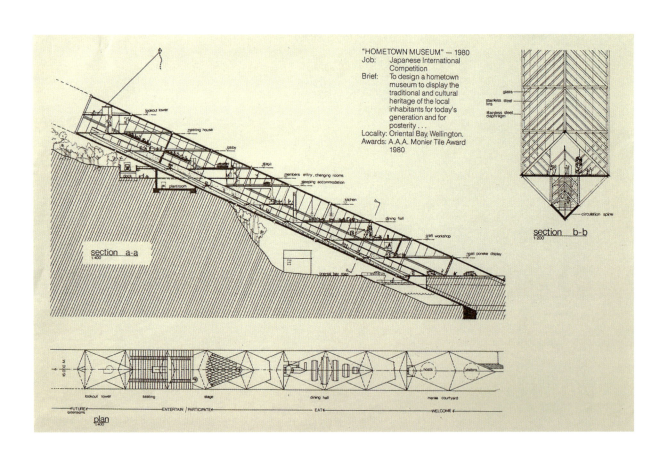

Speculative and unbuilt

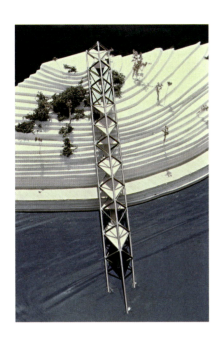

Opposite: The Ngāti Pōneke Marae received considerable media attention. *The Landscape*

Left: An archival photograph showing a model of the Ngāti Pōneke Marae astride the contours of Tangi-te-keo Mount Victoria. *Lucy Thompson collection*

Below: A model of the marae in Lucy Thompson's collection. *Samuel Hartnett*

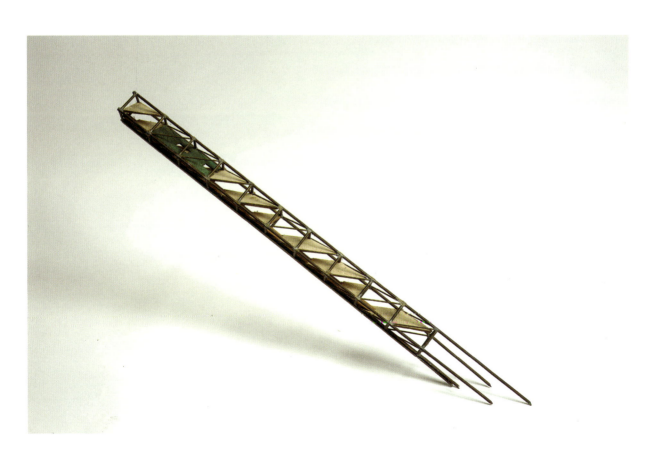

Cape Rēinga redevelopment

Cape Rēinga
Te Rerenga Wairua
Te Hiku o Te Ika

1983-89

Speculative and unbuilt

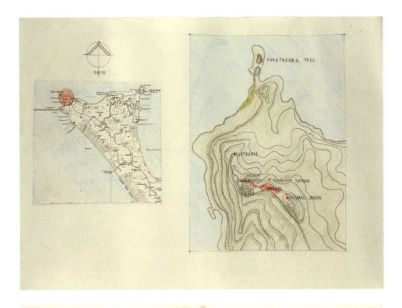

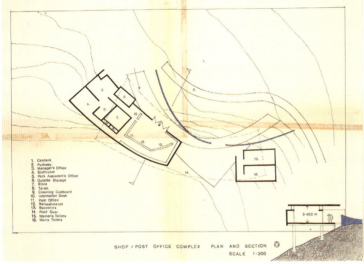

Sketches from Rewi's archives show renditions of the visitor centre hoisted on poles 'so as to further experience the hostility of the site', as Rewi put it. *Architecture Archive, University of Auckland*

Rewi Thompson's work at Cape Rēinga began with a three-bedroom ranger's house for the Department of Conservation, a simple, functional form that he said was a response to budget constraints and the wild weather at the site. 'The mainly inclement conditions make this house more of an interior,' he wrote in a 1988 edition of *The Landscape*. 'It is positioned to reinforce the relationship between sea/sky/land and provide a means of circulating ventilation.'

The ranger's house was built, and there are some beautifully abstract paintings of it in Rewi's archive at the University of Auckland. There are many more drawings of a larger project at the cape that was never realised: a visitor centre that was to include a shop, offices and public toilets. The curved building was to be held aloft on poles on the steep site, a form that found an echo almost 30 years later in the home and studio Rewi designed for artist Katharina Grosse on Auckland's west coast.

CARVED GATEWAY

Rewi later wrote about the Cape project in *The Landscape*: 'The "power and magnificence" of this special place "touches us" in different ways. For some it is primarily visual but for others it is far more meaningful in its interpretation. The structures and furniture that we hope to create are envisaged to reinforce these personal qualities. Seating and information posts are positioned and detailed so that the visitors' experience is more direct. The shop-office complex is propelled into space so as to further experience the hostility of the site.'

Speculative and unbuilt

The lavish curve of the building would have withheld the view of the cape until visitors entered.
Architecture Archive, University of Auckland

FirstCorp Tower

Tāmaki Makaurau Auckland

1983–89

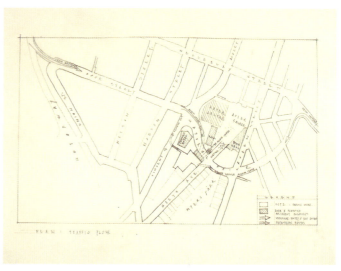

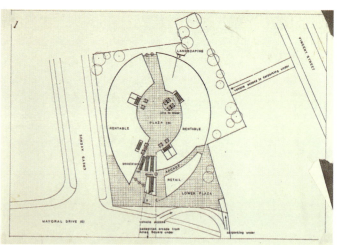

We're unclear on the origins of this speculative building, designed for a site on Auckland's Greys Avenue and labelled 'FirstCorp Tower' on some drawings, but several versions of it exist in Rewi's archive. It is almost 30 floors tall and backed by a slender tower that stretches much higher, and the name of the project suggests it was conceived in the city's go-go years of the late 1980s, when everything was named 'Corp' and outlandish structures seemed eminently possible. The site, just behind the Auckland Chamber of Commerce building on Mayoral Drive, is still empty at the time of writing, if an aspiring developer is interested.

Speculative and unbuilt

There are a number of renditions of the FirstCorp project in Rewi's archives, including a few in which a helicopter hovers above the development's incredibly slender tower. *Architecture Archive, University of Auckland*

Horouta ki Pōneke Marae Society

Porirua
Te Whanganui-a-Tara
Wellington

1983–89

Speculative and unbuilt

The Horouta ki Pōneke Marae Society is based in Porirua and was created as a temporary home away from home for whānau of *Horouta* waka (who hail from regions stretching from Te Whānau-ā-Apanui to Wairoa), a group of which Rewi, with his Ngāti Porou and Te Aitanga a Hauiti whakapapa, was part.

Rewi's archives contain an ambitious (and unrealised) scheme for new buildings to surround the society's existing wharenui. One iteration includes a hotel, an arts and crafts centre and a sports centre. In another drawing, the group of buildings is surrounded by a distinctive enclosure of red sail-like forms.

Pania Houkamau-Ngaheu, the manager of the marae, remembers working with Rewi on these concepts. 'I had the privilege of sitting in on three meetings between Rewi and Uncle Newton Crawford, Mereana Dakin and others about the initial designs,' she said. 'Rewi was very innovative, very persistent and had a brilliant mind for future-proofing any suggestions that were made by our kaumātua and committee. Dr Pat Ngata and Hirini Moko Mead were our leaders then, and after some time opted not to continue with his design. He was amazing as a person and as an architect.'

Rewi's vision for the Horouta ki Pōneke Marae Society included a dramatic red enclosure for the marae complex. *Architecture Archive,* University of Auckland

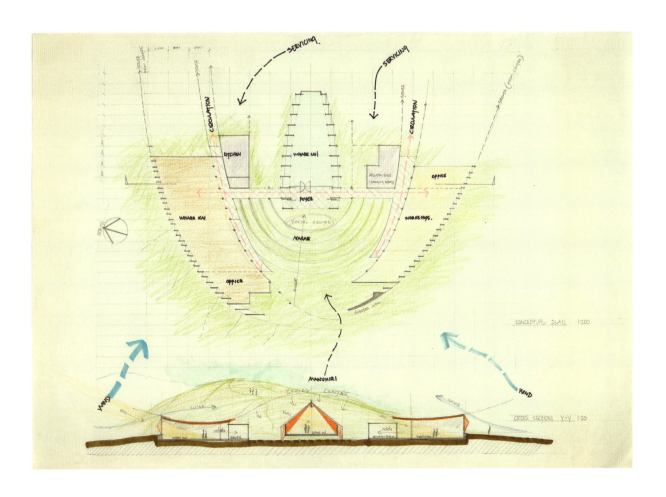

Rotorua Cultural Centre

1986

Speculative and unbuilt

This drawing of a hotel proposal from Rewi's archives was one of several suggestions for a site near Whakarewarewa. *Architecture Archive, University of Auckland*

According to a proposal we found in Rewi's archives, the Rotorua Cultural Centre was designed 'to provide visitors with an insight into Māori arts and life, presented in a living Arts Complex'.

The text in the brief says the complex would 'envelop a continuous, flexible space in a web-like glass and steel form', a design that would 'create a strong contemporary cultural identity for its users, and for New Zealand as a whole'. The drawings do look spectacular, with a single solid-timber pyramid form containing an auditorium and services nestling under the glass and steel canopy. The plans make provision for a future tower, which is illustrated in one sketch, while other drawings show what might have been an alternative design: a hotel whose shape appears as if it would fit the same site.

CULTURAL CENTRE ROTORUA 1986

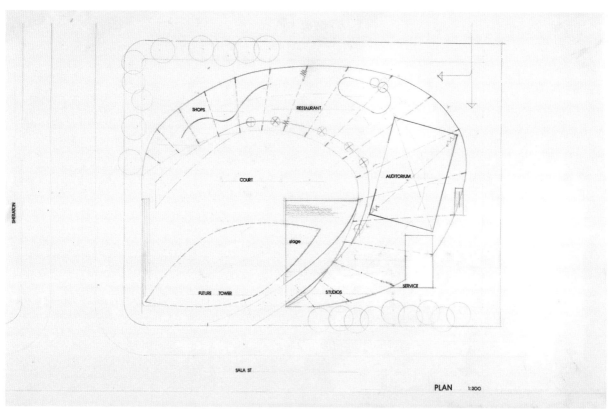

PLAN 1:200

Speculative and unbuilt

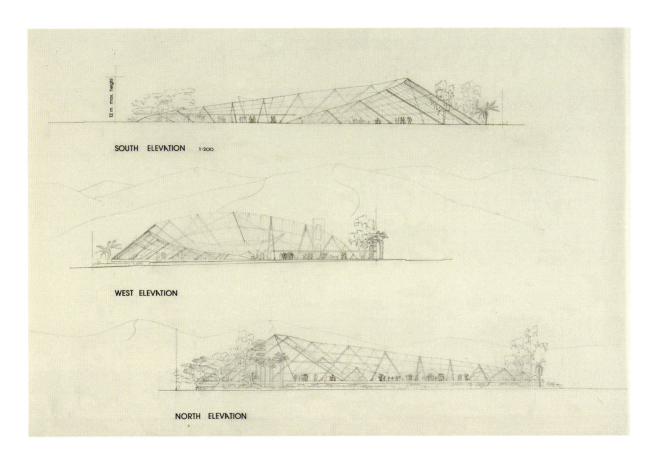

The Cultural Centre was to have been located near Whakarewarewa, bordered by Trigg and McKee Avenues and Sala Street. The introductory text of the proposal makes a case for a future-focused development that marries technology with tradition: 'If we are to "lean" too directly on tradition, we sadly deny ourselves the ability to demonstrate our own creativity, worthiness, significance . . . We must therefore begin to see our past with our minds rather than our eyes and not be scared to pick the "bare bones" of our past traditions and take in essence the "jewels" and be confident to engineer these treasures and manifest and mould our present and future built environment.'

The ambitious proposal for the Rotorua Cultural Centre featured a semi-circular glass and steel form containing an auditorium and other services. *Architecture Archive, University of Auckland*

Pacific Island Business and Cultural Centre

Location and date unknown

A spectacular series of atoll-like canopies and pavilions was to have made up the Pacific Island Business and Cultural Centre, a dream-like project from Rewi's archives.
Architecture Archive, University of Auckland

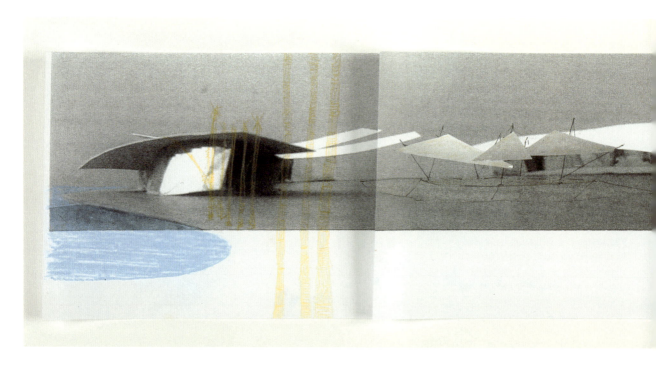

Speculative and unbuilt

'Welcome to Tropical Paradise', says the pitch document for the Pacific Island Business and Cultural Centre, a proposal we found in Rewi's archives that lacks information about its funders or its location (we presume that it was envisaged for a large site on Auckland's outskirts, but have been unable to confirm this). The ambitious complex was to be set amid a 'water theme park for families' featuring 'canoe voyaging, performance, "reef diving", an aquarium, hot pools for soothing and healing etc', as well as taro and banana plantations, vegetable gardens with attached research facilities, retail outlets and accommodation.

So far, so far-fetched. But what is interesting about the complex is the way Rewi's design gathered these disparate functions together into a single conceptual framework inspired by Polynesian navigational charts and

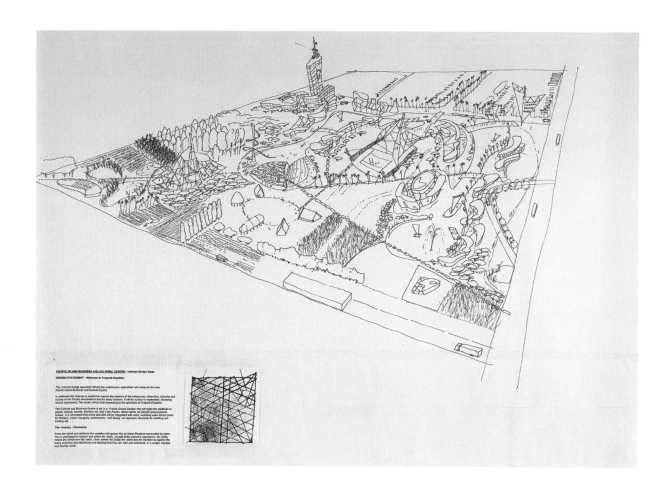

Speculative and unbuilt

the pathways they illustrate between islands. The first stage of the project was to feature four buildings — including a 1200-square-metre food court, 750 square metres of retail and an area devoted to performance and multimedia displays. The proposal states these buildings represent islands, and that they are linked by open and transparent structures with sail-like roofs that suggest connecting atolls.

'From the street,' the proposal says, 'the complex will appear like an Island Paradise surrounded by water. This is envisaged to seduce and entice the visitor. As part of the welcome experience, the visitor enters the island over water. Once across the bridge the visitor has the freedom to explore the many activities and attractions knowing that they are safe and welcomed in a unique, exciting and friendly world.'

The building at the heart of the Pacific Island Business and Cultural Centre proposal was to be part of a much larger site featuring, among other things, hot pools, a water theme park and taro and banana plantations. *Architecture Archive, University of Auckland*

Coastal Lodge

North Auckland

2000-01

Speculative and unbuilt

In the early 2000s, Laly and Sharley Haddon called Rewi Thompson with a suggestion. They were interested in creating a tourism venture on their farm on the coast north of Auckland: eco-friendly lodge-style accommodation that could take advantage of the incredible sea views from a promontory above the beach. Laly's connection to the land stretched back generations through his Ngāti Manuhiri and Ngāti Wai whakapapa, and Sharley had been running horse treks in the area since the 1980s. Farming wasn't an easy way to pay the bills, and they liked the idea of offering guests the opportunity to experience the place in specially designed accommodation.

They had first heard of Rewi some time in the 1990s through a mutual friend: Sharley remembers his name coming up in a conversation about 'Māori who were becoming successful without compromising their Māori integrity'. They met him soon afterward, and initially discussed the possibility of designing a small lodge and homestead. Those loose plans eventually developed into a string of small studios inspired by the pipi shells that are found in middens throughout the farm.

Rewi's vision 'blew us out of the water,' Sharley says. 'He didn't come here with the idea of the shells. We started talking and sharing meals and wine and then we started to really hit it and this concept came up. We all worked together and he drew it up. None of his other buildings are like that; this one is out of the box. It was Rewi at his most imaginative, and he really loved doing it. He was down to earth, but he had little flights of fancy that were beautiful.'

The diminutive shell-inspired structures started out as sketches on paper scraps at Sharley and Laly's dining-room table, before becoming more detailed drawings in Rewi's studio. The number of buildings envisioned for the project varies in the archival drawings; Sharley remembers the concept having 6–12 separate residential studios slung along the promontory, while guests would gather for meals in a central building containing a kitchen and dining room, lounge, outdoor patio and mezzanine-floor conference room. In some iterations, the studio units have beds and ensuite bathrooms on a mezzanine floor, while others have only a single level. The trio hoped that they could find a way to create pearlescent exteriors for the

The coastal lodge project 'was Rewi at his most imaginative,' Sharley Haddon says. 'He really loved doing it. He was down to earth, but he had little flights of fancy that were beautiful.' Courtesy of Sharley and Olivia Haddon

VIEW FROM BEACH UP ALONG THE RIDGE WITH THE BACKDROP OF DISTANT HILLS

buildings that might mimic that of the Sydney Opera House.

Laly and Sharley's daughter Olivia Haddon still has some of the original documentation relating to the project, including Rewi's project vision:

> The design approach will reflect an indigenous aesthetic.
>
> The site will be developed and landscaped to reinforce native coastal flora, in particular a pōhutukawa regenerative planting programme.
>
> The lodge will be domestic in size and accommodate a limited number of guests to generate a 'family perception', emphasising the 'personal' touch.
>
> Each accommodation unit will stand alone nestled in a coastal native landscape setting, to provide privacy to both indoor and outdoor areas. The interiors will be generous in size, planned to exploit the commanding views, containing all the comforts of home including spa, swimming pool and the latest in entertainment and communication technology.

It was a project on Māori land with a Māori client and a Māori architect. It also had a community focus: Laly (who died in 2013) and Sharley's vision involved producing food for guests on the farm and providing employment for local people. At the time they were contemplating the project, a rural downturn meant unemployment in their area was acute.

It seems like a logical proposal now, but Sharley says it was difficult to make headway with it 20 years ago, especially as they didn't want to put the farm up as security for the development. 'We were naive country people and what Rewi designed for us was way in excess of what we could cope with,' she says. 'We didn't know where to go for funding. But it was such a beautiful concept, and we could see how it could work so well. I would still really love to get it going, in the name of Rewi and Laly.'

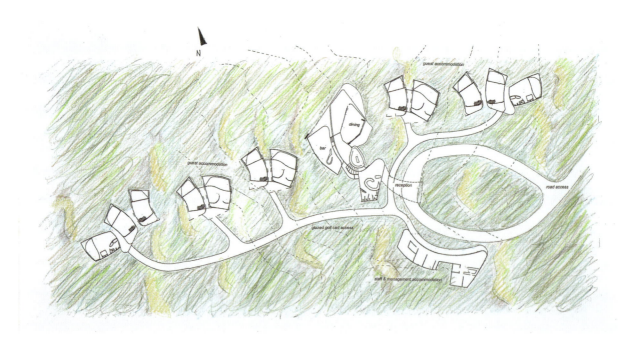

Speculative and unbuilt

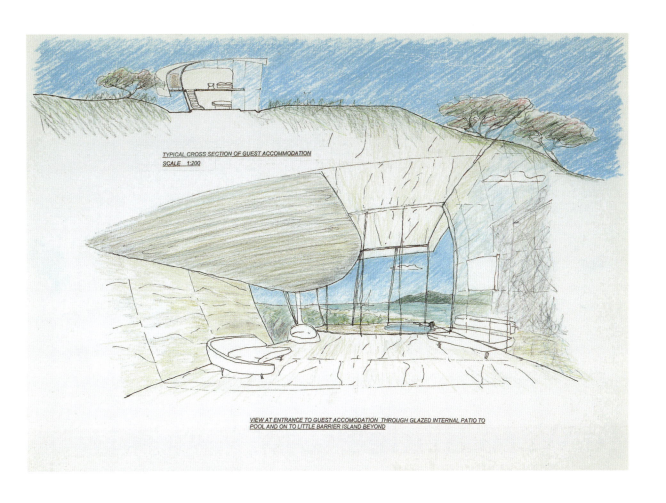

Individual studios were to be arranged on a promontory above the beach, with their interiors oriented to the view.
Courtesy of Sharley and Olivia Haddon

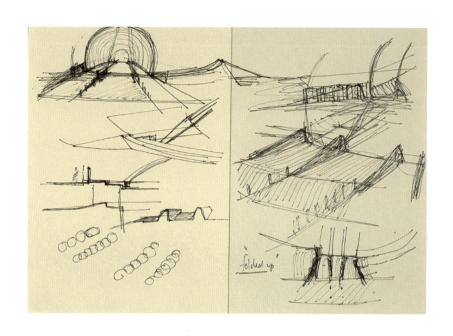

Te Wero Bridge

Quay Street West
Tāmaki Makaurau Auckland

2007

With Ngarimu Blair, Warren & Mahoney and Holmes Consulting

The Te Wero Bridge was a competition entry to connect Auckland's Te Wero Island and Wynyard Quarter, spanning the entrance to Viaduct Harbour. Inspired by the hīnaki (eel trap), the bridge was designed to rotate on a central pillar to allow boats to pass around it. Rewi's conceptual design was selected for the second stage of the competition, which he completed with Warren & Mahoney and Holmes Consulting. Another scheme was chosen as the winner but has never been built. This was the second competition entry Rewi worked on with Ngarimu Blair; the pair also teamed up for the competition to redesign Auckland's Queens Wharf, a competition which ended controversially when Auckland mayor John Banks and Auckland Regional Council chair Mike Lee declined to choose a winner.

Inspired by the form of an eel trap, Rewi's hīnaki bridge was to have turned on a central pivot to allow boats to pass by. *Architecture Archive, University of Auckland*

Rewi's love of a curve was expressed in especially glassy fashion in his proposal for this home in the Bay of Islands.
Architecture Archive, University of Auckland

Speculative and unbuilt

Campbell House

Kāretu
Te Pēwhairangi
Bay of Islands

2007

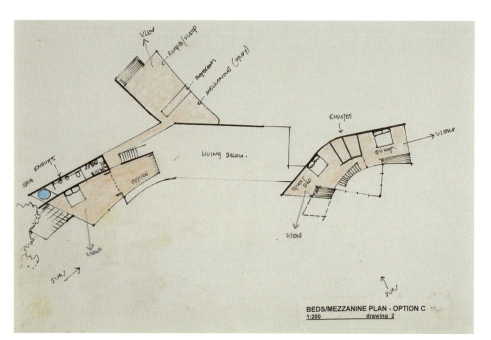

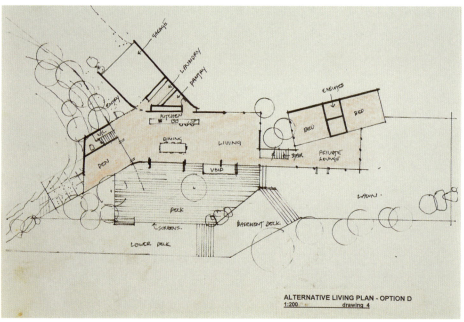

Speculative and unbuilt

The drawings of the Campbell House, designed in 2007, stood out in Rewi's archive because they had reached a fairly well-resolved stage — although we can't find any evidence that the house was ever built. Glassy and ambitious, the building was to stand on a site looking towards Ōpua across Te Tai Tokerau's Kawakawa River. The design contains echoes of the Wishart House, with its lofty living area, mezzanine bedrooms and carefully chosen views of the inlet and the hills behind the house.

As always, Rewi developed a range of layout options for his clients, mulling them over in a series of iterations.
Architecture Archive, University of Auckland

KOHA — creative responses

Ngā whakahoki auaha ā-tuhi

He pōkēkē uenuku i tū āi
Against a dark cloud a rainbow stands out brightly

KOHA

The discovery of a folder labelled KOHA was one of the most memorable moments of trawling through Rewi's archives. One drawing features prismatic buildings on water, one of them containing a Tyrannosaurus Rex; another shows totemic structures rising from the sea with birds swirling through a sunset sky. In the same folder, there is a clutch of drawings of a dramatic, transparent double-X-shaped tower in which a T-Rex shares a central atrium with an oversize take on Michelangelo's *David*. In another sketch, an aerial view shows concentric circles filling in parts of Auckland's St Marys Bay between the Harbour Bridge and the wharves of Wynyard Quarter. There are also drawings of enormous circular structures in the Waitematā Harbour with Rangitoto as a backdrop; ominous and thrilling, their purpose is unclear.

Nobody we've spoken to has been able to illuminate the origins of this project. It's possible that not all the drawings are by Rewi, as their style varies. But the drawings show something of Rewi's imaginative ability, his enthusiasm for the possibilities of imposing large structures on a landscape (or harbour) and his wit (the dinosaurs and *David*). They also set an idea in motion: What if we asked writers of fiction to respond to Rewi's drawings? Would they help us understand more of what was going on?

We decided to give this a try, sending sketches of Rewi's house to essa may ranapiri, of the prismatic structures with the T-Rex to Samuel Te Kani and of the totemic structures springing from the water to Gina Cole, asking them to inhabit Rewi's worlds and report back in writing. The results of their efforts are on the next few pages.

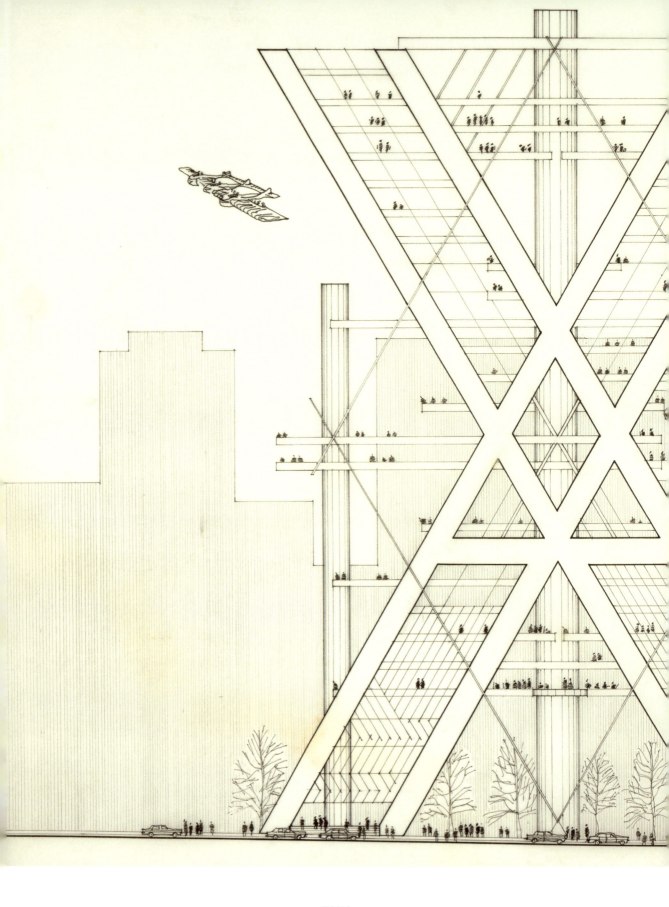

KOHA

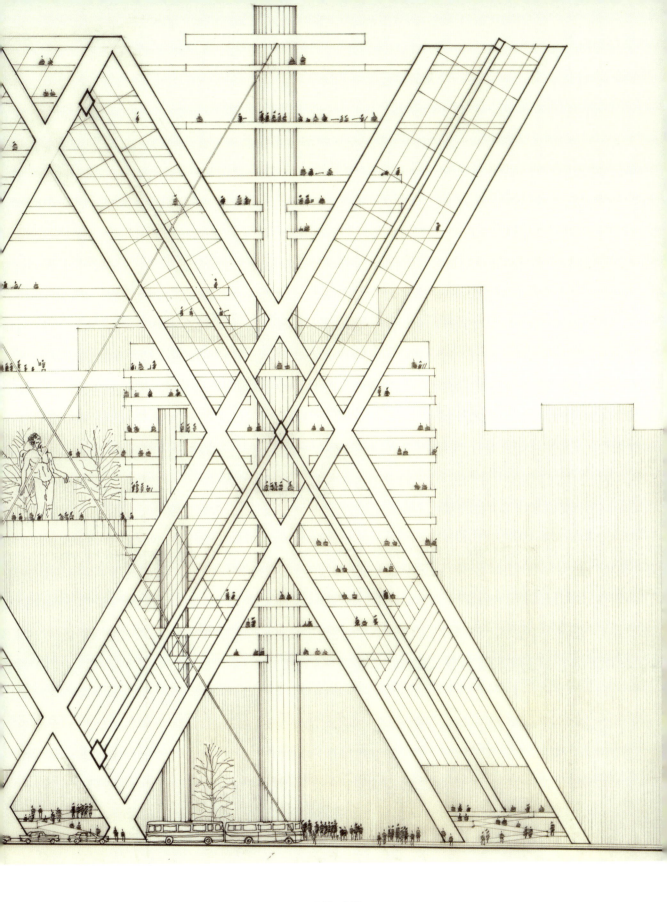

KOHA

KOHA

KOHA

KOHA

KOHA

POUTAMA

essa may ranapiri

I THINK OF OUR ANCESTOR
TUURONGO AND HIS
BUILDING OF A HOUSE OF
HIS TEARING DOWN OF A
HOUSE AND HIM BEING
TRICKED BY HIS BROTHER
TO BUILD A HOUSE TOO
SMALL TO FIT A FAMILY I

WHEN THEY MOVE IN ME THINK OF HIM TRAVELLING WHEN WILL THE DAY I BE
DO THEY MEAN TO ACROSS THE FISH TO MEET NOTHING COME WHEN WILL
COLONISE ME AGAIN AND HIS LOVE MAAHINAARANGI THE DAY I TURN INTO
AGAIN AS I SIT ON AN WHAT DOES LOVE SMELL SOIL AGAIN COME PAPA
ISLAND WHAT ISLANDS LIKE WELL HERE IS THE RANGI I HANG IN
HAVE BEEN BURNT TO RAUKAWA LEAF HERE IS THE BETWEEN YOU BOTH AS
NOTHING FOR THE RAUKAWA LEAF CRUSHED ON TIME AS TIME AS TIME

MY TEETH CONSTITUENT PARTS OF THE SIDE OF A ROAD SUSPENDS ITSELF FOR ME I HAVE BEEN
TASTE LIKE THIS BODY HOW ARE WE BUILT LIKE MANY OTHERS I CLIMB INTO THE MANY THINGS
WOOD MY THINKING ABOUT THIS COLONISING VEINS LASHED HEAVENS AND STEAL THE MOVING IN MANY
TONGUE TASTES BUILDING HOW DO WE ACROSS THE LAND AS THE KNOWLEDGE OF MYSELF DIRTS WILL I
LIKE TREE FEEL ABOUT THE HANDS HOUSE DISAPPEARS WITH FOR THE FUTURE I WOULD ONE DAY SWIM
KEEP MY THAT MAKE ME VERSUS THE BIRDS UNDER A FOREST LOVE TO BE DUST MOTE I IN A SEA WILL
FOREST INTACT THE HANDS THAT BUY THAT NEVER REALLY LEFT WOULD LOVE TO BE SMALL I BECOME WAKA

The Mysterious Case of the T-Rex in the Night: Rewi Thompson, Big Gay Dinosaurs, and You

Samuel Te Kani

If you haven't already, take time to note the T-Rex. Curious, isn't it. Perhaps Rewi Thompson only has a T-Rex inside his speculative architecture for purposes of scale. This would make sense, being an architect and all — scale in building design is crucial. But a T-Rex? Surely there could've been other landscape features available for similar effect. But Thompson made a very specific and endearingly idiosyncratic choice. Through the delicately rendered glass you can see little figures inside viewing the T-Rex, some on the ground, others on an elevated viewing platform. Is it a natural history museum? Is it a convention centre with a T-Rex installed to commemorate a generous deceased and dinosaur-crazy arts patron? Is it maybe a ticketed Jurassic Park experience, the kind with paid actors playing dime-store versions of John Hammond and whoever Jeff Goldblum's character was (and good luck finding a Laura Dern lookalike)?

Perhaps the building's imagined purpose is irrelevant. Perhaps what matters most is this T-Rex, a primordial anachronism in an otherwise aggressively modern glass structure biting into the open sky with jagged gables. Perhaps trying to contextualise the T-Rex is a red herring, and Thompson meant for this discordant intruder to stealthily supply some other liminal meaning. What's in a T-Rex?

In nineties cult movie *Tammy and the T-Rex* desire is ultimately amorphous. This is only after being stripped of its gendered-corporeal packaging, though, namely bodies, using a sci-fi/comedy set-up (and elaborate preposterousness) to unravel the dynamics of a conventional heteronormative teen movie for the bestial furies beneath. A speculation, perhaps, that in even the most proprietary relationships unplanned subjectivities are never completely disavowed, that in the morphology of desire the legible remains contaminated with that which it refuses to speak. The story centres on high-school cheerleader Tammy, opening with frank homage to that other American movie about supernaturally repressed sexuality, *Carrie* (Brian De Palma, 1976). Tammy and jock-type Michael are in love, but their love is dogged by Tammy's homicidally jealous ex Billy. Long story short, Billy and cohort abduct and beat Michael and leave him in a wildlife park where he's attacked by a lion, after which he has a brief stint in the hospital, then has his death faked by a mad scientist, only to finally be whisked off 'post-mortem' for said scientist's dastardly purpose — which is to transplant his living brain into a mechanical T-Rex.

Tammy and T-Rex-Michael reunite, but only after Michael slaughters his abductors and adjusts to his dysmorphic status with unlikely aptitude. Through an equally unlikely acumen for charades Tammy interprets Michael's reptilian grunts and realises her dead lover has come back to her as an extinct apex predator, and vows to force the scientist responsible to reverse the procedure. There's a minor snag, though. When they pop the ersatz grave, Michael's human body has already started to decompose. No longer an eligible candidate. Eligible being the operative word here, as a later scene in a morgue has Tammy and her painfully nineties gay-bestie Byron essentially body-shopping for a vessel befitting her preferences. Byron finds the corpse of a blonde girl in mint condition and Tammy is adamant she wants a boy, and even in jest there's the implication that Tammy's desire is necessitated by the body first, that Michael's personality is secondary to the physical attraction she feels — consummation of which they've denied themselves out of the threat from Billy (now dead).

What follows is a montage scene of potential host bodies for Michael in which difference in sex and race is conflated, identity itself become a consumer frenzy — or at least reduced to its visual signifiers, abstracted from the dialectical and aestheticised towards a mutually pleasurable romantic arrangement. As in love and sex and so here, difference is viewed exclusively through a lens of sensual utility, weighed for its fetish value. This might sound highly problematic, but the scene is a hammily comedic one, carnivalesque in its strangeness. The couple seem to be finding enjoyment in their predicament even while they try to rectify it. Despite the quote-unquote 'problem' of Michael's T-Rex body, the couple are momentarily outside the embodied essentialism of heterosexuality, even of identity itself. While here, even if for a short while, they are taking the time to breathe some fresh air and enjoy the spacious fun of the polymorphous perverse. Though never spoken it's as if they both know this, going through the motions of morphological correction like it was no more pressing than picking out ribbed condoms and a flavour of lube.

The film's climax sees T-Rex-Michael in a stand-off with both the mad scientist wanting his creation back, and some charmingly hapless police. In the ensuing shoot-out Michael is killed, or at least his bullet-riddled reptile form is unquestionably finished. Cutaway to Tammy coming home to her suburban parents with a spring in her step, like she hasn't just been subjected to a sequence of bizarre and potentially traumatic events. Her parents express concern she isn't more grieved, with her father making allusions to some horror upstairs he can barely conceive Tammy's happy to share space with.

The horror, of course, is Michael's disembodied brain, in a vat of life-support fluid and hooked up to a camera-eye so that he and Tammy can finally consummate — even if not in the ways of traditional embodied coupling. Instead, Tammy dances for Michael, putting on lingerie and doing a strip tease until sparks fly from Michael's exposed brain in apparently orgasmic audio-visual stimulation.

Besides being an incredibly prescient depiction of OnlyFans camming cultures, the film here reaches for Videodrome-levels of techno-commentary, eschewing Cronenberg's fatalism for something genuinely emancipatory. Tammy is, as her parents have already pointed out, strangely ecstatic, despite her beloved being reduced to a bowl of sentient brain-matter. As when morgue-shopping the pair allude to still being on the hunt for a suitable replacement body, and yet in this non-conventional set-up they seem happier than ever. There's clearly no rush. Just what is happening here?

Perhaps initially more a read of the ways in which cinema (and visual cultures broadly) traffic sex, and rejigger our consumptions thereof, the film nonetheless proffers a view of technology as concomitant with sexualities and their apparently limitless possibility. If Tammy showed hesitation in the morgue about having a gendered-embodied preference for a lover, by the film's close no such preference remains. Instead, Tammy is content with a love that is morphologically untethered, cavorting lasciviously within Michael's transition space as both its object of affection and its slippery enabler.

With more appealing naivete perhaps than author Maggie Nelson's chronicles of a transitioning partner (*The Argonauts*, 2015), the film here proclaims how the slippage from convention into queerness can be a ride first fraught then celebratory — an excavation not of love's essentialist core, but of a mutual expansion in love's egregiously ossified and compulsively heterosexual trenches. Unlike her ex Billy, whose addiction to heteronormative mores drove him insane with jealousy, Tammy and Michael are now entirely liberated therefrom, pursuing shapes and intimacies beyond the curtailments of given sex, gender, even personhood. Theirs is an unscripted love generating its own meaning, pioneers on the margin, drawing from a conjecturally bottomless well of morphological potential in the nexus of technology and desire.

This nexus itself has destabilised gender (both in the film and IRL), and rather than respond with immunological defence Tammy and Michael open themselves to being rewritten. Because desire as a dialectical force will always and ever subsume the structures of language with which puritanical counter-forces attempt to cage it. Such is the psychoanalytical grasp of the subconscious, as a super-processor enclosing more data than the conscious mind could ever hope to, and thusly (and thankfully) sabotaging more conscious orders with periodic liberatory destructions.

Caged is exactly how Thompson's dulcet T-Rex comes across to me. There's an implacable sadness to it. It might be a sadness connected to effigies, like some monument to the old ways Tammy and Michael have forgone, charging forth in queerness and love against the cat-calls of a decrepit guard of eroto-luddites. A dinosaur in more ways than one. A dead king, the world over which he once ruled long gone but remembered — despite its problems — for contemporary perspective. More to it then than trickery of architectural scale.

This is of course pure fabula and we can hardly credibly presume Thompson's intention was queer-coding à la *Tammy and the T-Rex*. Was he even alive when the film was released? Speculation is the writer's very pleasurable bread and butter, though, and it's what I indulge here with free rein, if only to productively bridge texts with seemingly nothing in common except a carnivorous prehistoric McGuffin (see Hitchcock).

What I can say, though, is he seems lonely. It's a large building and apart from a few curious visitors — no doubt selfie-ing up a storm — this T-Rex is by himself, looking out across the ocean with all the amorous grief of Dido (both the early noughties pop star and the war-widow from the *Aeneid*). I dread to imagine what happens in the night when sightseers are ushered out and the building's doors are closed and locked.

As cages go, one that might be worse for having walls of glass, reflective in the day and pitch black at night with only the sound of the steadily rising seas to keep him company. Poor thing. As public art goes, a reminder of what happens when we refuse our personal evolutions when they come calling. Stuck in a cage — even an architecturally flashy cage — forever.

The Bridge

Gina Cole

KOHA

I was built across the mouth of an estuary to save people the trouble of driving around the purple hills, a circuitous and dangerous route where many people have lost their lives miscalculating turns, driving over the edge into the harbour or smashing into each other in head-on collisions as they crossed the short one-lane bridge at the northern end of the inlet. The one-lane bridge is a concrete single-span which now sits in retirement with the old fishermen who cast their rods into the river below to catch eels on sunny days. It calls to me when the rain howls — thank the gods you are here.

Unlike the one-lane bridge I have many modern safety features — clear arching barriers to stop jumpers (because I have a very high span), split dual carriageways to prevent head-on collisions, and closed-in lookouts where people can view the surroundings: from the hills on one side, to the surf at the entrance of the bay on the other side, to the valleys, and the town and the marae nestled into the foothills. I also have my wings, vast inverted spans which some people call architectural folly and others call genius. Every time Pāpā Hone drives along my belly with his moko he tells the story about how my wings come from the tukutuku panels in the wharenui carved by his grandfather.

Not long after my opening ceremony I tried to fly away. The wind blew into the channel and hummed into my wings, lifting my spirit. My wiring vibrated and I struggled to lift off into the air to join the karoro. My belly rose, sending a truck careening into the barriers. My edges shook and people screamed and lost their balance on the pedestrian alley. Others fell and injured themselves in the stairwells leading up to the lookouts. But I am strung along twenty-three strong footings and five wide cylindrical pillars driven into the bedrock of the bay.

When I tried to escape, my feet betrayed me, digging into the mud and rock beneath blue estuarine water, dispersing my need to fly and keeping me grounded, refusing my efforts to break away. I didn't understand — I have wings. I wanted to fly with the birds. I know my job is to provide safe passage over the estuary for tourists and residents and vehicles and to stand bold and proud, an artistic monument for all to enjoy. But there is so much tension in my bones.

I called out to the ancient concrete bridge, settled and squat in the riverbed. It has neither the ability nor the inclination to lift off and fly. You are young and new. You will settle into the water and do your job. The hills huffed and grumbled and told me I was a selfish structure. They have stood guard over the estuary since time immemorial and will be here long after I have outlived my usefulness. The karoro, tara, tōrea, tākapu and toroa were evenly split. Half wanted me to stay put to ensure their roosts and colonies would remain safe within the ridges of my wings and the crevices beneath my spanned belly. The other half spurred me on to join them, telling me tales of the sights I would see flying into a velvet orange sunset and the wonder I would experience gliding on thermal uplifts over blue water that melded into blue sky.

The winds were the only ones that understood. They explained that I can take flight in myriad possibilities — in the imaginations of people who walk and ride on my belly, who love to climb to my lookouts, who find comfort in me as a guidance point from the valley. I can float in the wairua of the people taking their loved ones on their last journey over my belly. I can drift in the mauri of the waters swirling at my feet and the hills casting their protective shadows over me.

The hills groaned in agreement when the winds spoke this way. The winds promised to always sing to my wings — there is flight in singing, in laughter, in morning mist, in sea spray, in water trickling down the face of a rock high up in the valley, in a scatter of mountain flowers opening across the hills, in the humming of a truck driver, in anything at all.

My attempted lift-off brought together all the people in the valley for a meeting in the town hall. Newspaper reporters questioned the truck driver who'd smashed into the carriageway. He didn't tell them he'd taken a phone call from his distraught and pregnant wife who had gone into labour and had called an ambulance to transport her to the hospital. I'm okay, but please come straight to the birthing suite. I knew the truck driver's heart, but I wouldn't tell. Television news people questioned the pedestrians who fell on the undulating footpath. Yes, the bridge had lifted. They thought I might collapse and tip them into the sea. One woman arrived at the meeting on crutches. She gave a terrifying account on the 6 o'clock news of being thrown against the walls inside a stairwell, scrambling to hold on but there were no handrails.

The bridge inspectors arrived soon after. They closed me off to all traffic and pedestrian access, placed barriers at each end of me. They took samples, drilled holes and tested my strength with high-range conductivity machines. They closed the lookouts and talked about removing my wing spans.

The architect arrived flustered and frustrated. Had the builders placed the rivets at the correct intervals? Had they positioned the reinforced steel struts at the precise angles he had specified? Where were the handrails in the stairwells? The councillors met around a large wooden table and decided to commission an independent enquiry. They agreed for public safety I would be closed until they knew the outcome. The winds curled around my struts. I sang into the grottos deep in the hills and whistled to the waves crashing at the heads.

The old concrete bridge called out to me in a grumpy stony voice. Now look what you've gone and done with your modern flights of fancy. There was a terrible crash on me today. Three people were killed. Do your job! I flexed my wings a little, huffing into the breeze. The people at the marae told the inspectors they had to bury three people in the urupā. Those people would still be here if you hadn't shut the tukutuku bridge. The kuia cried. Pāpā Hone spoke with fire in his belly. My footings sank further into the rock and mud. It's a safety issue, said the engineers, and the councillors agreed. We'll have to wait for the findings of the enquiry.

When the judge and the lawyers arrived, everyone packed into the town hall. The councillors dragged their meeting table to the end of the room and four young men carried out a couple of formica tables from the dining room for the lawyers. The judge took her place in a square of sunlight falling through the north window. Everyone helped to bring chairs out from the cupboard at the back, placing them behind the lawyers, in bingo night rows. The truck driver hung his head, told the judge he was on his phone, it was an emergency, it wasn't the bridge that caused him to crash. People murmured and shifted in their seats.

The head builder answered questions from the lawyers while sweat circles formed in the armpits of his suit jacket. He admitted his company had tried to save costs by putting in fewer handrails than the plans required. A collective gasp rose from the people seated in the hall. One man stood up and shouted that the corrupt builder should be jailed. The judge raised her voice above the uproar, calling for silence.

I stretched my wings around everyone to protect them and sent my songs to them on the wind. They all heard me. They turned their heads this way and that, like tōrea listening for the gentle pop of crustaceans settling into the sand.

A report came out weeks later stating that traffic, pedestrians and tourists were safe to cross over me. The judge recommended that more safety rails be installed in the stairwells inside my wings. The next day townsfolk and farmers from both sides of the valley, fishermen from the boats and the truck driver with his wife and new baby joined people from the marae and marched to my eastern entrance.

They removed the barriers and walked across my belly. They chanted and performed haka to the hills. I escaped in their song and grief as the winds had promised. My feet sank deeper into the rocky layers beneath the estuary and I settled a little more into the silt, like the old concrete bridge had said I would.

That evening the people rested safe in their homes and the wind whistled through my wings. A group of karoro touched down in the mangroves on the far side of the bay. They flicked their heads to the hum of traffic travelling over my belly. One gull rose into the spring breeze carrying a live crab, its dangling pincers snapping at the air. The gull climbed higher, her wings beating in synchrony with my humming bridge spans. She released the crab to its fate. A Catherine wheel death tumble, orange shell smashing on a flat rock. Cawing gulls rushed to the feast.

It had been a satisfying day for them, full of grab, lift and smash, set against the imposing backdrop of the breakers at the heads. The hills turned mauve in lengthening evening light and the gulls flew from the muddy mangroves into cool airstreams, their bellies heavy with smashed crab meat.

They flew to my tallest wing span arching high above the water and sat with their wings tucked into their sides. On the next wing, my middle one, a tara colony roosted for the night, tightly packed in together. On my southern wing the toroa nested and waited for the planetary tip that would signal time for her to fly over the ocean to South America. The tākapu colony on my two north wings sat in their nests shaking their yellow heads. The tōrea remained in the mangroves facing into the onshore breeze while the wind buzzed between my wings, pāpā Hone sang to his moko, the architect sat in the darkened wharenui drawing tukutuku wing spans and the sunset cast a velvet orange display over the vast ocean expanse.

Koirak

auer

puna

meaners.

Design philosophy

Tautake hoahoa

Mā te tika o te toki o te tangere, me te tohu o te panoho,
ka pai te tere o te waka i ngā momo moana katoa
*Through the correctness of the adze that shapes the hull of the
waka, the waka will travel swiftly through every kind of ocean*

Architecture and translation

The exhibition *Now See Hear!: Art, Language, and Translation*, curated by Gregory Burke and Ian Wedde, ran from 15 July to 30 September 1990 at the Wellington City Art Gallery. *Now See Hear!* was 'assembled around the central rubric of translation',[1] and the essays in the accompanying publication address 'translations between art, language, advertising, television, graphic design, comics, videos, film, history, art-history, signs and symbols, landscape and architecture'.[2] Extracts from Rewi Thompson's essay explore the translation or interpretation of Māori cultural concepts into architecture (traditional and contemporary), and also interrogate the spatially mediated relationships between Māori and Pākehā: the differing spatial relationships that arise from differing cultural viewpoints, and the architectural conflict that sometimes occurs as a result.

Rewi Thompson
Ngāti Raukawa: Ngāti Ngarongo, Ngāiterangi; Ngāti Porou: Te Aitanga-a-Hauiti, Ngāi Tāmanuhiri

Māori architecture has been little theorised yet its presence and language have existed in New Zealand for hundreds of years, and its translation may be understood by only a few. Māori have strong ties to their ancestral land. This is not only portrayed in Māori mythology but is more significantly expressed in their daily lives. The meanings of marae, tāngata whenua, tūrangawaewae, are fundamental to Māori life and are expressed both physically and spiritually.

Often the physical aspect is misread or misunderstood. For example, the wharenui (meeting house) (fig. 1) is often visualised as a facade and labelled as a 'traditional form', with a door to the left and window to the right. The wharenui however is more symbolic and more expansive in its meaning. Basically it represents the tīpuna (ancestor) of that particular house.

1   Ian Wedde and Gregory Burke (eds), *Now See Hear!: Art, Language, and Translation* (Wellington: Victoria University Press for Wellington City Art Gallery, 1990), p. 8.
2   Ibid.

Design philosophy

fig. 1

fig. 2

The building components represent the body parts; for instance: the tekoteko (gable apex) represents the head, the maihi (barge board) represent the arms, the tāhuhu (ridge) represents the backbone, the heke (rafters) represent the ribs, etc. Traditionally, all the building components were carved, painted or woven to reinforce and complete the whakapapa (genealogy). (fig. 2)

Today we see our meeting houses not so much as *translations of the original* but more as *interpretations* based on tradition.

The structural integrity of our modern houses no longer relates to the traditional house. However, Māori it seems have accepted this, so long as the spiritual meaning and symbolism remain, and this is usually in the form of tekoteko, kōwhaiwhai and carving, applied as elements independent from structure and construction. (fig. 3)
This acceptance, in my view, separates the essence of the symbolism from the structure. If this is the case, then symbolism should decide the structure. However, the common practice is to build the house shell, then design the symbolism within the space.

There have been cases where carvings have been inappropriately sized for the space. How relevant does symbolism become then? What seems to have happened is that the master carver's role has changed.

This may suggest that as long as significance and symbolism are understood, the physical form or translation may be more a matter of interpretation and not fixed.

The spiritual and symbolic dimensions allow our interpretation or translation to be flexible and to accommodate compromised situations without losing the 'bare bones' or 'essence'.

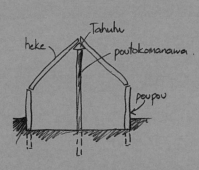
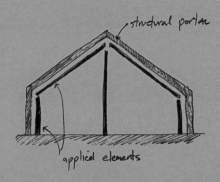

fig. 3

fig. 4

This wharenui is for Ngāti Ōtara Marae Society and breaks from the traditional door and window order. The door and window are conceived as one element. This acceptance illustrates the changing view of the Māori, and that tradition may only be a matter of interpretation. (fig. 4)

This design for a 'Hometown Museum' for Wellington, was based on the marae. The marae is symbolised in the form of a futuristic canoe beached within the harbour. (fig. 5) The spiritual significance and protocol of the marae still exist, but the architecture has been 'translated' in a contemporary form.

fig. 5

Pa & Mana

While the pā was primarily seen as a defence device, it also became an identity and therefore carried mana (prestige). Tribes associated themselves with their respective pā and these became symbolic landmarks. (fig. 6)

This symbolism attached to our 'landmarks' and pā sites is less obvious today, yet the translation of these places can suggest architecture which is more significant and relevant than is normally achieved.

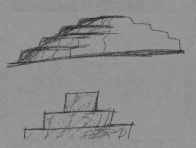
fig. 6

This design is for a prestigious office block development for Auckland. The form is dramatised by the volcanic cones of Auckland which also became pā sites for the Māori inhabitants. (fig. 7) (fig. 8)

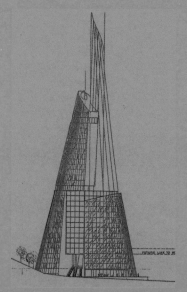
fig. 7

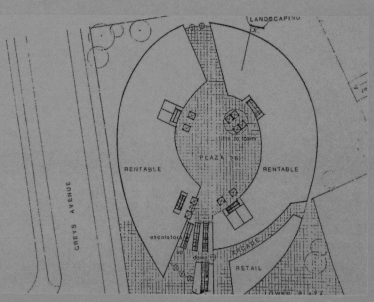
fig. 8

Design philosophy

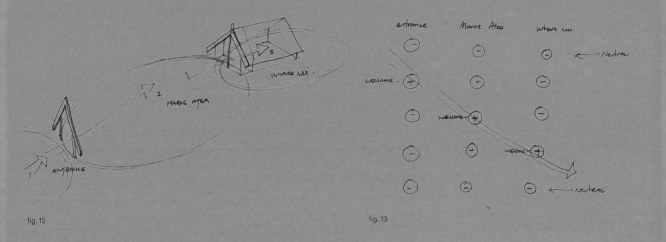

fig. 12

fig. 13

fig. 9

fig. 10

fig. 11

The Debating Chambers for the Auckland Regional Authority's new buildings (fig. 9) have been articulated to reflect the numerous volcanic cones and headlands. (fig. 10) The association of various areas is expressed as a city. This expression is sometimes difficult to visualise in architecture. The sketches and design illustrate that the various parts of the city are architecturally connected — connected physically, spatially, historically and spiritually. (fig. 11)

Marae & Space

The marae is a place for 'rituals of encounter', whether it be for tangi, hui, etc. The welcome process is formal and follows protocols and tradition. The architecture is interpreted not so much as building, but in spatial terms. (fig. 12)

    1st space — entrance
    2nd space — marae ātea
    3rd space — wharenui

The significance of each space is clearly defined during the welcome, by the protocol process. At times when there are no functions, the space is *unified*. Today the marae is used occasionally and therefore the spatial quality is always changing.

This diagram illustrates the change in spatial quality and relevance, dictated by formal occasions on the marae. Space is more dynamic and related to time. If space is three dimensional, this may suggest that space can be defined in a vertical direction, and related to the welcome process. (fig. 13)

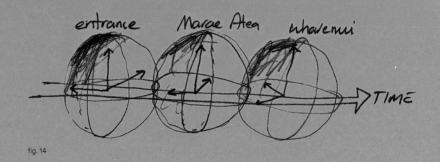

fig. 14

fig. 15

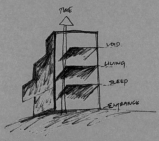

fig. 16

fig. 17

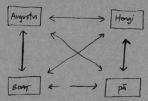

fig. 18

If the 'marae' can be translated into architectural space, then 'time' becomes a 4th dimension of (marae) architectural space. (fig. 14)

The house in Kohimarama, Auckland (fig. 15) has interpreted the marae as an architectural space in a vertical direction. (fig. 16) A four-storey void unifies the whole house as a space. (fig. 17)

As one ascends, the mezzanine levels define each space relative to the position of the person ascending.
The experience should be no different, whether moving vertically or horizontally.

Different Viewpoints

The arrival of the Pākehā resulted in architecture being seen as more absolute, more defined. Māori and Pākehā translations of architecture can be conflicting. However, architectural conflict can only be resolved in architectural terms. That is to say, in terms of the relationship between different viewpoints, or rather the spatial relationship between each viewpoint. This architectural conflict may not produce answers but will at least define differences.

Augustus Earle's painting *Meeting of the Artist with the Wounded Chief* allows us to translate this historic event in architectural terms.

Hongi's relationship with site — the land.

Hongi is looking out.

Augustus's relationship with site is not clear but we can assume that it is with his way out — the sea.

Earle is looking in.

The different relationships can be defined as outlined in the matrix. (fig. 18)

Design philosophy

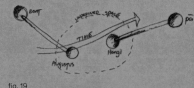

fig. 19

fig. 21

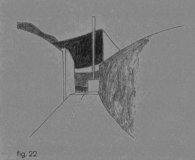

fig. 22

However, the relationships should be defined three-dimensionally, if we are to see things in architectural terms. (fig. 19)

Both Augustus and Hongi have clearly defined space relationships. The transitional space between them is more difficult to define but exists nevertheless. To illustrate this more physically, we can look at a house design for the Hokianga Harbour, Northland. (fig. 20)

The individual elements and their spaces respond to various aspects of the harbour and surrounding hills. They 'come together' at a particular point. Each element is a segment of a larger site and is represented by its shape and orientation. (fig. 21) (fig. 22)

The space created by the elements is undefined and transitional. Similar to the space created between Augustus and Hongi. This space could be informal, friendly, unpretentious, etc.

In creating architecture in New Zealand, the spiritual dimension is virtually untried. Yet it has existed here for hundreds of years. In my view it would be difficult to call New Zealand architecture authentic without coming to grips with the spiritual dimension. How one decides to translate this is a matter of interpretation. The architectural space created by Augustus and Hongi defined their relationship. It is not always necessary to see architecture as formal elements. As architects, we need to get used to this idea.

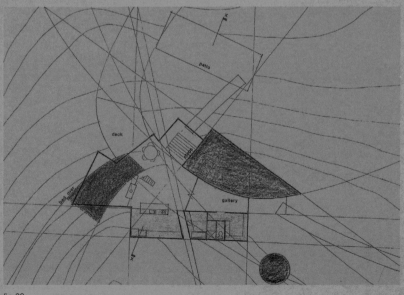

fig. 20

Māori architecture — a myth

This short article by Rewi was published in *NZ Architect* in 1987. In it Rewi expresses his views on the notion of defining a Māori-specific architecture or architectural style. He seems to be resisting easy categorisation, and instead encouraging readers to think more deeply about the contributions of Māori people and culture to New Zealand architecture.

Anthropology in this century has focused attention upon ethnic cultures and societies. The authenticity of expressions of these cultures within multicultural societies — of which everyone is also a part — has become a most important subject.

It is no coincidence, then, that with the travelling of the *Te Māori Exhibition*, and the new influx of adopted 'architectural styles' — the re-use of art deco, Gothic, and classical languages — speculation should arise concerning the possible emergence of more definite Māori influences in NZ architecture.

If it ever eventuates, then great!

But I think the days of labelling architectural styles after ethnic groups or minorities are all gone.

For instance, the notion of developing a Pākehā or Māori architecture sounds absurd (that happened two hundred years ago). It would be fair to say, however, that regardless of our individual backgrounds, ties with our pasts and continuity [are] still very strong.

In a rapidly changing society it seems an insult to our 'forebears' that we still maintain only their previous cultural style.

Further to this, it is no secret that most architectural critics require a 'reference point' to make statements or critical comments. Categorising or labelling architects work provides these limits or reference points. There are architects who deliberately label themselves or advocate a particular style. They are quite rightly criticised for their own actions.

There are some architects, however, who have no intention of belonging to any architectural style, but rather believe that an open ended approach, and developing work on its own merits, is a far better way of doing things. As individuals we have the freedom to choose our own approach to our work.

Design philosophy

For instance, because I'm Māori, that doesn't necessarily
mean that my work is Māori architecture. 'Sure, there are
times when Māori influence is appropriate, but not all the
bloody time mate.'

Architecture can be a lot more interesting than categorising
people and their work. Deep down 'cuzzies', we're all the
same whether physically or spiritually, it's only a matter of
degree.

To talk about the development or influence by Māori people in
architecture is a worthwhile and important task.

The above comments are made because they are immediately
relevant to our readers.

But it is the coming decade which will be of crucial
importance to this discussion.

New Zealand in America

In 1986, Rewi joined Roger Walker, John Blair and Ian Athfield on a lecture tour of the United States. In this abridged version of an article originally published in *NZ Architect* magazine, Rewi reflects on his shifting attitudes to life and practice as a result of this trip.

I couldn't foresee the impact the trip would have on my personal life. This article is a personal picture of those effects.

As the youngest architect of the group, I felt humble and was very much led, but I grew in confidence from talking about my work in the context of the others.

These were three very strong individuals in NZ architecture and that strength made us a strong voice in talking about NZ.

Although we were four people trying to create an authentic view of NZ architecture from different viewpoints, we were New Zealanders with a common landscape and environment, so we tried to represent ourselves as a group.

This forced us to reassess our work before we could talk about it to the Americans, and in turn reinforced our feeling of being Kiwi.

Travelling together, bundled in aeroplanes, taxis and hotels, we spent many hours reflecting on where we're at and where we're going in our work. It was like going to America to see ourselves.

Suddenly, for the first time, we began to see real meaning in our work. We'd never done that before because we were so used to getting our 'work out the door'.

As the trip progressed we built on each other's strengths.

Over a huge pizza and beer one night, we talked about our presentation at Yale and the difficulties Roger had speaking to a 'dead' audience. He was trying to make them laugh.

We all felt Roger had a lot to say about his work and underneath the humour was a serious man who had a lot to offer not only to NZ but Americans too.

As we sat around eating our pizza at one o'clock in the morning, trying to help Roger's presentation, it struck me here were four independent individuals who had a real desire to work as a unit and help each other.

Design philosophy

The real benefits of the trip for me came from just being with the group; sharing their experience, advice and friendship.

It was a new phase I entered in my work, and I think it was a new phase for the other guys as well.

I've formed a new direction and approach to my work, and I'm starting to see benefits, not so much architecturally, but as a person.

I think architecture will also be a reflection of the character of the person doing it.

So I've had to start looking at myself, my own intuitive feelings and assess what qualities and skills I have. I've never done that before, and I'm trying to develop qualities I have, rather than develop new ones.

When you look at Roger, John, and Ian, they've very strong people.

Take Roger, on the surface he's a colourful character and his work reflects that.

They're all three very serious architects and regardless of whether you like their work or not, you have to admire them as people.

What I was seeing in Roger's work wasn't necessarily a building but was Roger's qualities which ultimately became the building.

The building is the end product. There's a process in between which makes it good or bad, and unless you acknowledge and respect that process, together with people, it can still be a disaster.

As I develop as a person I think my architecture will develop from that.

The trip's also given me new confidence in my work. Whatever I feel intuitively I'll do it, and I'm not afraid of the outcome of my design.

Before the trip, the business was a private matter. I think it comes from my Māori upbringing, and being a minority I was reserved.

My parents were poor and we lived a sheltered life, but we knew the fundamental qualities of integrity, and I'm proud of that.

My whole life's been directed upward and I needed a trigger to accelerate the process. Travelling with Roger, John and Ian gave me that trigger.

So now I've opened up the business and we talk about everything.

We're using systems which are appropriate to the way we design, present and market our work, rather than be dictated by systems.

We think drawings as a tool to design aren't necessarily beneficial . . . and developing one's thinking is a more positive approach because until you get the ideas sorted out you can't talk about a building.

We talk about a job until we reach a consensus, and there's always a time when we come together to fine-tune a design. I haven't done this before.

Then we'll pick the most appropriate way of illustrating it rather than having the system dictate how we should do it, and the designs become ours rather than an individual's.

This means none of our jobs are the same, every problem's different and we have a different way of looking at it.

We're flexible and open minded but there's a loose framework and I've become more of a mobile resource person which my team can call upon.

Because I now have a certain direction I can choose people to work with me with similar ideas and attitude. In essence, they have taken over part of my design brain and this allows me to concentrate more on the business side of architecture which I'm enjoying . . . such as planning and marketing.

Whether we knew it or not, on the trip we were developing marketing skills — as a group and as individuals, and this has flowed into my business.

In a marketing sense, I'm aiming at people who'll be receptive to what I'm doing, rather than getting work for work's sake.

By targeting this way, I can direct my attention to the work I want and not waste time. There are a lot of people who've spent the last five years doing work which hasn't necessarily meant they're better off as architects. To my way of thinking that's five years wasted.

I'd hate to be in that situation, so the only way I can progress and develop is to get the work I want and market to people who'll benefit from my work.

Architects should be targeting themselves more to their individual qualities and intuition.

One of the nicest things that's happened since the trip is my business has become part of my family.

My family are already half of my life as my business is half of my life, but having accepted an openness on life, they're considered in all things.

Leona, my wife, is going to be involved in the administration side because she has those skills, as she'll be part of my business life as well as a mother to 18 month old Lucy.

Design philosophy

Extending from that, I'd like to involve more Māori people in
the business, not because they're Māori but because of what
they have to offer.

It's important that while I'm developing we offer a wide
range of options. Māori people have a different approach and
this will balance against some of my colleagues' ideas . . .
who are primarily Pākehā.

And it's not only on the design side, but all aspects of the
business. So what I'm developing is a unique business and
administration approach to an architectural practice.

From our visit, and in the wake of TE MĀORI, the Americans
started to see how the Māori was adapting in the Pākehā world
without losing their identity or integrity.

I spoke about how my work reflects the bi-culturalism of
Māori and Pākehā.

Being brought up in the more physical world of the Pākehā,
I learnt to deal with physical things, as opposed to the
Māori world which is a very metaphysical one, and I think a
lot of my work reflects the balance between things Māori and
Pākehā.

I was able to illustrate in my talks, that in the past
there's been an imbalance in cultural influence, and my work
now is showing some versatility that both Māori and European
people can enjoy.

I think that's unique to New Zealand and that's what I have
to offer as an architect.

And that motivates me to further my knowledge and experience
in both European and Māori worlds.

If you like, it's a matter of trying to do twice as much work
in half the time . . . and it's difficult.

Ian Athfield had a phrase he used a lot . . . 'It doesn't
matter'. At the time I couldn't come to grips with it, but I
understand it now.

For instance, being a 'Māori architect' doesn't matter so
much as what I believe in.

I believe in architecture . . . that's my product. Because I'm
Māori I just have a different approach.

Being called a Māori architect is just a label. We don't call
an architect who's Catholic, a 'Catholic architect' or a
woman a 'Woman architect'. . . we're all architects.

Creative process

Te hātepe auaha

Ko Tāne pupuke
Tāne is welling up (designs, thoughts and plans are springing up in profusion)

Rewi always seemed to be drawing, on big sheets of paper in his office or in the pocket notebooks he always carried with him. 'He never stopped,' his daughter Lucy says. 'We'd be sitting at a restaurant sometimes and he'd have left his pocketbook in the car, so he'd get the napkin out and he'd draw on it.' Lucy now has many of Rewi's notebooks — a rich assemblage of doodles, recipes, rugby tactics and other jottings — in her personal collection, and his archives at the University of Auckland are full of sheets on which he was attempting to figure out one architectural problem or another.

It's not straightforward to tie any of the sketches on the following pages to specific architectural projects, but we wanted to include a selection of them here because we felt they illuminated something of Rewi's process, and how he utilised pen and paper in his constant search for the right approach. All the material was photographed by Samuel Hartnett.

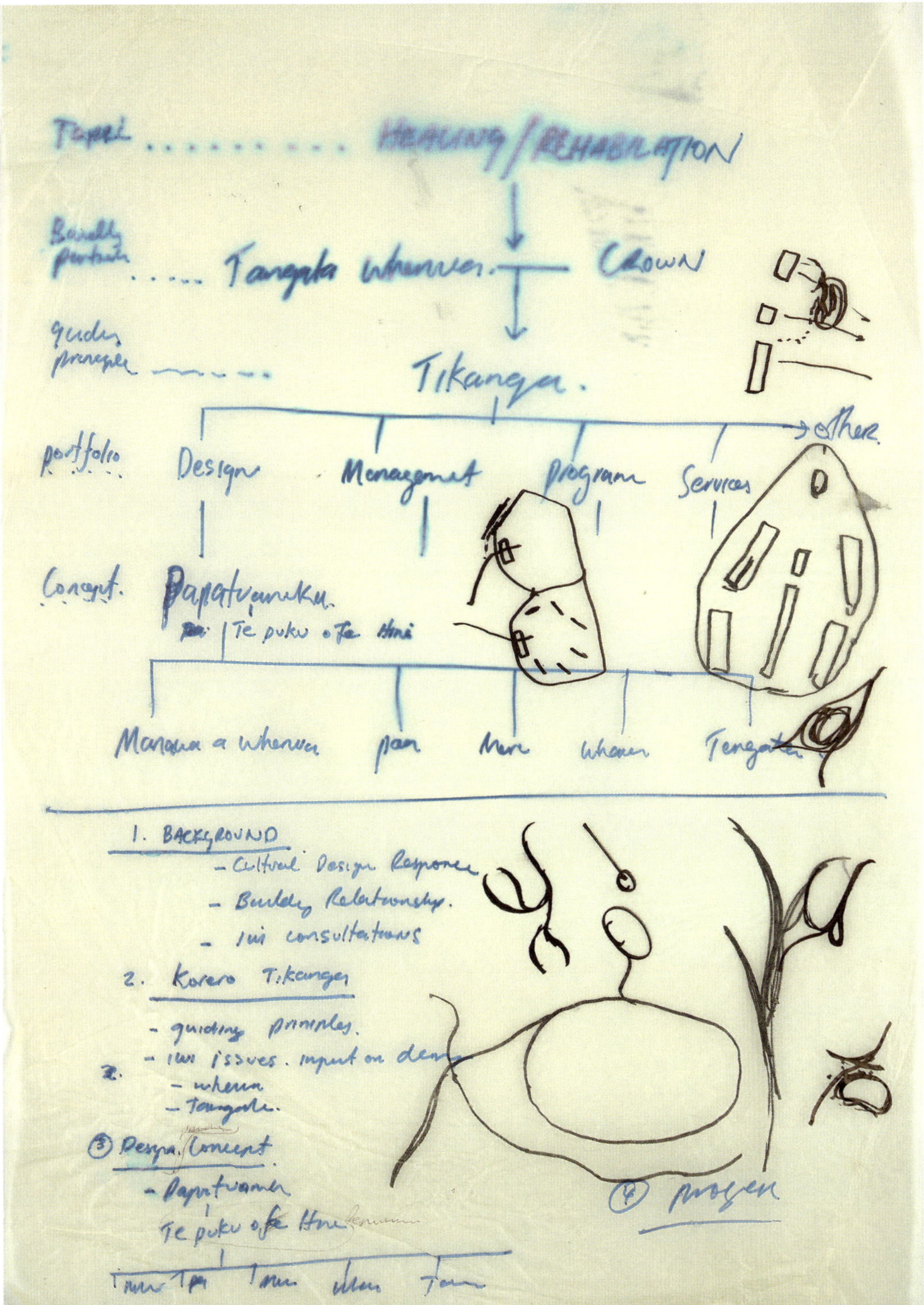

Topic .... HEALING / REHABILITATION

Broadly
pertains ..... Tangata whenua. — CROWN

guiding
principles — — — — — —

Tikanga.

portfolio   Design   Management   Program   Services   → other.

Concept.   Papatuanuku.
Ra: | Te puku o Te Hine

Manawa a whenua   pan   Mari   whenua   Tangata

---

1. BACKGROUND
   - Cultural Design Response.
   - Broadly Relationships.
   - iwi consultations

2. Korero Tikanga
   - guiding principles.
   - iwi issues. input on des—
      - whenua
      - Tangata.

③ Design / Concept
   - Papatuanuku
   Te puku o Te Hine —————

Taua Tai   Taua   whau   Tana

Creative process

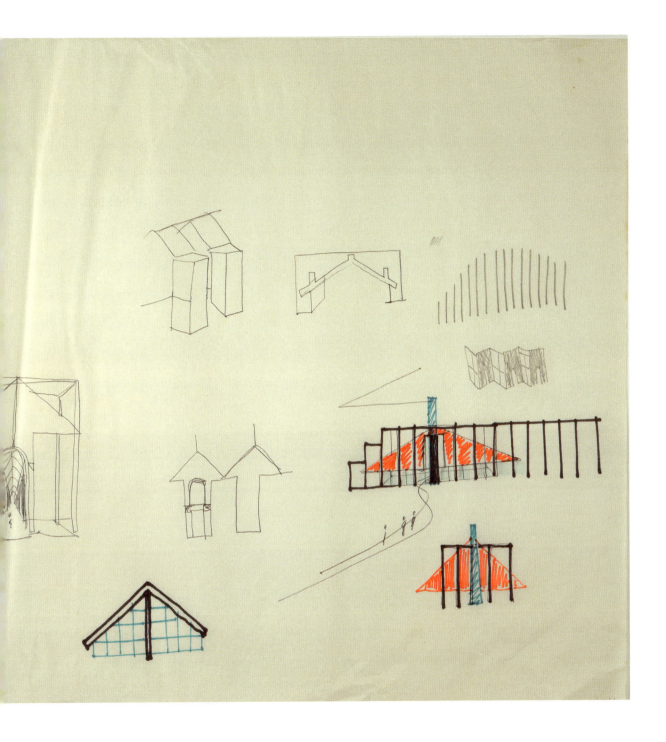

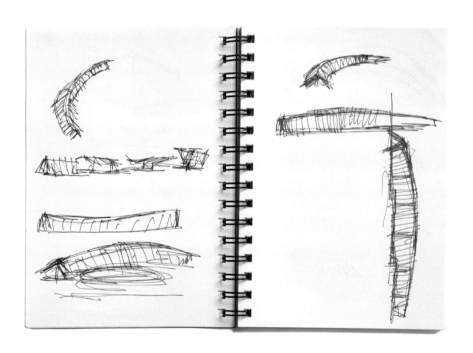
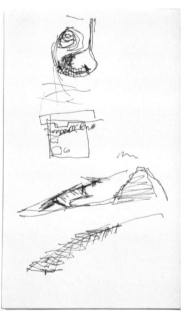

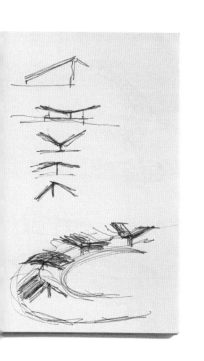
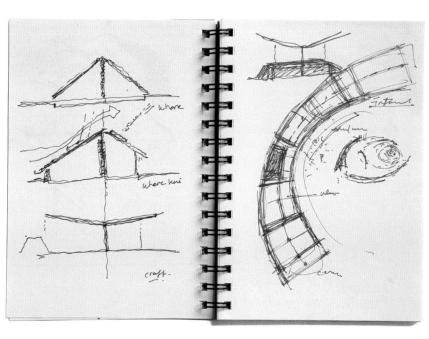

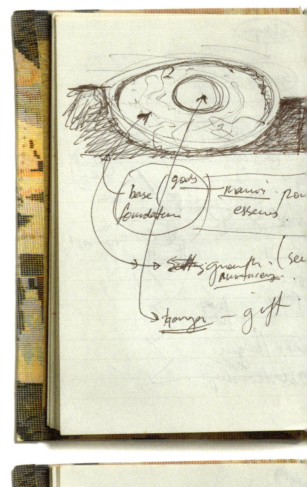

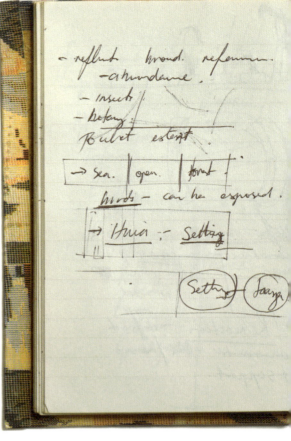

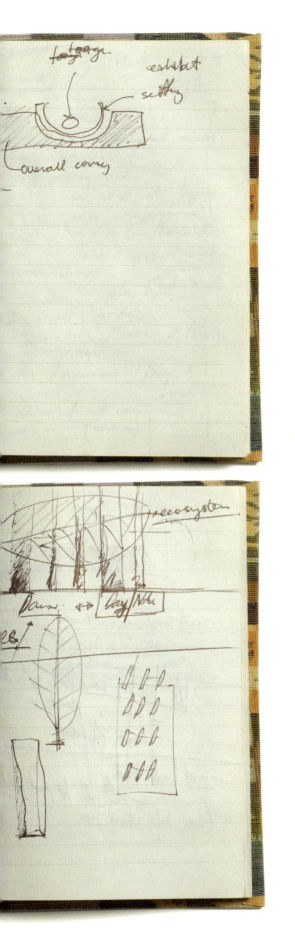

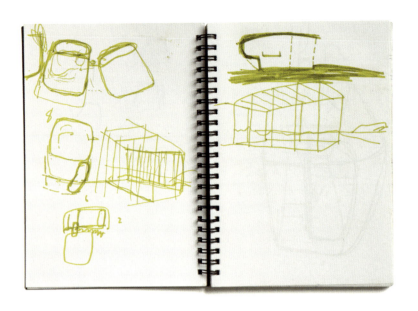

Creative process

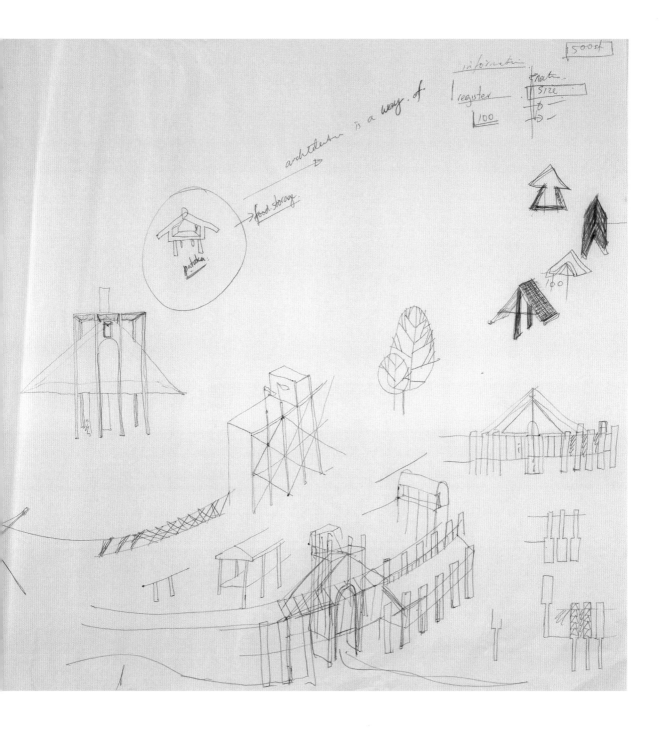

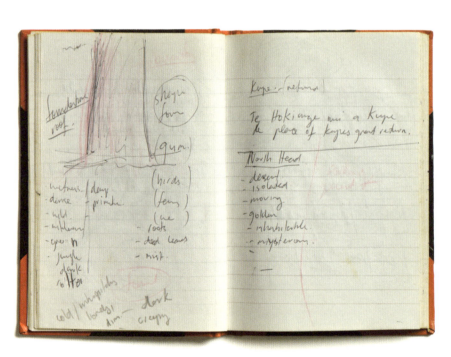

Creative process

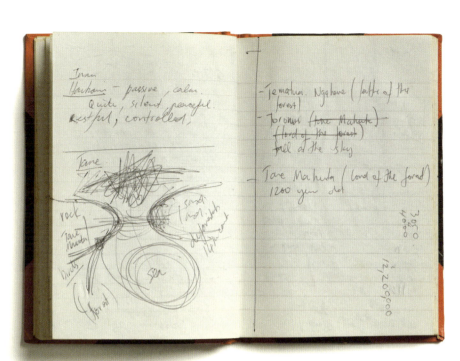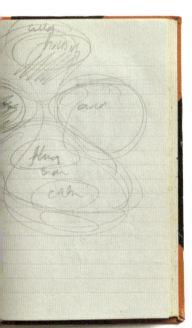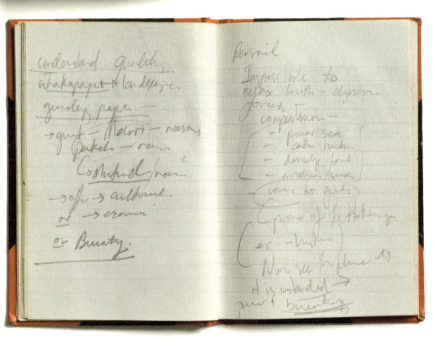

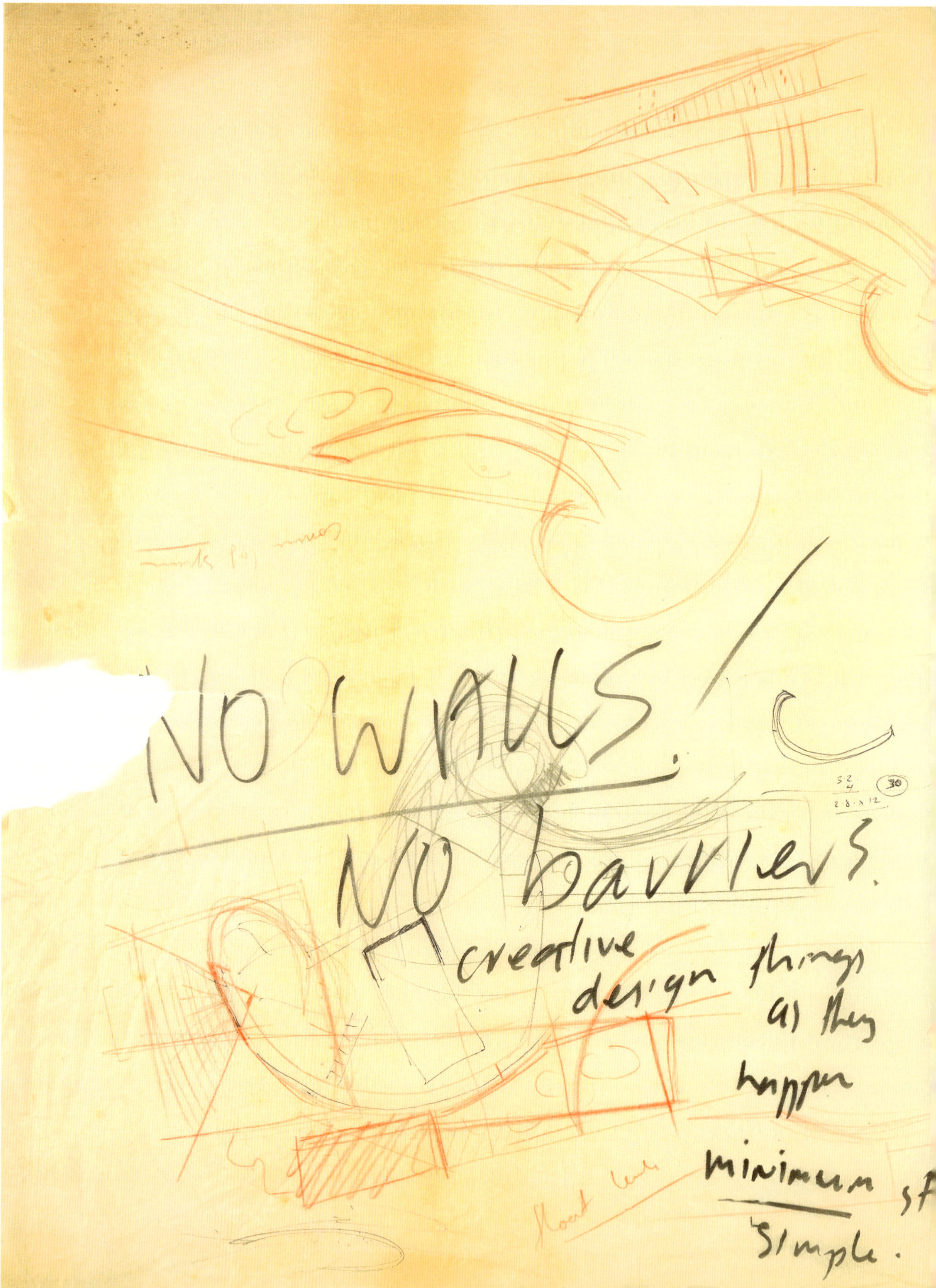

NO WALLS.

NO barriers.

creative
design things
as they
happen
minimum sf
Simple.

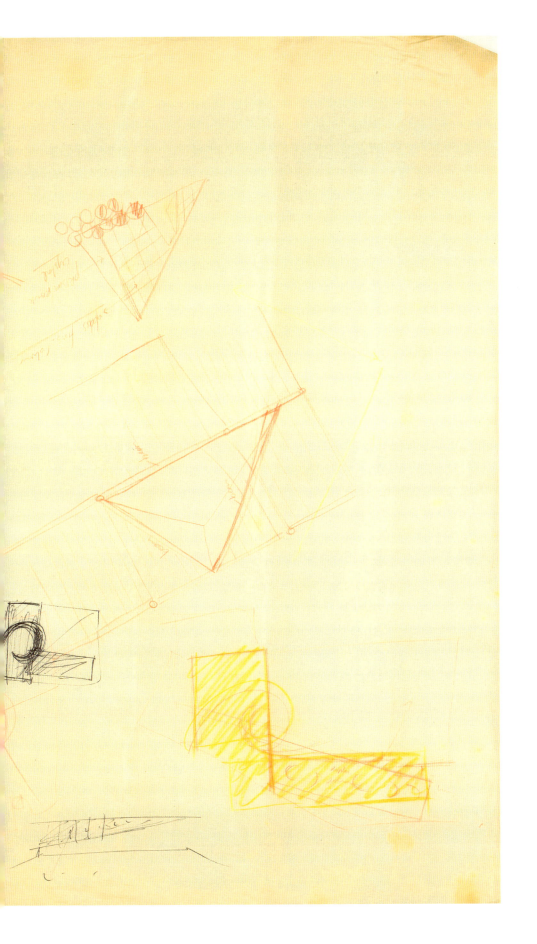

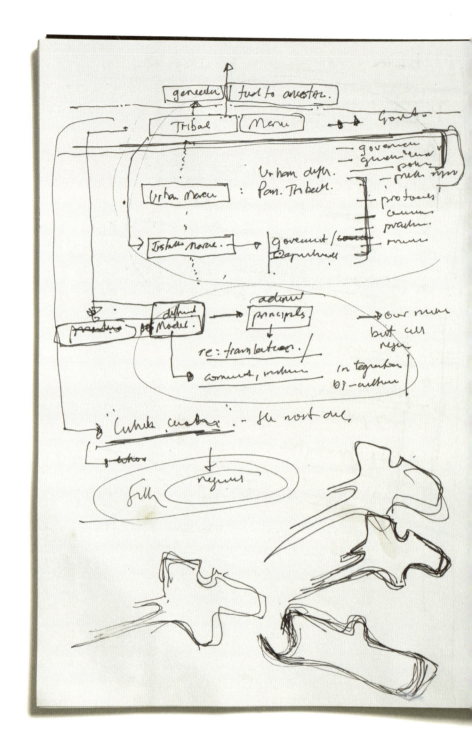

Creative process

REWI THOMPSON   ARCHITECT B.Arch (Hons)
PO Box 37-406 / 130 St. Georges Bay Road / Parnell / Auckland / NZ /
Telephone (09) 732-088, 732-090 / Fax 732-030

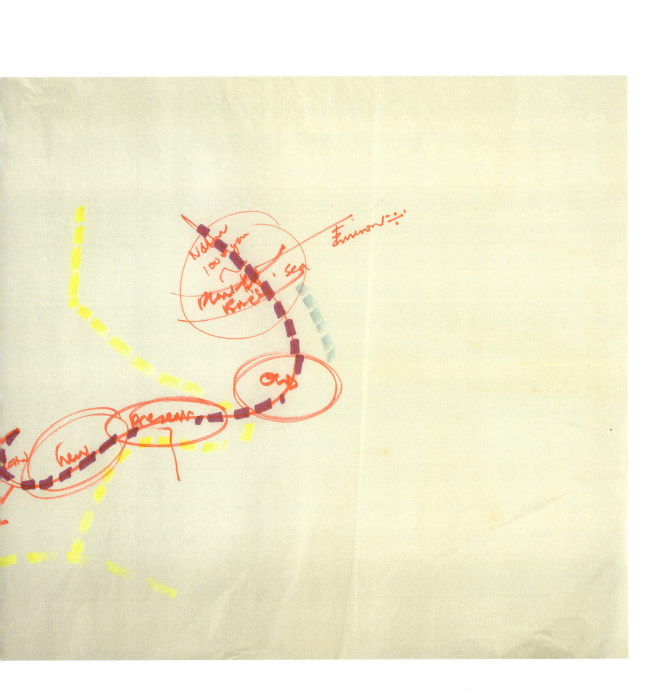

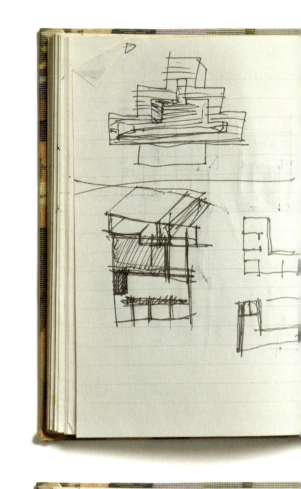
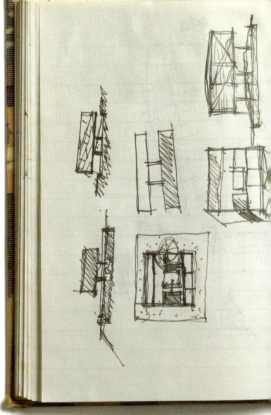

...dscoby with landscape
a house (or group)
individuals
ae. the spacial qualities
sch. — /intellect) — fuel.

...shape/qualities as fuel.
creative thought — relevth
mode, —
...lationship shop —
overall scheme

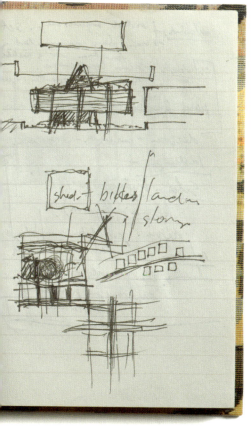

shed — bikes / landon
 stony

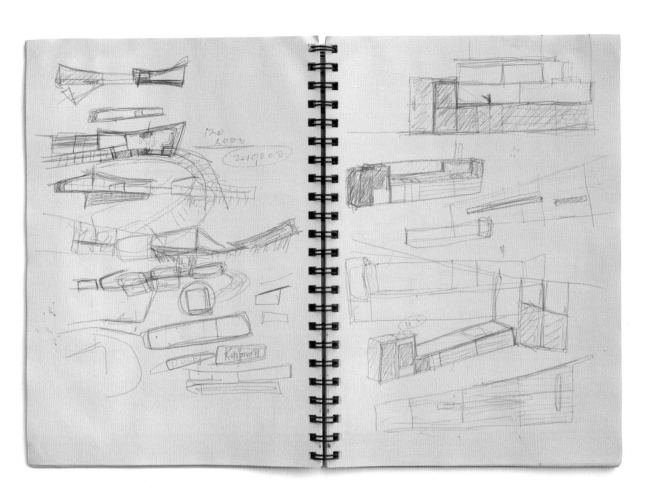

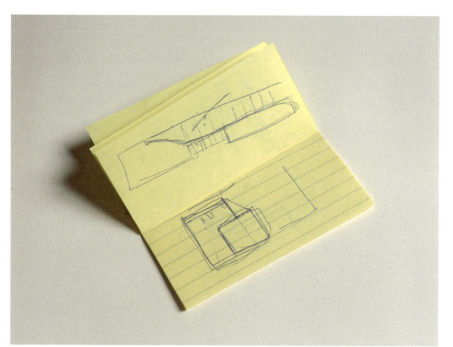
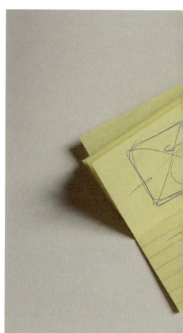

Creative process

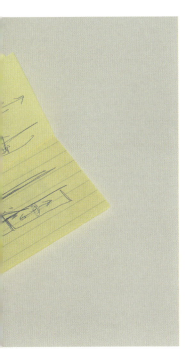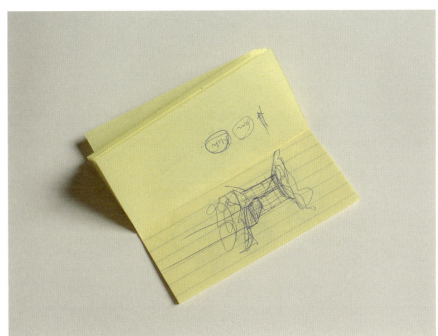

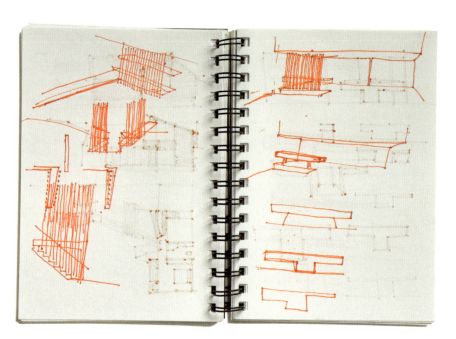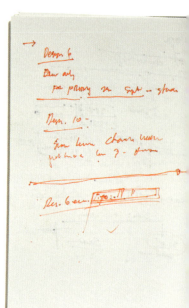

Creative process

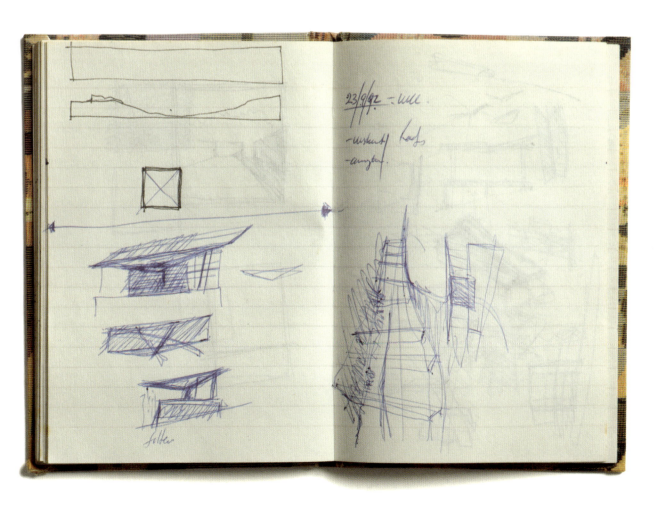

Creative process

Creative process

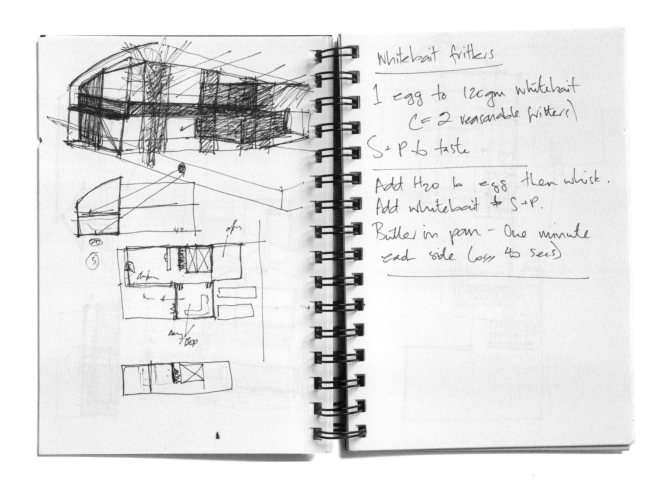

Whitebait fritters

1 egg to 120gm whitebait
(= 2 reasonable fritters)
S + P to taste

Add H2O to egg then whisk.
Add whitebait & S+P.
Butter in pan - One minute
each side (less 40 secs)

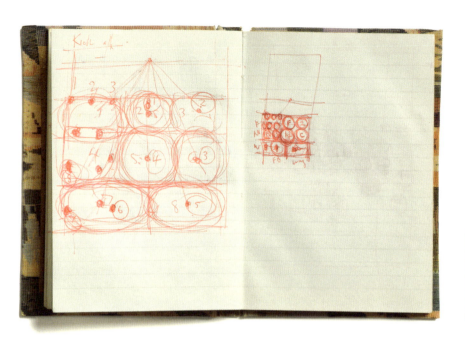
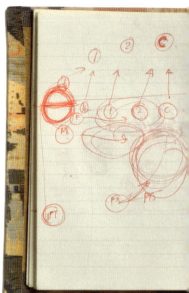

Creative process

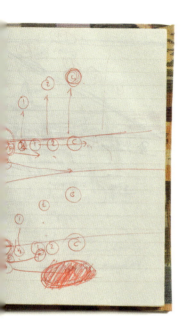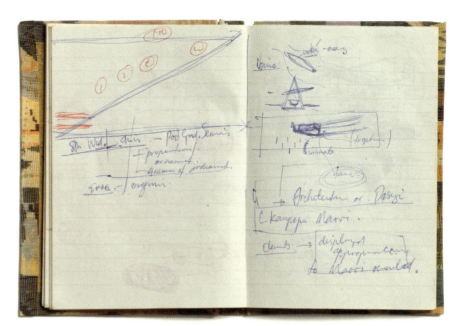

Creative process

Creative process

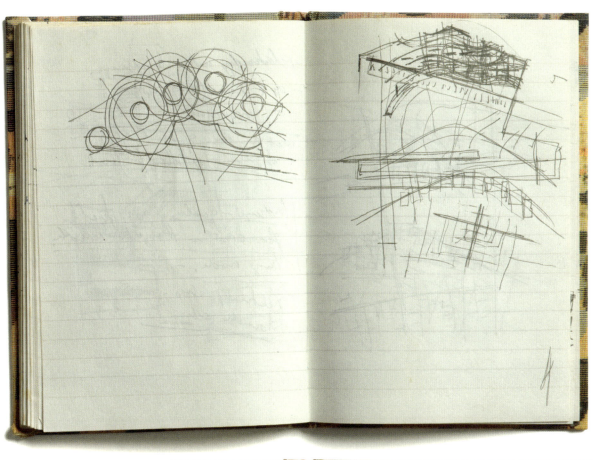
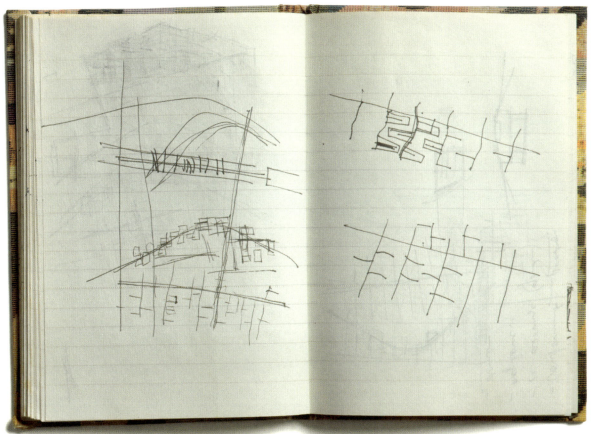

Creative process

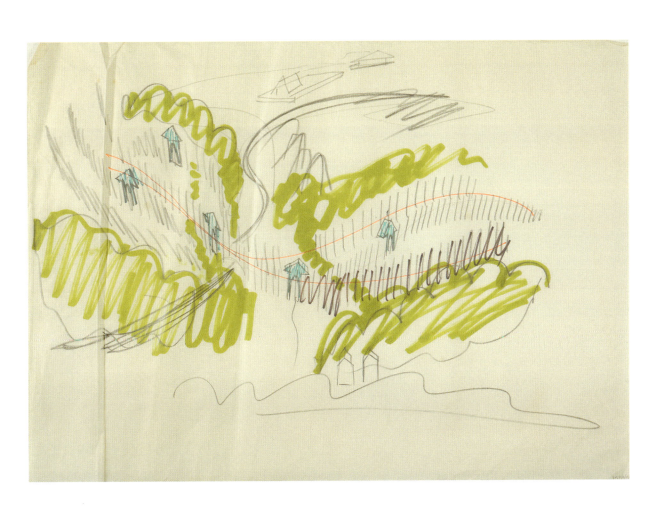

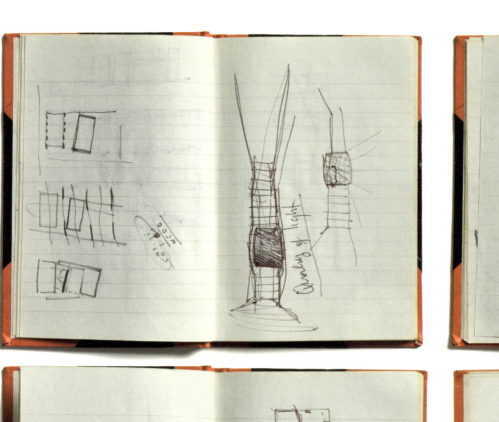

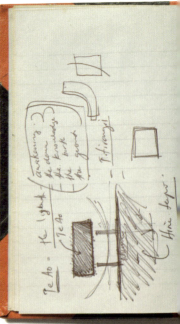

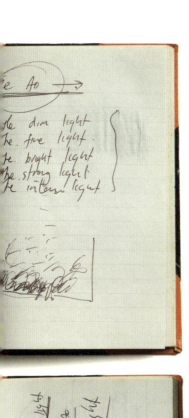

Te Ao →

- he dim light
- he fine light
- he bright light
- he strong light
- he intense light

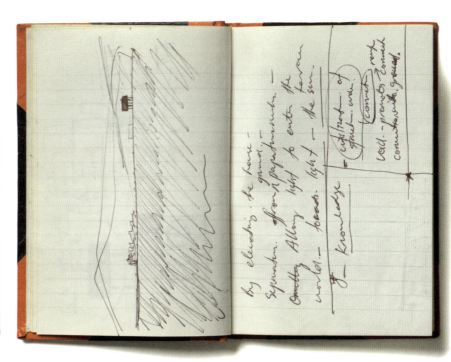

by electric. the house —
Speaker. of a department. —
Overtly Allowy light to enter the tavern
world. — foreran light — the sun.

knowledge — abstract of
 stock man.
 connect —
void — prompts connect
 connection with ground.

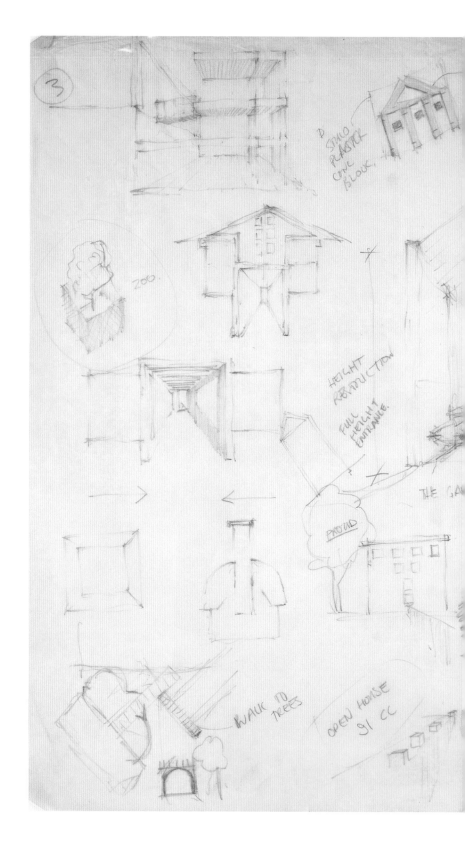

Creative process

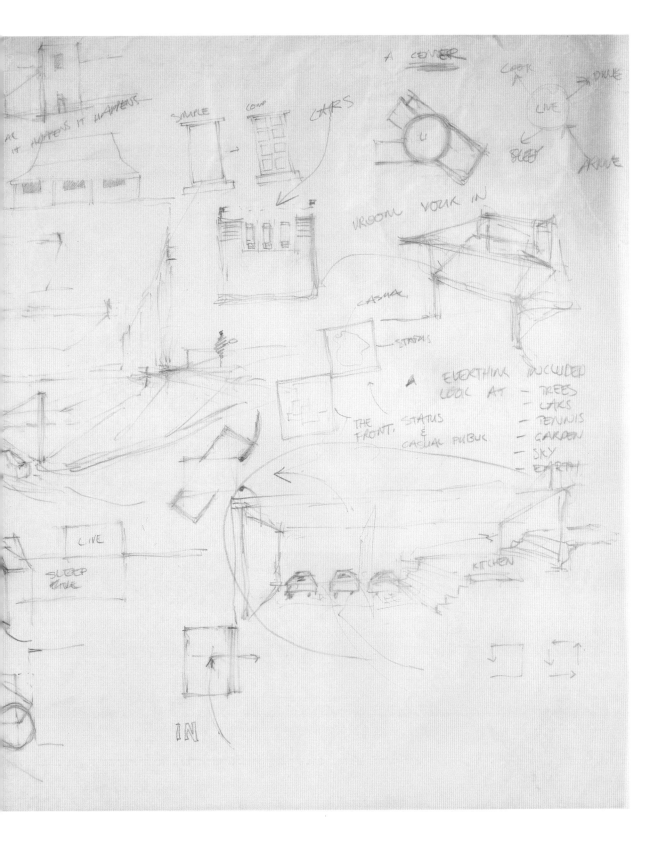

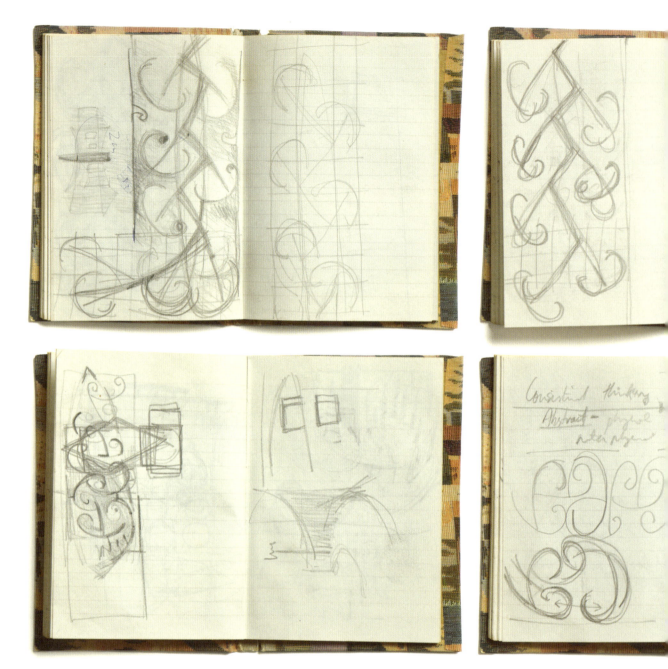

Creative process

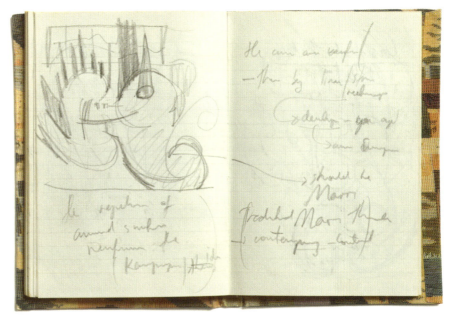

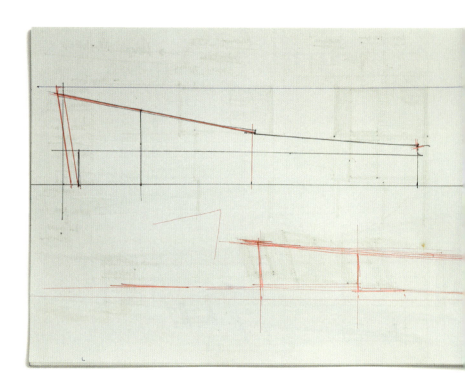

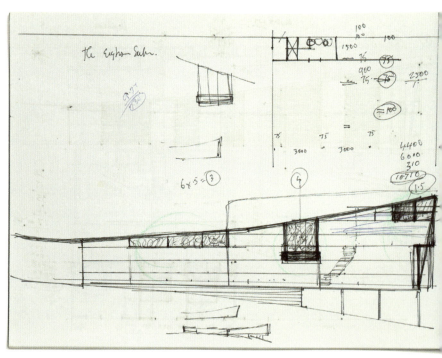

Creative process

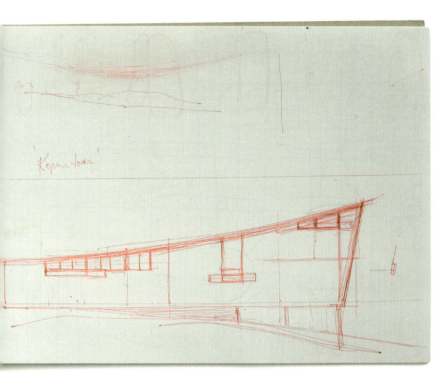
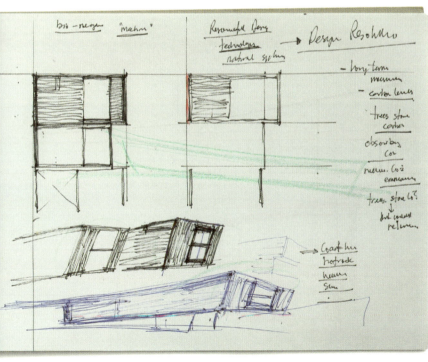

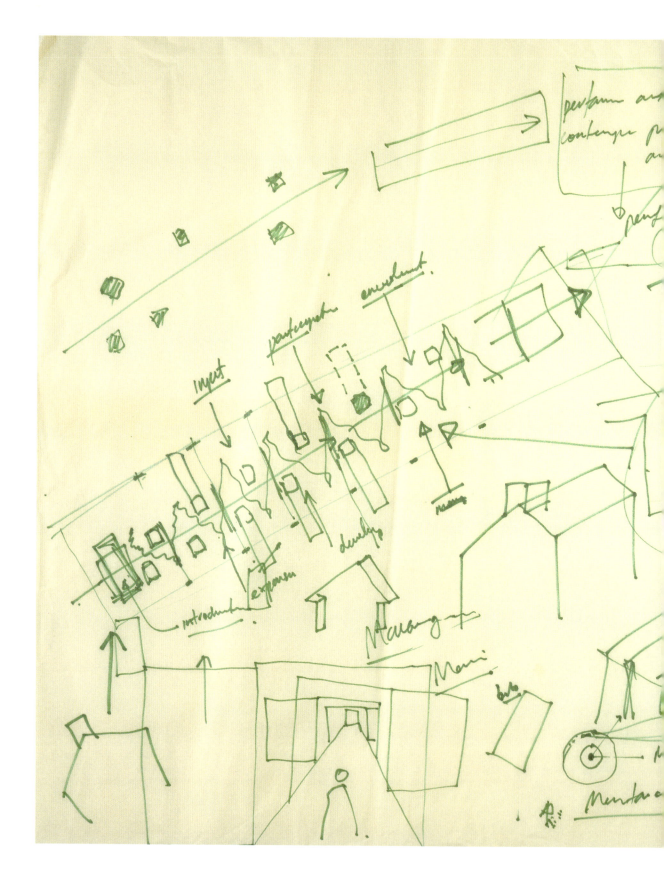

Creative process

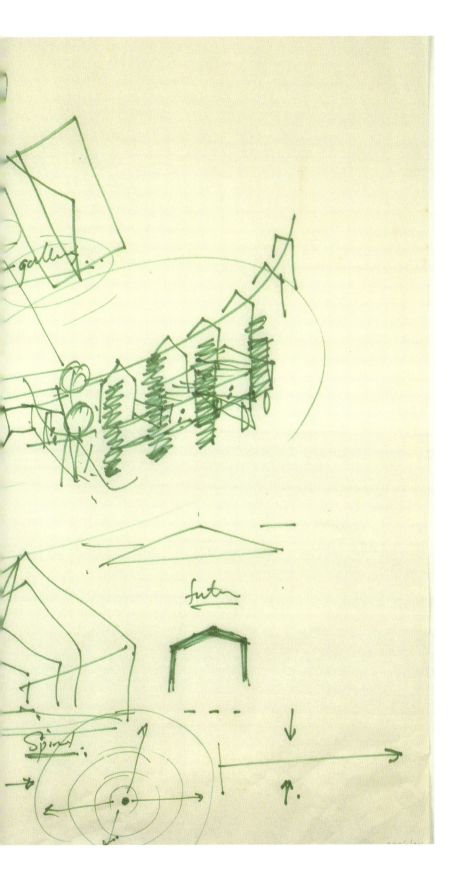

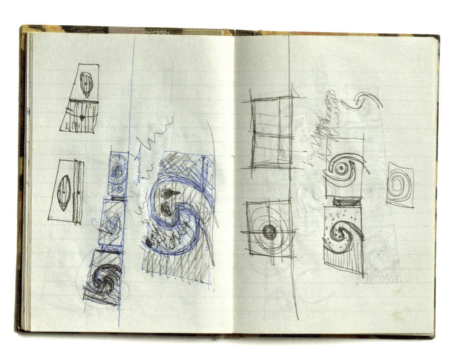

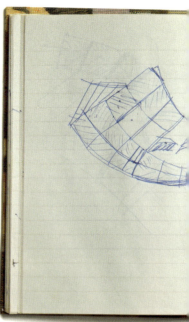

Creative process

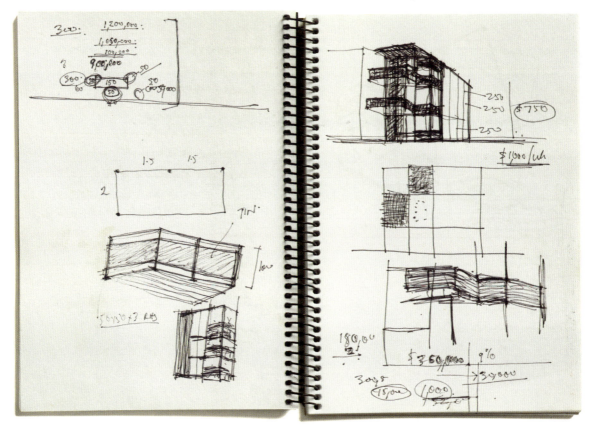

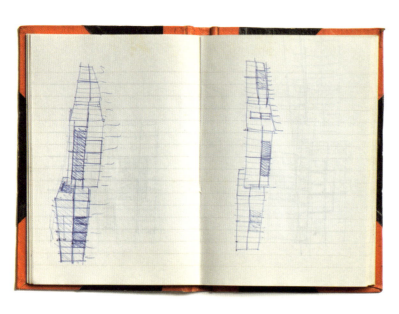
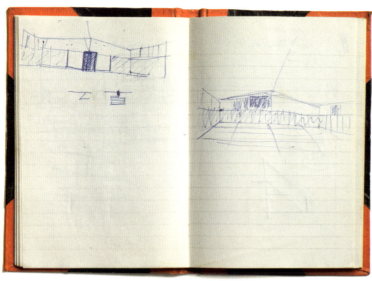

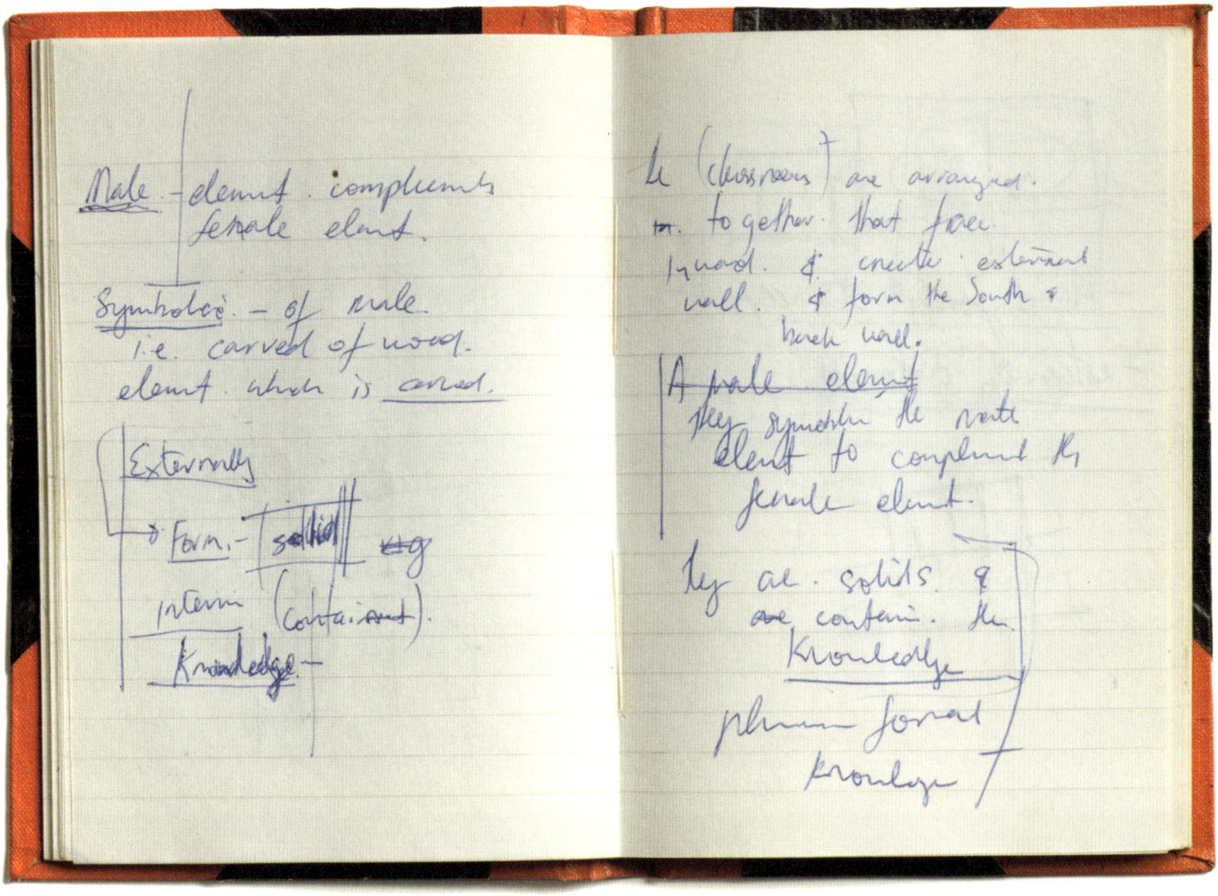

Male — element. complements
female element.

Symbolic. — of rule.
i.e. carved of wood.
element. which is carved.

Externally
→ Form. — solid +g
interior (containment).
Knowledge —

the (classrooms) are arranged.
together. that face.
inward. & create external
wall. & form the South &
back wall.

A male element
they symbolise the male
element to complement the
female element.

they are solids. &
are containing the
Knowledge

permanent formal
knowledge

Creative process

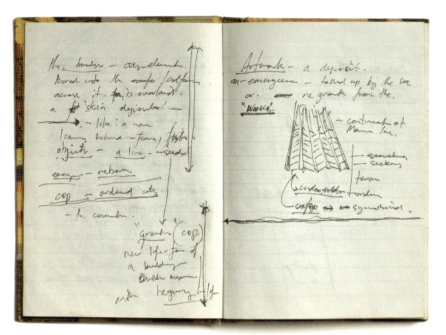

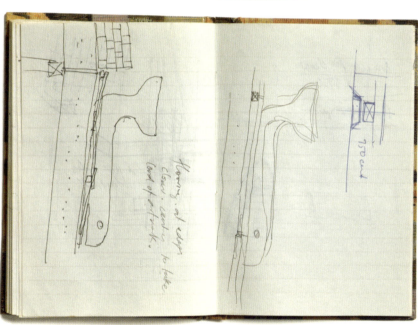

Creative process

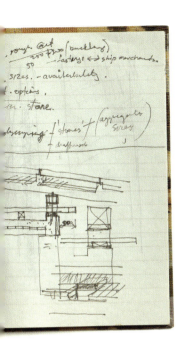

Creative process

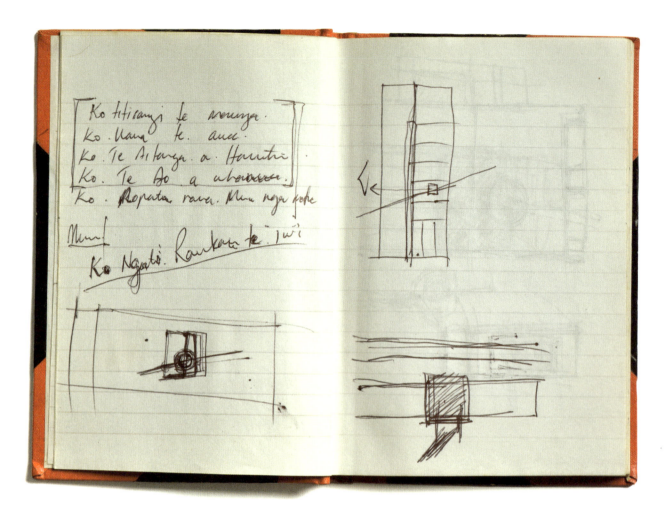

Creative process

About the authors

Jade Kake
Ngāpuhi, Te Whakatōhea, Ngāti Whakāue

Jade is an architectural designer and writer. She is the founder of Matakohe Architecture and Urbanism, a kaupapa Māori architecture studio, and a part-time lecturer at Huri Te Ao School of Future Environments at Auckland University of Technology Te Wānanga Aronui o Tāmaki Makaurau. She is the author of *Rebuilding the Kāinga: Lessons from Te Ao Hurihuri* (Bridget Williams Books, 2019) and has contributed articles and chapters to magazines and books on housing, architecture and urbanism. She is a two-time winner of Te Kāhui Whaihanga New Zealand Institute of Architects' Warren Trust Awards for Architectural Writing.

Jeremy Hansen

Jeremy is the co-author (with Jeremy Salmond and Patrick Reynolds) of *Villa: From Heritage to Contemporary* (Godwit, 2009), and editor of *Modern: New Zealand Architecture from 1938 to 1977* (Godwit, 2014). For 11 years he was the editor of *HOME* magazine. He was also the editor of *Paperboy*, a free Auckland weekly magazine, from 2016–18. He has been a contributor to *Metro*, *North & South*, *New Zealand Listener* and *The Spinoff*, and to US-based *Architectural Record* and *Dwell* magazines. He now works as a placemaker and facilitator of arts and culture projects in Auckland's Britomart precinct.

Samuel Te Kani
Ngāpuhi, Ngāti Porou

Samuel is a freelance writer, author and sexpert. His short story collection *Please, Call Me Jesus* was published by Dead Bird Books in 2021. He lives in Tāmaki Makaurau Auckland.

Gina Cole

Gina is a freelance writer of Fijian and Pākehā descent. Her collection *Black Ice Matter* won the Hubert Church Best First Book Award for Fiction at the 2017 Ockham New Zealand Book Awards. Her work has been widely anthologised and published in literary journals. She was the inaugural Pasifika curator at the Auckland Writers Festival in 2021. She is a qualified lawyer, holds a PhD in creative writing from Massey University Te Kunenga ki Pūrehuroa and is an Honorary Fellow in Writing at the University of Iowa. Her second book, *Na Viro* (Huia, 2022), is a science fiction fantasy novel and a work of Pasifikafuturism. She lives in Tāmaki Makaurau Auckland.

essa may ranapiri
Ngaati Wehi Wehi, Ngaati Raukawa-ki-te-Tonga, Te Arawa, Ngaati Puukeko, Ngaati Takataapui, Clan Gunn

essa is a poet who lives on whenua Ngaati Wairere. Their first book of poetry, *ransack* (Te Herenga Waka University Press, 2019), was longlisted for the 2020 Ockham New Zealand Book Awards. They are the featured writer in *Poetry New Zealand Yearbook 2020* (Massey University Press, 2020) with their work 'HAUNT|HUNT'. They also dabble in visual arts; their *redinblack* series of paintings was hosted in the Gus Fisher Gallery as part of the *queeralgorithms* exhibition in 2020. Their second book, *ECHIDNA*, was published in 2022 by Te Herenga Waka University Press. They are co-editor, with Michelle Rahurahu, of *Kupu Toi Takataapui*. They will write until they're dead.

Acknowledgements

The authors acknowledge the generous support of a CLNZ/NZSA Writers' Award from Copyright Licensing New Zealand in 2021, a Whiria Te Mahara New Zealand History Grant from New Zealand History Research Trust Fund in 2021, a grant from the Warren Trust and a grant from Creative New Zealand.

Many people contributed to this book. We offer our gratitude to all those involved in the research, development and production. Our thanks go to:

Professor Deidre Brown, Rewi's friend and university colleague, for her early guidance and support of this project.

Nicola Legat at Massey University Press, our publisher, for seeing the potential in our book and enthusiastically accepting our proposal, and Emily Goldthorpe for keeping us moving along.

Sarah Cox, Archivist, Cultural Collections at the University of Auckland Waipapa Taumata Rau, Zac Athfield and Esther Crookbain at Athfield Architects and Nathan Inkpen at AGM Publishing for their support in locating and accessing archival material. Special thanks to Bill McKay, Grant Bulley and Simon Twose for generously sharing photographs, plans and other material from their personal archives, and to Lucy Thompson for sharing treasured personal and whānau photos.

Those who agreed to be interviewed: Mike Austin, Mike Barns, Ngarimu Blair, Malcolm Bowes, Deidre Brown, Ross Brown, Grant Bulley, Graeme Burgess, Pip Cheshire, Patrick Clifford, Nick Dalton, Ken Davis, Wally Fitness, Matt Fleming, Katharina Grosse, David Irwin, Bill McKay, Melanie Mason, Karamia Müller, Pip Newman, Kevin O'Brien, Te Ari Prendergast, Albert Refiti, Amber Ruckes, Lucy Thompson, Michael Thomson, Sarah-Jane Tiakiwai, Lynda Toki, Lama Tone, Philip Tremewan, Simon Twose, Charles Walker and John and Pip Wishart.

Our photographers for new and relicensed images: Jamie Cobel, Samuel Hartnett, Paul McCredie, Grant Sheehan, Erica Sinclair, David St George, James Stokes, David Straight and Jane Ussher.

Phillip Kempster at Chow:Hill, Graeme Burgess at Burgess Treep & Knight Architects, Grace Wilfred and Andrew Mirams at Isthmus for providing base plans for redrawing for projects not in the archive.

Gina Cole, essa may ranapiri and Samuel Te Kani, who contributed new speculative creative writing.

Gordon Campbell and Tommy Honey for allowing us to republish previously published writing.

Our amazing design team at Extended Whānau — special thanks to Tyrone Ohia and Eva Charlton.

Zoe Black, Kim Paton, Micheal McCabe and the team at Objectspace for supporting the idea of an exhibition to coincide with the launch of the book.

Jade would like to thank Huri Te Ao at Auckland University of Technology Te Wānanga Aronui o Tāmaki Makaurau for the use of staff time towards research for this book, and her colleagues for their enthusiastic support for this book and accompanying exhibition.

Jeremy would like to thank his colleagues at Cooper and Company, as well as Cameron Law, Sarah Martin, Mei-Lin Hansen, Simon Hansen, Tim Hansen and Peter Hansen for their love and encouragement and helpful feedback on early drafts.

Finally, Lucy Thompson, thank you for trusting us to tell your dad's story. Without your support there would be no book.

Index

Page numbers in *italic* refer to images.

380 Group 140

AAA/Monier Design Award 16, 23, 237, 308, 310
Adam Art Gallery, Te Whanganui-a-Tara Wellington 304
Adam, Denis 198
AECOM 223, 224, 225
Allen, Desmond 291
Andrews, John 235
Ara Institute of Canterbury 304
Aravena, Alejandro 298
Architectural Group 18, 19
Architectus 96, 122, 139
Asian financial crisis 233
Athfield, Ian 14, 19, 237, 239, 240
    Capital Discovery Place Te Aho a Māui, Te Whanganui-a-Tara, Wellington (1988) 168, 169–70, 172
    City to Sea Bridge, Te Whanganui-a-Tara Wellington (1990) 168, 176, 178, 181, 182, 185
    house 300, 304
    lecture tour of United States (1986) 372–75
    Museum of New Zealand Te Papa Tongarewa competition entry (1989) 15, 17, 187, 188–91, 193–94, 197–99, 270
Athfield Architects 167, 174, 176, 178
Auckland City Mission, HomeGround building 110
Auckland Council, Te Aranga principles and design methodology 22
Auckland Regional Authority Debating Chambers 367
Austin, Mike 23, 25, 96, 283
    interview 284–85

Baldwin, Jane 240
Banks, John 333
Barns, Mike 19, 22, 23, 24, 43, 228, 233, 236, 284, 310
    interview 237–40
Barrie, Andrew 291
biculturalism 21, 168, 169–70, 181, 182, 190, 191, 194, 198, 199, 273, 375
Blair, John 372–75
Blair, Ngarimu 110, 112, 115–16, 332, 333
Boehringer Ingelheim warehouse, Wiri, Tāmaki Makaurau (1986–89) 154
Bossley, Pete 96, 137
Bowes, Malcolm, interview 139–41
Brick Studio *see under* University of Auckland School of Architecture [and Planning]

Brown, Deidre 15, 31, 210, 211, 212, 273, 277, 280, 281
    interview 268–70
Brown, Ross 143, 178, 230, 237, 238, 239
    interview 233–35
Bulley, Grant 206, 210
    interview 211–12
Burgess, Graeme 68, 86–89
Burke, Gregory 364

Campbell, Gordon: Ian Athfield interview 188–91, 193–94, 197–99
Campbell House, Kāretu, Te Pēwhairangi Bay of Islands (2007) 334–35, 335, 336, 337
canopy, altar and papal throne, Auckland Domain, Tāmaki Makaurau (1986) 17, 148, 154
    drawings 149
    photographs 146, 147, 151
    Pip Newman's recollections 148, 150
Cape Rēinga redevelopment, Te Rerenga Wairua, Te Hiku o Te Ika (1983–89) 17, 312, 313–14
    drawings, maps and plans 312, 313, 314, 315
Capital Discovery Place Te Aho a Māui, Te Whanganui-a-Tara, Wellington (1988) 17, 43, 168
    drawings 166–67, 170
    floor plan 171
    interview with Philip Tremewan 168, 169–70, 172
    photographs 169, 171
    Te Aho a Māui, narrative and illustrations 166–67, 168, 170, 172–73
Capital E, Te Whanganui-a-Tara Wellington 168, 172
Cheshire, Pip 96, 136
    interview 137–38
Chow:Hill Architects 258, 260, 261, 264
City to Sea Bridge, Te Whanganui-a-Tara Wellington (1990) 14, 43, 126, 168, 170, 176
    drawings and sketches 177, 178, 180
    interview with Ken Davis 176, 178, 181–82, 185
    model 185
    photographs 174–75, 179, 180, 183, 184
    split pyramid topped in pounamu 168, 170, 175, 180, 181
Clifford, Patrick 122, 139
    interview 139–41
Coastal Lodge, North Auckland (2000–01) 328, 328, 329, 329–30, 330, 331
Cole, Gina, *The Bridge* 358–61
Cook, Marsh 238

Corrections Department 233–35, 239
Couling, Nancy 92, 94, *96*, 161
Country, Australia 134–35
Cox Group 24, 228, 233
culture, as the origin of positioning 133, 134, 135

Daji, Mahendra 291
Dalton, Ben 23
Dalton, Nicholas 212
    interview 142–43
Davis, Ken, interview 176, 178, 181–82, 185
Department of Conservation 313
Designing with Country Framework 135

Earle, Augustus, *Meeting of the Artist with the Wounded Chief* 368–69
economic conditions, impact on architects 17, 233, 269, 270
Everyday Homes, Northcote Tāmaki Makaurau Auckland (2015–16) 12, 138
    drawings *123*, 125
    floor plans *123, 129–30*
    intergenerational occupation 138
    interview with David Irwin 120, 122, 125–26
    models *122, 123*
    photographs *118–19, 121, 127, 128*
    A Place Called Home (poem, Rewi Thompson) 125
    residents *124*

Far North District Council 52, 56, 61, 64
Ferguson, Bruce 303
FirstCorp Tower, Tāmaki Makaurau Auckland (1983–89) 316
    plans and drawing *316, 317*
Fitness, Wally 206, 211, 215, 219, 220, 224
    interview 225–26
Fleming, Matt 214
    interview 219–21
Future Islands, Venice Architecture Biennale, Venice, Italy (2016) 280, 296, 298
    fragment of a mihimihi 6–7
    haka pōwhiri *302*, 303
    interview with Charles Walker 298, 303–04
    New Zealand tour 304
    photographs *296–97, 299, 300–01*

Gallipoli memorial competition 291
Gehry, Frank 15, 17, 142, 168, 176, 181, 187, 188, 189–90, 191, 193, 194, 197–98, 270
Graham, Brett 264
Graham, Fred 264
Grant, Lyonel 246, 252

Gray, John 174, 176
Grosse, Katharina 18, 68–71, 87–88, 89
    see also West Coast Studio, Tāmaki Makaurau Auckland (2015–19)
Guggenheim Museum, Bilbao, Spain 188, 189–90, 194, 197

Haddon, Laly and Sharley 329–30
Haddon, Olivia 330
Halkyard, Hilda 23
Hansen, Jeremy 12–21, 34, 36, 40, 43, 44
Harawira, Hone 23
Harris, Anne 34
Hauiti 25
He Taua students group, University of Auckland 23
Henare, Denese 261
Hill, Richard 260, 261, 264
Hillmorton Hospital, Christchurch 215
Hīngāngāroa 25
Holmes Consulting 332, 333
Hometown Museum *see* Ngāti Pōneke Marae/Hometown Museum, Te Whanganui-a-Tara Wellington (1980)
Honey, Tommy 94, 95
Horouta ki Pōneke Marae Society, Porirua (1983–89) 318–19, *319*
Hoskins, Rau 22, 269
Hotere, Ralph 70
Houkamau-Ngaheu, Pania 319
Housing Corporation 94, 101, 140, 141, 235
Hudson, Grant 88

Indigenous architecture 134, 272, 277, 284
    see also Māori architecture
Indigenous creative practices 272
Insley, Tere 22, 23, 284
Ip, Minka 303
Irwin, David 120, 122, 125–26
Isthmus Group 12, 40, 118, 120, 122, 125–26, 154

Jackson, Moana 170
Japanese Metabolist movement 16
Jasmax 214, 216
    Waka Māia team 218
Jenner, Ross 20, 21, 148, 291
John Paul II, Pope, visit to New Zealand (1986) 17, 142, 148, 150, *150*
    see also canopy, altar and papal throne, Auckland Domain, Tāmaki Makaurau (1986)
    Māori welcome 148
Jones, Shane 226

Kaa, Keri 170
Kahukiwa, Robyn 270

Kāinga Ora 120
Kaitāia Hospital redevelopment, Te Hika o
Te Ika (2005)
community involvement 225–26
floor plan *227*
models *224*, 225
sketch *222–23*
wharehui 226
Kake, Jade 15, 22–25, 34, 36, 40, 43, 44
Kara, Eugene 264
Kawiti, Derek 22
Kenana Marae 284
Kingi, Wikuki, snr 264
Kīngitanga 260, 263, 264
Kofoed, Rory 88
KOHA, Tāmaki Makaurau Auckland 15,
126, 340, *340*, 341, *342–51*
response from writers of fiction 341,
353–61
Kombumerri, Dylan 132, 133

Lambton Harbour Management 181–82
landmarks, symbolism in
architecture 366–67
Laurelia Place state houses, Wiri, Tāmaki
Makaurau (1986–89) 17, 92, 140, 154
drawings and sketch plans *97*, *102*,
103
floor plans *105*, *106*, *107*
interview with Bill McKay 95, 101, 104
landscaping 94–95
model *103*
photographs *92–93*, *98*, *99*, *100*
Pip Newman's recollections 94–95
Lee, Mike 333
Lloyd Jenkins, Douglas 12
Lloyd Wright, Frank 198

Mahuika, Api 240
Mahuta, Sir Robert 25, 260, 261, 264
mana 366
Manukau City Council 154
Māori
see also te ao Māori
contemporary expression of culture in
the built environment 182
identity 238
importance of ancestral land 20, 137
imprisonment 230, 233, 239
key force in New Zealand's identity 182
within a majority Pākehā
environment 22–23, 96, 142–43
mental health 211, 215, 218, 220, 221
narratives in creating urban forms 15,
192–93
renaissance and political awareness 22,
23, 104

rise of economy 137
symbolism 191
Māori architecture 137, 143, 170, 240, 278,
284
growth of legitimacy 23
Māori students 15, 19, 22, 23, 24, 135,
142, 237, 238, 268, 271–74, 278,
280–82, 284–85
modernism 101, 273–74, 278
role in returning identity and well-being
to Māori 15, 24
significance of affiliation with the
land 18, 20, 70, 81, 364
spiritual dimension 20
Māori architecture: Rewi Thompson's
views, influence and legacy 15, 20,
22–23, 70, 237, 238, 272, 273, 274,
284–85, 375
see also Thompson, Rewi — as a Māori
architect
Rewi Thompson, 'Māori Architecture
— A Myth', *NZ Architect*, 1987 20,
370–71
Rewi Thompson's essay for *Now See
Hear!: Art, Language, and Translation*
exhibition, Wellington City Art
Gallery (1990) 364–69
Māori design principles 15, 16, 18, 22, 70,
101, 138, 210, 235, 240, 268, 272, 273,
364–68
marae 17, 104, 143, 261, 284, 364
see also Ngāti Pōneke Marae/Hometown
Museum, Te Whanganui-a-Tara
Wellington (1980)
concept in mental health
architecture 211, 216, 220
spatial quality and relevance 367–68
Marsden, Māori 239
Mason Clinic, Point Chevalier Tāmaki
Makaurau Auckland
Extension (1999) 206, 209, 210, 211, 269
nature of a forensic facility 215, 216, 220
site plan *213*, *221*
Te Aka Forensic Mental Health Unit 214
Te Papakāinga o Tāne Whakapiripiri
(2003–06) 206, *208–09*, 209, 214,
214, 215–16, *217*, 218, *218*, 219–21,
225, 269, 270
wharenui 211–12, 214, *214*, 215, 270
Mason, Melanie 214
interview 215–16, 218
Mason Report (1988) 211, 269
mātauranga Māori 25, 255, 261, 294
Matchitt, Paratene 70, 170, 172, 174, 176,
180, 182, 183, 184
Maunsell 209, 215, 216, 219, 224
McCahon Place project, Titirangi 88

Index

McColl, Michael 92, 94, *96*, 161
McGrath, Warren 264
McKay, Bill 12, 43, 95, 101, 104
McMillian, Elizabeth 194
Mead, Hirini Moko 319
Mead, June 169
Meier, Richard 194, 234
mental health architecture 215, 218, 225
  courtyard concept 216, 220
  marae concept 211, 216, 220
Middemore Hospital *see* Tiaho Mai Acute
  Mental Health Facility, Middlemore
  Hospital, Ōtahuhu, Tāmaki Makaurau
  Auckland (1995–96)
Mikaere, Buddy 194
Milan Triennial *see* Triennale de Milano,
  Milan, Italy (1996)
Millar, Judy 69, 71, 72, 75, 87
Mitchell, David 96, 140
Mitchell, Manning 95, 101
modernism 101, 138, 162, 269, 273–74,
  278
Moller, Gordon 176
Morrow, Kerry 23, 96, 140, 178, 237–38,
  291, 310
Müller, Karamia 18
  interview 271–74
multiculturalism 21, 199, 370
Museum of New Zealand Te Papa
  Tongarewa competition entry
  (1989) 15, 17, 168, 170, 176, 181, 187,
  188, 270, 278
  drawings *192–93*, *195*, *196*, *200–01*
  feather element *186*, 193, *193*, 194, *195*,
  270
  Gordon Campbell's interview with Ian
  Athfield 188–91, 193–94, 197–99
  model *186*, *190*

New Zealand architecture 19, 212, 370
  see also Māori architecture; Pasifika
  architecture
  cultural simplification 18–19
  Māori and Pākehā translations of
  architecture 15, 21, 368–69, 375
  Māori influences 15, 216, 370, 371
  mental health architecture 211, 215, 216,
  218, 225
  neo-Colonial approaches 19
  primacy of landscape 18
  spiritual dimension 369
  US lecture tour by Roger Walker,
  John Blair, Ian Athfield and Rewi
  Thompson 372–75
Newman, Pip 41, 44, 45
  canopy, altar and papal throne,
  Auckland Domain, Tāmaki

Makaurau (1986) 148, 150
Laurelia Place state houses, Wiri,
  Tāmaki Makaurau (1986–89) 92,
  94–95, *96*
Ngā Aho 22
Ngākete whānau 264
Ngata, Pat 319
Ngāti Ōtara Marae Society 366
Ngāti Pōneke Marae/Hometown Museum,
  Te Whanganui-a-Tara Wellington
  (1980) 16, 23, *23*, 138, 141, 237, 308,
  310, 366
  drawing and plans *309*, *310*
  models *311*
Ngāti Porou 16, 240, 319, 364
Ngāti Rangi 24
Ngāti Raukawa 16, 25, 112, 260, 364
Ngāti Whātua housing, Takaparawhau,
  Tāmaki Makaurau Auckland (2000–
  04) 12, 110
  drawings and sketch plans *111*, *112–13*,
  114–15, 115, *117*
  Kāinga Tuatahi project, Kupe Street 110,
  112, 115–16
  model *108–09*, *366*
  Ngarimu Blair's memories 110, 112,
  115–16
Northland Region Corrections Facility,
  Ngāwhā (1999–2005) 24, 220, 269,
  270
  drawings and sketch *229–30*, *232*
  interview with Mike Barns 237–40
  interview with Ross Brown 233–35
  involvement of mana whenua 239
  photographs *231*, *232*, *234*, *236*, *241*
  wharehui *252*, 253, 270
Now See Hear!: Art, Language, and Translation
  exhibition, Wellington City Art
  Gallery (1990) 364
  Rewi Thompson's essay 364–69

Objectspace gallery, Ponsonby, Tāmaki
  Makaurau Auckland 304
O'Brien, Kevin, interview 132–35
Ōmāpere, Hokianga 50–51, 55
Oriental-Rongotai rugby club 17, 34
  Rewi Thompson as team vice-captain,
  1972 16
Ōtara Town Centre canopies, Ōtara,
  Tāmaki Makaurau Auckland (1987) 14,
  24, 43, 138, 154, 240, 278, 292
  adaptation of the fale form 158, 161
  drawings *152*, *156–57*, *159*, *164–65*
  fish motif 154, *154*, 158, 161–62, 270
  interview with Albert Refiti 158,
  161–62
  photographs *153*, *154*, *155*, *160*, *162*, *163*

pā 366
Pacific Island Business and Cultural
    Centre 324, *324*, 325, *325*, 326, 327,
    327
Pasifika
    identity 238
    mental health 211
Pasifika architecture 23, 276, 277–78, 284
    students 15, 268, 271, 276–78
Patumāhoe house rebuild 140
Piha beach house 140
Pine, Matt 182
    sculptures, City to Sea Bridge *180*
Pope's visit, 1986 *see* canopy, altar and
    papal throne, Auckland Domain,
    Tāmaki Makaurau (1986)
Post Office Building, Waterloo Quay, Te
    Whanganui-a-Tara Wellington 198
post-modernism 19, 101, 143, 162, 269
public works projects, reluctance to
    appoint Māori architects 239, 240
Puukenga School of Māori Studies,
    Unitec Institute of Technology,
    Ōwairaka Tāmaki Makaurau
    Auckland (1993) 14, 43, 126, 132, 141,
    246, 278
    article by Rewi Thompson on aspects of
        the design concept 254–56
    drawings and sketches *244, 250–51*
    ground floor plan *257*
    interview with Lynda Toki 246, 247,
        251–52
    lighting design 251, 254
    Ngākau Māhaki wharenui 246
    photographs *246, 248, 249, 253*
    pouihi (Blaine Te Rito) *246, 249,* 251,
        255, 256
    Te Noho Kotahitanga Marae 246,
        251–52
    whakapapa 255
    whakapapa (pouihi) 256

Queen's Wharf redevelopment, Tāmaki
    Makaurau Auckland 110, 333

racism 18, 23, 96, 137, 170
ranapiri, essa may, *Poutama* 353
Rangihoua pā site 270
Rata Vine project *see* Laurelia Place state
    houses, Wiri, Tāmaki Makaurau
    (1986–89)
Rawiri whānau 264
Reedy, Sir Tamati 240
Refiti, Albert 158, 161–62
Rotorua Cultural Centre (1986) 17, 320,
    321, 323
    sketches and plans *320–21, 322, 323*

Rowling, Bill 194, 197, 199
Roy McKenzie Trust 168, 169
Royal Associates 270
Royal, Wiremu (Bill) 233, 239
Ruckes, Amber, interview 279–82

Scott, John 23, 70, 233, 235, 237–38, 269,
    310
social change 25
Sotheran, Dame Cheryll 198
Southcombe, McLean and Co. 245
Southgate, Wade 88
speculative and unbuilt projects 298, 303,
    354
    see also KOHA, Tāmaki Makaurau
        Auckland; and names of individual
        projects
Spence, Sir Basil 198
The Spinoff, 'Cursed Slides of Aotearoa',
    2021 168
Spring Hill Prison, Waikato 234, 239
Stanish, Nick 96
state housing 18, 95, 101, 120
    see also Everyday Homes, Northcote,
        Tāmaki Makaurau Auckland
        (2015–16); Laurelia Place state
        houses, Wiri, Tāmaki Makaurau
        Auckland (1986–89)
Stephenson & Turner 24, 211, 226, 228
Stevens Lawson Architects 110, 116
Stevenson, Allan 24, 34
stock market crash (1987) 17, 233, 269,
    270
Stokes, James 13
Structon Group, Wellington 16, 24, 140,
    143, 178, 230, 233, 235, 237, 238, 284
Sumich House, Newmarket 12, *12–13,* 13,
    270
Sutherland, Oliver 170

Takaparawhau *see* Ngāti Whātua housing,
    Takaparawhau, Tāmaki Makaurau
    Auckland (2000–04)
Talbot, Bruce 220
Tāmaki Makaurau Auckland
    see also names of individual projects
    a desirable place to live 32
    vernacular 32–33
    violence 20, 32
Taumata o Kupe education centre,
    Te Mahurehure marae, Point
    Chevalier 212
Te Aka Whai Ora 218
te ao Māori 87, 210, 211, 246, 272, 278,
    280, 282, 294
Te Kāhui Waihanga New Zealand Institute
    of Architects 22, 136

Index

Te Kanawa, Kahu 254

Te Kani, Samuel, *The Mysterious Case of the T-Rex in the Night: Rewi Thompson, Big Gay Dinosaurs, and You* 354–57

Te Kawenata o Rata 22, 136

Te Kura Kaupapa Māori o Te Rawhiti Roa 31

Te Miringa Te Kakara 247, 251, 252

Te Papa Tongarewa *see* Museum of New Zealand Te Papa Tongarewa competition entry (1989)

Te Puea Marae 280

Te Rāwheoro Marae and whare wānanga 25

Te Rito, Blaine, pouihi *246, 249*, 251, 255, 256

Te Wero Bridge, Quay Street West, Tāmaki Makaurau Auckland (2007) 110, 116, 332, *333*

Te Whanganui-a-Tara Wellington, civic works 14, 17, 24, 43

Te Wïata, Inia 264

Tebbs, Maurice 176

Tennent, Hugh 61

Thompson, Bobby and Mei 16, 25, 140, 237, 238

Thompson House, Kohimarama, Tāmaki Makaurau Auckland (1985) 12, 15, 20–21, 28, 31, 101, 104, 126, 132, 133, 138, 140–41, 212, 235, 270, 278
  as an architectural space 368, *368*
  drawings and sketches *28, 30, 33, 38–39, 41–42,* 44, *46, 352, 368*
  floor plans *46*
  in *Future Islands*, Venice Architecture Biennale, Venice, Italy (2016) *296–97,* 298, *301,* 303–04, *305*
  Lucy Thompson's memories 34, 36, 40, 43
  name, 'The Warrior' 44, 140
  photographs *28, 29, 35, 37, 45*
  Pip Newman's memories 44
  ranapiri, essa may, *Poutama* 353
  Rewi Thompson's description 31–33

Thompson, Leona 17, *17,* 25, 31, 34, *35,* 36, 55, 56, 64, 134, 140, 237, 238, 240

Thompson, Lucy *14,* 15, 19, 31, 55, 134, 238, 281
  involvement in Rewi Thompson's work 36, *36,* 40, 43, 374
  memories 34, 36, 40, 43

Thompson, Rewi
  architectural career (*see also under* names of individual projects)
    approach to architecture 15, 22, 23, 31–32, 40, 70, 88, 101, 134–35, 269–70, 281–82

built output 17–18, 104, 110, 126, 137, 233, 239, 278
  collaboration 15, 24–25, 87–88, 94, 110, 141, 176 (*see also under* individual collaborative projects)
  consultant model 24, 120, 168, 211
  giftedness 269, 272
  Isthmus Group, Auckland 12, 40, 118, 120, 122 125–26, 154
  lack of logistical capability for large, complex projects 17, 116, 120, 122, 141, 233
  radicality 14, 25, 94, 125, 126, 168, 185, 272, 291
  relationships 43, 61, 70, 88, 96, 110, 115, 170
  on shifting attitudes to life and practice following US lecture tour (1986) 372–75
  Structon Group, Wellington 16, 24, 140, 143, 178, 230, 233, 235, 237, 238, 284
  style of architecture 19, 21, 61, 101, 138, 143, 278, 370
  views on impermanence of buildings 18, 40, 70, 94, 212, 274
  vision 137, 185, 269, 329, 330
articles
  on aspects of the design concept for Puukenga (1995) 254–56
  The Landscape (New Zealand Institute of Landscape Architects Tuia Pito Ora, 1988) 20, 23, 308, 314
  'Māori Architecture — A Myth', *NZ Architect* (1987) 20, 370–71
  on shifting attitudes to life and practice following US lecture tour, *NZ Architect* 372–75
  Transition (1995) 20
awards 16, 23, 61, 237, 308, 310
creative process 44, 61, 341, 373 (*see also* Thompson, Rewi — drawings and sketches)
  conceptual thinking 25, 44, 61, 88, 126, 238, 239, 240, 272, 273, 292, 294
  gaps in using technology 122, 125
  model-making 44, 55–56, *85,* 141 (*see also under* individual projects)
  space/time diagrams 133–34
  taking time 44, 280–81, 292
cultural consultancy work 17, 24, 25, 143, 168, 169–70, 211, 214, 215–16, 219–20, 225, 226, 233–35, 261, 264, 269
death and tangi 12, 15, 25, 31, 68, 86, 87, 89, 120, 126, 132, 143, 149, 169, 304

design philosophy
  enthusiasm for large structures on
    a landscape or harbour 16, 270,
    310, 341
  Māori cultural concepts in
    architecture 364–68
  relationship to land 18, 25, 69, 95,
    122, 126, 134, 212, 230, 233, 270,
    276, 308
  settings and connections of
    buildings 18, 50–51, 56, 61, 64, 68,
    69–70, 72, 78, 134, 135, 191, 194, 197,
    269, 270
  spatial terms and relationships 12,
    25, 61, 64, 75, 82, 126, 190, 216, 256,
    269, 272, 364, 367–69
    time, as fourth dimension of
      architectural space 368
drawings and sketches 15, 16, 19, *19*, 23,
    40, 43, 44, 56, 101, 115, 125, 133, 161,
    281, 284 (*see also* KOHA, Tāmaki
    Makaurau Auckland; and under
    individual projects)
  selection of sketches and jottings
    from notebooks 378, *379–444*
early life and training 16, 23–24, 25, 44,
    70, 139–40, 143, 237
interviews
  interview for TV show *Koha* 50, 55
  Ross Jenner for article in *Lotus
    International*, 2000 20
lecture tour of the United States
    (1986) 372–75
legacy 25, 43, 44, 104, 110, 116, 135,
    137–38, 143, 162, 212, 218, 220–21,
    226, 264, 272, 278, 285
as a Māori architect 15, 16, 20, 22–24,
    25, 43, 70–71, 84, 101, 104, 116, 138,
    170, 212, 218, 238, 240, 263, 284–85,
    310, 371, 375
  in teaching and mentoring 142, 272,
    278
personal life 162 (*see also* Thompson,
    Leona; Thompson, Lucy)
  friendships 14, 15, 19, 22, *24*, 43, 52,
    86, 95, 110, 120, 132, 134, 139, 140,
    141, 230, 236, 240, 268, 291, 373
  grounding 25, 126, 133, 172, 178
  health 17, 87, 122, 138, 239–40, 272
  identity 19, 23, 24, 25, 238
  love of rugby 16, *16*, 34, 133, 162,
    235
  marriage and family life 17, *17*, 34, *35*,
    36, 43, 134, 140, 238, 240, 374
  surfing 139, 235
    values 120, 122, 138, 143, 274
    whakapapa 25, 263, 264, 319

photographs of
  in Auckland Studio, 1980s *17*
  with friends, 1970s *24*
  in kapa haka group when a child *17*
  with Leona and Lucy Thompson *14*
  photograph by Jane Ussher *9*
  with team members of Laurelia Place
    state housing project *96*
  vice-captain, Oriental-Rongotai rugby
    club, 1972 *16*
  wedding day with Leona, 1970s *17*
poem, *A Place Called Home* 125
teaching and mentoring 25, 61, 141, 162,
    178, 182, 239, 240, 273, 291
  centredness in the Māori
    environment 96
  'gentle navigation' approach 279–80,
    281–82, 304
  influence 18, 104, 212, 215–16, 219,
    273, 274, 276, 277, 280–81, 282, 292,
    294
  Kevin O'Brien 133–35
  Lama Tone 276, 278
  listening 280
  making safe spaces 273, 280, 281–82
  Māori concepts and design
    principles 269–70, 272, 273
  Māori students 15, 135, 142, 268,
    271–74, 278, 280–82
  Pākehā students 15, 268, 273
  Pasifika students 15, 268, 271, 276–78
  studio projects 269, 270, 272–73,
    280–81
  Tauiwi students 15, 268, 269–70, 273,
    277
  thesis supervision 281–82
Thomson, Michael, interview 139–41
Tiaho Mai Acute Mental Health Facility,
    Middlemore Hospital, Ōtahuhu,
    Tāmaki Makaurau Auckland (1995–
    96) 204, *205*, 206, *207*, 210, 214, 215,
    216, 225, 226
  involvement of mana whenua and
    community 206, 225
  wharenui 206, 225
Tiakiwai, Sarah-Jane, interview 260, 261,
    263–64
Toki, Lynda, interview 246, 247, 251–52
Tone, Lama, interview 275–78
Toomath, Bill 176
Treadwell, Sarah 291
Treaty of Waitangi 142–43, 170, 191, 198,
    211, 290, 292
Tremewan, Philip 168
  interview 169–70, 172
Triennale de Milano, Milan, Italy
    (1996) 289–90, 303

Index

drawings 291, *293*, *294–95*
interview with Simon Twose 291–92, 294
photographs *288*, *289*, *290*
Tūrangi township glass canopy project 40, 120, 122, 154
Turei, John 251–52, 254
Turei, Pita 89
Tūwharetoa 263, 264
Twose, Simon, interview 291–92, 294
Tyrannosaurus Rex, in KOHA drawings 15, 341, 354–57

Ūawa Tolaga Bay 25, 43, 140
Unitec Institute of Technology
    see also Puukenga School of Māori Studies, Unitec Institute of Technology, Ōwairaka Tāmaki Makaurau Auckland (1993)
    School of Architecture 94
    student housing 291
University of Auckland School of Architecture [and Planning] 15, 16, 86, 87, 95, 120, 137, 142, 210, 219, 235, 239, 240, 269–70, 271–74, 275, 276, 279–82, 291, 294
    see also Thompson, Rewi — teaching and mentoring
    Brick Studio 16, 96, 139–40, 178
    Māori students 19, 22, 23, 24, 237, 238, 284–85
    Rewi Thompson archives 15
    Rewi Thompson as adjunct professor 18, 268, 272

Van Lieshout, Father Theo 148
Venice Biennale
    see also Future Islands, Venice Architecture Biennale, Venice, Italy (2016)
    1991 291, 303
    2012 134
vernacular as a language 32

Waikato Museum
    extension 291
    Future Islands exhibition 304
Waikato Raupatu Claim 260, 261
Waikato-Tainui College for Research and Development, Hopuhopu, Ngāruawāhia (2000) 25, 258, 260, 291
    drawings *265*
    floor plans *266*
    interview with Sarah-Jane Tiakiwai 260, 261, 263–64
    photographs *258–59*, *262–63*
    pou *260*, 264

Walker, Charles, interview 298, 303–04
Walker, Paul 181
Walker, Roger 14, 19, 240, 372–75
Walsh, John 230
Ward, Tony 219
Warren & Mahoney 291, 332, 333
Warren, Miles 55
Watene, Susan 251
Wedde, Ian 364
Wellington Public Library 181, 182
West Coast Studio, Tāmaki Makaurau Auckland (2015–19) 18, 68–69, 270, 313
    consent process 88
    drawings and sketch plans *66–67*, 70, *73*, *77*, *80*, *81*, *82*, *83*, *84*, *85*, 88, *89*
    emails from Rewi Thompson to Katharina Grosse 72–85
    floor plan *71*, 88
    interview with Graeme Burgess 86–89
    interview with Katharina Grosse 69–71
    models *85*, *86*
    whakatau and blessings 89
whakapapa 25, 255, 256, 260, 365
whānau 31, 32, 110, 112, 115, 211, 269, 278
    extended family living 138, 270, 277
whare wānanga 261, 264
wharenui and wharehui 364–66, *365*, 367
    in correctional facilities 232, 233, 270
    in educational facilities 246
    in mental health facilities 206, 211–12, 214, *214*, 215
    modern interpretations based on tradition *365*, 365–66, *366*
    symbolism and structure 365–66
Wild, Allan 284
Wilson, Carin 22
Wilson, Derek 176
Wishart House, Ōmāpere, Hokianga (1989–98) 12, 40, 43, 52, 234, 270, 337
    consent process 52, 56, 61
    drawings 44, *54*, 61, 64
    floor plans *65*
    individual elements and their spaces 369
    interview with John and Pip Wishart 52, 55–56, 61, 64
    photographs *48–49*, *53*, *57*, *58*, *59*, *60*, *62*, *63*
    Pip Wishart's aspirations 50–52, 55, 64
Woolford-Roa, Beryl 251
Wootton, Peter 225
Worley Architects 204, 209, 211, 224
Wyeth, Sue 225

First published in 2023 by Massey University Press
Private Bag 102904, North Shore Mail Centre
Auckland 0745, New Zealand
www.masseypress.ac.nz

Text copyright © individual contributors, 2023
Images copyright © as credited, 2023

Design by Extended Whānau
Typesetting by Katrina Duncan

The moral right of the authors has been asserted

All rights reserved. Except as provided by the Copyright Act 1994, no part of this book may be reproduced, stored in or introduced into a retrieval system or transmitted in any form or by any means (electronic, mechanical, photocopying, recording or otherwise) without the prior written permission of both the copyright owner(s) and the publisher.

A catalogue record for this book is available from the
National Library of New Zealand

Printed and bound in China by Everbest Printing Investment Limited

ISBN: 978-1-99-101641-6

The assistance of Copyright Licensing New Zealand, Creative New Zealand and the Warren Trust is gratefully acknowledged by the authors and publisher.